KANT'S REFORM OF METAPHYSICS

Scholarly debates on the *Critique of Pure Reason* have largely been shaped by epistemological questions. Challenging this prevailing trend, *Kant's Reform of Metaphysics* is the first book-length study to interpret Kant's *Critique* in view of his efforts to turn Christian Wolff's highly influential metaphysics into a science. Karin de Boer situates Kant's pivotal work in the context of eighteenth-century German philosophy, traces the development of Kant's conception of critique, and offers fresh and in-depth analyses of key parts of the *Critique of Pure Reason*, including the Transcendental Deduction, the Schematism Chapter, the Appendix to the Transcendental Analytic, and the Architectonic. The book not only brings out the coherence of Kant's project but also reconstructs the outline of the 'system of pure reason' for which the *Critique* was to pave the way, but which never saw the light.

KARIN DE BOER is Professor of Philosophy at the University of Leuven, Belgium. She is the author of *Thinking in the Light of Time: Heidegger's Encounter with Hegel* (2000) and *On Hegel: The Sway of the Negative* (2010), as well as numerous articles on Kant, Hegel, classical German philosophy, and Heidegger. She also coedited, with Tinca Prunea-Bretonnet, *The Experiential Turn in Eighteenth-Century German Philosophy* (2020).

T0381879

KANT'S REFORM OF METAPHYSICS

The Critique of Pure Reason *Reconsidered*

KARIN DE BOER

University of Leuven

CAMBRIDGE UNIVERSITY PRESS

CAMBRIDGE
UNIVERSITY PRESS

University Printing House, Cambridge CB2 8BS, United Kingdom

One Liberty Plaza, 20th Floor, New York, NY 10006, USA

477 Williamstown Road, Port Melbourne, VIC 3207, Australia

314-321, 3rd Floor, Plot 3, Splendor Forum, Jasola District Centre, New Delhi - 110025, India

103 Penang Road, #05-06/07, Visioncrest Commercial, Singapore 238467

Cambridge University Press is part of the University of Cambridge.

It furthers the University's mission by disseminating knowledge in the pursuit of
education, learning and research at the highest international levels of excellence.

www.cambridge.org
Information on this title: www.cambridge.org/9781108820110
DOI: 10.1017/9781108897983

© Karin de Boer 2020

First published 2020
First paperback edition 2022

A catalogue record for this publication is available from the British Library

Library of Congress Cataloging in Publication data
NAMES: Boer, Karin de, author.
TITLE: Kant's reform of metaphysics : the Critique of pure reason reconsidered / Karin de Boer,
Katholieke Universiteit Leuven, Belgium.
DESCRIPTION: Cambridge, United Kingdom ; New York, NY, USA : Cambridge University Press,
2020. | Includes bibliographical references and index.
IDENTIFIERS: LCCN 2020009143 (print) | LCCN 2020009144 (ebook) | ISBN 9781108842174
(hardback) | ISBN 9781108820110 (paperback) | ISBN 9781108897983 (epub)
SUBJECTS: LCSH: Kant, Immanuel, 1724-1804. Kritik der reinen Vernunft.
CLASSIFICATION: LCC B2779 .B646 2020 (print) | LCC B2779 (ebook) | DDC 121–dc21
LC record available at https://lccn.loc.gov/2020009143
LC ebook record available at https://lccn.loc.gov/2020009144

ISBN 978-1-108-84217-4 Hardback
ISBN 978-1-108-82011-0 Paperback

Contents

Acknowledgments

Like a river, this book owes its life to many sources, some of which gave rise to small currents that for years hardly came to the surface, if at all. One of these currents can be traced back to the time I taught a course on the history of metaphysics at the University of Amsterdam. In 1998, Chris Doude van Troostwijk suggested I include excerpts from Wolff's *German Metaphysics* to clarify Kant's critique of the metaphysical tradition. I would like to thank him for making me aware of Wolff's work. I started teaching advanced courses on the *Critique of Pure Reason* at the University of Groningen in 2007, and I am indebted to Job Zinkstok and Johan Blok for the inspiring discussions on the *Critique* we had during the years that followed.

From 2008 onward, my ideas on Kant began to come together and find their way to audiences and readers, all of whom I would like to acknowledge. I am grateful to my critics, including the many anonymous referees who read versions of articles and the present book, for challenging me to make my account more clear and compelling. Among the many researchers from whose comments and questions my work on Kant has benefited, or who provided advice and support, I would like to thank in particular Juan Bonaccini, Emanuele Cafagna, Mario Caimi, Brian Chance, Corey Dyck, Miguel Herszenbaun, Stephen Houlgate, Julia Jansen, Guido Kreis, Thomas Land, Colin Mcquillan, James Messina, Fernando Moledo, Angelica Nuzzo, Arnaud Pelletier, Tinca Prunea-Bretonnet, Pavel Reichl, Oliver Sensen, Camilla Serck-Hanssen, Kristi Sweet, Henning Tegtmeyer, and Eric Watkins.

I am grateful to my colleagues and supporting staff at the Institute of Philosophy of the University of Leuven for their dedication and the friendly atmosphere, and to the many students who took the classes on the *Critique of Pure Reason* that I taught at this institute from 2012 onward. Special thanks are due to my past and present doctoral students Elise Frketich, Simon Truwant, Sean Winkler, Gesa Wellmann, Cody

Staton, Yannick Van den Abbeel, Mihaela Vatavu, Markos Feseha, Kwangchul Kim, Luciano Perulli, Pierpaolo Betti, and Wai Lam Foo, as well as to Dennis Vanden Auweele, Henny Blomme, Stephen Howard, David Wood, and Laure Cahen-Maurel, for their trust, the spirited conversations, and their cooperation on a number of workshops and conferences devoted to Kant and classical German philosophy. I am also grateful to Stephen Howard for his perspicuous comments on the final draft of this manuscript. Finally, I would like to express my gratitude to Karel, my husband, to whom I owe so much of my non-philosophical life.

Earlier versions of a number of chapters, or parts of them, have been published previously. All texts have been substantially revised. I wish to thank the editors and publishers for their permission to reuse (parts of) the following articles and chapters: "Pure Reason's Enlightenment: Transcendental Reflection in Kant's First *Critique*," *Kant Yearbook* 2, 2010, 53–73; "Kant, Hegel, and the System of Pure Reason," in Elena Ficara (ed.), *Die Begründung der Philosophie im Deutschen Idealismus* (Würzburg: Königshausen und Neumann, 2010), 77–87; "Transformations of Transcendental Philosophy: Wolff, Kant, and Hegel," *Bulletin of the Hegel Society of Great Britain* 32/1–2, 2011, 50–79; "Kant's Multi-Layered Conception of Things-in-Themselves, Transcendental Objects, and Monads," *Kant-Studien* 105/2, 2014, 221–60; "Categories versus Schemata: Kant's Two-Aspect Theory of Pure Concepts and his Critique of Wolffian Metaphysics," *Journal of the History of Philosophy* 54/3, 2016, 441–68; "Kant's Account of Sensible Concepts in the *Inaugural Dissertation* and the *Critique of Pure Reason*," in Violetta Waibel, Margit Ruffing, and David Wagner (eds.), *Natur und Freiheit. Akten des XII. Internationalen Kant-Kongresses* (Berlin: De Gruyter, 2018), 1015–22.

Abbreviations

Works that consist of numbered paragraphs are cited by the numbers of the paragraphs alone.

Abbreviations of Kant's Works

A/B	*Critique of Pure Reason* [1781/1789]
Announcement	*Announcement of the Organisation of His Lectures in the Winter Semester 1765–66* [1765]
CJ	*Critique of the Power of Judgment* [1790]
CPrR	*Critique of Practical Reason* [1788]
Diss	*Concerning the Form and Principles of the Sensible and Intelligible World (Inaugural Dissertation)* [1770]
Dreams	*Dreams of a Spirit-Seer* [1766]
Inquiry	*Inquiry Concerning the Distinctness of the Principles of Natural Theology and Morals (Prize Essay)* [1764]
LM	*Lectures on Metaphysics*
LRT	*Lectures on Rational Theology*
MFNS	*Metaphysical Foundations of Natural Science* [1786]
NE	*A New Elucidation of the First Principles of Metaphysical Cognition* [1755]
PM	*The Employment in Natural Philosophy of Metaphysics Combined with Geometry, of Which Sample I Contains the Physical Monadology* [1756]
Prol	*Prolegomena to Any Future Metaphysics That Will Be Able to Present Itself as a Science* [1783]
R	*Notes and Fragments*

Other Abbreviations

AN   Wolff, *Ausführliche Nachricht von seinen eigenen Schriften, die er in Deutscher Sprache herausgegeben* [Detailed Report on the Author's Own Writings] [1733]

Anm   Wolff, *Der Vernünftige Gedancken von Gott, der Welt und der Seele des Menschen, auch allen Dingen überhaupt, Anderer Theil, bestehend in Ausfuhrlichen Anmerckungen* (Detailed Remarks on the German Metaphysics) [1740]

Arch   Lambert, *Anlage zur Architektonik oder Theorie des Einfachen und Ersten in der philosophischen und mathematischen Erkenntnis* [Groundwork of the Architectonic or Theory of the Simple and First in Philosophical and Mathematical Cognition] [1771]

ASP   Tetens, *Über die allgemeine speculativische Philosophie* [On General Speculative Philosophy] [1775]

DP   Wolff, *Discursus praeliminaris de philosophia in genere* [Preliminary Discourse on Philosophy in General] [1728]

EDR   Meier, *Auszug aus der Vernunftlehre* [Excerpts from the Doctrine of Reason] [1752]

Essay   Locke, *An Essay Concerning Human Understanding* [1690]

GL   Wolff, *Vernünfftige Gedanken von der Kräften des menschlichen Verstandes und ihrem richtigen Gebrauche in Erkänntnis der Wahrheit* (German Logic) [1712]

GM   Wolff, *Vernünfftige Gedanken von Gott, der Welt und der Seele des Menschen, auch allen Dingen überhaupt* (German Metaphysics) [1719–20]

LC   Wolff, *Cosmologia generalis* (Latin Cosmology) [1731]

LL   Wolff, *Philosophia rationalis sive logica methodo scientifica pertractata* (Latin Logic) [1728]

LO   Wolff, *Philosophia Prima sive ontologica methodo scientifica pertractata* (Latin Ontology) [1730]

M   Baumgarten, *Metaphysics* [1739]

O   Crusius, *Entwurf der notwendigen Vernunft-Wahrheiten, wiefern sie den Zufälligen entgegen gesetzet werden* [Outline of the Necessary Truths of Reason] [1745]

P   Crusius, *Weg zur Gewissheit und Zuverlässigkeit der menschlichen Erkenntniss* [Path to the Certainty and Reliability of Human Cognition] [1747]

Introduction

Four years after the publication of the *Critique of Pure Reason*, Moses Mendelssohn noted in his *Morning Hours: Lectures on God's Existence* that his weak nerves had prevented him from reading the recent works in metaphysics by Lambert, Tetens, Plattner, "and even the all-crushing Kant," works that he admitted to knowing through "inadequate reports of friends and reviews" only.[1]

As poor as Mendelssohn's sources may have been, Kant's *Critique of Pure Reason* had indeed sought to crush the assumption that the human mind can obtain a priori knowledge of things such as the soul and God. But is that 'all'? In my opinion, Mendelssohn's worn-out but frequently cited words do not account for Kant's lifelong effort to turn metaphysics into a science. Contra Mendelssohn and the scholarship that followed in his tracks, I argue in the present book that the *Critique of Pure Reason* seeks to reform rather than abolish the metaphysical systems exemplified by the one that Christian Wolff published in 1719–20. This is to say that I consider Kant's *Critique* to dissect Wolffian metaphysics in order to discard its dogmatist assumptions and appropriate those of its elements that he took to be vital to the further enlightenment of the sciences and humanity at large.[2]

Since metaphysics meant something else in eighteenth-century Germany than it does in many contemporary contexts, it is useful to specify the main features of the post-Leibnizian metaphysics Kant engaged with from the time he was a student. Wolff's metaphysical system relies on the twofold division common in seventeenth-century metaphysical treatises. The first part, called fundamental science, general metaphysics, or

---

[1] Mendelssohn (1979: 5), my translation.
[2] In what follows, I will often refer to Wolffian and post-Leibnizian metaphysics indiscriminately. The latter term has the advantage of not excluding early critics of Wolff such as Crusius. However, since Crusius is deeply indebted to Wolff, he might be considered a proponent of Wolffian metaphysics broadly conceived.

ontology, consists in a comprehensive treatment of the concepts and principles that inform any cognition of objects whatsoever and, accordingly, cannot be treated within disciplines devoted to a particular kind of object. This part can be said to treat the determinations proper to things as such, regardless of whether they are simple or composite, mental or physical, immaterial or material. Accordingly, it was considered to prepare the ground for the second and main part. Often called special or applied metaphysics, this part consists in a comprehensive account of the determinations proper to a number of particular things, namely, the soul, the world as such, and God.³ Even though Wolff drew importantly on inner observations of the cognitive activities carried out by the human mind, he held that metaphysical truths could be obtained, at least in principle, by means of the intellect alone, that is, by means of inferences based on indubitable premises.

Given this preliminary sketch, the task Kant refers to as critique in the *Critique of Pure Reason* can be clarified in somewhat more specific terms. As was suggested above, critique, for Kant, is a matter of sifting the wheat from the chaff. This means with regard to the first part of Wolffian metaphysics, I will argue, that Kant embraced the idea of a discipline devoted to the concepts and principles presupposed in any cognition of objects, but shed the assumption that these cognitive elements amount to determinations of things. Put briefly, Kant's reform of former ontology consists in restricting the scope of these cognitive elements to possible objects of experience.

My take on Kant's critique of the second part of Wolffian metaphysics is perhaps more controversial. As I see it, Kant aimed to preserve what he took to be the rational core of the metaphysical disciplines devoted to the soul, the world as such, and God. Drawing on his critique of Wolffian ontology, he merely rejected the assumption that the treatment of these ideas and their determinations amounts to the cognition of *objects*. Kant's main reason to hold on to reformed versions of the rational psychology, general cosmology, and natural theology elaborated by his predecessors was

---

³ See Wolff, DP 56, 73, 99. Wolff here and elsewhere does not use a term such as 'special metaphysics,' but only refers to the particular disciplines that fall under it. In his commentary on his own German writings, Wolff notes in relation to his *German Metaphysics*: "I consider metaphysics ... , if it is to be truly comprehensive, to include 1. the foundational science or ontology ... ; 2. the doctrine of spirits or pneumatology ... ; 3. the general doctrine of the world or cosmology ... ; and 4. the natural knowledge of God or theology" (AN 4). See Vollrath (1962), Mora (1963), Sala (1988), and Ficara (2006: 83–106) for accounts of the intricate history of the distinction between general and special metaphysics up to Wolff and Baumgarten. See Baum (2015) for a helpful overview of Kant's conception of metaphysics.

his belief that the rational core of these disciplines must undergird the efforts on the part of philosophy to further the moral improvement of mankind and quell threats stemming from currents such as skepticism and materialism (cf. Bxxv, Bxxxiv).

Accordingly, the chapters that follow challenge not only the assumption that the *Critique of Pure Reason* destroyed metaphysics, but also the more widespread one that it established a 'metaphysics of experience' and eradicated any 'transcendent' metaphysics. The term 'metaphysics of experience' is mostly used to refer to Kant's investigation into the conditions of possibility of empirical knowledge.[4] However, apart from the fact that Kant does not use the terms 'metaphysics of experience' and 'transcendent metaphysics,' I hold that they obscure the logic behind his arguments in a number of ways.

First, the term 'metaphysics of experience' obfuscates the affinity between, on the one hand, the account of the categories and their corresponding principles elaborated in the Transcendental Analytic and, on the other hand, the content of Wolffian ontology.

Second, the term does not account for the two strands of which the Transcendental Analytic consists. This part of the *Critique* not only provides an account of the concepts and principles constitutive of any type of cognition, but also investigates if and how the human mind can obtain a priori cognitions of objects at all. Kant needs to answer the latter question, I contend, in order to determine to what extent, or under which conditions, metaphysics can achieve the a priori cognitions of objects it has always aspired to, that is, a priori cognitions that pertain either to any thing whatsoever or to things such as the soul and God. Evidently, I do not deny that the Transcendental Aesthetic and Transcendental Analytic provide an account of the conditions of possibility of experience. I will argue, however, that this account is not so much an end in itself as a means to get clear on the conditions under which metaphysics can be "brought onto the secure path of a science" (Bxxiii). Seen from this vantage point, the Transcendental Analytic and Transcendental Dialectic are not concerned

---

[4] The term was introduced by Paton. Contrasting Kant's "metaphysic of experience" and "the speculative metaphysics of the past," Paton (1936a: 72) takes the former discipline to be carried out in the Transcendental Aesthetic and Transcendental Analytic. He calls it a metaphysics because he mistakenly identifies it with the discipline that Kant at Bxviii calls "metaphysics in its first part." As I will argue in Chapter 2, Section 2, this passage is concerned with the first part of Kant's projected metaphysical system. The term 'transcendent metaphysics' is used by Kemp Smith (1923: 19). Both terms obtained wide currency through Strawson (1966).

with different topics, but elaborate a critique of general metaphysics and special metaphysics, respectively.

Third, I hold that the term 'transcendent metaphysics' is unhelpful as well, and this for a reason already mentioned above: the term obscures Kant's intention to carry out a reform of both main parts of former metaphysics. Clearly, as far as the negative strand of Kant's critique is concerned, the Transcendental Dialectic analyzes in great detail what goes wrong if metaphysics seeks to obtain a priori cognitions of quasi-objects such as the soul, the zzworld as such, and God. As far as its positive strand is concerned, there is agreement on Kant's affirmation of the ideas that refer to these quasi-objects as regulatory principles. However, few commentators have seriously considered Kant's plan, outlined in the Architectonic, to elaborate a metaphysical system the structure of which largely corresponds to Wolff's and Baumgarten's. For the most part, this plan is either ignored or regarded as a remnant of Kant's pre-critical dogmatism that inexplicably resurfaces in a work presumed to have cut all ties to Wolffian metaphysics.[5]

Since my reading of the *Critique of Pure Reason* hinges importantly on Kant's stated intention to publish a comprehensive metaphysical system, a few more remarks on this issue are in order. In both versions of the Preface and Introduction, Kant unambiguously presents the *Critique of Pure Reason* as a work intended to prepare the ground for such a system. On his conception of metaphysics, he writes in the 1781 Preface, the discipline "is the only one of all the sciences that can rightly expect to be able to reach ... completion." The metaphysics he envisions can be completed, he asserts, because it

> is nothing but the inventory of everything we possess through pure reason, ordered systematically.... Such a system of pure (speculative) reason I hope myself to deliver under the title Metaphysics of Nature, which will be ... incomparably richer in content than this critique, which had first to display its *sources and conditions of its possibility*, and needed to clear and level a ground that was completely overgrown.[6]

---

[5] See A841–47/B869–75. As far as Anglophone literature is concerned, Kemp Smith set the tone by noting that the Architectonic "is of slight scientific importance, and is chiefly of interest for the light which it casts upon Kant's personality." He adds that Kant's account of the various parts of the system "are for the most part not his own philosophical property, but are taken over from the Wolffian system" (1923: 579). More recent literature will be considered in Chapter 8.

[6] Axx–xxi, emphasis mine, translation modified; cf. Bxxxvi, Bxliii–xliv, A11–12/B25–26. Further relevant passages will be discussed in Chapter 8.

It is noteworthy that Kant here considers the *Critique of Pure Reason* to be concerned with the conditions of possibility not of experience but of metaphysics.

For reasons that will be discussed in due course, Kant never carried out his plan. However, various texts, including the *Critique* itself, provide material that makes it possible to reconstruct the outline of Kant's projected "system of pure reason."[7] According to the Architectonic, Kant intended to divide his metaphysical system into a theoretical and a practical part, called metaphysics of nature and metaphysics of morals, respectively.[8] Like most of the Architectonic, the passage cited above addresses the theoretical part of the system alone. I would like to stress, however, that Kant uses the term 'metaphysics of nature' in a very broad sense. The part of the system to which it refers was to contain both an ontology and disciplines concerned with nature qua object of outer sense, the soul qua object of inner sense, the world as such, and God (A845–46/ B873–74). Kant held that versions of the latter disciplines, however minimal, must be preserved not only because of the regulative function of the ideas of reason, but also for the sake of morality: the practical part of the system must rely on the results obtained in the theoretical part, and, conversely, the practical part provides these results with a content – or objective reality – that theoretical reason itself is unable to procure.[9]

In the 1787 Preface, Kant not only reiterates his ambition to publish a metaphysical system, but explicitly relates his projected system to Wolff's:

> The *Critique* is the preparatory work (*vorläufige Veranstaltung*) required for the advancement of a rigorous metaphysics as science, a science that must necessarily be carried out dogmatically and, complying with the strictest requirement, systematically, hence in the manner of the schools (*schulgerecht*); for this requirement is one that metaphysics may not neglect, since it takes it upon itself to carry out its task wholly a priori and thus to the full satisfaction of speculative reason. In the execution of the plan that the *Critique* prescribes, i.e., in the future system of metaphysics, we will have to follow the strict method of the famous Wolff, the greatest among all dogmatic philosophers.[10]

---

[7] See A11/B25, A204/B249, A841/B869.

[8] A841/B869. Kant's *Metaphysical Foundations of the Natural Sciences* (1786) can be considered to elaborate the first part of what the Architectonic calls rational physiology (A845/B873), but Kant's own remarks on the status of this work are somewhat equivocal. I discuss this problem in Chapter 8, Section 4.1.

[9] Cf. Bxx–xxi, A641/B669, A807–8/B835–36.   [10] Bxxxvi, translation modified.

Clearly, passages such as these are hard to square with the assumption that Kant intended, if not to destroy metaphysics completely, at least to reduce it to the account of the conditions of possibility of experience put forward in the Transcendental Aesthetic and Transcendental Analytic.

Given Kant's stated aim to elaborate a metaphysical system, I hold that he in the *Critique of Pure Reason* primarily engages with Wolff and Baumgarten, whose works he had studied more thoroughly than those of Leibniz or Descartes. As is well known, throughout his long career Kant mostly used Baumgarten's *Metaphysics* (1739) for his classes on metaphysics. However, I consider the negative strand of his critique to be ultimately aimed at an assumption common to Leibniz, Wolff, and the metaphysical tradition as such, namely, the assumption that knowledge of objects can be obtained by the intellect alone.

The fact that Kant's projected system never saw the light of day has contributed importantly to the prevailing trend among commentators to marginalize or ignore Kant's remarks on the subject and treat the *Critique of Pure Reason* as an end in itself. This holds true not only of the Architectonic but also of the Transcendental Doctrine of Method of which it is part. Even though the structure of this final main part of the work is rather elusive, I take it to contain important clues as to the larger context of Kant's critical project.

Kant's remarks on the relation between critique and system in the Doctrine of Method cohere with his presentation of the aim of the *Critique* in the two Prefaces and the Introduction. None of the passages on this subject refers to conditions of possibility of experience. Rather, Kant considers the "main question" at stake in this work to be the question as to "what and how much the understanding and reason can know free of all experience," in other words, the question as to what can be known a priori (Axvii). Examining the human mind in view of this question, the *Critique* is said to be concerned with the "decision about the possibility or impossibility of a metaphysics as such, and the determination of its sources, as well as its extent and boundaries."[11] Similarly, Kant notes that metaphysics "stands or falls" with the solution to the problem as to how we can make judgments about objects independently of experience, that is, judgments that are synthetic and a priori (B19). The examples taken from physics and mathematics (B14–18) clearly serve the purpose of determining

---

[11] Axii, cf. A11/B25, Bxxii. In the same vein, Kant considers transcendental logic to "determine the origin, extension, and objective validity" of the cognitions "by means of which we think objects completely a priori" (A57/B81, translation modified).

whether metaphysics is capable of "extending its a priori cognition synthetically" (B23) and, thus, of determining "how metaphysics is possible as a science."[12]

But if the *Critique* aims to identify the conditions under which Wolffian metaphysics can become a science, one might ask why Kant compares its task to the revolution achieved by Copernicus (Bxxii). Does not this suggest he took his critical philosophy to be completely novel? In my view, however, Kant's comparison concerns his decision to restrict the domain of his propaedeutic investigation to the cognitive elements that allow the human mind to turn representations into objects of cognition at all. This "reversal," as he calls it (Bxvi), does not entail there is no continuity between the version of metaphysics that the *Critique of Pure Reason* subjects to critique and the version Kant intended to elaborate on its basis. Indeed, the *Prolegomena* puts into perspective Kant's alleged break with the past by asserting that the *Critique* undertakes "a complete reform or rather a rebirth of metaphysics" that nothing will be able to halt.[13] As will be argued in Chapter 8, Kant's projected metaphysics would have resembled its pre-critical counterparts not only in terms of its overall structure but also in terms of its content. On this account, the view that Kant gradually weaned himself from Wolffian metaphysics up to the point of abandoning it altogether is unwarranted.

The present work uses Kant's implicit and explicit engagement with Wolffian metaphysics as a foil to interpret the *Critique of Pure Reason* as a work intended to turn metaphysics such as it was known to him into a science. Given this focus, the approach defended in this book deviates from many past and present accounts of the work. Regardless of the numerous tangled controversies among twentieth-century and contemporary commentators, most accounts concentrate on the investigation into the conditions of possibility of experience carried out in the Transcendental Aesthetic and Transcendental Analytic. This approach can be traced back to at least Cohen's *Kant's Theory of Experience*, published in 1871, and neo-Kantianism more generally.

According to Cohen, the *Critique of Pure Reason* seeks to ground Newtonian physics by identifying those "elements of consciousness" that

---

[12] B22, cf. A10, Prol, 4:274.

[13] Prol, 4:257. The German term is *Reform*. Passages that likewise refer to Kant's indented reform of metaphysics, using this term, include 4:258 and (in the Appendix) 373 and 382. In a letter to Bernouilli dated November 16, 1781, Kant refers to Lambert's invitation, in 1765, to "collaborate on the reform of metaphysics" (10:277, cf. Kant to Lambert, December 31, 1765, 10:57).

are "sufficient and necessary to establish and ground the fact of science."[14] Whether or not the role Cohen granted to Newton is accepted, the assumption that the main aim of the *Critique* consists in accounting for the a priori principles of empirical science informs a large range of more recent commentaries.

For example, in *The Bounds of Sense*, Strawson values Kant's investigation into "that limiting framework of ideas and principles the use and application of which are essential to empirical knowledge."[15] Similarly, Allison's widely shared epistemological reading considers the *Critique* to demonstrate that human knowledge is based on epistemic conditions "without which our representations would not relate to objects."[16] Tacitly identifying this knowledge with experience, Allison takes Kant to be concerned with the a priori elements constitutive of the latter. While this claim is, of course, not false, I maintain that what Allison and others fail to see is that Kant conceived of the categories and the principles of the pure understanding as instances of a priori cognition that first and foremost need to be scrutinized for their own sake and, ultimately, for the sake of determining to what extent metaphysics can avail itself of these instances.

The assumption that the *Critique* turns on the a priori elements of empirical knowledge also informs recent so-called metaphysical approaches to the *Critique of Pure Reason*.[17] Drawing on Strawson and Guyer, among others, proponents of this approach frame Kant's text in view of questions and terms derived from the analytic tradition. Thus, in her *Manifest Reality: Kant's Idealism and His Realism*, Allais presents what she calls a "moderate metaphysical interpretation" (2015: 8). In line with classical scholarship, she considers Kant's *Critique* to contain a "metaphysics of

---

[14] See Cohen (1871/1987: 108). Cohen's reading of Kant is discussed in more detail in De Boer and Howard (2019). In this article, we also examine the so-called metaphysical readings of Kant elaborated in the 1910s and 1920s, including Heidegger's, which took issue with neo-Kantianism.

[15] Strawson (1966: 18, cf. 44).

[16] Allison (2004: 11). See Ameriks (2000: 59) for a similar view. Ameriks has taken a more controversial stance in other works, arguing that Kant's critique of Wolffian metaphysics went hand in hand with the effort to preserve some of its ideas and doctrines. The present work shares common ground with his in this regard. However, since Ameriks's studies are mostly concerned with the Transcendental Dialectic (Ameriks 1982/2000) and Kant's lectures on Baumgarten (Ameriks 1992), it is unclear how he conceives of the relation between the two strands of the *Critique of Pure Reason* that he deals with in his various works.

[17] More generally, I consider the very opposition between metaphysics and epistemology to be misguided if used in relation to Kant. As was mentioned above, what is currently meant by metaphysics differs substantially from the discipline Kant was familiar with. The term 'epistemology' refers to a discipline not known to Kant either, although elements of it were elaborated in Wolffian logic and empirical psychology.

experience" (6). Unlike Paton and others, however, she uses the term 'metaphysics' to denote "what philosophers generally mean by the term today," which is to say that she takes Kant's investigation to be "concerned with the nature of reality." More specifically, she considers Kant's account to be metaphysical in that it seeks to determine, for example, whether "every event has a cause" or the extent to which spatiotemporal objects are mind-independent.[18]

While Allais convincingly rebuts a number of alternative accounts, I disagree with her apparent view, shared by many contemporary scholars, that the arguments put forward in the *Critique of Pure Reason* can be understood without reference to the immediate historical context within which they were developed.[19] As regards the content at stake in the debate in which she is engaged, moreover, I do not believe that Kant's arguments essentially concern the triangular relation between the a priori elements of the human mind, its representations of the things it encounters by means of the senses, and mind-independent things that must somehow be posited even though they cannot be known. Put in contemporary terms, the present book, rather, focuses on Kant's meta-metaphysical concerns, even if one of the challenges of the *Critique* will precisely turn out to be the intricate relationship between Kant's first-order account of the a priori elements of any type of cognition and his second-order investigation into the conditions under which metaphysics' use of such elements is warranted.[20]

Focusing as it does on the problem of metaphysics presented in the introductory sections of the *Critique of Pure Reason*, my reading has more affinity with the metaphysical interpretations defended in the 1910s and 1920s by authors such as Pichler, Wundt, Heimsoeth, and Heidegger.[21] Regardless of their disagreements on particular issues, they consider the *Critique* to be continuous with Wolffian general or special metaphysics.

[18] Allais (2015: 7). Most commentators would agree, against Allais, that Kant rather seeks to determine what it means to employ a principle such as 'all events have a cause' in the sciences and/or metaphysics at all.

[19] Accordingly, the reading elaborated in the chapters to come also avoids labels such as realism, anti-realism, phenomenalism, idealism, and skepticism.

[20] What I call 'first-order metaphysics' refers to former general and special metaphysics as well as to the reformed versions of these disciplines that Kant intended to elaborate in a comprehensive fashion in his projected system. These disciplines are contrasted with what I take to be the main aim of the *Critique*, namely, Kant's second-order investigation into the very possibility of first-order metaphysics.

[21] See Heimsoeth (1924/1956), Wundt (1924), and Heidegger (1929/1997). In his pioneering work, published in 1910, Pichler argues that Wolff's ontology and Kant's *Critique of Pure Reason* are both concerned with the "rules of the pure thinking of an object" (Pichler 1910: 73–74, cf. 4).

However, since their readings are largely shaped by their opposition to neo-Kantianism, they tend to err on the other side, namely, by down-playing the distance between Kant and his German predecessors. Apart from more specific hermeneutical problems with their works, these authors therefore no less than their opponents tend to misconstrue the goal of Kant's intended reform of metaphysics. Notwithstanding the insightful elements contained in *Kant and the Problem of Metaphysics*, I hold that this is also true of Heidegger's account of the *Critique* as a work concerned with the inner possibility, ground, or foundation of metaphysics rather than with a thoroughgoing critique of its premises.[22]

Where relevant, more recent approaches to Kant will be discussed in the chapters that follow. I merely want to note at this point that *Kant's Reform of Metaphysics* ties in with two relatively new trends in Kant scholarship, namely, to pay heed to the immediate intellectual context from which Kant's philosophy emerged and, more specifically, to interpret his writings in light of Wolff and Baumgarten's logical and metaphysical treatises. Yet since studies that do so tend to focus on Kant's early works, his lectures on Baumgarten, or a specific aspect of the *Critique*, they as yet have had little impact on the very framing of Kant's critical endeavor.[23] The present book

---

[22] While my approach to Kant is indebted to Heidegger's as regards the main direction of the *Critique of Pure Reason*, I disagree with a number of features of his interpretation, including his focus on the subjective elements of the Transcendental Deduction, his account of the imagination, and the idea of transcendence he projects onto Kant's text. Moreover, his initial remarks on Kant's engagement with the Wolffian tradition do not have any clear bearing on the work as a whole. On my assessment of Heidegger's reading of Kant, see De Boer (2015) and De Boer and Howard (2019).

[23] Studies that interpret the *Critique of Pure Reason* by taking recourse to Wolffian logic include Longuenesse (1998), Lanier Anderson (2015), and Lu-Adler (2018). A number of recent publications testify to the growing interest in Kant's engagement with the metaphysics of his German predecessors, including translations into German and English of Baumgarten's *Metaphysica*, a collection of essays on Kant's lectures on metaphysics (Fugate 2019), and a collection on Baumgarten and Kant (Fugate and Hymers 2018). However, very few of the essays in the latter volume deal with the *Critique of Pure Reason* and none of them takes into consideration the Transcendental Analytic or Kant's projected system. See Heimsoeth (1924/1956), Fulda (1988), Grondin (1989), Ameriks (1982/2000, 1992), Zöller (2004), Ficara (2006), and Baum (2015), among others, for earlier studies that underscore Kant's indebtedness to Wolffian metaphysics or interpret Kant's innovations in light of the latter. Elaborating on a number of Kant's German predecessors, Watkins (2005) focuses on an issue relevant to metaphysics – causality – rather than the question concerning the possibility of the discipline as such. However, I agree with his emphasis on the continuity between Kant's early works and the *Critique* (cf. 182). Dyck (2014) likewise tackles Kant's engagement with Wolff and his followers in relation to a particular metaphysical discipline rather than the problem of metaphysics as such. Moreover, his excellent study is concerned with the Transcendental Dialectic rather than the Transcendental Analytic.

seeks to redress this situation by reinterpreting the *Critique of Pure Reason* in light of Kant's engagement with Wolff and the tradition he initiated.

As I hope has become clear from the discussion so far, I intend to frame the *Critique of Pure Reason* in a way that brings out the unity of its various elements. This is to say that I reject the tendency among earlier commentators, including Kemp Smith, to identify particular strands of the work as critical and dismiss others as relics of Kant's allegedly dogmatic writings. Of course, it cannot be denied that the *Critique* brings together insights developed over more than a decade. Yet those who see the work as a patchwork of seemingly incongruous elements fail to see the pattern by dint of which they constitute elements of a whole. In this regard, we can take a cue from one of Kant's early letters to Herz:

> Insight into the matters at hand cannot be compelled or precipitated by force, but requires quite a long time, since one *examines one and the same concept intermittently and with regard to many relations and in as many contexts as possible.*[24]

Evidently, Kant in this passage reflects on the way he proceeded during the years leading up to 1771. Yet I hold that, in a similar way, the *Critique* examines a single problem from a number of complementary perspectives, namely, the problem concerning the conditions under which metaphysics is possible as a science.

Discussing a number of these perspectives in depth, the present book considers each of them to uncover an aspect of Kant's proposed solution. However, I largely abstract from Kant's practical philosophy, from the teleological orientation of his theoretical as well as practical works, and, more generally, from works published after the *Critique of Pure Reason*.[25] As far as the *Critique* itself is concerned, the eight chapters of which the present book consists deal most extensively with the Transcendental Analytic. A more than marginal discussion of the Transcendental Aesthetic and the chapter known as the Metaphysical Deduction is beyond its scope. What I do treat is outlined in the remainder of this introduction.

Chapter 1 elaborates on the historical context within which Kant developed his critique of early post-Leibnizian philosophy. It presents the pertinent elements of Wolff's highly influential metaphysics and theory

---

[24] Kant to Herz, June 7, 1771 (10:122, emphasis mine, translation modified).

[25] See Dörflinger (2000) and Fugate (2014) for illuminating studies of the teleological orientation of Kant's *Critique of Pure Reason* and his critical works in general. The holistic interpretation of Kant's practical philosophy provided by Sweet (2013) likewise stresses the role of reason's end-directedness.

of cognition as well as the main thrust of Crusius's critique of Wolff. Since I consider Kant's critique to target both Wolff, Crusius, and those who followed in their wake, the chapter also discusses the main tenets of Crusius's own metaphysics and the controversies that resulted from efforts among early post-Wolffian philosophers to reconcile Leibnizian monadology and Newtonian physics.

The second chapter seeks to clarify, against the background of the first, how Kant in the late 1760s and early 1770s came to conceive of the aim and main arguments of what was to become the *Critique of Pure Reason*. I focus in particular on Kant's evolving understanding of the act of critique and the criteria on which this act must rely in order to distinguish the viable core of metaphysics from its unfounded assumptions. The heart of the chapter consists in an analysis of the *Inaugural Dissertation*. Unlike most commentators, I highlight the critical impetus of this pivotal treatise by arguing that the specific criterion it employs to curb the ambitions of metaphysics – intellectual purity – is directed against an assumption common to Wolff, Crusius, and early post-Leibnizian philosophy in general. Moreover, I put into perspective the alleged break between the *Dissertation* and the *Critique* by arguing that this early instance of critique is preserved in the *Critique of Pure Reason*. Evidently, the *Critique* also marks a break with the earlier works: the new form of critique introduced in the Transcendental Analytic seeks to establish that any a priori cognition of objects rests on pure intuition. Preparing the ground for Chapter 8, I contend that these two complementary types of critique do not entail the impossibility of metaphysics, but specify the conditions under which the discipline might be turned into a science.

Chapter 3 addresses the relationship between the various tasks carried out in the *Critique of Pure Reason* by analyzing Kant's multifaceted use of the term 'transcendental.' Challenging the received view, I argue that this term does not primarily denote Kant's investigation into the conditions of possibility of experience, but has a much broader scope. I maintain that Kant's seemingly divergent accounts of the subject hinge on his conception of transcendental philosophy proper and transcendental critique as first-order and second-order branches of transcendental cognition, respectively. Drawing on a brief account of the seventeenth- and eighteenth-century history of the term 'transcendental,' I seek to show that Wolffian ontology and transcendental philosophy proper have more in common than is widely assumed: both disciplines can be said to provide a comprehensive account of the cognitive elements presupposed in any cognition of objects. I argue that the novelty of the *Critique* consists primarily in the second-order investigation into metaphysics that Kant calls transcendental critique. The chapter concludes by examining Kant's criticism of the way his predecessors and contemporaries understood the terms 'ontology' and 'transcendental philosophy.' In this context, I also consider his understanding of the intricate relationship between first-order and second-order transcendental cognition.

Chapter 4 is devoted to one of the most contentious elements of the *Critique*, namely, Kant's account of the thing in itself. From the late 1780s onward, many commentators have argued that Kant contradicts himself by claiming both that things in themselves cannot be known and that they cause our sense perceptions. In order to resolve the tangle that Kant's account has produced, I dissociate his remarks on the objects that affect our senses from his use of the term 'thing in itself' and its cognates in the context of his critique of Wolffian and post-Wolffian metaphysics. In the latter context, I argue, the term refers to things that can be thought but cannot constitute objects of cognition. I show that Kant's account of the thing in itself in this sense and, hence, the distinction between phenomena and noumena, allows him at once to limit the scope of former ontology to possible objects of experience and to affirm the ideas of the soul, the world as such, and God as noumena that can be thought but not known.

Focusing on its 1781 version, Chapter 5 interprets the Transcendental Deduction in light of Kant's overall investigation into the conditions under which metaphysics is possible. Whereas most commentators take the text to be mainly concerned with the conditions of possibility of empirical cognition, I seek to demonstrate that the various strands of Kant's tortuous investigation primarily aim to identify the conditions under which categories can be used to produce objects of a priori cognition as such. On Kant's account, categories can contribute to the production of such objects only if they function as a priori rules for the thoroughgoing unification of successive representations, which is not the case if they are used to determine alleged objects such as the soul, the world as such, and God. Thus, I contend that the transcendental deduction passes a balanced judgment on Wolff's unqualified affirmation of the possibility of a priori cognition of objects and Hume's unqualified rejection of the same.

Chapter 6 seeks to establish that Kant's account of the schematism of the pure understanding yields the same result as the transcendental deduction, but does so by approaching the question concerning the legitimate use of categories from the angle of time qua pure form of intuition. On my reading, Kant conceives of transcendental schemata and categories as different instances of the a priori rules that determine how the mind can unify a manifold at all. Since transcendental schemata present these rules as ways of unifying successive representations, they can be said to constitute the sensible condition of any a priori cognition of objects. I take Kant to argue that Wolffian metaphysics ought to use categories independently of this condition in order to establish itself as a purely intellectual discipline and, hence, that a priori judgments about the soul or God do not amount to cognitions of objects.

Zooming out, Chapter 7 turns to a section of the *Critique* in which Kant seeks to account for the ultimate premises of his critique and intended reform of metaphysics, namely, the Appendix to the Transcendental Analytic entitled "On the Amphiboly of the Concepts of Reflection." Using Leibniz's monadology as a prism, this section contains Kant's most systematic critique of the ontologies known to him. Kant conceives of this critique as a variety of transcendental reflection that is guided by four pairs of concepts, including sameness and difference. In order to contextualize this account, I briefly discuss Wolff and Baumgarten's treatment of these concepts. Commentators generally assume that the activity called transcendental reflection is carried out in the *Critique* alone. I contend, by contrast, that Kant distinguishes the version of transcendental reflection that informs the ontology of his predecessors from the critical version enacted in the *Critique*. On this basis, I outline Kant's understanding of the difference between a Leibnizian employment of the concepts of reflection and his own.

Chapter 8, finally, is devoted to the positive goal of Kant's reform of the theoretical part of metaphysics, namely, the system of pure reason he intended to elaborate on the basis of the propaedeutic investigation carried out in the *Critique*. On my account, the latter investigation aims to redirect the intellectual activity carried out by pure reason from quasi-objects such as the soul and God to the totality of a priori elements that any cognition of objects presupposes. Drawing on the outline provided in the Architectonic and other relevant texts, I maintain that Kant's critique of Wolffian metaphysics paves the way not only for a reformed version of general metaphysics or ontology but also for a reformed version of special metaphysics. As regards the latter, I argue that the *Critique* does not preclude the possibility of a comprehensive account of the purely intellectual determinations of the ideas of reason themselves and, hence, is much less detrimental to former special metaphysics than is generally assumed. Thus, the chapter seeks to bring out the common ground of Kant's projected system and the metaphysical systems put forward by Wolff and Baumgarten. I conclude the chapter by arguing that his later accounts of his intentions in this regard do not deviate from the plan outlined in the *Critique of Pure Reason*.

I hope to shed new light on Kant's pivotal work, in sum, by framing the text not in view of epistemological questions that took center stage after Kant, but in view of the past to which he responded and the future such as he envisioned it.

Wolff, Crusius, and Kant

1 Introduction

In order to interpret the *Critique of Pure Reason* as a work aimed at a thoroughgoing reform of metaphysics, the first task to be carried out consists in clarifying which metaphysical system or systems Kant considered to call for such a reform. Preparing the ground for the chapters to come, the present chapter does so by contextualizing Kant's critical project in four respects.

The first section seeks to support the claim that the *Critique of Pure Reason* is first and foremost intended to turn Wolff's metaphysics into a proper science. To this end, I examine Kant's explicit assessment of Wolff in this work and texts from the same period.

The second section presents the relevant elements of Wolff's own metaphysics. This will allow me to show, I hope, that Kant and Wolff had more in common than is often assumed: like Kant, Wolff sought to reform the metaphysics of his predecessors and to treat the concepts and principles presupposed in the other sciences in a rigorous and comprehensive way. Building on the account put forward in the present chapter, I will discuss further elements of Wolff's philosophy that shed light on Kant's arguments throughout this book.

Kant's evolving view on the questionable aspects of Wolff's metaphysics was fed by a decade-long debate among Wolffians and anti-Wolffians. There is no doubt that the most prominent representative of the latter, Crusius, had an impact on Kant's critical engagement with Wolff during the 1750s and 1760s. In order to contextualize the critical strand of Kant's effort to reform Wolffian metaphysics, the third section briefly discusses Crusius's criticisms of Wolff. However, the section focuses on the eclectic and rather elusive metaphysical system that Crusius published with the aim of vanquishing his adversary. I will argue that the extravagant elements of this system contributed importantly to Kant's insight into the pernicious assumption common to the metaphysical systems of Wolff, Crusius, and the tradition they drew on, namely, the assumption that sensibility and thought are nothing but two different ways to obtain knowledge of things. I will refer to this assumption as 'continuism.'

As I see it, Kant also came to identify the detrimental effects of this assumption on the efforts of his immediate predecessors and contemporaries to reconcile Leibnizian monadology with the premises of Newtonian physics. These efforts had led to a number of controversies that involved Wolff, Crusius, Kant's own earlier self, and various lesser known philosophers. The final section sketches the contours of these controversies because they shed additional light on the immediate reason of Kant's growing frustration with the state of metaphysics as well as on the increasingly radical solutions presented in the *Inaugural Dissertation* (1770) and the *Critique of Pure Reason* (1781).

Evidently, my account of Wolff's metaphysics and its reception is geared toward the interpretation of Kant's philosophy at stake in this book as a whole. In this respect it is not neutral, but driven by a specific aim. Yet as regards my presentation of Wolff and Crusius, though necessarily concise, I have tried to move away from the one-sided or even misguided images of them that are partly due to Kant's own scant remarks on the subject.

2   Kant's Assessment of Wolff in the 1780s

At the outset of the *Critique of Pure Reason*, Kant paints a grim picture of the metaphysics of his time. Despite Locke's efforts, he writes in its first Preface, the discipline is haunted by "endless controversies" and, as a result, met with scorn and indifference (Aviii–x). On Kant's account, metaphysics seeks to obtain cognitions independently of experience (Axii), that is, by "mere concepts" (Bxiv). If metaphysics is to have a future at all, one ought to determine to what extent this kind of cognition is possible in the first place.

Since the *Critique* seeks to determine "the possibility or impossibility of a metaphysics as such" rather than assess particular "books and systems" (Axii), it contains very few explicit references to Wolff and none to Baumgarten or Crusius. This reticence on Kant's part may have several additional reasons. First, he addressed a readership he could assume was familiar with the main traits of Wolffian and post-Wolffian German philosophy. Second, by referring to metaphysics in general terms, Kant may well have tried to preclude the misguided conclusion that the *Critique* attacked a movement that had suffered many blows already and had lost most of its relevance.

Both Prefaces to the *Critique of Pure Reason* make it clear that Kant's negative remarks represent just one strand of his effort to emancipate the discipline from its "worm-eaten dogmatism" (Ax) and elevate it to a proper science (Bxiv, cf. Axx). That he did not intend to beat a dead horse, but rather sought to reanimate the discipline, is confirmed by a letter to Kästner written in 1790:

> [T]he efforts at critique I have heretofore made are in no way meant ... to attack the Leibniz-Wolffian philosophy (for I find the latter neglected in recent times). The aim of these efforts is rather to reach the same goal, but to do so ... on the basis of a detour that those great men seem to have regarded as superfluous.... This intention of mine will become clearer when, if I live long enough, I carry out my plan of establishing metaphysics in a coherent system.[1]

Transcripts of lectures Kant gave during the first half of the 1780s support the view that the *Critique of Pure Reason* primarily engages with Wolff, who was generally considered to have systematized Leibniz's philosophy, and his followers. They also present the *Critique of Pure Reason* as a detour rather than an end in itself.

Thus, Kant told his students in 1780 that "the dogmatic philosophizing characteristic of Leibniz and Wolff ... contains so much that is misleading that it is necessary to suspend their procedure."[2] In the same context, he deplored the "indifferentism" of his contemporaries, that is, their open contempt of metaphysical ruminations and neglect of metaphysics considered as philosophy proper. The 1781 Preface to the *Critique*, as seen, mentions both the problems afflicting metaphysics and the indifferentism resulting from this predicament in similar terms (cf. Ax). Moreover, the Introduction considers the act of critique to suspend the activity of metaphysics for the sake of an investigation into its capacity or incapacity to erect a building made of concepts alone (A5/B9).

Similarly, in lectures delivered in 1784–85, Kant refers to Wolff in terms that closely resemble those that are used time and again in the *Critique of Pure Reason* to explain the aim of the work:

> Wolff ... did not investigate how we can attain concepts, but presents them in a system that he called metaphysics. Yet he does not investigate to what extent we can use our concepts, what their limits are, and whether we can judge about objects of experience alone or about other things as well. The critique of reason, by contrast, asks: how far does our cognition reach and to

---

[1] Kant to Kästner, August 5 (?), 1790 (11:186, translation modified).
[2] LL Pölitz, PM 16 (dated around 1780).

what extent are we licensed to make use of purely rational cognition (*reine Vernunft-Erkentniß*)?... One therefore should not start thinking about a system of reason without having carried out a critique of reason.[3]

Written in a similar vein, an unpublished note dated 1776–78 has it that

> Wolff did great things in philosophy, but got ahead of himself and extended cognition without securing, altering, and reforming it through a special critique. His works are therefore very useful as a storehouse of reason (*Magazin der Vernunft*), but not as an architectonic of the latter.[4]

In this note, Kant charges Wolff not only with ignoring the boundaries within which a priori cognition of objects can be obtained but also with failing to treat the concepts and principles involved in this mode of cognition in a rigorous fashion.

As I will argue in Chapter 2, Kant's critique of the former feature hinges importantly on his account of the distinction between sensibility and thought. From the *Inaugural Dissertation* onward, Kant takes issue with the assumption that sensibility and thought are part of a single continuum because, on his account, metaphysics ought to be a purely intellectual endeavor. In the *Critique of Pure Reason*, Kant complicates his initial position by arguing that sensibility is a necessary condition of any cognition of objects and, hence, that purely intellectual cognition of objects is impossible.

In one of the two passages in the *Critique of Pure Reason* that explicitly address Wolff, Kant discusses the distinction between sensibility and thought from the latter perspective:

> In considering the distinction between sensibility and the intellectual as merely logical, the Leibnizian-Wolffian philosophy has ... assigned all investigations into the nature and origin of our cognitions an entirely unjust point of view, since this distinction ... does not concern merely the form of distinctness or indistinctness, but the origin and content of these cognitions, such that through sensibility we do not cognize the constitution of things in themselves merely indistinctly, but rather not at all, and, as soon as we take away our subjective constitution, the represented object with the properties that sensible intuition attributes to it, is nowhere to be encountered, nor can it be encountered, for it is precisely this subjective constitution that determines its form as appearance.[5]

---

[3] LM Volckmann, 28:377–78 (my translation). See also, among other passages, Axii, A11/B25, B23–24, A63/B87–88. These will be discussed in due course.

[4] R5035, translation modified; see also R4446 (dated 1772), R4866 (dated 1766–78).

[5] A44/B61–62, cf. A43/B60, A270/B326; Diss, 2: 394–95.

The other passage in which Wolff is mentioned, in the 1787 Preface, refers not so much to the critique carried out in the *Critique of Pure Reason* as to the scientific metaphysical system that Kant intended to elaborate on its basis. Such a metaphysics, he notes, "must necessarily be carried out dogmatically and ... systematically" (Bxxxvi). As was mentioned in the Introduction, Kant fully acknowledges Wolff's merits in this regard:

> In the execution of the plan that the critique prescribes, i.e., in the future system of metaphysics, we will have to follow the strict method of the famous Wolff, the greatest among all dogmatic philosophers, who gave us the first example ... of the way in which the secure course of a science is to be taken, namely, through the regular ascertainment of the principles, the clear determination of concepts, the attempt at strictness in the proofs, and the prevention of audacious leaps in inferences; for these reasons he would have been most suited to bring a science such as metaphysics into this condition, if only it had occurred to him to prepare the field for it by a critique of the organ, namely, of pure reason itself.[6]

In this passage, Kant merely blames Wolff for his lack of insight into the limits within which the a priori cognition of objects is possible. This criticism is extended to Baumgarten, to whom Kant in a private note refers as "a Cyclops among metaphysicians, who was missing one eye, namely critique."[7]

The second Preface explains this point by distinguishing between "dogmatism" considered as the un-critical employment of the dogmatic method to obtain cognitions of immaterial things and, on the other hand, the employment of the latter method as such.[8] On Kant's understanding, the dogmatic method simply consists in the elaboration of strict a priori proofs on the basis of secure principles (Bxxxv). In line with the passages

---

[6] Bxxxvi–xxxvii, translation modified, cf. A856/B884.   [7] R5081 (dated 1776–78).

[8] Bxxxv. Kemp Smith's influential commentary exemplifies the response to such passages of commentators directly or indirectly informed by neo-Kantianism. Noting with regard to Bxxxvii that, for Kant, "the method of the Critique must be akin to that of dogmatism" (1923: 21), he ignores the distinction between dogmatism and the employment of the dogmatic method, mistakenly relates Kant's remark to the *Critique of Pure Reason* itself rather than the metaphysical system for which it prepares the ground, and does not mention Kant's explicit reference to Wolff. Commenting on another, perfectly genuine, passage from the second Preface, Bxxiii–xxiv, which he associates with Wolff's "ultra-rationalistic attitude," Kemp Smith charges Kant with failing "to appreciate the full extent of the revolutionary consequences which his teaching was destined to produce" (35). The widespread view that Kant failed to emancipate himself sufficiently from dogmatic metaphysics is, of course, a very convenient way of modeling the text after one's own image of Kant's real achievement.

cited above, Kant denounces Wolff's dogmatism, but does not disavow this method per se.[9]

What emerges from this discussion is, first, that Wolffian metaphysics is the main subtext of Kant's account of metaphysics in the *Critique of Pure Reason*; second, that Kant considered Wolff to have moved metaphysics in the right direction even though his actual treatises fall short of the criteria he himself established; and, third, that he first and foremost took issue with Wolff's assumption that metaphysics can obtain purely intellectual cognitions of alleged objects such as the soul and God. Seen in this way, the *Critique of Pure Reason* is not opposed to Wolffian metaphysics as such, but aims to let metaphysics take the "secure course of a science" in a more adequate and more radical way than his predecessor had done. In order to clarify the significance of this radicalization, the section that follows discusses the relevant elements of Wolff's conception of metaphysics.

3 Wolff's Overhaul of Seventeenth-Century Scholasticism

Christian Wolff was a professor at the newly founded university of Halle from 1706 to 1723 and, after the reversal of his ban from Prussia, from 1740 to his death in 1754. While he started out as a mathematician, he became the first to elaborate a full-fledged metaphysical system – as well as a number of works in other disciplines – in German. Emerging from the early Enlightenment, his work became very influential both in Protestant Germany and throughout Europe, especially because of his so-called *German Logic* (1712), *German Metaphysics* (1719), and the multivolume *Latin Metaphysics* (1728–37). Despite the many attacks on Wolff's alleged determinism, his ideas lived on in the works and teaching of his students, among

---

[9] In the Doctrine of Method, Kant seems to take up a more negative stance on the method that Wolff called mathematical. On closer inspection, however, he here takes issue with Wolff's use of this method in philosophy on three counts, but does not reject it in all regards. First, Kant argues that the term 'mathematical' is misguided insofar as the method is employed in philosophy. Clearly addressing Wolff, though without mentioning him, Kant proposes that the method "by means of which one seeks the same certainty in philosophy" as in mathematics rather be called "dogmatic" (A713/B741). As was seen above, Kant does not oppose the very idea of a dogmatic method. Second, since philosophy cannot rely on intuition, Kant holds that it should not seek "definitions, axioms, and demonstrations . . . in the sense in which the mathematician takes them" (A726/B754). Evidently, this does not imply that philosophy cannot provide definitions, axioms, or demonstrations at all. Third, Kant objects to the use of the dogmatic method in philosophy as a means to "get beyond the bounds of experience into the enchanting regions of the intellectual" (A726/B754), that is, to obtain knowledge of the soul and God. It is primarily in this regard, I take him to hold, that philosophy should resist the temptation of emulating the "resplendent example" offered by mathematics (A712/B740–41). See Zöller (2001: 55–56), Paccioni (2011), and Gava (2018) for discussions of this topic along similar lines.

whom was Alexander Gottlieb Baumgarten.[10] Although a number of Wolffians remained active into the 1790s, after Wolff's death his intellectualist
approach to philosophy increasingly lost ground to currents such as British
empiricism, Newtonianism, and Scottish common sense philosophy.

The significance of Wolff's philosophy for Kant cannot be understood if
it is one-sidedly identified with rationalism or, more specifically, the
Protestant scholasticism that dominated seventeenth-century German uni-
versities. At the time Wolff started teaching in Halle, the latter tradition
had more or less fallen apart. As Max Wundt explains, metaphysics was
increasingly considered to have nothing more on offer than a lexicon of
basic concepts, and so lost most of its terrain to logic, on the one hand, and
applied modes of philosophy such as psychology and physics, on the
other.[11] Due to the great impact of Pietist theologians on the university
of Halle at the turn of the eighteenth century, many of its professors
treated scholastic metaphysics with greater contempt than elsewhere.

In the face of this indifferentism, to use Kant's term, Wolff took up the
challenge of developing a comprehensive metaphysical system not suscep-
tible to the criticisms and ridicule aimed at its seventeenth-century counterparts. According to his own description, his main motive for
undertaking this reform was a moral and religious one. In the commentary
on his German works published in 1726, he explains that he wrote his
metaphysics in order to fight "atheism and profanity and establish the
ground for a rational morality."[12] In this sense, the task he set himself can
be compared to the one Kant took upon himself fifty years later.

Wolff's main criticism of the scholastic metaphysics known to him
concerned its lack of scientific rigor. In the first Preface to the *German
Metaphysics*, Wolff describes the situation as follows:

> Until now, the matter treated [in metaphysics] has been full of obscurity
> and chaos. It has lacked clear concepts, thorough proofs, and the connec-
> tion of the truths among one another. Consequently, one has regarded
> many truths as mistakes, and rejected them because they were considered to
> contradict others, even though they not only are perfectly correct, but also
> need to be counted among the most important and most useful ones.[13]

---

[10] In the Preface to the first edition, Baumgarten presents his *Metaphysics* as a work indebted to
    "celebrated reformers of metaphysics" such as Leibniz and Wolff.
[11] See Wundt (1939: 152–60). I also draw on the helpful account in Schwaiger (2019).
[12] Wolff, AN 8–9, cf. Anm 932.
[13] Wolff, GM, Preface 1719. In the *Latin Ontology*, Wolff writes with regard to ontology that the
    scholastics had invited the condemnation of this "very useful and foundational part of philosophy."
    He takes his work to vindicate the discipline by converting its sterile investigations into fertile ones
    (LO 1), explicitly acknowledging Leibniz's *On the Emendation of First Philosophy* (1694) as source of

This passage is remarkably similar to both Kant's negative assessment of the metaphysical systems developed thus far, including Wolff's, and his praise of the latter's "strict method" in the second Preface of the *Critique* (Bxxxvi). Contrary to Kant, however, Wolff employed this method to rescue alleged truths such as the immortality of the soul and the existence of God from the misguided judgment of his contemporaries. Far from rejecting metaphysics, Wolff sought to bring it in line with Enlightenment culture by incorporating ideas about cognition, science, and methodology stemming from such thinkers as Bacon, Descartes, Locke, Leibniz, and Newton. Thus, responding to the latter, he was the first to include a discipline devoted to the world as such, called general cosmology, in the part of metaphysics that used to be devoted to the soul and God alone.[14] More generally, Wolff was a child of the early Enlightenment in the sense that he continually emphasized the usefulness of logic, metaphysics, and the applied parts of philosophy.

But how did Wolff think he could create order in the chaos left by his predecessors? As was mentioned in the Introduction, the structure of his metaphysics rests on a distinction that was established in the seventeenth century, namely, that between a foundational discipline called general metaphysics, first philosophy, or ontology and, on the other hand, a number of disciplines that together make up special or applied metaphysics. Whereas the former part treats those concepts that can be predicated of all things, the latter part is concerned with the subject matter of theology, cosmology, and psychology.

Even though Wolff does not use the terms 'general metaphysics' and 'special metaphysics,' this division is clearly reflected in the title of his *German Metaphysics*, namely, *Rational Thoughts on God, the World, and the Human Soul, as Well as All Things as Such*. Apart from an introductory chapter, the main text consists of an ontology, empirical psychology, general cosmology, rational psychology, and natural theology.[15]

The part of the *German Metaphysics* that contains Wolff's ontology is titled "On the First Grounds of Our Knowledge and All Things as Such." As he puts it later in the *Discursus praeliminaris*, ontology treats "the

---

inspiration (LO 7). A discussion of the extent of Wolff's indebtedness to Leibniz and other predecessors is beyond the scope of this chapter.

[14] See Simmert (2018) and Leduc (2020) for recent discussions of Wolff's cosmology.

[15] The *Latin Metaphysics* (1730–37), which will be largely disregarded here, consists of voluminous books devoted to the same disciplines, albeit that general cosmology and empirical psychology are swapped. The order in which concepts and principles are treated also differs to some extent. For a comparison of both versions of the ontology, see Schnepf (2007b).

general properties of things," that is, those concepts "that are predicated of souls as well as physical things, be they natural or produced." The concepts of "essence, existence, property, mode, necessity, contingence, place, time, perfection, order, the simple, the composite, etc." need to be treated separately, he adds, because all sciences "require these concepts and the principles derived from them and because they cannot be adequately explained in sciences such as psychology or physics."[16]

The ontology contained in the *German Metaphysics* sets out from the indubitable truth that we are conscious of ourselves and other things, a truth that according to Wolff necessarily entails that something cannot exist and not exist simultaneously. In this way, he derives the principle of non-contradiction (GM 10) and, subsequently, the concepts of possibility, impossibility, actuality, and thing (12–16). Other concepts include whole and part (24), nothing (28), ground (29), essence (33–35), and necessity (36). Even though this order is perhaps not perfectly transparent, it is clear why Wolff discusses the concept of essence after concepts such as possibility and ground: he needs the latter to explain what is meant by the essence of a thing. Thus, he writes that "that in which the ground can be found of the other characteristics of a thing, is called the essence" (33).

As this passage illustrates, Wolff's ontology provides definitions of such concepts as are mentioned above. However, the chapter is not merely a lexicon of ontological concepts, but also contains a priori judgments about things, for instance, about the characteristics that must be attributed to things of which we are conscious as things that are external to us (45). In this context, Wolff not only explains what is meant by concepts such as space (46), place (47), and time (94), but also posits that the things of which we are conscious as external to ourselves are composite (51), fill a space (52), are three-dimensional (53), can come into being and perish (64), and so on. Likewise, relying on the principle of sufficient reason, he infers from the existence of composite things that there must be simple things as well (76–77, cf. 582–85). All in all, Wolff's ontology appears to treat of the concepts and principles involved in our cognition of anything whatsoever, of those involved in our cognition of the composite things given to the senses, and of those involved in our non-sensible cognition of

---

[16] Wolff, DP 73. In the *Discursus praeliminaris*, intended to introduce the reader to the Latin works, Wolff offers an account of what he takes philosophy to be, which parts it consists in, and how philosophy needs to be practiced.

simple things. However, this threefold distinction is neither reflected by the structure of the text nor explicitly discussed.[17]

It is noteworthy, finally, that Wolff presents a proof of the principle of sufficient reason right after his discussion of the concept of ground (30), but does not posit it as indubitable principle until much later. What Wolff announces as a sufficient "proof" of the principle (30) comes down to the assertion that without it "truth and dreams can no longer be distinguished" (144). In other words, one of Wolff's alleged proofs is based on what the human mind must necessarily posit in order to conceive of things as elements of a rationally ordered whole.[18]

This example suggests that Wolff understood the concepts and principles treated in the ontology to ground our cognition of things rather than these things themselves. Yet the very title of the ontology included in the *German Metaphysics*, "On the First Grounds of Our Cognition and All Things as Such," indicates that he considered the basic principles of our cognition to coincide with the grounds of the things themselves.[19] Similarly, while the *Discursus praeliminaris* defines ontology as the discipline concerned with "being as such and its general properties," Wolff immediately identifies these properties with the "general concepts" presupposed in all other parts of philosophy.[20] The *Latin Ontology* even maintains that ontology "reveals the sources (*fontes*) of all human cognitions."[21] Seen in this way, as various commentators have argued, the gnoseological conception of ontology at stake in Kant's *Critique of Pure Reason* goes back to Wolff's and, from there, to Suarez and Scotus.[22]

---

[17] Wolff's *Latin Ontology* remedies this problem by dividing its subject matter into a part devoted to those concepts that concern any thing whatsoever and a part of which the various sections are devoted to concepts that concern (1) composite things, (2) simple things, and (3) the mutual relations of things. On this, see Marty (2011). Baumgarten's ontology, for its part, distinguishes between the inner predicates of things (which are said to be either universal or disjunctive) and their external or relative predicates.

[18] Similarly, Wolff notes in the *Latin Ontology* that it would be impossible to support the system of principles and laws treated in cosmology if the principle of sufficient reason were not accepted as axiom (LO 75).

[19] In this regard, I disagree with Schnepf (2007b: 187), according to whom "the transition from epistemological principles to ontological determinations" constitutes "the basic methodological problem of Wolffian ontology."

[20] Wolff, DP 73, cf. LO 1. Similarly, Baumgarten's *Metaphysics* defines metaphysics as the science of the first principles of human cognition (M 1) and its first part, called ontology, general metaphysics, or first philosophy, as the science of the more general predicates of things (M 4).

[21] Wolff, LO 219. This passage is quoted by Prunea-Bretonnet (2011a). My reading is largely in agreement with hers.

[22] See Courtine (1990) for a detailed and insightful account of the transformation of metaphysics into a theory of the object from Suarez to Leibniz. Honnefelder (1990: 321–22), Benoist (1996),

Evidently, this is not to say that Kant accepted all premises of Wolffian ontology. However, since Kant's critique is most visibly aimed at the assumption that metaphysics can acquire knowledge of the soul, the world as such, and God, it is useful to briefly consider Wolff's conception of the disciplines that make up special metaphysics.

The first of these disciplines is empirical psychology. According to Wolff, both empirical and rational psychology deal with the soul considered as the thing "that is conscious of itself and other things outside of itself" (GM 192), but treat their subject matter from complementary perspectives. Empirical psychology turns those perceptions of one's own thoughts that anyone can obtain into clear concepts and subsequently derives a number of truths from them (191, cf. DP 111). In this context, Wolff examines cognitive activities such as sensation (GM 220–34), imagination (235–45), memory (248–53), the capacity to produce concepts (273), the understanding (277–90), experience (325–31), and reason (368–83).

Rational psychology, for its part, conceives of the various aspects of the soul treated in empirical psychology as effects grounded in the essence of the soul. For this reason, the two disciplines overlap considerably in terms of content.[23] Supposedly anchored in indubitable inner perceptions, empirical psychology is said to guarantee that the purely rational account of the soul provided in rational psychology does not deviate from its proper course. As Wolff puts it,

> [W]hat was said earlier about the soul by drawing on experience is the touchstone of that which is here taught about its nature and essence, as well as the effects grounded therein, but that what we treat here is by no means the touchstone of what experience teaches us. (727)

However, much of the content of the rational psychology does not seem to be amenable to testing by means of inner perception. Thus, on the basis of his earlier definition of the kind of change that can occur in a composite thing (615), Wolff purports to demonstrate that bodies cannot think (738) and that the soul, defined as a thing capable of thinking, is a simple

---

Bouton (1996), and Prunea-Bretonnet (2011a) likewise underline Wolff's role in what Bouton refers to as the "noetization" of ontology initiated by Suarez and Descartes (250, cf. 253, 258). Stressing the proximity between Wolff and Kant even more, Schnepf (2007b) interestingly argues that Wolff's ontology conceives of principles such as that of non-contradiction and sufficient reason as "conditions of possibility" of the fact that we are conscious of ourselves and other things (88).

[23] Apart from this overlap, rational psychology discusses a wide range of problems, including the problem of the relation between body and soul and that of the difference between animals and human beings. These will not be taken into consideration here.

thing (742). He further infers that the essence of the soul consists in its power to represent the world (753–55), a power that manifests itself in a variety of ways (744–47). Finally, Wolff infers from the definition of the soul as a simple thing that the soul does not perish with the body (922) and is immortal (926).

Sandwiched between the two psychologies, Wolff's general cosmology is concerned with the "general cognition of the world" that both physics and natural theology presuppose (541). It conceives of the world as a composite thing (551) of which the parts are connected in terms of space and time (546–48) and constitute a whole (550). As seen above, Wolff infers the existence of simple things from the existence of composite things (582). The former are further defined as elements that possess the power to modify their inner state (584). Explicitly referring to Leibniz's principle of indiscernibles, he draws on the principle of sufficient reason to assert that two things cannot be similar in all regards (586–90). After a further discussion of the simple things Leibniz called monads, Wolff turns to composite things considered as material bodies (606–7). In this context, he clearly aims to clarify the basic presuppositions of Newtonian science (cf. 608–10), but also draws on Leibnizian ideas (cf. 660, 685). As in the case of psychology, Wolff repeatedly supports his rational inferences with examples taken from experience, which, in this case, take the form of experiments (cf. 649–51, 674). Wolff's descriptions of the latter appear increasingly to blur the distinction between, on the one hand, the purely rational account of the world he started out from and, on the other, empirical physics.

Its empirical strand notwithstanding, the final sections of the chapter deal extensively with the order and perfection of the world, that is, with the idea that the laws governing particular phenomena can be traced back to general ones (701–21). According to Wolff, the order of the world cannot be fully grasped through experience, but ultimately must be derived from God's properties (722).

At one point in the general cosmology, Wolff states that even though everything in the world that follows from the world's essence is necessary (578), the very existence of the world is not (576–78). Taking up this result, the natural theology that closes the system seeks to ward off Spinozism by proving that the autonomous being that is commonly called God does not coincide with the world (939). Wolff's proofs of the existence and properties of God rely heavily on the principle of sufficient reason (cf. DP 131). Since this principle entails, for Wolff, the impossibility of infinite regress, he can infer that our contingent existence must ultimately be grounded in a thing that is itself not contingent, but contains the ground of its actuality within itself (GM 928). This being is said to also contain the ground of the existence of all other things (930), to be eternal (931), immaterial (935), simple (936), and to exist through a force of its own (937).

Whereas Wolff infers these non-anthropomorphic properties from the mere fact of our contingent existence (cf. Anm 557), he appears to infer from the assumed perfection of the actual world that God possesses an intellect (GM 954), knows itself (979), and possesses a free will (980), the greatest power possible (1025), highest wisdom (1048), eternity (1072), and so on. For we can account for the perfection of the world, I take him to mean, only by conceiving of God as a being that "can clearly represent all worlds at once" so as to choose the most perfect one (952). Moreover, we actually *can* conceive of God in this way by transferring features that our own soul possesses in a finite way to God considered as infinite being. In the 1729 Preface, Wolff explains this as follows:

> Since I have most clearly shown . . . the difference between an infinite and a finite being, . . . one can free (*befreien*) the concepts of that which is found in the soul of their imperfection. In this way, we can not only obtain a rational clarification of the divine attributes, . . . but also demonstrate that they possess the greatest possible degree.[24]

Thus, the concepts of our own soul obtained in empirical psychology can be turned into concepts of those of God's attributes that do not follow from the sheer fact that something exists. God can subsequently be proven to possess these attributes by means of inferences based on the principle of sufficient reason.

Evidently, the results of Wolff's natural theology converge with Christian doctrine. In his *Anmerckungen*, a commentary on the *German Metaphysics*, Wolff acknowledges that this is no coincidence:

> [P]art of my aim has been to ensure that reason brings out those aspects of God's properties that can be found in the revealed word of God, because for those who sympathize with Christian religion, the harmony between God's word and reason is very plausible. (Anm 577)

This passage testifies to an important feature of Wolff's philosophy, namely, its assumption of a single rational world that can be grasped from a number of different perspectives. Just as reason and faith provide

---

[24] Wolff, GM, Preface 1729, 4; cf. DP 96.

different perspectives on God, the world, and the human soul, so too do sense perception and reason.

Wolff's continuism is supported by his so-called *German Logic*, which deals with the rules that any mode of cognition requires. More specifically, Wolff here discusses the production of concepts, the clarification of given concepts, the combination of concepts in judgments, and the production of new judgments out of given judgments through syllogistic reasoning.

Drawing on Leibniz, Wolff takes it for granted that the understanding is able, at least in principle, to clarify the concepts of singular things obtained by the senses by distinguishing the marks they contain (GL 1.13), a procedure that results in definitions. By subsequently comparing the marks contained in the concepts of singular things and singling out what they have in common, the understanding can produce general concepts (1.26, cf. GM 286). Further, since "one can take away from those things that determine the matter at hand as much as one pleases," one can "ascend to ever more general concepts" (GL 1.27), concepts that subsequently can be used in judgments and syllogistic inferences that belong to abstract disciplines such as ontology (cf. DP 12). As Paccioni aptly remarks, "ontological concepts ... are therefore not defined by their purity."[25]

The continuism that the *German Logic* presupposes fits hand in glove with Wolff's conception of the role of experience in metaphysics. In order to preclude the aberrations of his scholastic predecessors, Wolff considers clear or indubitable experiences of our own cognitive activities both as a crucial source of concepts and principles and as a check on at least part of the truths to be obtained in the discipline.[26] Thus, as was noted above, the *German Metaphysics* relies on the allegedly indubitable consciousness of ourselves and other things to deduce principles such as that of non-contradiction and sufficient reason, and sees no gap between disciplines such as empirical and rational psychology. Similarly, Wolff notes, for example, that we obtain the concept of space by paying attention to ourselves insofar as we are conscious of things as external to ourselves (GM 45).

---

[25] Paccioni (2006: 30); see also Paccioni (2011: 106–12). See Pelletier (2017) for a clear account of the continuism presupposed in Wolff's *German Logic*. Noting that Wolff regarded abstraction as a means to move from sensible to intellectual cognition (57), École (1979) considers him to be a rationalist in this specific sense (60). Commentators who stress the weight Wolff gives to experience include Wundt (1924), Arndt (1983), Engfer (1996: 268–83), Kreimendahl (2007), and Dyck (2014: 19–42).

[26] Along Cartesian lines, the *German Metaphysics* adduces the "indubitable experience" that we are conscious of ourselves and other things to infer that we exist (GM 7). On this, see Dyck (2014: 176–79).

However, anchoring metaphysical truths in the inner observation of our own cognitive activities is only one element of Wolff's methodology. Once the relevant truths have been secured, on his account, reason has the capacity to grasp the sufficient reason, or ground, of these truths independently of experience, in which case it comprehends them in view of the rationally ordered totality of which they are part. According to the *German Metaphysics*, mathematics provides the best example of this a priori procedure:

> If one grasps the connections between things by relating the truths without assuming propositions stemming from experience, then reason is pure (*so ist die Vernunft lauter*). If, by contrast, one also takes recourse to empirical propositions, ... then we do not fully grasp the connections among the truths.... The sciences provide us with sufficient evidence that our reason is not always pure, especially as regards our cognition of nature and ourselves.... Arithmetic and geometry, as well as algebra, provide examples of pure reason.[27]

Given the finitude of our intellectual capacities, I take Wolff to hold, metaphysics must rely on inner experience to generate its most basic concepts. In this regard it is impure. However, metaphysics can approximate the purity of mathematics by deriving further concepts and truths from these concepts by means of the principles of non-contradiction and sufficient reason. This is, at least, what can be inferred from a comment of Wolff on the procedure employed in rational psychology:

> In rational psychology, we derive a priori from the mere concept of the human soul everything of which one can observe that it belongs to the soul as well as what is derived from these observations, as befits the philosopher. (DP 112)

Whether or not Wolff believed that metaphysics can attain the same degree of purity as mathematics, he clearly tried to elaborate the discipline according to the demonstrative or scientific method that mathematics carries out in an exemplary manner (cf. LO 4). This means that the most basic concepts treated in metaphysics must stem from clear or indubitable inner experiences, that the definitions derived from these concepts must not contain concepts that have not yet been clarified, and that the truths derived from these definitions must be processed according to strict logical rules so as to generate purely rational cognitions of things as such as well as

---

[27] GM 382, cf. DP 139; Wolff distinguishes between a pure and impure mode of the understanding along the same lines at GM 282. On this topic, see Paccioni (2011: 102–6).

the soul, the world as such, and God. As seen, the inferences by means of which Wolff's metaphysics establishes cognitions of this kind presuppose the absolute validity of the principle of sufficient reason. The latter, he notes in the *Latin Ontology*, must be considered to be "without any limitation and restriction" (LO 75).

In the first Preface to the *German Metaphysics*, Wolff states with regard to ontology that this is indeed what he sought to achieve:

> As regards these [first general] concepts, I have done what I could to assume nothing without proof: my every assertion is either grounded on clear experiences (*klare Erfahrungen*) or demonstrated (*erwiesen*) by means of solid inferences.... First and foremost, however, I have made sure that all truths are interconnected and that the whole work resembles a chain in which each link is connected to another and, hence, every link is connected to all others.[28]

Ten years later, Wolff admitted that "the scientific treatment of first philosophy is ... more difficult than that of mathematics," since it cannot take recourse to "the senses and the imagination" and since its subject matter cannot be examined as easily (LO 7). Yet even if Wolff's actual treatment of metaphysics does not always meet the requirements he establishes, there is no doubt that the method he employs dispels at least part of the "tenebrity" he attributes to scholastic elaborations of the discipline (LO 6–7). As said, Wolff owed his great success to this achievement. However, his metaphysics can also be assessed in view of criteria very different from the ones he himself sought to meet. This is where Crusius comes in.

4   Crusius's Challenge to Wolffian Metaphysics

Whatever one's assessment of Christian August Crusius's philosophical works, there is no doubt that his anti-Wolffianism pushed Kant toward the critique of metaphysics that culminated in the *Critique of Pure Reason*.[29] Kant repeatedly acknowledged his debt in this regard.[30] By contrast,

---

[28] Wolff, GM, 1719 Preface, cf. AN 22, LO 4 and 7. The description cited above matches the one Kant presents and endorses in the second Preface of the *Critique of Pure Reason*. See LO 115–20 for a more detailed description of the demonstrative method to be employed in philosophy.

[29] While Wundt (1924: 60) claims that Crusius was highly influential during the 1750s and 1760s, albeit mainly because of his early writings, Kuehn (1987: 264–69) sheds doubt on this view. Yet even if Crusius's metaphysics had few direct followers, his ideas may well have had an impact on philosophers such as Lambert, Tetens, and Kant in less perspicuous ways.

[30] See, for example, NE, 1:398, and *Inquiry*, 2:293n.

Crusius's own extravagant claims are likely to have catalyzed the more radical guise of critique that Kant elaborated in *Dreams of a Spirit-Seer* (1766), the *Inaugural Dissertation* (1770), and the *Critique of Pure Reason*. In this section, I will focus on aspects of Crusius's metaphysics that I believe became a crucial eye-opener for Kant during the latter half of the 1760s. Apart from the insightful essay on Crusius and Kant that Heimsoeth published in 1926, to which my reading is indebted, these aspects do not seem to have drawn much attention from commentators.

Crusius was a professor of philosophy in Leipzig from 1744 to 1750, after which he took up a professorship in theology and stopped publishing philosophical texts. The main treatises he wrote on behalf of his courses in philosophy are titled *Directions for a Rational Life* (1744), *Outline of the Necessary Truths of Reason* (1745), and *Path to the Certainty and Reliability of Human Cognition* (1747). Crusius's critique of Wolff in these and other works testifies to his affinity with the Pietist current within German reformed theology, which is to say that he followed in the track of those of Wolff's antirationalist colleagues in Halle who had attacked his alleged determinism from the 1720s onward.[31]

Crusius's philosophy is a case apart, however, because both his criticisms and the eclectic system he presented as alternative are much more sophisticated. What Crusius sought to achieve, briefly put, was a philosophical system that could compete with Wolff's in terms of style, structure, and rigor but, unlike the latter, could account for the possibility of spontaneous action, or freedom, on the part of human souls and God. Driven by this overarching aim, Crusius turns against what he saw as Wolff's logicism in a number of ways, of which I will mention three.

First, Crusius drives a wedge between "objective truths" said to be grounded in the possibility or actuality of the object itself and "subjective truths" that the human mind can actually know to be true (P 52). Seen from the latter perspective, true knowledge is achieved if "the understanding operates according to the laws of its nature" (P 53). According to Crusius, metaphysics needs to investigate the necessary truths that constitute its object (cf. O 1) in view of the way in which the mind actually operates. Thus, in the *Outline*, Crusius presents the principle of non-contradiction as

---

[31] I will disregard the influence on Crusius of Thomasius, his teacher Hoffmann, and others. On this background, see Wundt (1924: 52–81) and Carboncini (1986). See Fugate (2014: 130–42) for a helpful account of the impact of Hofmann's conception of experience on Crusius and, through the latter, on Kant. As Fugate explains, Crusius argues against Wolff, in an empiricist vein, that cognition proper requires that the understanding add cognitive elements to sensible representations instead of clarifying those alleged to be contained in the latter (132).

one element of the more general principle that follows from the "essence of the understanding," namely, that whatever can be thought is possible and that whatever must be conceived as true is actual.[32] For this reason, he might be considered an early proponent of psychologism.[33] Crusius does not seem to acknowledge that Wolff himself, as seen, regarded inner experience as a source of metaphysical truths.

Second, based on this quasi-psychological perspective, Crusius drives a wedge between logical truths considered to follow from the principle of non-contradiction alone and truths about objects that we become aware of through sense perception. In this context, he distinguishes Wolff's merely logical notion of possibility from the "real possibility" of those things that are "external to thought" (O 56). On his account, we posit something as actual, or as existing, by dint of our inner or outer sensation of it, for only in this case "are we forced to think something immediately as existing."[34] Thus, Crusius clarifies what we mean by a concept such as existence by appealing to this subjective necessity.

Third, Crusius opposes what he takes to be Wolff's methodology by driving a wedge between the method to be employed in philosophy and the one employed in mathematics.[35] As regards his own ontology, accordingly, he does not derive the concepts that are presupposed in all sciences from the principle of non-contradiction, as he took Wolff to have done, but instead identifies a small number of simple concepts by analyzing the elements contained or presupposed in any cognition of an actual object.[36] Due to their simplicity, the concepts at which we arrive by using this analytic method need not be defined in order to be clear (O 8).

The elementary concepts Crusius thus identifies are subsistence, somewhere, outside one another, succession, causality, outside one another in a non-spatial sense, unity, negation, and contained in something.[37] On their

---

[32] Crusius, O 15. Unless noted otherwise, the translations from *Outline of the Necessary Truths of Reason* are taken from the excerpts in Watkins (2009).

[33] See Tonelli (1969: xxiii). His view is in line with Heimsoeth (1926/1956: 161–62), who, however, does not use the term 'psychologism.'

[34] Crusius, O 16. Crusius writes in *Path* that "all first truths are sensations" and that both outer and inner sensations can provide secure guidance on the condition that one exercise one's intellectual capacities (P 30, cf. 56).

[35] Opposing "a few famous men" without mentioning Wolff by name, Crusius writes in *Path* that mathematics differs from philosophy insofar as it requires only a single example to produce the definition of the object. He further rejects the view that philosophy ought to proceed by means of demonstrations (P 10).

[36] Crusius, O 7, cf. Preface.

[37] Crusius, O 102. The rationale behind this list is not very clear. One might ask, for example, why concepts such as possibility, essence, and existence are not included.

own or combined, they give rise to the material principles that the *Outline* considers to be necessary or a priori truths and at one point refers to as "postulates of inner sensation."[38] Crusius suggests that all other concepts treated in metaphysics result from combinations of these elementary concepts (O 7).

Each of these features of Crusius's critique of Wolff left traces on Kant's early works as well as on the *Critique of Pure Reason*.[39] Kant also seems to accept Crusius's distorted image of Wolff as arch-rationalist. As was mentioned above, however, Kant became increasingly skeptical of Crusius's own position. Before turning to the aspects of the *Outline of the Necessary Truths of Reason* that are most relevant in this regard, I will briefly consider a number of passages in which Kant contrasts Wolff's and Crusius's positions and expresses his dissatisfaction with both.

According to Herder's transcript of Kant's earliest lectures on metaphysics dated 1762–64, Kant considered both Wolff and Crusius to have held erroneous views on the basic principles to be treated in metaphysics. Whereas Wolff wrongly assumed that all of these principles can be demonstrated, Crusius admitted principles that lacked absolute certainty.[40] Crusius did so, Kant adds, by assuming that the truth of such principles can be derived from "inner sensation" alone, in other words, by assuming that "what I cannot but hold to be true, must be true."[41] Kant values Crusius's view that metaphysics contains indemonstrable, material principles, but takes him to have endorsed such principles as are either

---

[38] Crusius, O 8, my translation, cf. Preface and P 39, 259–60. On this, see Heimsoeth (1926/1956: 165–69).

[39] In the *Inquiry* (1764), Kant turns against Wolffianism by distinguishing the methods to be employed in philosophy and mathematics along the lines of Crusius (2:276–79, 281–82, 283–84) and by explicitly endorsing Crusius's view that the first truths to be treated in metaphysics include "material principles of the human intellect" that are indemonstrable (295, cf. 293–94) and must be obtained through analysis (290). However, here as elsewhere, he rejects Crusius's claim that such principles can be true by dint of a strong feeling on our part (295). For a helpful analysis of the *Inquiry* in view of Kant's relationship to Crusius, see Prunea-Bretonnet (2011b). In my opinion, Kanzian (1993) underestimates the extent of Kant's debt to Crusius in the *Inquiry* and works from the 1750s and 1760s such as *New Elucidation*, *The Only Possible Argument*, and *Negative Magnitudes*. Perin (2015) analyzes Kant's response in the latter text to Crusius's 1743 attack on Wolff's allegedly unbridled use of the principle of sufficient reason. See Rumore (2018) for a helpful discussion of Crusius's influence on Kant's practical philosophy, in particular with regard to the idea that the immortality of the soul cannot be demonstrated by theoretical means, but must be postulated on moral grounds.

[40] LM Herder, 28:5, cf. 9.

[41] LM Herder, 28:10. Kant here seems to identify the derivation of material principles from inner sensation with their derivation "from the nature of the soul" (LM Herder, 28:10). As seen, both ideas can be found in Crusius's *Outline*.

underdetermined or downright false.[42] The same line of criticism recurs in a number of later lectures and texts. Thus, Kant notes in his letter to Herz from 1772 that Crusius resorted to concepts and rules allegedly implanted in the human mind by God. As he sees it, it is absurd to try to determine "the origin and validity of our cognitions" by means of this "deus ex machina," because it opens the gate to vacuous whims and figments of the brain.[43]

One of Crusius's material principles that Kant discusses in his early lectures is the principle according to which "everything that is, is somewhere and somewhen."[44] Since this principle became pivotal to Kant's critique of Crusius from at least 1770 onward, it is worth considering in some detail.

As was mentioned above, Crusius conceives of 'existence' as a concept that we use with regard to objects we are immediately aware of by means of inner or outer sensation. In the *Outline*, he further specifies what the concept of existence entails by tying the immediate sensation of something to space and time:

> If we represent something as existing, then the essence of our understanding requires us … to think … that it *exists somewhere and at some time*, and thus we must also add in thought, beyond the metaphysical essence of the thing, an *ubi* and *quando* that belongs to it. For that reason 'existence' is the predicate of a thing due to which it can also be found outside of thought somewhere and at some time.… It is impossible for us to think something other than this.[45]

From the concept of existence thus defined, Crusius derives two material principles, which he also calls axioms (cf. P 42). These principles specify that attributing 'existence' to something means conceiving of it as in space and time:

> The two main axioms [that follow] from the concept of existence are these, that everything that exists must be somewhere … and, further, that everything that exists is sometime or at some time.[46]

Accordingly, Crusius defines space, according to its "primary concept," as "that in which we think that substances exist" (O 48) and time as "that in

---

[42] LM Herder, 28:10, cf. 156–57. See also Kant's discussion of Crusius in the *Inquiry* (2:295).

[43] Kant to Herz, February 21, 1772 (10:131).

[44] LM Herder, 28:9. Both in the lectures and in the *Inquiry*, Kant adduces this principle as an example of the material principles put forward by Crusius without expressing his agreement or disagreement with its content (cf. 2:294).

[45] Crusius, O 46, first emphasis mine, cf. 54, 59.

[46] Crusius, O 48. In what follows I will treat the two axioms as one.

which we think the succession of things that follow each other" (54). Appealing to "inner experience" as criterion, he claims moreover that we necessarily "represent all substances, even simple ones, as somewhere" (50).

In line with Kant's later account of space and time in the *Critique*, Crusius stresses that what we mean by time pertains not to the "actual sequence of things one after another" (54). On his account, time is rather a sequence that we necessarily think when we think of something as existing.[47] Similarly, space is said to be a feature that we necessarily add in thought to anything of which we think as existing. Since we can treat these features separately, as we do in philosophy, Crusius calls them *abstracta* of existence (51, cf. 54).

In sum, Crusius attempts to restrict, in empiricist fashion, our use of the term 'existence' to that which is thought by means of inner or outer sensation.[48] In this regard, even Kant's mature position seems to be indebted to Crusius: according to one of the synthetic principles of the pure understanding treated in the *Critique of Pure Reason*, we posit something as actual if it "is connected with the material conditions of experience (of sensation)" (A218/B219). Like Crusius, Kant anchors his account of the principles constitutive of empirical knowledge in an account of the operations carried out by the understanding.[49]

However, seen from Kant's perspective, not all is well with Crusius's examination of the cognitive activity carried out by the human mind, for it is the breeding ground of contorted metaphysical speculations. The claim alone that we must conceive of all substances, including simple substances, as present in space entails, as Heimsoeth writes, "extraordinary ontological difficulties."[50] Apparently without noticing it, he adds, Crusius transfers "the forms and concepts of our sensible knowledge to immaterial and 'supersensible' beings" by appealing to the alleged 'essence of the understanding.'"[51]

---

[47] Crusius, O 48. See Fugate (2014: 135–36). In order to preclude potential objections against his subjectivism, Crusius asserts, as he does in many other cases, that his conception of time "does not stem from the imagination, but rather from the essence of the understanding" (O 54).

[48] Cf. Crusius, P 534. On this, see Kanzian (1993: 403).

[49] Crusius refers in this regard to "laws" that determine "how the inner acts and modifications of spirits follow from one another" (O 365). In *Path*, he notes that "rules" can be derived from the "nature of the understanding" that concern the use of our intellectual powers (P 53, cf. 54–56).

[50] Heimsoeth (1926/1956: 180).

[51] Heimsoeth (1926/1956: 186). I agree with Heimsoeth that Kant's account of space and time in the *Inaugural Dissertation* must be considered in light of his critique of Crusius's extravagant speculations (185). I will come back to this in Chapter 2.

What are the effects of this transferral on Crusius's conception of the soul and God? In many respects, Crusius follows Wolff's natural theology and rational psychology. Yet his *Outline* also yields a number of more unusual results. Since we must conceive of any substance as being somewhere, Crusius writes with regard to God, an "infinite substance cannot be thought if it is not necessarily ... present in any possible 'somewhere' whatsoever" (O 251). This can be done only if God "fills (*erfüllt*) all merely possible space in the most perfect manner" (250). According to Crusius, God's perfect manner of filling space does not entail his extension or divisibility, because our view of space as something that consists of parts is relevant only with regard to finite substances (253). Similarly, souls, which Crusius calls finite spirits, are said to fill "the space in which they are present, ... but in a manner that is much more perfect than that of bodies" and accordingly does not entail their extension in space (253).[52] If these assertions seem rather obscure, we must grant Crusius that they are not self-contradictory and, hence, might be known to be true by an intellect not hampered by the restrictions imposed on the human mind, that is, by God (cf. 14).

When we conceive of bodies as filling a space, we necessarily conceive of them as capable of movement and as impenetrable as well.[53] But should we do so in the case of material bodies alone? As was to be expected, Crusius posits that souls likewise possess the capacity to move and are impenetrable, albeit in a more ethereal way than bodies (364). Throughout, his strategy consists in attributing a number of capacities to any substance whatsoever – as Leibniz had done as well – and subsequently distinguishing matter and spirit in terms of the specific way in which they exert these capacities.[54]

---

[52] The same holds true of all simple substances: they are said to be in space, albeit "in a different way than composite things" (O 50). The translation of these passages on God is mine. Heimsoeth (1926/1956: 188) rightly asks what remains spatial about the concept of space if we empty it of the sensibility known to us.

[53] Crusius's idea that in philosophy we cannot but think together the concepts of substance, spatiality, impenetrability, and so on illustrates an important element of his methodology. He seems to hold that the tendency to associate these concepts stems from the realm of empirical cognition.

[54] Crusius, O 364. This strategy allows Crusius to distinguish his position from materialism: as he points out, positing that both matter and soul are impenetrable does not mean that the soul itself is material (cf. 440). Crusius's strategy differs from Leibniz's in that he transfers the properties we normally attribute to matter to all substances, whereas Leibniz attributed the capacity to perceive to the ultimate elements of matter. Crusius's strategy also shares common ground with Wolff's. As seen, Wolff's *German Metaphysics* establishes the divine attributes by emptying the concepts of attributes of the human soul of their imperfection.

Crusius not only conceives of the soul as impenetrable, but also allows for its real interaction with matter:

> No substance can be understood otherwise than as impenetrable.... Now since finite spirits are thus also impenetrable, just as matter is, matter must yield when there is a sufficiently strong effort in spirits to occupy the place of matter. Similarly, spirits must yield and thus be moved if a sufficiently strong effort is present in matter to move to the place where they are currently found.[55]

These assertions are consistent with Crusius's rejection of pre-established harmony (363–64). Nevertheless, the thought of an immaterial and immortal soul pushed out of its place by a body is extremely obscure.

In the passage quoted above, Crusius allows for one exception: he attributes impenetrability to finite substances alone. God, qua infinite substance, fills space in such a manner that he cannot be penetrated by any finite substance. Rather, we are told that "all creatures are penetrated by him, and that he is with them at the same time in the same place that they are."[56]

One might object to Crusius, of course, that these assertions about the soul and God are not derived from inner sensations and, hence, cannot be said to follow from the essence of the understanding. Does Crusius not fall prey, at this point, to vacuous speculations of the kind he purported to have rooted out, as Kant held was the case?

From the outset, Crusius seeks to preclude criticisms of this kind by distinguishing truths that can be known to be true by finite minds from truths that must be affirmed even though they cannot be known to be true by finite minds. According to one of these caveats, we may be obliged to consider

> something to be possible or actual that is incomprehensible to us, in order not to endanger our ultimate ends and violate the most important rules of human perfection.[57]

Put simply: theology ultimately trumps a metaphysics based on inner sensation, for Crusius, because only it allows us to conceive of ourselves in light of God's infinite wisdom and to act accordingly. Thus,

---

[55] Crusius, O 364, cf. 402 and P 80. On Crusius's account of mind–body interaction in these and other passages, see Watkins (2005: 89–93), who, however, does not comment on the extravagance of Crusius's ideas. Moreover, whereas Watkins takes Crusius to defend a specific mode of physical influx (93), it seems to me that the influence Crusius considers soul and body to exert on each other is real but not physical: the soul is not a physical substance on his account.

[56] Crusius, O 364, my translation, cf. 250.   [57] Crusius, O 14, my translation.

anticipating the *Critique of Pure Reason*, and in keeping with the Pietist tradition, Crusius seeks to safeguard morality and faith by pointing out the limits of human cognition and distinguishing between that which can be thought and that which can be known.[58]

As seen, however, Crusius's plea for intellectual modesty does not prevent him from making a number of claims about the soul and God that do not seem to serve the practical ends of humankind in any clear sense. These claims, rather, follow from the ontological axiom according to which everything that exists must be somewhere and somewhen. As will be shown in the next chapter, Kant came to see this axiom as a sign of the pernicious assumption, common to Wolff, Crusius, and their contemporaries, that sensibility and thought are nothing but two ways in which we can come to know things. Targeting this assumption, but without mentioning Crusius, the *Critique of Pure Reason* claims that things can be held to be "next to one another in space" only on the condition that they "be taken as objects of our sensible intuition."[59] If this is the case, then obviously monads, souls, and God cannot be considered to be in space or time (cf. A34–35/B51).

However, Kant's critique of the continuism presupposed by Crusius's axiom had a much wider scope. In order to further contextualize this critique, the next and final section briefly sketches some of the debates that followed in the wake of Wolff's cosmology and rational psychology.

5 Post-Leibnizian Monadologies

From the 1720s onward, efforts to reconcile a monadological account of the world with the principles of Newtonian physics gave rise to a number of interrelated debates on the nature and properties of the ultimate elements of matter and the soul, on the relationship between corporal bodies, and on the relationship between body and soul.[60] While many proponents of these debates rejected Leibniz's view that all things are

---

[58] See Bxxviii–xxx. See *Dreams* for a similar argument (cf. 2:349, 372).

[59] A27/B43, cf. LM Mrongovius, 29:833 (1782–83), where Crusius is mentioned by name. Kant's critique of Crusius in the *Inaugural Dissertation* will be discussed in Chapter 2, Section 4.

[60] For clear and convincing accounts of the reception of Leibniz's philosophy up to the early Kant, see Watkins (2005: 23–100) and Watkins (2006). While the former text puts the debate on preestablished harmony center stage, the latter focuses on the problem of monads. Laywine (1993: 25–42) discusses the competing theories of pre-established harmony and physical influx in view of Kant's *Dreams of a Spirit-Seer*. See also Gerlach (1998). I will disregard attacks by Euler and others on monadology as such. Because of the role played by the Berlin Academy, such attacks became more widespread from the 1740s onward. On this, see, for example, Hahmann (2009a).

ultimately constituted by monads capable of some degree of perception, they did not want to give in to materialism.[61] The tension between these two extremes gave rise to a variety of intricate theories about the ultimate elements of corporal bodies deemed compatible with Newtonian physics.

Wolff's cosmology contributed importantly to this development. While Wolff accepted a number of features of Leibniz's conception of monads, which he called elements, he came to deny that the elements constitutive of corporal things must possess the same kind of force as monads such as the soul or God. According to the *Anmerckungen* (1724), he considered it likely that "the elements of corporal things contain a force from which . . . the force that bodies manifest insofar as they are in movement can be derived in an intelligible way."[62] This is to say that Wolff sacrificed the common ground of non-corporal monads and the ultimate elements of matter – that is, perception – in order to account for the continuity between the force constitutive of these ultimate elements and the force proper to the corporal things studied in physics.

While Wolff left open what kind of non-representational force these elements possessed, he argued that they do not fill a space by themselves, but are rather like points in a space (GM 602, cf. 81). Nevertheless, he took these elements to be outside one another and to fill a space insofar as they coalesce (602–3). Presumably, he considered their force to consist precisely in their capacity to fill a space and, thus, to constitute the corporal things that can be perceived by the senses.

In the wake of Wolff's partial departure from Leibniz, the debate came to turn on questions such as whether the elements constitutive of matter are in space, fill a space, are impenetrable, possess one or more forces, and so on. In short, Leibnizian monadology gave way to theories that considered the ultimate elements of matter to be both monad-like and somehow part of matter itself, that is to say, real.[63]

---

[61] As Watkins (2006: 290–98) and Hahmann (2009b: 30–35) point out, Baumgarten was an exception in this regard. Curiously, his *Metaphysics* considers all monads both to be impenetrable (M 398) and to possess the capacity to represent the universe with some degree of clarity (400).

[62] Wolff, Anm 215, emphasis mine. This passage is cited and discussed in Watkins (2006: 281–82) and Hahmann (2020). They also note that the *German Metaphysics* itself takes up a more agnostic position on this point (cf. GM 600). In contrast to his reputation, Wolff's contributions to the debates repeatedly testify to methodological caution. Thus, he notes that the fact that I can decide to move my arm does not warrant the conclusion that the soul acts on the body (536), for the alleged interaction between soul and body cannot itself be experienced (529). He points out, however, that its possibility should neither be ruled out (530, cf. 598).

[63] Wolff notes at one point that these elements are simply too tiny to be perceived, which suggests that he considered them to be on a par with composite things (GM 83–86). On the other hand, he distinguishes elements from corpuscles conceived as parts of matter itself (613). Watkins (2006:

Proponents of these so-called physical monadologies faced the following problem: a body must be considered to be divisible ad infinitum by dint of the space that it occupies, but must also be considered to consist of a determinate number of discrete, indivisible elements. Kant's first attempt to untangle this knot, in a text known as *Physical Monadology* (1756), hinges on the distinction between the indivisibility of the physical monad itself and the infinitely divisible "sphere of its activity" (2:481), a sphere he considered to ensue from the interplay of forces – repulsion and attraction – that the monad exerts.[64]

The details of Kant's early reflections on this issue need not concern us here. What matters, rather, is that Kant during the second half of the 1760s came to realize that the attempts of Wolff, his followers, and his own earlier self to align Leibniz and Newton had created a tangle of contentious speculations that made metaphysics highly vulnerable to attacks from without. As he came to see it, this tangle could be resolved only by cutting the umbilical cord between noumena and phenomena, that is, by abolishing the continuism underlying Wolff's and Crusius's systems alike. Once this was done, a concept such as that of a physical monad would turn out to be completely empty.

Yet issues in cosmology were probably not Kant's main concern. The continuism he came to reject had also had a detrimental impact on debates concerned with the relationship between soul and body and, hence, the plausibility of pre-established harmony. As seen, Crusius took souls not only to occupy a place but also to be impenetrable and capable of real interaction with bodies. As Heßbrüggen-Walter has shown, from the 1720s onward a number of German philosophers, including Kant's teacher Knutzen, had proposed intricate arguments to assert that the soul is present in a place without filling it, that it fills a space without therefore possessing extension, that we cannot know whether it fills a space, that it is present in the body as a whole or in a part of the body, and so on.[65]

---

288) rightly notes that the simples Wolff considered to be non-mental cannot for that matter "be physical *in the same sense* in which bodies are." It follows that Wolff faces the same difficulty as Leibniz, namely, to explain "how something that is not physical is supposed to give rise to something else that is." This problem, a version of continuism, can be said to be at the core of any physical monadology.

[64] PM, 2:484, cf. 480–83. See Schönfeld (2000: 161–79) for a helpful contextualization of Kant's essay, and Engelhard (2009: 301–38) for an illuminating discussion of Kant's early physical monadology and his criticism of it in the Antinomy of Pure Reason. See also Edwards (2000: 118–23).

[65] See Heßbruggen-Walter (2014). The article also discusses Crusius's position and Kant's evolving view on the subject up to and including the *Dissertation*. Unmistakably targeting Crusius, Kant

Obviously, the controversy on the soul considered as spiritual monad presupposes the same continuism as the one on physical monads and can therefore be shown to be fruitless on the same ground. Kant's first attack on the underlying premise of this debate is carried out in *Dreams of a Spirit-Seer* (1766), a text that arguably marks the beginning of his efforts to divorce metaphysics from any form of continuism. While a discussion of this text falls outside the scope of this chapter, the following passage makes it clear that Kant around this time believed that he had found a way to arouse both Wolff and Crusius from their dogmatic slumber:

> [I]f we consider those who build their various thought-up worlds in the sky, each happily inhabiting his own to the exclusion of the others – if we consider, for example, the one who inhabits the world known as the order of things, a world tinkered together by Wolff from a few building-materials derived from experience and a larger amount of surreptitious concepts, or the one who inhabits the world which was conjured out of nothing by Crusius employing the magical power of a few formulae concerning what can and what cannot be thought – then we shall be patient with their contradictory visions, until these gentlemen have finished their dreams.[66]

However, notwithstanding Kant's increasingly radical critique of dogmatist metaphysics, there is no doubt that he borrowed extensively from the storehouses of ideas built by Wolff, Crusius, and others, and this not only in the works he wrote prior to the *Dissertation*. As Kant notes somewhere between 1776 and 1778, "I have not cited anyone from reading whom I have learned something. I have found it good to omit everything foreign and to follow my own ideas" (R5019).

From Wolff, briefly put, Kant at least took over the idea of metaphysics as a comprehensive system of the concepts and principles constitutive of any cognition of objects as well as the idea that such a system ought to be established by means of a strict method. For this reason, the reform of metaphysics to be achieved by means of the *Critique of Pure Reason* is first and foremost concerned with Wolffian metaphysics. From Crusius, Hume, and, ultimately, Locke, on the other hand, Kant at least took over the idea that metaphysics needs to set its own boundaries by carefully

---

maintains in *Dreams* that souls are present in space without therefore being impenetrable (2:321, cf. 327–28).

[66] *Dreams*, 2:342, translation modified. See also R4936 (dated 1776–78). I discuss Kant's critique of Wolffian metaphysics in *Dreams of a Spirit-Seer* in De Boer (2018b).

examining how the human mind actually brings about the concepts and principles constitutive of any mode of cognition. Evidently, this program constitutes the core of the *Critique of Pure Reason*. However, Kant's examination of the human mind in this work seeks to stay clear of the psychologism that the approach of his predecessors appears to involve. How Kant reached this position will be examined in the next chapter.

CHAPTER 2

The "Thorny Paths of Critique"

1 Introduction

Kant's critique of metaphysics is mostly known for its claim that we cannot know the soul, the world as such, and God. While this account is not exactly false, I hold that it does not do justice to the intricate arguments deployed in the *Critique of Pure Reason*, nor to the unity of its various parts, nor to its intended result. This chapter aims to prepare a more nuanced interpretation of this work by examining Kant's critique of post-Leibnizian metaphysics from the perspective of its genesis.

As was mentioned in the Introduction, I hold that Kant never purported to break with his German predecessors completely. Moving away from the common distinction between a pre-critical, critical, and post-critical phase, this chapter contends that the various phases of his career, including the one defined by the *Critique of Pure Reason*, rather consist in increasingly radical efforts to reform the metaphysics of his predecessors.[1] Giving pride of place to the *Inaugural Dissertation* (1770), I will argue that each of these phases testifies to a critical impetus, albeit one that was aimed to defend core elements of post-Leibnizian metaphysics against a variety of attacks. Accordingly, this chapter also puts into perspective the assumption, shared

---

[1] While taking a different route, my interpretation shares common ground with Ameriks (1982/2000: xxii–xxiii, cf. 97), who considers Kant's critique of rational psychology in the Transcendental Dialectic to be compatible with a moderate form of rationalism. Kant held on to the latter, he rightly points out, in order to ward off materialism and other threats to morality. Other Anglophone authors who challenge the view that Kant came to completely reject the metaphysics represented by Leibniz and Wolff include Jauernig (2008) and McQuillan (2016). However, I do not share Jauernig's assumption that transcendental philosophy is "non- or antimetaphysical" (44). Conversely, I hold that McQuillan does not give enough weight to Kant's increasingly radical criticism of the assumptions underlying Wolffian metaphysics. Laywine (1993) offers insightful accounts of Kant's early engagement with particular metaphysical issues such as force, causality, and the relation between body and soul, but fails to relate them to Kant's various efforts to reform Wolffian metaphysics as a whole. Her claim that everything Kant undertook up to 1781 was aimed at a "credible system of physical influx" (123, cf. 3) is highly contentious. Other relevant studies that examine Kant's development during the 1760s and 1770s will be taken into account over the course of this chapter.

by many commentators, that the *Dissertation* is a dogmatic treatise that inexplicably interrupts the antimetaphysical thrust of *Dreams of a Spirit-Seer* (1766) and the *Critique of Pure Reason*.[2]

My sketch of the "thorny paths of critique" (Bxliii) that Kant pursued during the 1760s and early 1770s is intended to pave the way – as a propaedeutic of sorts – for the interpretation of the *Critique of Pure Reason* elaborated throughout this book. Drawing on an idea that I take to inform the *Dissertation*, namely, the idea that the suitability of pure concepts for a particular purpose depends on whether their use does or does not rest on time qua pure intuition, I contend that Kant's mature critique seeks not only to wean post-Leibnizian metaphysics from its tendency to objectify the unconditioned but also to turn it into a purely intellectual discipline.[3] Accordingly, I consider the *Dissertation* to be the breeding ground of Kant's critical distinction between phenomena and noumena, the account of transcendental schemata elaborated in the Transcendental Analytic, and Kant's mature critique of post-Leibnizian metaphysics.

Clearly, Kant's increasingly radical critique of this tradition went hand in hand with instances of self-criticism. Given the already large scope of this chapter, this issue will largely be disregarded. Kant, for his part, likewise abstracted as much as possible from the peculiarities of particular systems, presenting the *Critique* as a work that lets pure reason – and, hence, metaphysics as such – engage in a thoroughgoing self-criticism.[4]

In order to clarify the genesis and significance of this endeavor, Section 2 offers a brief sketch of Kant's early intellectual trajectory, mostly by means of his own reminiscences. Focusing on Kant's idea of a critique of metaphysics, Sections 3–5 zoom in on the years between 1765 and 1772.

---

[2] For example, Beck (1969) writes that Kant, after having been aroused from his dogmatic slumber, took a "nap" around the time of the *Dissertation* and, after its publication, saw the "sweet dreams which he enjoyed in 1770" destroyed once and for all (439, cf. 455–57). This view does not sit well with a letter, cited by Beck, in which Kant asks his editor Tieftrunk to include the *Dissertation* in a one-volume edition of his critical writings. See Kant to Tieftrunk, October 13, 1797 (12:208). Moreover, Kant told Herz already in 1781 that he considered the *Critique* to result from "all of the manifold investigations that ensued from the concepts we debated together under the heading *mundi sensibilis* and *intelligibilis*." See Kant to Herz, May 1, 1781 (10:266). Further literature on this topic will be discussed in Section 4 of this chapter.

[3] The current chapter draws on earlier work on Kant's notion of sensible concepts in the *Inaugural Dissertation* and the *Critique of Pure Reason* (De Boer 2018a) and is intimately connected to Chapter 6 of the present book. In De Boer (2020) I develop the core idea of the present chapter by interpreting the Antinomy of Pure Reason in light of the distinction between the twofold use of pure concepts put forward in the *Inaugural Dissertation*.

[4] As Kant puts it, the *Critique of Pure Reason* does not target "books and systems" (Axii), but demands that reason take on "the most difficult of all its tasks, namely, that of self-knowledge" (Axi, cf. Prol, 4:329). See also R5019, dated 1776–78.

Drawing on the preceding chapter, my reading of the *Dissertation*, in Section 4, gives much weight to Kant's critique of Crusius's identification of existence with spatiotemporal existence. Sections 6 and 7 seek to bring out the continuity between the *Dissertation* and the *Critique of Pure Reason* by examining Kant's mature notion of critique and the two-pronged critique he actually carries out in latter work, respectively.

2 Kant's Intellectual Trajectory in a Nutshell (1755–1770)

In an unpublished note dated 1776–78, Kant writes that all efforts of metaphysics to obtain "cognitions of objects about which we cannot be instructed by any sense" prove to be vain (R5115, 18:94). The subsequent note, R5116, provides an account of the trajectory that led him to this position. In this account, five phases can be distinguished and, roughly, mapped onto the works Kant had published up to that point.[5] Taking its lead from this note, this section discusses a number of retrospective notes and letters in order to reconstruct Kant's evolving view on the task of a critique of metaphysics.

[1] In R5116, Kant points out that his various efforts to "improve" metaphysics were initially geared toward the acquisition of "dogmatic insights" (18:95). This approach can be traced back to at least 1755: already in *New Elucidation*, Kant compares his position to that of an impartial judge who carries out a "modest assessment" of proofs put forward by others.[6] At this stage, according to the note, Kant "gave no hearing" to the "boldly stated doubt" about metaphysical truths raised by his contemporaries (18:95). Since Kant was almost certainly familiar with the German translation of Hume's *Enquiry* from 1755 onward, this remark may well refer to his decision to ignore the latter's attack on metaphysics.[7] Rather than

---

[5] These phases are not necessarily distinguished by clear breaks. In a letter to Lambert dated December 31, 1765, Kant sketches his development so far by referring to "a number of reversals," each of which is said to concern his effort to discover "the sources of the mistake or insight" in the "procedure" of metaphysics (10:55). As I see it, however, this description does not entail that Kant thought these reversals were random or that his texts defy a developmental account.

[6] Similarly, Kant presents *The Only Possible Argument* (1763) as a work that contains a critical examination (*Prüfung*) of the principles assumed in alleged proofs of the existence of God (2:156). Stressing the continuity in Kant's development, Hinske (1970a: 114) points out that Kant adopted this critical attitude from the publication of *Thoughts on the True Estimation of Living Forces* (1747) onward (121–23).

[7] I will largely disregard the question concerning Hume's impact on Kant and the literature on this issue. On this, see De Boer (2019a). In line with the present book, this article treats Kant's relationship to Hume from the perspective of their critique of metaphysics.

abandoning the core assets of Wolffian metaphysics to the enemy, Kant's strategy consisted in fortifying the building intended to protect them.

[2] The second phase Kant distinguishes consisted in subjecting "what one has learned or even thought for oneself entirely to critique," not even sparing "one's own products" (18:95). As seen in Chapter 1, Kant, spurred by Crusius and others, gradually emancipated himself from a number of assumptions of Wolffian metaphysics, a process that can be traced back to the early 1760s and culminated in *Dreams of a Spirit-Seer* (1766). In 1768, Kant refers in a letter to Herder to the period between 1764 and 1768 as a period in which he changed his mind in a number of ways:

> I am committed to nothing and, deeply indifferent toward my own and others' opinions, often turn the whole edifice (*Gebäude*) upside down, observing it from a variety of perspectives in order finally to discover one that hopefully will allow me to sketch this edifice (*es*) in a truthful manner. For this reason, I have, since we parted, replaced my insights on many issues (*in vielen Stücken*) by other ones.[8]

[3] Yet for a number of years – roughly, from 1765 to 1769 – Kant's critique targeted specific aspects of metaphysics rather than the very possibility of a priori cognition of objects. It "took a long while," he writes in R5116, before he found "the whole dogmatic theory to be dialectical" and, hence, untenable (18:95). In a late letter to Garve, Kant refers to this skeptical insight as the insight into the antinomy that pure reason produces whenever it seeks to determine non-sensible objects such as the world as such. In this letter, Kant writes that it was

> the antinomy of pure reason – "The world has a beginning; it has no beginning, and so on, right up to the fourth: There is freedom in man, vs. there is no freedom, only the necessity of nature" – that first aroused me from my dogmatic slumber and drove me to the critique of reason itself, in order to resolve the scandal of the ostensible contradiction of reason with itself.[9]

A letter to Bernoulli, sent in 1781, suggests that Kant, at least according to his own recollection, had begun to consider this matter around 1765, that is, around the time Lambert had proposed that they cooperate on a

---

[8] Kant to Herder, May 9, 1768 (10:74), translation modified. Since Kant goes on to mention his work on a metaphysics of morals, I take it that the term 'edifice' refers to both the theoretical and practical part of metaphysics.

[9] Kant to Garve, September 21, 1798 (12:257–58), cf. A407/B433–34, A757/B785, Prol, 4:338. In his letter to Garve, Kant mentions the first three of the cosmological conflicts presented in the *Critique of Pure Reason*, mistakenly referring to the third as the fourth.

"reform of metaphysics" (10:277). At that point, Kant tells Bernoulli, he had realized that

> this putative science lacked a reliable touchstone with which to distinguish truth from illusion, since different but equally persuasive metaphysical propositions lead inescapably to contradictory conclusions, with the result that one proposition inevitably casts doubt on the other. I had some ideas for a possible improvement of this science then, but I wanted my ideas to mature first.[10]

Kant's ideas seem to have reached maturity in 1769, that is to say, shortly before publishing the *Inaugural Dissertation*. This can be seen from a set of notes likewise dated 1776–78. In one of them, partly quoted in the preceding chapter, Kant writes that Wolff "extended cognition without securing, altering, and reforming it through a special critique" and so failed to bring the "experiments of the understanding ... under rules."[11] Remedying this, Kant writes in a subsequent note, requires that "the boundaries of every science must be precisely observed," since "mixing them together only results in illusions" (R5036, 18:69).

In the most famous note from the set, Kant suggests he developed his insight into the illusions produced by metaphysics by reflecting on the contradictions produced by reason that the *Critique of Pure Reason* treats in the chapter titled "The Antinomy of Pure Reason." In accordance with the two letters cited above, Kant writes:

> Initially ... I tried quite earnestly to prove propositions and their opposite, not in order to establish a skeptical doctrine, but rather because I suspected I could discover in what an illusion of the understanding was hiding. The year '69 gave me a great light.[12]

---

[10] Kant to Bernoulli, November 16, 1781 (10:277). This passage speaks against Ertl's assumption of a radical break in Kant's development around 1769. See Ertl (2002: 635).

[11] R5035, cf. R4866 (also dated 1776–78).

[12] R5037. If the letter to Bernouilli quoted above is correct, Kant must have carried out this examination of contrary metaphysical claims during the years 1765–69. He can indeed be said to have done so from at least 1766 onward. Thus, *Dreams of a Spirit-Seer* treats a conflict internal to metaphysics by subsequently affirming (2:347) and denying (2:352) the existence of unembodied spirits. Kant comments on this procedure at 2:366–68. Earlier texts, including the *Physical Monadology* (1756), do not treat conflicts internal to metaphysics, but seek to solve a particular problem by disentangling a mathematical from a metaphysical approach. Early versions of the cosmological conflicts treated in the Antinomy of Pure Reason can be found in notes dated 1764–68 (R3841, R3860), notes dated 1769–70 (including R3976, R4000, R4007, R4271), and the *Inaugural Dissertation* (2:391–92, 415). For discussions of Kant's development in this regard, see Hinske (1970a), Schmucker (1974: 272–73), Gawlick and Kreimendahl (1987: 197), Kreimendahl (1990), Ertl (2002), Chance (2012: 323–28), and De Boer (2019a).

Once Kant had identified the ubiquous illusions that metaphysics produces quasi-naturally, he may well have been ready, finally, to confront
rather than dismiss Hume's denial of the capacity of the human mind to
obtain cognitions of objects independently of experience. Seen in this way,
Kant's famous remark in the *Prolegomena* that thinking anew of David
Hume interrupted his "dogmatic slumber" (4:260) is not at odds with his
assertions that it was his critical examination of the cosmological conflicts
produced by metaphysics that led to this awakening.[13]

Even though Kant never accepted Hume's skeptical conclusions
(cf. Prol, 2:260), various texts from 1765 to 1769 testify to Kant's
increasing exasperation about the unfounded speculations that abounded
in the metaphysical treatises of his days. In a letter sent to Mendelssohn in
1766, for instance, Kant denounces "the inflated arrogance of whole
volumes full of what are passed off as insights nowadays." Yet he notes
in the same letter that the "true and lasting welfare of mankind" depends
on metaphysics "objectively considered" and that the latter ought to be
elaborated on the basis of a completely new "guiding thread" or "plan."[14]
Likewise, Kant wrote to Lambert the year before that the wished-for
"euthanasia of false philosophy" is the precondition of its rebirth:

> Before true philosophy can come to life, the old one must destroy itself; and
> just as putrefaction signifies the total dissolution that always precedes the
> start of a new creation, so the current *crisis* in learning causes me to hope
> that the great, long-awaited *revolution* in the sciences is not too far off.[15]

However, it is unclear how Kant thought he could actually achieve this
lofty goal. Evidently, doing so requires that one assess the various elements
of metaphysics by means of an infallible criterion.

[4] Kant clearly believed to have found such a criterion in 1769, that is
to say, the year of the "great light." In a letter sent to Lambert together
with a copy of the *Dissertation*, dated September 2, 1770, he writes:

---

[13] Kreimendahl (1990: 188, 192) defends a similar position, though by different means. I am not
convinced by the role he here and elsewhere grants to Kant's alleged knowledge of Hume's *Treatise*.
I deal with this point and the debate on the issue of Kant's awakening more generally in De Boer
(2019a).

[14] Kant to Mendelssohn, April 8, 1766 (10:70).

[15] Kant to Lambert, December 31, 1765, 10:57, cf. A407/B434. Earlier on in the letter (10:55–56),
he refers to a projected work devoted to the proper method of metaphysics. Evidently, this plan
contains the seeds of the *Critique of Pure Reason*. De Vleeschauwer (1939/1962: 39–41) and Beiser
(1992: 43–46), among others, refer to the impact Rousseau had on Kant around 1764. In my
opinion, the passages quoted above do not suffice to infer, as these commentators do, that Kant
went through a deep and sudden crisis at the time.

> For perhaps a year now, I believe I have arrived at a position that, I flatter myself, I shall never have to change, even though extensions will be needed, a position from which all sorts of metaphysical questions can be examined according to wholly certain and easy criteria, and the extent to which these questions can or cannot be resolved will be decidable with certainty. (10:97)

While Kant does not mention any texts in R5116, it seems to me that his description of the phase initiated by this new insight fits the 1770 *Dissertation* very well. At a certain point, he writes in the note, he sought to achieve certainty not with regard to objects but "with regard to the nature and boundaries of this kind of cognition," that is, of metaphysics qua putative a priori cognition of objects. Through this new investigation into the human mind, Kant "gradually" realized – along the lines of Crusius and Hume – "that many of the propositions we regard as objective are in fact subjective, i.e., contain the *conditiones* under which alone we can ... comprehend the object."[16] I consider this insight to be pivotal to the critique of metaphysics put forward in the *Dissertation*. Before turning to this work, however, I briefly consider Kant's thoughts on the task of a critique of a metaphysics in the years prior to 1770.

3   Kant's Early Notion of Critique

In the spirit of the letters to Mendelssohn and Lambert mentioned above, Kant started using the term 'critique' to refer to the act of disentangling the rational core of metaphysics from its unfounded assumptions and inferences. The terms in which he does so are very similar to the ones used in 1781. Thus, *Dreams of a Spirit-Seer*, albeit rather inconspicuously, considers the act of "critique" to resolve "the ambivalent mixture of reason and credulity into its elements" (2:356). Toward the end of the text, Kant writes that metaphysics must carry out this act with regard to itself in order to eradicate "the fathomless projects ... that ... lie outside the sphere of man" so as to "enhance the wisdom of which humankind is capable" (369). The discipline should step back from its first-order activity in order to "pass judgment on its own procedure" (369–70), that is, to establish itself as a "science of the boundaries of human reason" (368). If, Kant writes, philosophy

---

[16] Diss, 2:18:95. The name of Locke, whose work Crusius must have known at least indirectly, might be added here (see Carboncini 1986).

achieves knowledge not only of the objects, but also of their relation to the human understanding, then its boundaries (*Grenze*) contract in size and those boundary-stones (*Marksteine*) are placed that will never again permit the enquiry to leave the realm proper to it. (369–70, translation modified)

The first printed text in which Kant discusses the idea of a critique of metaphysics is not *Dreams*, but his announcement of his lectures on metaphysics, logic, and ethics for the winter semester of 1765–66.[17] In this text, he claims to have discovered for some time both "the source of the errors which have been committed" in metaphysics and the "criterion (*Richtmaß*) of judgment by reference to which alone those errors can be avoided, if they can be avoided at all" (2:308).

Kant introduces the idea of a "critique and canon" of metaphysics by drawing an analogy with the preparatory task assigned to general logic. Whereas the study of any science must be preceded by a "critique and canon" of the common use of the understanding, metaphysics, qua particular science, calls for a "critique and canon" of its own, namely, an examination of the "method which is peculiar to it, and which can serve as an organon of this science."[18] Thus, metaphysics must be preceded by a discipline that establishes the rules it ought to follow by means of an

---

[17] Unpublished notes that deal with the notion of critique include R3716 (probably stemming from 1768–69; see Ertl 2002), R3970 (1769), and R4146 (1769–70). The latter note conceives of metaphysics as "the critique of pure reason" and considers it to be concerned with "the conditions under which alone human pure reason can make judgments." On possible sources of Kant's conception of critique, including Henry Home's *Elements of Criticism*, which was published in German between 1763 and 1766, see Tonelli (1978) and McQuillan (2016: 3–20). According to Tonelli, Kant's use of the term 'critique' stems from the inclusion into logic, from the sixteenth century onward, of a part – called critique – concerned with the act of assessing the opinions of others. Yet obviously it does not follow from this history, as Tonelli claims, that Kant saw the *Critique of Pure Reason* "as a work primarily on Logic" (147).

[18] *Announcement*, 2:310. The *Critique of Pure Reason* likewise distinguishes between a logic concerned with the general use of the understanding and a logic concerned with the rules required to think correctly about a particular kind of object (A52/B76–77, cf. A12/B26, A708/B736). In this sense, the critique carried out in the *Critique of Pure Reason* is a logic concerned with the way in which metaphysics, qua particular discipline, ought to think about its objects. This does not entail, however, that what Kant means by critique can be understood on the model of formal logic in all respects. See Tolley (2012) for a discussion of the long-standing debate on this issue, a debate that in my view rests on overly narrow accounts of what Kant means by a logic tailored to a particular science. While I agree with many of Tolley's criticisms, I am not convinced by his alternative framing of the problem in terms of the universality of the concepts and judgments considered in transcendental logic: although general metaphysics, like general logic, indeed deals with modes of thought that pervade all sciences, general and special metaphysics are also disciplines distinguished from others by their type of cognition (a priori) and objects (all things and the various modes of the unconditioned). Tolley does not take into account that it is metaphysics *in this regard* that calls for a second-order investigation into the legitimacy of its use of concepts and principles, in other words, for the logic that the *Critique of Pure Reason* calls transcendental logic (cf. A64/B88).

investigation into the activities carried out by the human mind.[19] Kant's insights in this regard, he asserts at one point, will allow him to improve the textbook he intends to use for his classes: he considers a "small flexion" to suffice to steer Baumgarten's *Metaphysics* into the right direction (308–9).

Unlike *Dreams*, the *Announcement* makes it clear that Kant did not regard the negative strand of his projected science of the boundaries of human reason as an end in itself. Referring to the philosophical disciplines taken together, he notes that the critique proper to metaphysics ought to be geared toward the elaboration of a canon, that is, "a precise ground-plan, on the basis of which such an edifice of reason (*Gebäude der Vernunft*) can be erected in a lasting and rule-bound way (*dauerhaft und regelmäßig*)."[20] Combined with the reference to Baumgarten mentioned above, this passage strongly suggests that Kant saw his projected critique of metaphysics as a means to improve rather than abolish the metaphysics exemplified by Baumgarten's system. It is clear, however, that Kant went on to spend most of his time on the critical, second-order examination of metaphysics outlined in texts such as the *Announcement* and *Dreams*. The next section will argue that this also holds for the *Inaugural Dissertation*.

4   The *Inaugural Dissertation*

As was mentioned in the introduction to this chapter, many commentators consider the *Inaugural Dissertation* to inexplicably deviate from the critical path set out in *Dreams*.[21] It is true that Kant's treatise – titled *On the Form*

---

[19]   Kant notes that, for didactic purposes, the reflection on the method of metaphysics must come at the end of the course (*Announcement*, 2:310). In my view, however, this remark is not at odds with the idea that metaphysics as such must be preceded by a critical investigation into its method and principles.

[20]   *Announcement*, 2:310, translation modified.

[21]   Echoing Beck (1969: 439), and in accordance with, among others, De Vleeschauwer (1939/1962: 56) and Kuehn (1983: 183), Ertl (2002: 635) asserts that Kant interrupted his dogmatic slumber in 1768–69 "only temporarily" because of "the utterly un-Kantian view that the human understanding has access to the world of *noumena*" put forward in the *Dissertation*. Similarly, Kreimendahl (1990: 224–32) claims that the treatise cannot reflect Kant's considered position at the time because its dogmatic and progressive strands do not cohere. By contrast, Beiser (1992: 48) puts into perspective the apparent gap between *Dreams* and the *Dissertation* by arguing that the former does not proscribe the "new metaphysics" elaborated in the latter, which he considers to be "first and foremost an ontology" (49). I agree on many points with Schmucker (1974), who defends Kant's text against charges of dogmatism (276). However, mostly drawing on Kant's notes and letters, he does not offer an innovative reading of the *Dissertation* itself. Moreover, he no less than his opponents seems to measure the critical nature of the text in terms of, first, its account of space and time and, second, the question concerning the conditions of possibility of experience alleged to be pivotal to the transcendental deduction (cf. 276–77). My reading is in line with Moledo (2016), who likewise

and Principles of the Sensible and the Intelligible World – does not immediately betray its critical impetus. But first impressions can be deceptive: in
§ 8 Kant presents the text as a "specimen" of the "propaedeutic science"
that in his view has to precede metaphysics (2:395, cf. 419). Even though
the *Dissertation* develops in a very different intellectual element, it no less
than *Dreams* seeks to introduce the reader to a critical, second-order
investigation into the conditions under which a rigorous metaphysics is
possible. Whereas *Dreams* does so by focusing on rational psychology, the
Dissertation uses Wolffian general cosmology as an example to show how
metaphysics might be turned into a science.[22] In order to foreground the
critical thrust of the text, I will start from Kant's criticism of dogmatic
metaphysics in its final section and consider earlier key passages in
this light.

In line with the notion of critique presented in the *Announcement*,
Kant's criticism in the *Dissertation* is not directed against the mathematical
method that according to Wolff ought to be used in any science, but rather
aims at a procedure that belongs to metaphysics alone and was not even
identified as such by his predecessor.[23] Metaphysics calls for special scrutiny, Kant maintains, because it does not start from intuitions and accordingly must generate the content of its cognitions all by itself. Unlike
empirical science, metaphysics cannot proceed by subordinating particular
cognitions under more general ones in accordance with the principle of
non-contradiction, which is to say that its use of the intellect is not merely
"logical" (2:410–11). It is for this reason, it seems to me, that Kant
considers metaphysics to rest on a "real" use of the intellect, that is, on
the production of purely intellectual concepts such as composition, existence, substance, and causality as well as on the conception of purely
intellectual objects such as the world by means of these concepts.[24] Since
in this case the use of the intellect cannot be kept in check by sensible

---

    considers Kant's effort to establish metaphysics as a purely intellectual discipline to testify to the
    critical impetus of the text.

[22] Kant's sketchy discussion of first-order general cosmology, in section IV (2:406–9), is heavily
    indebted to Wolff and Baumgarten. Abstracting from spatial and temporal determinations, it treats
    the world in view of the way in which "a connection between a plurality of substances comes to be,
    and how a totality between them is brought about" (2:407). Earlier texts that contain similar
    expositions include *New Elucidation* (1755).

[23] Thus, Kant writes that the method actually employed in metaphysics is "not well known at the
    present time, apart, that is, from the kind which logic teaches generally to all the sciences," and that
    "the method which is suited to the particular nature of metaphysics" is even "wholly unknown"
    (Diss, 2:411).

[24] "As far as intellectual thoughts (*intellectualia*) as such are concerned, in respect to which *the use of
    the intellect is real*, the concepts of objects as well as of their relations are given by the nature of the

intuitions, metaphysics risks becoming a mere "play of the intellect" (411). I take Kant to hold that the correct use of the mathematical method promoted by Wolff does not necessarily prevent the particular kind of errors to which metaphysics is prone. In order to avoid the latter, therefore, metaphysics ought to begin by investigating the way it uses concepts and principles that are generated by the intellect itself (411). Clearly, this is the task Kant assigns to the "propaedeutic science" mentioned above (cf. 395).

For Kant, "a considerable part" of the method actually employed in metaphysics is defective because it rests on "the contagion of intellectual cognition by sensible cognition."[25] This method is said to concern not only the unwarranted use of accepted principles but also the invention of spurious ones (411). The *Dissertation* explores a number of principles and judgments infected with sensibility, moving from rather obvious cases to cases that are hard to detect.

The first example of a spurious axiom that Kant mentions, in a footnote, is the "common" axiom according to which "everything that exists is somewhere" (412n). As was seen in Chapter 1, this is one of Crusius's principles.[26] The principle is spurious, according to Kant, because the predicate 'somewhere,' just as any other sensible concept that functions as predicate of a judgment, is nothing but a "condition of sensible cognition." Positing that things are 'somewhere' allows us to make judgments about things that present themselves to the senses, but the predicate 'somewhere' cannot be attributed to things insofar as they are thought by the intellect, which means that it cannot be asserted "objectively" (412n). The problem with Crusius's principle, on Kant's account, is that it purports to obtain of anything whatsoever, including things such as the soul and God, whereas it rests on space qua condition of sensible cognition alone:

> intellect itself: they contain no form of sensible cognition and they have been abstracted from no use of the senses" (Diss, 2:394, translation modified, cf. 411). The *Critique of Pure Reason* also connects the real use of reason to its capacity to generate concepts and principles all by itself (A299/B355). At 2:392, the term *intellectualia* clearly refers not to things but to a specific kind of representation. Similarly, in his 1772 letter to Herz, Kant uses the expression "intellectual representations" to refer to what the *Dissertation* called *intellectualia* (10:130–31). Since the *Dissertation* does not yet clearly distinguish between the understanding and reason, I will translate 'intellectualis' as 'intellectual' throughout: what Kant calls intellectual concepts or thoughts (*intellectualia*) includes both pure concepts and what he will come to call ideas of reason.

25 Diss, 2:411, translation modified. I will translate 'sensitivus' as 'sensible' rather than 'sensitive' because the latter term means something else than the Latin version. Moreover, the German equivalent 'sinnlich' is normally translated as 'sensible.'

26 Kant's critical discussion of metaphysical fallacies in section V starts from Crusius's principle according to which "what is, is somewhere and somewhen" (2:413), but does not mention his name. Evidently, Kant's criticism of this principle does not entail that he came to reject Crusius's idea of material principles as such.

> [S]ince the predicate contains the conditions of sensible cognition, it will not be possible to assert it of the subject of the judgment in general, namely, of anything that exists whatsoever. Accordingly, this formula, if understood objectively, is false.[27]

Thus, the judgment 'everything that exists is somewhere' involves a sensible predicate, yet purports to obtain of things as they are in themselves. Kant refers to any judgment that does so as a "metaphysical fallacy of subreption" and to those judgments that function as principles of other metaphysical judgments as "subreptic axioms" (412). Principles that draw on the latter, Kant writes, "deceive the understanding and ... have disastrously permeated the whole of metaphysics" (412).

Kant thought that his discovery made it possible to root out a variety of fallacious metaphysical judgments, including "idle questions about the places in the corporeal universe of immaterial substances, ... about the seat of the soul, and about other questions of the kind" (414). As seen in Chapter 1, these questions were the subject of a number of controversies that involved Wolff, Crusius, and their followers. Most likely including Crusius among his targets, Kant specifically denounces efforts to conceive of God as spatial in any sense. It is impossible, he writes,

> to express the extent to which one has been deluded by the shadows which flit before the understanding. One ... has enfolded God in the world as if he were contained all at once in infinite space; to compensate for this limitation, one has, of course, conceived of this local presence as an eminent one (*per eminentia*), that is to say, as infinite.[28]

However, Kant's discussion is not exclusively or even primarily concerned with judgments that predicate sensible determinations of non-sensible things in such an obvious way. These clear cases rather point the way to "prejudices ... that conceal themselves to a ... greater extent" (415). This second kind of spurious judgment does not explicitly involve spatial or temporal predicates, but rather employs purely intellectual concepts such as quantity and quality in a surreptitious way.

---

[27] Diss, 2:412n. By contrast, if the purely intellectual concept 'existence' is used as a predicate and attributed to 'everything that is somewhere,' that is, to phenomena, Kant continues, then the proposition is perfectly justified (412n). Thus, whereas purely intellectual concepts can be used to determine phenomena as well as noumena, sensible concepts are suitable with regard to the former alone. Similarly, but without mentioning Crusius, Kant notes in the Transcendental Aesthetic of the *Critique of Pure Reason* that if space and time are conceived as "conditions of all existence as such, they would also have to be conditions of the existence of God." To avoid this result, they must be considered mere forms of intuition (B71–72).

[28] Diss, 2:414, translation modified. As was seen in Chapter 1, Crusius held that God "fills all merely possible space in the most perfect manner" (O 250).

As regards the concept of quantity, to which I will limit my account, Kant distinguishes an approach to the world based on purely intellectual laws from an approach based on sensible laws. According to a purely intellectual approach, any series of effects can be traced to a first principle, which is to say that it denies the possibility of an infinite regress. This approach is guided by the principle of sufficient reason. According to an approach that relies on sensible principles, by contrast, any series of things can be measured (415). Kant claims that these two propositions "are mistakenly supposed to be identical" (415). Metaphysicians who fail to distinguish the two, I take it, confuse the finitude of any causal chain posited by the intellect with a conception of quantity that presupposes measurability. This confusion results in spurious judgments about the world that concern its extension, duration, and the indivisibility of its elements. As Kant puts it:

> [T]hat the universe, in respect of its mass, is *mathematically* finite, that its past duration can be *measured*, that there is a *definite* number of simples constituting any body whatsoever – these are propositions which openly proclaim their origin in the nature of sensible cognition and . . . suffer from the unmistaken blemish of their origin.[29]

What ought to be removed from a purely intellectual account of the world, accordingly, is any determination that surreptitiously presupposes the mental act of counting, that is, the act of adding one element to another ad infinitum. By relying exclusively on the intellectual principle according to which any causal series is limited, Kant writes, metaphysics is licensed to claim that the world is finite with regard to time, space, and the divisibility of its elements:

> [T]hat the magnitude of the world is limited . . . , that bodies consist of simples – these things can, indeed, be known (*cognosci*) under the certain sign of reason. (416)

Evidently, Kant no longer accepts this position – the theses of the first two cosmological conflicts – in the chapter of the *Critique of Pure Reason* titled "The Antinomy of Pure Reason." Targeting the cosmological principles represented by the antitheses alone, the *Dissertation* seeks to preserve the intellectual core of Wolffian metaphysics and to reject a wide range of positions adopted by Wolff, Crusius, or their followers – including Kant's

---

[29] Diss, 2:416, emphasis mine. In this case, Kant's target clearly includes an earlier position of his own: according to the *Physical Monadology*, all bodies "consist of a determinate number of simple elements" (2:480).

earlier intellectual self. This difference notwithstanding, I hold that both the *Dissertation* and the *Critique of Pure Reason* defend the position that metaphysics ought to purge itself of any concepts and judgments tainted by sensibility in order to resolve its internal conflicts.[30] This is, in my view, the insight that Kant referred to as the "great light." Since I believe that the argument that supports the critical task carried out in the *Dissertation* is key to understanding the *Critique of Pure Reason*, I will examine it in somewhat more detail.

Kant argues in the *Dissertation*, first, that the concepts employed in metaphysics must stem from the intellect itself (cf. 395) and, second, that they can acquire two different meanings: either a purely intellectual one or one that refers to the mental act of adding one element to another. In the first section of the treatise, Kant clarifies his idea of a "double genesis" (387) by distinguishing two ways in which the mind can conceive of the world as such by means of the concept of composition:

> It is one thing, given the parts, to conceive (*concipere*) the composition of the whole by using an abstract concept of the intellect, and another thing to carry out this general concept by means of the sensible faculty of cognition, ... that is to say, to represent it concretely in a determinate intuition. The former is done by means of the concept of composition in general, ... and thus by means of universal ideas of the intellect. The latter case rests upon the *conditions of time*, insofar as it is possible, by the successive addition of part to part, to arrive genetically, that is to say, by synthesis, at the concept of a compound; this case falls under the laws of intuition.[31]

Thus, Kant argues that the mind can conceive of the world by using a purely intellectual concept such as composition in a purely intellectual way. If it uses such a 'thin' mode of the concept of composition, nothing

---

[30] While there is no doubt that the *Dissertation* targets Crusius, it is hard to determine to what extent the text targets Wolff's own doctrines or rather those of his followers alone. This question will be left open here. Hinske (1970a: 109–10) argues that the *Dissertation* contains a preliminary version of the problem that the *Critique of Pure Reason* refers to as the antinomy of pure reason, but one that as yet merely concerns the discrepancy between laws of sensibility and laws of the understanding. On my account, by contrast, Kant already in the *Dissertation* holds that the intellect can be governed by either purely intellectual laws or intellectual laws informed by sensibility. Seen in this way, there is much more continuity between the *Dissertation* and the *Critique of Pure Reason*. Ertl (2002) convincingly challenges the discontinuity Hinske identifies by drawing on notes he believes to stem from the late 1760s. I also agree with Ertl that the *Dissertation* scrutinizes the real use of the intellect in order to solve an early version of the antinomies (631–32). As was mentioned above, however, I disagree with his claim that the *Dissertation* is an anomaly in Kant's otherwise smooth development.

[31] Diss, 2:387, emphasis mine.

prevents the mind from conceiving of the world as limited or of its
ultimate elements as indivisible. According to Kant, however, the mind
can also conceive of 'composition' by representing its content in an
intuitive manner, that is, as the act of adding one part to another that
can be repeated ad infinitum. Since this 'thick' mode of the concept of
composition presupposes sensibility, it can be used with regard to things
that appear, but not in order to conceive of the world as such as limited or
as constituted by indivisible substances.[32] Metaphysics errs, I take Kant to
mean, insofar as it involves the surreptitious use of 'thick' concepts.

Seen in this light, the distinction Kant draws in the *Dissertation* between
our cognition of appearances and of things in themselves turns out to be
motivated by his critique of metaphysicians who generate concepts the
meaning of which inconspicuously rests on sensibility and who subsequently employ them in general cosmology and, by extension, rational
psychology, and natural theology. In my view, it is first and foremost to
counter this continuism that Kant's propaedeutic treatise "teaches the
distinction between sensible and intellectual cognition" (395) and presents
space and time as the "absolutely primary and universal ... conditions of
everything sensible in human cognition" (398).

As I see it, the first step of this teaching consists in applying the
distinction between primary and secondary qualities to the purely intellectual mode of cognition that metaphysics aspires to, which is to say that
Kant implicitly combines a Lockean and a Platonic account of cognition:

> Since whatever in cognition is sensible depends upon the particular nature
> of the subject ... , and whatever cognition is exempt from such subjective
> conditions relates only to the object, it is clear that sensible thoughts
> (*sensitive cogitata*) are representations of things *such as they appear*, while
> intellectual thoughts (*intellectualia*) are representations of things *such as
> they are*.[33]

Drawing on this distinction between sensible and intellectual thoughts,
Kant's actual argument hinges on time considered as the "pure intuition"
that allows the human mind to represent things as simultaneous or successive (399). In the final section of the text, partly discussed above, he

---

[32] Diss, 2:388, cf. 391. On this, see Laywine (1993: 115–20), who argues that Kant's criticisms apply
to views he himself held in texts such as *New Elucidation* (1755) and the *Physical
Monadology* (1756).

[33] Diss, 2:392, translation modified. Alluding to Plato, Kant also refers to these intellectual thoughts as
noumena (395, 396, cf. 392). He amends his position in the *Critique of Pure Reason* by suggesting
that it concerns the Lockean distinction between primary and secondary qualities alone (A258/
B313).

transfers the partial result of his earlier account of time to the main problem of the *Dissertation*, namely, the capacity of the human mind to generate purely intellectual cognitions of things such as the world considered as object of rational cosmology.

In this section, Kant clarifies what he means by the "conditions of time" mentioned at the very beginning of the treatise. If a purely intellectual concept such as 'composition' actually pertains to the mental act of adding one element to another, then predicating it of a subject such as the world presupposes time, which entails that time 'affects' our conception of the world:

> [A]lthough the concept of time is not contained in the concept itself of the predicate, and although it is not considered to be a characteristic of the subject, it nevertheless *serves as a means for forming the concept of the predicate*, thus affecting, as a condition, the intellectual concept of the subject, for it is only by relying on this condition that we can arrive at the latter concept. (415, emphasis mine)

Thus, we can use the concept of composition in judgments about the world as such by conceiving of composition – the predicate – either in purely intellectual terms or by representing its content as the act of generating a series of elements, in which case its meaning presupposes time and, hence, is not purely intellectual. The import of this passage cannot be overestimated: it contains the seeds not only of Kant's critique of special metaphysics in the Transcendental Dialectic but also of his account of the schematism of the pure understanding in the Transcendental Analytic.[34]

As regards the latter point, Kant suggests already in the *Dissertation* that the use of intellectual concepts such as causality for the sake of empirical cognition involves time. Relations such as that between cause and effect, he notes, can be known only "with the assistance of the relation of time," because only in this way can the mind actually determine what precedes and what follows.[35] Although the *Dissertation* does not focus on the use of intellectual concepts with regard to appearances, Kant by no means excludes it.[36]

---

[34] As far as Kant's Schematism Chapter is concerned, this point will be elaborated in Chapter 6.

[35] Diss, 2:406, cf. R3932 (dated 1769–71), R4054, and R4156 (dated 1769–70). In the latter note, Kant distinguishes between "rules of pure reason" and "rules of reason" employed by reason insofar as it rests on "concepts of appearance." This pivotal insight can be traced back to the claim in *New Elucidation* (1755) that the concept of causality presupposes a temporal difference between cause and effect and therefore cannot be used with regard to God (1:394).

[36] On this, see Wunsch (2013). By contrast, Watkins (2001) maintains that the *Dissertation* does not take into account the intellect's use of pure concepts with regard to phenomena. Arguably, the use of intellectual concepts with regard to appearances to which the *Dissertation* alludes at various points does not fit Kant's distinction between the logical and real use of the intellect in the same text.

As regards the former point, more relevant here, Kant maintains in the passage quoted above that if metaphysicians unknowingly rely on time, qua sensible condition of the judgment, in their use of intellectual concepts such as composition, then the meaning of the latter concept is unwarrantedly infected with sensibility. Just as a genuinely sensible concept, an intellectual concept the meaning of which presupposes time *actually functions as a sensible predicate* and is accordingly nothing but a particular way in which the human mind processes given representations. Such a predicate, Kant writes,

> may not be affirmed objectively of an intellectual concept (*conceptus intellectualis*); it may be affirmed only as a *condition* in the absence of which sensible cognition of the given concept cannot occur.[37]

According to Kant, therefore, the "criterion" or "touchstone" (412) by means of which metaphysics as a whole can be assessed consists in the purely intellectual nature of the concepts that function as predicates in the judgments it produces:

> The whole method employed by metaphysics ... amounts to this essential prescription: great care must be taken that the principles native to sensible cognition do not transgress their limits and affect intellectual cognitions.[38]

Kant was convinced that if metaphysics abided by this maxim, the futile debates among his contemporaries on, for example, the spatiality of the ultimate elements of matter, the soul, or God would become a thing of the past.

A cosmology based on this same maxim would rid concepts such as composition, divisibility, and cause of any reference to temporal succession and, accordingly, conceive of the world as a totality of things constituted by indivisible elements and grounded on an ultimate cause. This is, of course, precisely the thrust of the purely intellectual cosmology sketched out in section IV of the text.

More generally, I hold that Kant considered the critique at the heart of the *Dissertation* to pave the way for a metaphysics limited to, first, a systematic treatment of the purely intellectual concepts generated by the human mind and, second, their purely intellectual use with regard to purely intellectual concepts such as the soul, the world as such, and God. The gains of this purified metaphysics would extend beyond the

---

[37] Diss, 2:412, emphasis mine, original emphasis omitted.
[38] Diss, 2:411, cf. 419. See also Kant's letter to Lambert, September 2, 1770, 10:98.

sphere of theoretical cognition, for the purely intellectual concepts this metaphysics establishes would allow it to ward off attacks stemming from skepticism, determinism, and materialism and so to put itself in the service of the moral ends of mankind. As Kant told Herz in 1773, he believed that his account of the mode of reason that "isolates itself" from sensibility would give a "turn" to philosophy "much more favorable to religion and morality."[39] Earlier letters to his former pupil make it clear, however, that Kant around 1771 decided to postpone the elaboration of this original plan in order to confront head-on a question that may have been on his mind for a while but was "silently passed over" in the *Dissertation*.[40]

5   Toward a Two-Pronged Critique of Metaphysics

Clearly, the idea of a purely intellectual metaphysics put forward in 1770 called at least for a comprehensive account of those concepts that, as Kant mentions in *Dissertation*, stem from "the very nature of the pure intellect" and include "possibility, existence, necessity, substance, cause, etc." (2:395). Although the *Dissertation* does not provide an exhaustive list, Kant did not seem to have foreseen any problems here. On the contrary: he wrote to Herz in February 1772 that he had been able "to identify all concepts belonging to completely pure reason," and this by arranging them "according to the way they classify themselves by their own nature."[41] A systematic elaboration of his propaedeutic critique of metaphysics, on the other hand, would definitely have included an account of the two complementary ways in which the human mind can employ these intellectual concepts – namely, either by relying on

---

[39] Kant to Herz, 10:144. Translation modified. The term 'sensibility' is not mentioned in the letter, but the *Critique of Pure Reason* (A62/B87 and A65/89–90) uses similar expressions (*isolieren* and *sich aussondern*) in relation to sensibility.

[40] Kant to Herz, 10:130–31.

[41] Kant to Herz, February 21, 1772 (10:132, cf. 130). Passages in the *Dissertation* suggest that Kant already in 1770 regarded quantity (2:415), the simple, composition, and totality (2:387–388, cf. 415–16) as pure concepts as well. See also a number of notes dated 1769 (R3927, R3930, R3941, R3946) and Carl (1989a: 34–37). A note dated 1770–71 conceives of Aristotle's categories as "acts of the intellect" that allow us to refer our representations to an object (R4276). Whether the classification Kant refers to in his letter to Herz is the one put forward in the Metaphysical Deduction of the *Critique of Pure Reason* need not concern us here. Thöle (1991: 29), among others, assumes that Kant's account of purely intellectual root concepts was indebted to Leibniz's *Nouveaux essais sur l'entendement humain*, which was published in 1765. While this may well be true, we have seen in Chapter 1 that Kant argues already in his 1762–64 lectures on metaphysics, with reference to Crusius, that metaphysics ought to establish a number of indemonstrable material principles (LM Herder 28:10, cf. 157). Already in the *Inquiry* (1764), he maintains that such principles ought to be presented in a table (2:281, 295–96).

sensibility or by abstaining from the latter – and would have assigned each of them its proper sphere.[42]

As was seen above, the *Dissertation* differs from the *Critique of Pure Reason* in that it affirms the possibility of purely intellectual cognitions of the soul, the world as such, and God. Because of this feature, most commentators consider the two texts to be worlds apart. Yet I hold that even in this regard the *Dissertation* is less dogmatic than seems to be the case: Kant states that since "an intellectual concept is devoid of all that is given in human intuition," the human mind is granted only "symbolic cognition" of intellectual things.[43] Moreover, he considers cognition of phenomena to be "in the highest degree true" (397, cf. 417).

What the *Dissertation* does seem to avoid, in my view, is the question as to whether the symbolic cognitions obtained by predicating purely intellectual concepts of purely intellectual things amount to *cognitions of objects at all*.[44] Spurred, perhaps, by his exchanges with Herz on the *Dissertation*, Kant must have decided to turn his attention to this question.[45] As he tells his friend in 1772, he "silently passed over the … question of how a representation that relates to (*sich bezieht auf*) an object without being in

---

[42] I take this point to be supported by the division of his project, as he conceived of it between 1770 and 1772, into a phenomenology and a metaphysics. See Kant to Lambert, September 2, 1770, 10:98, and Kant to Herz, February 21, 1772, 10:129.

[43] Diss, 2:396. Kant here seems to use *intellectualia* to refer to things rather than representations. As Favaretti Camposampiero (2015: 316–24) explains, Leibniz's distinction between intuitive and symbolic cognition became current because of Wolff's treatment of it in his *German Metaphysics*.

[44] The *Dissertation* does not explicitly maintain that the act of predicating purely intellectual concepts of purely intellectual things results in the cognition *of objects*. Although the term 'cognition' is used on several occasions (cf. 2:392), Kant at important junctures uses the broader term *concipere* and merely refers to *intellectualia* as "representations" of things such as they are (2:392). Some of the notes dated 1769–70 suggest that Kant's rejection of the possibility of cognition proper of things such as God predates the *Dissertation*. One of these notes maintains that "all synthetic judgments of pure reason are … subjective" (R3938, dated 1769, cf. R3948). Another one, on God, states that "we do not cognize the original being … through the concepts that we somehow possess of the inner predicates of a being, but … through its relation to our concepts of the possibility of all things; the concept of an original being is an a priori limit concept. We assume it without contradiction, we need it on behalf of the completion of our reason" (R4248, dated 1769–70, cf. R4242). Possibly, Kant in the *Dissertation* held back this view in order to comply with the expectations of his readers.

[45] Kant writes in R5116, discussed in Section 2, that determining to what extent non-analytical "a priori cognition" can be achieved in metaphysics requires considering "how a cognition a priori is possible" in the first place (18:95) and, hence, the elaboration of "a critique of pure reason" and "above all a canon thereof" (18:95–96). See Watkins (2001) for a brief but informative account of the commentary on the *Dissertation* Herz published and sent to Kant in July 1771. However, I do not agree with his inference that Kant in 1772 did not yet realize that "one must prove that we cannot know things in themselves" (77). Whereas Watkins considers Herz's skeptical worry to have had an impact on Kant's position around 1772, I hold that Kant could have reached it merely by thinking through the analyses he had carried out from at least 1769 onward.

any way affected by it can be possible."[46] Famously, Kant also articulates this question by inquiring into the ground of the relation between the "intellectual representations" stemming from the "inner activity" of the understanding and the object.[47] In accordance with the *Dissertation*, he appears to accept that the use of principles that stem from the "nature of our soul" is warranted with regard to things qua objects of the senses: he does not doubt that a concept such as causality can be used to conceive of two moving billiard balls as a unity.[48] What is at stake, rather, is the *ground* of this possibility. For what if this ground were lacking in the case of the purely intellectual cognitions of objects to which metaphysics aspires? Although Kant's letter does not provide an answer to the question he raises, his account in the *Dissertation* of how the mind generates sensible cognitions points in the direction of one.

In the case of sensible cognition, Kant argues in the *Dissertation*, the mind uses an intellectual concept such as composition as a task to be carried out, namely, the act of unifying representations that present themselves in time qua pure intuition. Reconsidering this account, as well as the results of various earlier investigations, Kant must have realized, I submit, that *pure sensibility is indispensable to obtain cognition proper* because it is precisely the act of synthesis carried out in pure time that

---

[46] Kant to Herz, June 7, 1772, 10:130–31. This passage is in line with Kant's remark in R5116, discussed above, that the question as to "how a cognition a priori is possible" took center stage at some point (18:95).

[47] Kant to Herz, February 21, 1772 (10:130), cf. R4473 and R4634 (dated 1772). More specifically, Kant asks how representations can be related to objects in cases where they are not caused by given objects nor themselves create objects (10:130–31). On my reading, it is crucial that Kant does not specify whether the question he raises concerns appearances or things in themselves, since the task at hand consists in determining to what extent the use of intellectual concepts on behalf of our a priori cognition of objects as such is warranted. A dispute about the passage in terms of the opposition between appearances and noumena is therefore unhelpful. The letter to Herz is neither future-directed because of Kant's alleged turn to the problem of empirical cognition in the 1781 Transcendental Deduction (Carl 1989b, Mensch 2007) nor past-directed because of his alleged worry about cognition of things in themselves such as the soul and God (De Vleeschauwer 1939/1962: 59; Beck 1989; Ertl 2002).

[48] Kant writes in this regard that "the principles that are derived from the nature of our soul have an understandable validity for all things insofar as those things are supposed to be objects of the senses" (10:130). Similarly, he notes in a draft very similar to the letter to Herz that "there must be cognitive acts (*Handlungen der Erkenntnis*) that precede experience and by means of which these cognitions are possible." In the same text, he writes that while "it can be learned from pure mathematics and metaphysics *that* there are such a priori cognitions," it is important to obtain "insight into *the ground of their possibility*" (R4473, dated 1772, emphasis mine). These passages support the view that the term 'principles' in the letter does not refer to space and time. In Chapter 5, I likewise maintain that the Transcendental Deduction seeks to demonstrate not so much that pure concepts can be used with regard to objects of experience as to identify the very ground of their use with regard to objects at all.

allows the mind to objectify its representations, that is, to attribute them to an *object*.[49] Seen in this way, intellectual concepts that are used in a way not tainted by sensibility do not for that reason constitute determinations of things as they are in themselves, but merely represent ways in which objects can be *thought*. If this is true, then they are no less subjective than concepts infused with sensibility. Contrary to the latter, however, purely intellectual concepts are not capable of generating cognitions of objects as such and, hence, of purported objects such as the soul and God. Kant clearly articulates this view in a note dated 1772–73:

> If certain concepts in us do not contain anything other than that by means of which all experiences are possible on our part, then they can be asserted a priori prior to experience and yet with complete validity for everything that may ever come before us.... However, things that cannot be given to us through any experience are nothing for us; hence, while we can very well employ (*brauchen*) such propositions as universal from a practical point of view, they *cannot be employed as principles of speculation about objects as such.*[50]

This passage arguably constitutes an early version of the answer to the question as to how purely intellectual concepts can have a bearing on objects, an answer that the *Critique of Pure Reason*, as we will see, elaborates and supports by means of a number of complementary argumentative strategies.

It follows from Kant's new perspective – which can be considered phase [5] in his development – that metaphysics can err in two principal ways. According to the 1770 strand of Kant's critique, metaphysics errs if it lets sensible determinations infuse its allegedly intellectual judgments about the soul, the world, and God. I will call this strand [1]. According to the strand developed – or asserted – some time after 1770, on the other hand, metaphysics also errs if it alleges that its purely intellectual judgments constitute cognitions of objects, in other words, cognition proper. This new insight, which I will call strand [2], entails that the purely intellectual

---

[49] In a note dated 1776–78, Kant writes that he initially regarded the "distinction between the sensible and the intellectual" established in the *Dissertation* as "merely negative" (18:60): it was drawn in order to exclude sensibility from metaphysics, not to account for the possibility of objective judgments about appearances.

[50] R4634, 17:618, emphasis mine, translation modified. Theis (1982: 214–18) and Beck (1989:7–8) discuss this note, as well as notes stemming from the same period, apparently without regarding the problem of objectivity and Kant's critique of former special metaphysics as two sides of the same coin. Already in his 1771 letter to Herz, Kant distinguishes between subjective principles belonging to sensibility and subjective principles belonging to the intellect (10:122). In a note dated 1772, Kant states that metaphysics falsely treated *intellectualia* as objects (R4445, 17:553).

version of Wolffian metaphysics Kant aimed to develop in the *Dissertation* must yet be purged of the assumption that the noumena it generates and determines amount to objects of cognition.[51] I contend, however, that Kant never abandoned the idea presented in the *Dissertation* that metaphysics must be turned into a purely intellectual discipline.

It is unclear when exactly Kant saw the need to develop this two-pronged critique of metaphysics. He wrote to Herz in 1772 that the *Dissertation* still lacked "the key to the whole secret of metaphysics" (10:130) and that he now, in the possession of this key, was ready "to bring out a critique of pure reason that will deal with the nature of theoretical as well as practical knowledge," the first part of which was to be concerned with "the sources of metaphysics, its method and limits."[52] Yet whether or not the solution Kant grasped at this point already included the second strand of his critique, it is clear that over the years the project Kant came to refer to as the *Critique of Pure Reason* became much more complex than he had initially envisioned.

Clearly, the question as to what it takes to conceive of something as an object independently of experience called for an in-depth examination of the assumptions of Wolffian ontology or general metaphysics rather than special metaphysics, which is to say that Kant went on to develop his critique of metaphysics primarily within the element, as it were, of former ontology.[53] While this question is at the origin of both the transcendental deduction and the account of the schematism of the pure understanding, neither of these accounts seems to be even on the horizon in 1772. This also holds for Kant's investigation into the conditions of possibility of experience that is usually identified with transcendental philosophy. However, rather than considering the notes and drafts Kant wrote after 1773, the following sections turn to the critique of metaphysics actually carried out in the *Critique of Pure Reason* as well as, to begin with, Kant's own presentation of this task.

---

[51] Thus, Kant writes in the *Critique of Pure Reason* that "through a pure category, in which abstraction is made from any condition of sensible intuition … no object a is determined, rather only the thought of an object in general is expressed in accordance with different modi" (A247/B304, cf. A44/B61–62, A92–93/B125). Clearly, this position goes beyond the one defended in the *Dissertation*.

[52] Kant to Herz, February 21, 1772 (10:132). Similarly, in a letter to Herz dated the end of 1773, Kant purports to be "in possession of a principle that will completely solve what has hitherto been a riddle and bring the procedure of the mode of reason that isolates itself under certain and easily applied rules" (10:144, translation modified).

[53] I elaborate on this issue in Chapter 3.

6   Kant's Conception of Critique in the *Critique of Pure Reason*

Adopting a more radical tone than earlier texts, the 1781 Preface presents the *Critique of Pure Reason* as a work aimed at deciding the "possibility or impossibility of a metaphysics as such," a decision that, Kant writes, calls for the determination of "its sources, as well as its extent and boundaries."[54] Carrying out a critique in this sense requires that one trace back the propositions put forward in metaphysics to the efforts of the human mind to obtain a priori cognitions, that is, to pure reason taken in the broad sense of the term.[55] As Kant puts it, this decision requires a "critique of the faculty of reason as such" in respect of the cognitions it seeks to obtain "independently of all experience."[56]

Kant's clarification of the task at hand contains a number of elements familiar from earlier texts. The *Critique of Pure Reason* takes aim at the controversies that jeopardize the reputation of metaphysics[57] and is presented as a "propaedeutic"[58] intended to put metaphysics on "the secure path of a science."[59] In agreement with texts such as *Dreams*, moreover, Kant considers the scientific metaphysics he envisions to serve the moral ends of humankind. For as long as metaphysics employs principles that "in fact reach only to objects of possible experience" to obtain cognitions of things in themselves, it precludes the possibility "of assuming God, freedom and immortality for the sake of the necessary practical use of . . . reason."[60]

As far as its theoretical part is concerned, metaphysics is called upon to interrupt its usual activity in order to reflect on the nature of its ultimate premises[61] and, hence, to obtain knowledge of its proper capacity to obtain knowledge (Bxxxvi). Accordingly, Kant refers to critique as the "scientific and fully illuminating self-knowledge" of reason.[62] Famously comparing

---

[54] Axii, cf. Axxi, A3/B7, A11/B25, B23. I will largely limit my account to the introductory sections of the *Critique of Pure Reason*. For a more extensive treatment, see McQuillan (2016).

[55] Kant calls "pure reason" the form of reason that contains "the principles for cognizing something absolutely a priori" (A11/B24). As is well known, he uses the term 'reason' sometimes in the broad sense of 'intellect,' such that it encompasses reason and the understanding (A835/B863), and sometimes in a sense that excludes the understanding (qua capacity to determine objects) (cf. Axvii, A302/B359, A702/B730). It is not always clear when Kant intends the broad or narrow meaning of the term.

[56] Axii, cf. Axvii, Bxxxvi–xxxvii, A12, B22–23.   [57] Aviii, cf. Bxv, A710–11/B738–39.

[58] A11–12/B25–26, cf. B27, Bxliii.   [59] Bvii, cf. Bxiv–xv, B22.

[60] Bxxx, cf. Bxxi, Bxxiv–xxv, Bxxxii–xxxiv, A319/B376, A463–64/B491–92, A799–801/B827–29, CPrR 54–57. Stressing its negative element, Kant does not address the ultimately moral end of his critique in the first Preface and Introduction (cf. A11).

[61] Bxxxv, cf. Bxxxii, A3/B7.   [62] A849/B877, cf. Axi, A485/B513.

this propaedeutic investigation to a tribunal, he asserts that pure reason must disentangle its "rightful claims" from its "groundless pretensions"[63] and, similarly, that critique is "to supply the touchstone of the worth or worthlessness of all cognitions a priori" (A12/B26).

However, the introductory sections of the *Critique of Pure Reason* do not seem to specify which touchstone pure reason, in its capacity as impartial judge, must use in order to pass judgment on the first-order claims about things as such, the soul, the world, and God put forward in former metaphysics. On Kant's understanding, metaphysics consists in "a wholly isolated speculative rational knowledge that elevates itself entirely above all instruction from experience."[64] But if metaphysical claims cannot be assessed by the "touchstone of experience" (Aviii), which other touchstone or touchstones ought to be appealed to for this purpose?

Unlike the *Dissertation* (cf. 2:411–12), the introductory parts of the *Critique* are rather elusive in this regard. Kant clearly and repeatedly considers the work to pave the way for a "purified" metaphysics (Bxxiv) or a system of pure reason.[65] Yet although the second Preface mentions the need to push back principles that belong to sensibility for the sake of morality (Bxxiv–xxv), intellectual purity is not explicitly presented as a touchstone for metaphysical propositions. As regards the post-1770 touchstone discussed above, Kant points out, albeit only in the second Preface, that a priori cognition of things in themselves is impossible.[66] Since this latter strand of his critique suggests that former special metaphysics must be abolished in all respects, Kant's remarks on this point are difficult to square with his confidence that a purely intellectual system of pure reason can be erected on the basis of the first *Critique*. In order to solve this problem, we need to turn to the content of Kant's twofold critique of metaphysics.

7 Kant's Two-Pronged Critique of Metaphysics in the *Critique of Pure Reason*

Drawing on the results obtained so far, this section argues that Kant's mature critique of metaphysics rests on the two strands discussed in

---

[63] Axi, cf. Axx, A501/B529, A751/B779, A787/B815.   [64] Bxiv, cf. Axii, A11/B24, A713/B741.

[65] Axx–xxi, Bxxiii, Bxxx, Bxxxvi, A11–12/B26, A83/B109. This issue will be discussed most extensively in Chapter 8.

[66] Bxxvi, cf. Bxiv, Bxix, Bxxix. The 1781 Preface and Introduction do not touch on this subject, except insofar as the latter suggests that the a priori cognition of objects aspired to in metaphysics requires a non-intellectual condition different from experience (A9/B13–14).

Section 5. This is to say that I take the *Critique of Pure Reason* to require of a scientific metaphysics that it [1] shed its dependence on pure sensibility as well as [2] acknowledge that cognitions generated by purely intellectual means do not amount to cognitions of objects.

As regards strand [2], which will be discussed in more detail in the coming chapters, Kant notes in the 1787 Preface that he considers the "analytical part" of the work to prove that "we can have cognition of no object as a thing in itself, but only insofar as it is an object of sensible intuition, i.e. as an appearance" (Bxxv–xxvi). Pure concepts such as substance and causality cannot be used to determine "objects in themselves" because, as Kant seeks to show in the Schematism Chapter, such concepts,

> in addition to the function of the understanding in the category, must also contain *a priori formal conditions of sensibility* (namely of inner sense), conditions that contain the general condition under which alone the category can be applied to any object. (A139–40/B178–79, emphasis mine)

Thus, according to strand [2] of Kant's critique of metaphysics, we cannot obtain a priori cognitions of objects by means of the intellect alone. Such cognitions rest on the employment of pure concepts as rules that allow the mind to unify a manifold of successive representations and, hence, to establish transcendental unity of apperception.[67]

As was argued in Section 4, Kant maintains already in the *Dissertation* that the use of pure concepts for the purpose of unifying a sensible manifold relies on pure time. While this treatise used this insight to purge metaphysics from the influence of pure sensibility, the Transcendental Analytic uses this very insight for a different purpose, namely, to argue that only 'thick' versions of pure concepts such as substance and causality can be used to obtain a priori cognitions of objects. This insight entails that the cognitions of the soul, the world as such, and God to which former special metaphysics aspired do not amount to cognitions of objects.

However, the upshot of strand [2] does not substantially differ from the position Kant defended in the *Dissertation*, because, as is well known, the *Critique* does not exclude the use of purely intellectual or 'thin' versions of pure concepts to conceive of things such as the soul, the world as such, and God. Even though these things cannot be known, Kant writes, we "must be able to think them as things in themselves" as long as their concepts are not self-contradictory (Bxxvi, cf. Bxxviii). As long as metaphysics does not

---

[67] The transcendental unity of apperception, Kant writes, "is that unity through which all of the manifold given in an intuition is united in a concept of the object" (B139, cf. A103–5). I consider this issue in Chapter 5.

mistake such thoughts for objective cognitions, there is no reason to reject its capacity to conceive of things by means of the intellect alone.

But how can metaphysics actually conceive of something by means of the intellect alone? The answer to this question leads us to strand [1], that is, to Kant's view that metaphysics must be purged from concepts the meaning of which presupposes pure sensibility. While, as was seen above, this strand is pivotal to the *Dissertation*, it resurfaces in various parts of the *Critique of Pure Reason*. Thus, Kant notes in the Architectonic that reason has not yet elaborated a metaphysics "in a manner sufficiently purified of everything foreign to it" (A842/B870). Similarly, a passage from the 1787 Preface has it that

> the principles with which speculative reason ventures beyond its boundaries ... threaten to extend the boundaries of sensibility, *to which these principles really belong*, beyond everything, and so to shut out (*verdrängen*) the use of pure (practical) reason. (Bxxiv–xxv, emphasis mine)

While Kant does not specify which principles should be used within the boundaries of sensibility alone, one of the subtexts of this passage is certainly his rejection in the *Dissertation* of Crusius's claim that space and time must be attributed to any substance, including the soul and God.[68]

Like the *Dissertation*, however, the *Critique of Pure Reason* does not aim at Crusius's principle alone, but considers the latter to exemplify a feature that one way or another informs the metaphysical tradition as such. As will be argued in Chapter 6, Kant also considered Wolff and his followers to unwarrantedly attribute 'thick' versions of concepts such as substance – that is, versions that inconspicuously rely on time – to things as such and, hence, to supersensible things such as monads, the soul, and God.

A dense passage from the final chapter of the Transcendental Analytic brings together strands [1] and [2].[69] Starting from strand [1], Kant here claims that the pure understanding must posit things that can only be

---

[68] That Crusius's metaphysics was one of Kant's targets is also suggested by a passage in the Transcendental Aesthetic that deals explicitly with the improper use of the concept of space. Kant notes to this effect that "pure concepts of the understanding" are inclined to use the concept of space "beyond the conditions of sensible intuition" (A88/B120–21), that is, with regard to things in themselves. Considered in this way, the Transcendental Aesthetic, like its counterpart in the *Dissertation*, discusses space and time not primarily to identify the conditions of possibility of empirical cognition but to limit the use of a priori principles affected by pure sensibility to the realm of appearances. The assumption that principles relevant to representations given in intuition can be used with regard to things as such is the assumption that Kant calls transcendental realism (A369, cf. A491/B519) and rejects throughout the *Critique of Pure Reason*.

[69] This chapter, entitled "On the Ground of the Distinction of All Objects in General into Phenomena and Noumena," will be discussed in Chapters 4 and 7.

thought, or noumena, in order to defend the terrain of special metaphysics against inroads from sensible cognition. If considered mere "limit concepts" (A255/B310), these noumena are

> necessary in order not to extend sensible intuition to things in themselves, and thus to limit the objective validity of sensible cognition. (A254/B309)

Thus, if the concept of the soul functions as a boundary stone that keeps sensibility at bay, it precludes judgments that determine the soul as substance, as spatial, or even as material. By positing noumena in this negative sense, Kant continues, the understanding "is not restricted by sensibility, but rather restricts the latter" (A256/B312). Clearly, passages such as these defy the assumption that Kant's mature critique of metaphysics consists in restricting the scope of the intellect alone.

In the same breath, Kant turns to the constraint on metaphysics imposed by strand [2] of his critique. The understanding, he notes, not only restricts the scope of sensible principles by positing noumena, but

> also immediately sets boundaries for itself, not cognizing these things through categories, hence merely thinking them under the name of an unknown something. (A256/B312)

Thus, according to strand [1], the pure understanding can establish metaphysics as a science by isolating its cognitions from the surreptitious impact of pure sensibility (cf. Bxiv). According to strand [2], conversely, this very isolation deprives the pure understanding of the capacity to obtain cognitions of the noumena it posits, for any cognition of objects requires categories the meaning of which relies on pure time. In other words, by expelling sensibility from its domain, as it has to, metaphysics *at once* expels itself from the domain within which theoretical cognitions of objects can be obtained. While the result of this critical act may appear to be "very disadvantageous" to former special metaphysics (Bxix), Kant considers it to have the advantage of staking out a realm within which the ideas of reason – the soul, the world as such, and God – can be determined in purely moral terms (Bxxi).

8   Conclusion

This chapter has traced Kant's critical engagement with post-Leibnizian metaphysics from his attempts to replace some of its doctrines by better ones to his decision to interrupt first-order metaphysics for the sake of a propaedeutic investigation into the capacity of the human mind to obtain a priori cognitions of objects at all.

Focusing on the *Dissertation*, I have identified two mutually exclusive criteria by means of which the *Critique* assesses the systems of his predecessors, namely, intellectual purity and objectivity. As seen, Kant derives these criteria from his 1770 analysis of the two ways in which pure concepts can be employed. According to the first criterion, metaphysics can become a science insofar as it is purely intellectual. In this regard, Kant throughout the *Critique of Pure Reason* seeks to disentangle the capacity of pure reason to think the unconditioned in purely intellectual terms from the mode of the pure understanding that, relying on pure time, is suited to turn manifolds of sensible representations into objects of cognition. According to the second criterion, conversely, the human mind is capable of a priori cognitions of objects insofar as the concepts it employs presuppose pure time. This second criterion, which takes center stage in the Transcendental Deduction and the Schematism Chapter, entails that metaphysics, qua theoretical discipline, is incapable of a priori cognitions of objects. Nevertheless, this criterion does not preclude the elaboration of a metaphysical system concerned with the a priori concepts and principles constitutive of any cognition of objects. For this reason, the *Critique of Pure Reason* answers its main question by arguing that metaphysics is possible as a science on the condition that it abandon its efforts to obtain knowledge of the quasi-objects of special metaphysics.

In my opinion, these are the contours of the project that Kant envisioned from at least 1769 onward, actually embarked on in the early 1770s, and held on to even when its elaboration demanded that he explore paths and overcome obstacles he had not anticipated. Seen in this light, the idea of a reform of metaphysics can be said to function as the "inner end" (A833/B861) of the *Critique of Pure Reason*, that is, as the idea that determines a priori "the domain of the manifold as well as the position of the parts with respect to each other" (A832/B860).

Taking this idea as a guiding thread makes it easier to grasp the unity of the analyses carried out in the *Critique of Pure Reason*. The Transcendental Analytic requires the account of space and time elaborated in the Transcendental Aesthetic in order to demonstrate that any a priori cognition of objects rests on pure time and, accordingly, is limited to objects of possible experience. General metaphysics, I take Kant to demonstrate in the Transcendental Analytic, can be turned into a science by restricting itself to a systematic treatment of the a priori elements of any cognition of objects. The Transcendental Dialectic, in turn, demonstrates that special metaphysics cannot become a science as long as it seeks to determine the unconditioned by means of pure concepts the meaning of which presupposes pure time. Finally, the Doctrine of Method, as will be shown in Chapter 8, indicates how metaphysics, once it has overcome its objectifying tendency, can actually establish a comprehensive system of the a priori elements presupposed in any cognition of objects.

Whereas the current chapter has framed the *Critique of Pure Reason* in terms of Kant's long-term inquiry into the conditions under which metaphysics can become a science, the five chapters that follow treat various aspects of the Transcendental Analytic in view of Kant's intended reform of Wolffian general metaphysics. The next chapter seeks to clarify the main thrust of this part by examining Kant's notion of transcendental philosophy and related terms in light of the Wolffian tradition.

CHAPTER 3

Ontology, Metaphysics, and Transcendental Philosophy

1 Introduction

So far I have examined Kant's efforts to reform post-Leibnizian metaphysics without considering the term by which his critical philosophy is commonly identified, namely, transcendental philosophy. Regardless of its ubiquity in the literature, however, it is far from clear what the term actually stands for in the *Critique of Pure Reason*, and the same can be said of other terms modified by the adjective 'transcendental.' Neither is it clear, finally, whether the various ways in which Kant uses these terms are compatible.[1]

Whatever their views on these issues, most commentators seem to assume that the term 'transcendental philosophy' basically refers to the inquiry into the conditions of possibility of empirical knowledge carried out in the *Critique of Pure Reason* and other works from the critical period. This assumption is shared by scholars who relate Kant's transcendental philosophy to the scholastic treatment of so-called transcendentals such as unity, truth, and perfection. Seen from their perspective, there is

---

[1] Hinske (1970a: 24), among others, considers Kant's use of the term 'transcendental philosophy' to be highly ambivalent. Deploring the lack of a unifying meaning of the term 'transcendental' in *the Critique of Pure Reason*, Hinske (1998: 1382) does not mention that Kant refers to his investigation into the possibility of a priori cognition as transcendental critique rather than transcendental philosophy. What seems to be missing from Hinske's account, moreover, is the instance of transcendental philosophy of which Kant conceived as the first part of his metaphysical system, that is, the instance that in my view shares common ground with Wolffian ontology. Following Tonelli (1994), Ferrarin (2015: 235–52) lists the widely diverging meanings in which Kant uses terms such as critique, metaphysics, and transcendental philosophy without a clear attempt to sort them out. If Kant's intellectual trajectory is taken into account, Ferrarin writes, the changes in his use of these terms are "little short of incredible" (236). In this chapter, I will largely disregard Kant's evolving understanding of terms such as metaphysics, ontology, and transcendental philosophy in his unpublished notes, published writings, and lectures from the 1760s and 1770s. Studies that do so include Ficara (2006) and Rivero (2014). Commentaries that treat Kant's lectures on Baumgarten's *Metaphysics* in this regard include Ameriks (1992), Fugate (2015), Lorini (2015), De Boer (2019b), and Lu-Adler (2019).

a puzzling gap between, on the one hand, the scholastic conception of the most general determinations of all beings and, on the other hand, Kant's investigation into the subjective conditions of possibility of experience.[2]

In this chapter, I aim to untangle at least part of this knot by examining Kant's innovative conception of ontology, metaphysics, and transcendental philosophy in light of the ways in which the terms were coined and transformed in the seventeenth and eighteenth centuries. On this basis, I argue that Kant, first, reconceived of the core task of the first part of Wolffian metaphysics – ontology or general metaphysics – as transcendental cognition and, second, considered the latter to branch out into transcendental philosophy and transcendental critique. On my reading, Kant considered transcendental philosophy in the strict sense to be a first-order investigation into the a priori concepts and principles constitutive of any cognition of objects. This task is carried out – albeit in a defective manner – in the first main part of Wolff and Baumgarten's metaphysics and is elaborated to some degree in the *Critique of Pure Reason*. The mode of transcendental cognition that Kant calls 'transcendental critique,' conversely, consists in a propaedeutic, second-order investigation into the conditions under which the use of a priori concepts and principles is warranted. Unlike first-order transcendental cognition, this discipline is carried out in the *Critique of Pure Reason* alone.

Considered in this way, there is more continuity than is commonly assumed between the disciplines that used to be called *scientia transcendens*, ontology, or general metaphysics and Kant's first-order investigation into the concepts and principles constitutive of any cognition of objects.[3] More

---

[2] For example, the editors of the *Historisches Wörterbuch der Philosophie*, drawing on the contribution by Hinske, claim that "[f]rom the time of its origination until immediately prior to Kant, the concept of *transcendentia* . . . referred ontologically to the most general determinations of beings.. . . In Kantian and post-Kantian philosophy, by contrast, the term is used as a predicate of the cognition that is concerned with the a priori conditions of possibility of experience" (Ritter and Gründer 1998: 1358–59). I concur with Demange (2009) that Kant's own remarks in the *Critique of Pure Reason* on the "transcendental philosophy of the ancients" (B113–16) are not very relevant to the conception of transcendental philosophy at stake in this work. Commentators who interpret Kant's account of transcendental philosophy in light of the scholastic tradition without referring to Wolff include Knittermeyer (1953/54) and Doyle (1997). Bärthlein (1976) discusses Wolff's ontology primarily with regard to its account of the scholastic doctrine of the transcendentals. Angelelli (1972) does the same with Baumgarten's *Metaphysics*.

[3] My approach concurs with Fulda (1988) and Schnepf (2007a) to the extent that they consider Kant's transcendental philosophy, qua theory of objects as such, to ensue from a transformation of Wolffian ontology. However, they take into account neither Kant's notion of transcendental critique nor his reason for restricting the scope of former ontology to possible objects of experience. Similarly, Ficara (2006), among others, collapses the two modes of transcendental cognition into

generally, I hope to show that the various ways in which the *Critique of Pure Reason* uses the adjective 'transcendental' are less incoherent than might appear at first sight.

Although the term 'transcendental' is relevant to the *Critique* as a whole, Kant's notion of transcendental philosophy first and foremost concerns the reform of former ontology at stake in the Transcendental Analytic, in particular what I have called strand [2] of Kant's critique in the preceding chapter. Concentrating on this part of the work, the present chapter seeks to clarify Kant's use of the term 'transcendental' as well as his account of the complementary tasks to be carried out by transcendental philosophy and transcendental critique.

Covering themes that readers are likely to be familiar with, Section 2 relates Kant's conception of the relationship between general and special metaphysics to the task he attributes to transcendental logic. Section 3 provides some of the historical background to Kant's use of the term 'transcendental.' Returning to Kant, Sections 4 and 5 examine the various accounts of transcendental philosophy and transcendental critique in the first *Critique*. Section 6, finally, considers Kant's comments on Wolff's and Tetens's understanding of transcendental philosophy in some of his lectures on metaphysics from the 1780s.

2 The Task of Transcendental Logic

One of the problems with the prevailing understanding of the term 'transcendental philosophy' is that neither version of the Preface and Introduction of the *Critique of Pure Reason* explains the aim of the work by referring to conditions of possibility of experience. As was mentioned in the Introduction to the present book, I hold that Kant rather intended the *Critique of Pure Reason* as a propaedeutic investigation into the condition of possibility of metaphysics itself, that is, into the mode of cognition that the *Dissertation* assigns to the real use of the intellect (2:394). Seen from Kant's perspective, Wolffian metaphysics calls for a propaedeutic investigation because it ignored the conditions under which the a priori cognitions of things as such as well as things such as the soul and God is warranted.

a broad notion of transcendental philosophy. On this basis, she more or less identifies this "new" notion of transcendental philosophy (191) with Kant's conception of ontology qua investigation into a priori principles (12, 29) and stresses the similarities with Wolff's conception of ontology (122–24). On my reading, by contrast, this continuity concerns transcendental philosophy only qua first-order mode of transcendental cognition.

In the Introduction, Kant frames this second-order investigation into the condition of possibility of metaphysics in terms of the problem of synthetic a priori judgments. What needs to be done, Kant writes, is

> to uncover the ground of the possibility of synthetic a priori judgments with appropriate generality, to gain insight into the conditions that make every kind of them possible, and to determine, in a system, ... this entire cognition completely and, with regard to its usage, sufficiently.[4]

As is well known, Kant considers synthetic judgments to connect a predicate to a subject the content of which is not contained in the subject itself (A7/B10–11). If such a judgment is a priori, that is, cannot take recourse to experience, it is unclear, Kant writes, what the "X" is "on which the understanding depends when it believes itself to discover beyond the concept of A a predicate that is foreign to it and *that is yet connected to it*" (A9, cf. B13).

Notwithstanding Kant's references to mathematics and physics, the synthetic a priori judgments he is primarily concerned with are the ones that – warranted or unwarranted – make up metaphysics (B18, cf. B23), that is, judgments that predicate, for instance, causality of all things or immortality of the soul. According to Kant, these synthetic a priori judgments differ from the ones of which mathematics consists in that the latter spring from pure intuitions rather than pure concepts (A159/B198–99). A synthetic a priori judgment such as 'any event has a cause' differs from synthetic a priori judgments that belong to physics alone, on the other hand, in that they are not grounded in higher ones (A148/B188).

By considering the judgments enacted in metaphysics as synthetic a priori judgments, Kant establishes a vantage point from which it can inquire into the ground – or X – that allows the mind to make synthetic a priori judgments at all. More precisely, Kant's second-order investigation into the activities carried out by the human mind is supposed to demonstrate why principles derived from pure concepts such as substance or causality are absolutely necessary to turn appearances into objects of cognition, but cannot be used to achieve cognition of supersensible objects (cf. Bxxvii).

Kant uses the term 'transcendental critique' to refer to this investigation. As he puts it, "transcendental critique ... does not aim at the amplification of the cognitions themselves, but only at their correction, and is to supply

---

[4] A10, translation modified, cf. B73, A761/B789, Prol, 4:274. Chapter 6, Section 2, discusses this part of the Introduction in somewhat more detail.

the touchstone of the worth or worthlessness of all cognitions a priori" (A12/B26). In line with the analyses carried out by Locke and Hume, this critique examines the various activities carried out by the human mind in order to determine the limits within which cognition of objects is possible at all and, thus, rule out vacuous speculations. Unlike his empiricist precursors, however, Kant does so in order to analyze the way in which the mental faculties contribute to our *a priori* cognition of objects.[5]

Insofar as transcendental critique treats the rules that govern a particular kind of cognition, it can be said to share certain features with general logic. However, since general logic is not concerned with objects, it is not suitable, according to Kant, to investigate the human mind with the aim of determining under which conditions metaphysics is possible. In the following passage, he attributes this critical task to transcendental logic:

> The explanation of the possibility of synthetic judgments is a problem with which general logic has nothing to do.... But in a transcendental logic it is the most important business of all, and indeed the only business if the issue is the possibility of synthetic a priori judgments and likewise the conditions and the domain of their validity. For by completing this task, transcendental logic can fully satisfy its goal of determining the domain and boundaries of the pure understanding.[6]

Thus, transcendental logic is the branch of transcendental cognition that is carried out in the *Critique of Pure Reason* and examines the role of pure thought in the a priori cognition of objects. This logic, Kant writes elsewhere, seeks to determine "the origin, the domain, and the objective validity of the cognitions "by means of which we think objects completely a priori" (A57/B81). It does so by determining the boundaries within which pure reason – considered as the source of any a priori cognition – can lawfully exert its synthetic activity. As he puts it in the second Preface,

> [T]he real problem of pure reason is contained in the question: how are synthetic a priori judgments possible?... Metaphysics stands or falls with the solution to this problem.[7]

The two parts of transcendental logic that Kant distinguishes – an analytic and a dialectic – correspond to general and special metaphysics, respectively. Thus, a synthetic a priori judgment such as 'any event has a cause' specifies what counts as an object in the first place. Accordingly, it

---

[5] While Kant is sympathetic to Locke's "physiology of the human understanding" (Aix), he rejects its empiricist elaboration (A86–87/B118–19).
[6] A154/B193, cf. A14/B28, Prol, 4:324.   [7] B19, cf. Axii, Prol, 4:274–76.

constitutes a principle of cognition that used to be treated in general metaphysics or ontology. In the Transcendental Analytic, Kant considers these principles to rest on the pure concepts listed in the Metaphysical Deduction and treats them under the heading of principles of the pure understanding.[8]

Drawing on these principles, a second kind of synthetic a priori judgment seeks to determine supersensible things such as the soul or God by means of the intellect alone. These judgments, and the concepts on which they are based, used to be treated in the various parts of special metaphysics and are scrutinized in the Transcendental Dialectic.

In a passage from the Preface to the second edition partly quoted in the preceding chapter, Kant obliquely explains the task of critique in relation to this distinction between general and special metaphysics.[9] If we were to adopt the view that objects conform to our cognition, rather than the other way round, he notes, the first part of metaphysics – that is, the discipline formerly called general metaphysics – might well be raised into a science:

> This experiment . . . promises the secure course of a science to *metaphysics in its first part*, where it concerns itself with concepts *a priori* to which the corresponding objects appropriate to them can be given in experience. For after this alteration in our way of thinking we can very well explain the possibility of a cognition *a priori* and, what is still more, we can provide satisfactory proofs of the *a priori* laws constitutive of nature qua sum total of objects of experience. (Bxviii-xix, emphasis mine)

No less than the Wolffian tradition, Kant considers the first part of metaphysics to treat concepts constitutive of any cognition of objects such as substance, causality, and necessity. Yet Kant here refers only implicitly to former general metaphysics or ontology, because he seeks to demonstrate, according to strand [2] of his critique, that the use of these concepts is warranted with regard to possible objects of experience alone. The difference between 'things' or 'beings' and 'objects of experience' is a crucial one, for in this context the term 'object' refers exclusively to the content of judgments brought about by the human mind.

If the scope of the first part of metaphysics were restricted in this regard, Kant maintains, then its second part – former *special* metaphysics – would be deprived of the means to make synthetic a priori judgments about the soul, the world as such, and God. As he puts it,

---

[8] A148–235/B187–287. I consider Kant's discussion of this topic in Chapter 6.
[9] Texts in which Kant draws this connection explicitly include R4855 (dated 1776), R4851 (dated 1776–78), and LM Mrongovius (1782–83), 29:768. On this, see Höffe (2003: 19).

this deduction of our faculty of cognizing *a priori* in the first part of metaphysics yields a … result … that appears very disadvantageous to the whole purpose with which *the second part of metaphysics* is concerned, namely, that with this faculty we can never get beyond the boundaries of possible experience, which is nevertheless precisely the most essential occupation of this science. (Bxix, emphasis mine)

However, it does not follow from this that Kant is prepared to give up the main assets of former special metaphysics completely. As was argued in Chapter 2, he considers critique to disentangle the rational core of a discipline from its untenable elements. What ought to be preserved in the case of special metaphysics are the ideas of reason, in their capacity as regulative principles, as well as a number of their purely intellectual determinations. A priori judgments about human freedom, the soul, and God, conversely, ought to be transferred to a discipline supposedly immune to skeptical attacks on the theoretical part of metaphysics, namely, its practical part:

> [A]fter speculative reason has been denied all advance in this field of the supersensible, what remains to be tried is whether there are not data in reason's practical cognition (*praktische Erkenntnis*) for determining the transcendent rational concept of the unconditioned mentioned above and, thus, in accordance with the wish of metaphysics, to move beyond the boundaries of all possible experience with our cognitions a priori, which are, however, possible only insofar as they have a practical aim.[10]

For now, I will disregard the way Kant actually carries out the first part of the investigation he calls transcendental logic, and focus on his reason for conceiving of the various aspects of his critical project as modes of transcendental cognition. Since Kant's use of the term 'transcendental' seems to create more problems than it resolves, a brief discussion of the term's history is warranted.

3   'Transcendental Philosophy' Prior to Kant

By the time Wolff published his metaphysical treatises, the term *transcendens* was no longer used primarily to refer to the determinations of being – including unity, truth, and perfection – that thirteenth-century scholars such as Aquinas and Duns Scotus considered to transcend the generality of

---

[10]   Bxxi, translation modified (the translation has 'practical data' for *praktische Erkenntnis* and the final clause, unlike the German, is ungrammatical). Cf. Bxxxii–xxxiv.

the categories listed by Aristotle.[11] Duns Scotus had already enlarged the domain of *transcendentalia* with further predicates, coining the term *scientia transcendens* to refer to the discipline concerned with any determinations of being qua being.

During the seventeenth century, the discipline called ontology or general metaphysics also became known as *scientia transcendentalis*, a term that goes back to Duns Scotus's conception of metaphysics as *scientia transcendens*. Thus, the terms 'transcendental science' and 'ontology' both came to refer to the part of metaphysics concerned with concepts that can be predicated of all beings and, as such, provide the other disciplines with their basic principles.

As seen, the first part of Wolff's German *Metaphysics* is simply called "On the First Grounds of Our Knowledge and All Things as Such." Even though Wolff must have been familiar with the term *scientia transcendentalis*, he chose to call the Latin version of his first philosophy *Philosophia prima sive ontologia* rather than transcendental science or something to that effect. That is why commentators who deal with this issue tend to ignore Wolff's works and, instead, compare Kant's conception of transcendental philosophy with the Scholastic treatment of transcendentals and Kant's discussion of them in the second edition of the first *Critique* (cf. B113–17). If, by contrast, one takes into account Wolff's reason for referring to the first part of his metaphysics as ontology, as I will do in what follows, then Kant's conception of transcendental philosophy – qua first-order investigation into basic concepts and principles – may well turn out to be more akin to that of his German predecessors.

In his Latin works, Wolff uses the term 'transcendental' to denote a doctrine that treats those concepts and principles that are presupposed in the applied part of the discipline and possibly in other disciplines. Thus, he refers to the Latin version of his general cosmology as *cosmologia transcendentalis* because it is concerned with the most general, or essential,

---

[11] Aquinas distinguished six transcendentals (*ens, res, aliquid, unum, verum, bonum*), that is, determinations that transcend the difference between infinite and finite beings and accordingly must be predicated of all beings. Duns Scotus enlarged the number of *transcendentia* by including conceptual determinations that come into pairs, such as necessity and possibility, and finite and infinite, because one of them can always be predicated of a being. He was the first to refer to the science that is concerned with the transcendentals as *scientia transcendens*, identifying this science with metaphysics. Thanks to Suarez, among others, this conception of metaphysics became influential during the seventeenth and early eighteenth centuries. The same discipline also became known as *theoria, scientia*, or *philosophia transcendentalis* (rather than *transcendens*), terms that were known to Wolff. The accounts of these developments from which I have drawn include Vollrath (1962), Courtine (1990), Honnefelder (1990), Honnefelder (1995), and the works by Hinske, Bärthlein, and Demange mentioned in the introduction to this chapter.

determinations of the world as such. This transcendental cosmology differs from ontology in that it deals with the world as such rather than all beings. In this capacity, it provides the hinge between ontology, on the one hand, and physics, on the other.[12] As Wolff explains in the *Latin Cosmology*, he called the discipline

> transcendental, because in it only such things are demonstrated of the world that accrue to it as to a composite and modifiable being, so that indeed it stands to physics in the same manner as ontology or first philosophy to universal philosophy.[13]

Accordingly, it seems to me that Wolff might have used the term 'transcendental science' rather than 'ontology' to refer to the Latin version of his first philosophy.

Wolff notes in his *Anmerckungen* that he decided to use the term *Grundwissenschaft* as the German equivalent of *ontologia* to dissociate the discipline from its bad reputation among the Cartesians:

> In German I call the *ontologia* fundamental science (*Grundwissenschaft*).... I need the term 'fundamental science' because in this part of philosophy one clarifies the first grounds of cognition.... [A]part from this reason, I also took into account the circumstance that one has currently thrown out the baby with the bathwater, at the expense of the sciences, and I have therefore chosen a name that indicates the utility of this science.[14]

What should be retained from these passages is that Wolff conceived of ontology as a foundational discipline *that treats the most general concepts and principles relevant to a particular domain* and for that reason might as well be called transcendental science. Seen in this way, the meaning the term 'transcendental' received within the Wolffian tradition is akin to that of the scholastic notion of *scientia transcendens* – at least if we abstract from the fact that the latter dealt with determinations that transcend *any* particular domain. Clearly, in neither case does the term 'transcendental' denote an investigation into the conditions of possibility of empirical cognition. So what happened to the meaning of the term between Wolff and Kant?

---

[12] Cf. Wolff, DP 94, 97.

[13] Wolff, LC, 1n, cf. DP 78. On this, see Vollrath (1962: 261–62), Hinske (1968: 98–103), and Bärthlein (1976: 357–58). Kant refers implicitly to Wolff's transcendental cosmology at A334/B391–92. Seen in this light, it makes sense that Kant uses the term 'transcendental' not only to denote the mode of philosophy that was to constitute the first part of his projected metaphysics, but, analogously, also to denote disciplines such as transcendental theology (A580/B608).

[14] Wolff, AN 17, 32–33, cf. LO 1. Thus, Wolff held that the best way to save ontology (the child) from its scholastic elaboration (the bathwater) was to provide it with an untainted name.

4 Kant's Conception of Transcendental Philosophy

In 1773, Kant told Herz about his attempt "to design an entirely new science" and the difficulties involved in "considering the method, the divisions, the search for exactly appropriate terms."[15] Rather than coining new words, he later wrote in the *Critique of Pure Reason*, one should "look around in a dead and learned language" for expressions that can be used for one's own purposes (A312/B368–69).

This is clearly something Kant did with the term 'transcendental' and concepts modified by it. Kant was dissatisfied with Wolff's distinction between a general and an applied part of a particular discipline because it does not entail a clear-cut demarcation of the principles treated in these parts in terms of their origin.[16] Rather than equating 'most general' and 'transcendental,' as Wolff had done, Kant calls a philosophical discipline transcendental if it deals with cognitive activity or its products from a perspective that is purely intellectual rather than empirical, but differs from general logic because it is concerned with the way in which the mind turns representations into objects of cognition.[17] Because a transcendental discipline abstracts from any empirical content, it treats concepts and principles that are presupposed in the applied part of a particular science. For this reason, Wolffian transcendental cosmology can count as a transcendental discipline in Kant's sense on the condition that its content does not stem from the senses.[18]

One of Kant's remarkable innovations in the *Critique of Pure Reason* consists in transferring the term 'transcendental' from the disciplines at stake to their subject matter, that is, to the elements involved in the a priori cognition of objects. Thus, those concepts and principles are called transcendental that, first, cannot be treated in general logic because they contribute to the a priori cognition of objects and, second, cannot be

---

[15] Kant to Herz, toward the end of 1773 (10:144).

[16] See Diss, 2:394 and A843–44/B871–72. I elaborate on this issue in De Boer (2019b).

[17] This description also excludes mathematics, which according to Kant rests on pure intuition (A713/B741). Kant's definition of transcendental philosophy at A11–12 will be discussed below. For Kant's distinction between a logical and transcendental approach to cognition, see A44/B61, A55–56/B79–80, A262/B318–19, A574/B602. For the distinction between an empirical and transcendental approach, see A14/B28, A801/B829.

[18] According to Hinske (1968: 102), Wolff uses the term 'transcendental' in a way that is close to the original meaning of *transscendere*, since his cosmology can be said to treat of concepts and principles that "move beyond" empirical knowledge. However, I consider this approach unhelpful. As will be argued below, Kant associates only the transcendental *use* of pure concepts with the act of transcending the realm of experience, and does so in the context of his critique of Wolffian ontology.

treated in sciences such as physics or psychology because they are not empirical. Moreover, Kant applies the term 'transcendental' in this sense not only to products of cognitive activity such as concepts, schemata, or ideas but also to the activities and faculties from which they stem.

Understood in a minimal sense, accordingly, the adjective 'transcendental' denotes any cognitive element, whether an activity or a product of the latter, that is considered neither from a logical nor from an empirical perspective. If the term modifies a mode of philosophical cognition, on the other hand, it denotes this non-logical and non-empirical consideration of a priori cognitive elements itself.

This description holds true of all elements treated in the Transcendental Doctrine of Elements. The Transcendental Aesthetic and the Transcendental Logic – its two main parts – differ insofar as the former treats elements that stem from intuition, whereas the latter treats elements that stem from the understanding taken in the broad sense of intellect (cf. A22/B36). Within the scope of the Transcendental Logic, accordingly, cognitive elements can be called transcendental if they are considered to be purely intellectual, yet not purely logical.

These elements used to be treated in the first part of Wolffian metaphysics. One of the advantages of the term 'transcendental' over 'metaphysics' is surely that it is dissociated from Wolff's assumption that things can be known by means of the intellect alone. Thus, radicalizing Wolff's own gesture, Kant may well have taken recourse to the term 'transcendental' to distinguish the rational core of metaphysics from the bathwater of this dogmatist assumption. However, much more needs to be said about Kant's efforts to fill terms such as 'transcendental philosophy' with new meaning.

These efforts can be traced back to the end of the 1760s. Already in his Latin *Physical Monadology* (1756), Kant identified metaphysics and transcendental philosophy, apparently assuming that his readers were familiar with the latter title:

> Metaphysics, therefore, which many say may be properly absent from physics, is, in fact, its only support.... For bodies consist of parts; it is certainly of no little importance that it be clearly established of which parts, and in what way they are combined together.... But how, in this business, can metaphysics be married to geometry, when it seems easier to mate griffins with horses than to unite transcendental philosophy with geometry? (1:475)

In this passage, Kant does not explicitly distinguish between general and special metaphysics. After 1769, by contrast, the terms 'transcendental philosophy' and 'transcendental logic' tend to refer to Kant's conception of general metaphysics, or ontology, considered as a first-order discipline concerned with the concepts and principles constitutive of any cognition of objects. As Kant notes around 1769–70, "ontology is nothing other than a transcendental logic."[19] Similarly, he wrote to Herz in 1772 that he "sought to reduce transcendental philosophy (that is to say, all concepts belonging to completely pure reason) to a certain number of categories."[20]

Evidently, these early passages do not allow us to draw conclusions as to the meaning or meanings of the term 'transcendental philosophy' in the *Critique of Pure Reason*. Kant's use of the term – and related ones – in this work is far from straightforward because he had to account for the difference between, on the one hand, the first-order investigation into pure concepts that he shares with earlier instances of general metaphysics and, on the other, his "completely new" second-order investigation into the conditions under which these concepts can actually be employed.[21]

In the following passage from the *Prolegomena*, concerned with the question as to the possibility of synthetic a priori cognition, Kant shifts the received meaning of the term 'transcendental philosophy' to the latter sense:

> It can be said that the whole of transcendental philosophy, which necessarily precedes all of metaphysics, is itself nothing other than simply the complete solution of the question presented here . . . , and that until now there has therefore been no transcendental philosophy; for *what goes under this name* is really a part of metaphysics, but this science is to settle the possibility of metaphysics in the first place, and therefore must precede all metaphysics.[22]

Kant here explicitly contrasts the received meaning of transcendental philosophy, that is, general metaphysics or ontology, with transcendental philosophy considered as second-order investigation into the very possibility of metaphysics. However, I hold that the *Critique of Pure Reason* itself rather uses the term 'transcendental philosophy' to denote the first-order investigation into the a priori elements of any cognition of objects that used to be called general metaphysics or ontology. In the *Critique*, I will argue in what follows, Kant attempts to account for both disciplines

---

[19] R4152 (dated 1769–70).   [20] Kant to Herz, February 21, 1772 (10:132).
[21] Prol, 4:279, cf. Kant to Herz, 1773 (10:144–45), Kant to Garve, August 7, 1783 (10:40). Similarly, a note dated 1772 has it that transcendental philosophy "is the critique of pure reason. *Studium* of the subject, mistaking the subjective for the objective, prevention" (R4455).
[22] Prol, 4:279, emphasis mine. Clearly, Kant here uses the term 'transcendental philosophy' to denote the second-order discipline that the Introduction to the *Critique of Pure Reason* calls transcendental critique and distinguishes from transcendental philosophy proper (cf. A12/B26).

by conceiving of transcendental philosophy and transcendental critique as two particular instances of transcendental cognition.

According to the first edition of the *Critique*, transcendental cognition, to begin with, is a form of cognition that treats a priori – or purely intellectual – concepts of objects as such, which is an activity carried out in philosophy alone. Transcendental philosophy is subsequently defined as the system treating the sum total of these concepts, that is, I add, as the discipline that must constitute the first part of any metaphysical system:

> I call all cognition (*Erkenntnis*) transcendental that is occupied not so much with objects *but rather with our a priori concepts of objects as such*. A system of such concepts would be called transcendental philosophy.[23]

Kant notes that the *Critique of Pure Reason* itself does not yet contain a full-fledged transcendental philosophy (A12/B25–26). Even so, one might hold on to the view that he here and elsewhere opposes transcendental philosophy to the discipline that used to be called ontology.[24] I have argued, however, that Wolffian ontology no less deals with the conceptual determinations of any object – from which the other sciences draw their principles – rather than actual objects. Considered in this way, Kant's conception of transcendental philosophy and Wolff's conception of ontology have much more in common than may appear at first sight.

Arguably, Kant's initial definition is a partial one because it is merely intended to distinguish transcendental cognition from sciences that seek

---

[23] A11–12. Clearly, Kant uses the term *Erkenntnis* in a broad sense in this context. On this definition, the two branches of transcendental logic carried out in the *Critique of Pure Reason*, the analytic and the dialectic, constitute modes of transcendental cognition. In the second edition, the clause "our a priori concepts of objects as such" is replaced by "our mode of cognition (*Erkenntnisart*) of objects insofar as this is to be possible a priori" (B25). Clearly, the term 'a priori mode of cognition' covers more than 'a priori concepts' alone: it does not exclude the investigation into the pure forms of intuition carried out in the Transcendental Aesthetic. The *Critique* uses the term 'mode of cognition' with regard to intuition and thought qua activities exerted by the human mind (A262/B318) as well as with regard to products of these activities such as pure concepts (B306), judgments (A6/B10), and experience (A157/B196). Thus, while the phrase in the first edition is closer to the traditional conception of transcendental philosophy, the phrase in the second edition encompasses more adequately both transcendental philosophy qua first part of a metaphysical system and the mode of transcendental cognition Kant calls transcendental critique, that is, the investigation of pure concepts in light of the various faculties involved in their production and application (cf. A12/B26). See Pinder (1986) for a detailed discussion of these passages, especially of the peculiar expression "nicht so wohl … sondern." I doubt, however, that Kant intended the subtle nuances Pinder attributes to the text. An unpublished note dated 1776–79 states unambiguously that transcendental philosophy examines not objects, but the human mind (R4873). Passages from his lectures confirm that Kant considered neither mode of transcendental cognition to be concerned with objects (see Section 6 of this chapter). In this regard, I disagree with Schnepf (2007a: 75–83, 103–6).

[24] This is the view of Hinske (1970a: 28, 33n).

the cognition of *objects* (empirical sciences and special metaphysics). Moreover, I take him to deliberately leave open whether transcendental cognition deals with the a priori concepts of objects as such in a dogmatic or critical fashion and, which is not the same, whether it takes the form of a first-order account of these concepts (transcendental philosophy qua first part of metaphysics) or a second-order investigation into their warranted use (transcendental critique).

An oft-cited passage from the Architectonic of Pure Reason almost identifies transcendental philosophy and former ontology qua first part of metaphysics. In this chapter, Kant sketches the structure of the metaphysical system he intended to elaborate on the basis of the propaedeutic task carried out in the *Critique of Pure Reason*, a topic that will be discussed in detail in Chapter 8. In this context, Kant defines metaphysics as a discipline that provides a systematic account of the pure concepts and a priori principles that allow us to achieve cognition of something at all (A845/B873). In line with the classical distinction between ontology or general metaphysics and special metaphysics, he refers to the first part of metaphysics as transcendental philosophy and to its second part as rational physiology:

> Metaphysics is the kind of philosophy that is to present [a priori] cognition in this systematic unity.... Metaphysics in a narrower sense consists of *transcendental philosophy* and the physiology of pure reason. The former considers only the understanding and reason itself in a system of all concepts and principles that are related to objects as such, *without assuming objects that would be given* (*Ontologia*); the latter considers nature, i.e., the sum total of *given* objects ... and is therefore physiology (though only *rationalis*).[25]

In accordance with his initial definition of transcendental philosophy as a system of "our a priori concepts of objects as such" (A11–12), Kant here conceives of transcendental philosophy as a first-order metaphysical discipline that does not presuppose given objects, but treats the concepts and principles constitutive of any cognition of objects in a systematic manner. Contrary to his initial definition, however, this passage explicitly states that transcendental philosophy, qua first part of metaphysics, used to be called

---

[25] A845/B837, emphasis mine, cf. A290/B346. In a similar, but more schematic note dated 1776–78, R4851, the terms *metaphysica generalis* and *metaphysica specialis* are added to the diagram as equivalents to (1) transcendental philosophy qua investigation into reason and the concepts it produces and (2) rational physiology qua investigation into objects that differ from reason itself. I discuss this passage in more detail in Chapter 8, Section 2.

ontology. Thus, Kant here affirms the continuity between his first-order transcendental philosophy and Wolff's ontology without a qualm.

Yet elsewhere in the *Critique of Pure Reason* – one might object – Kant famously maintains that his analysis of the pure understanding *replaces* former ontology. The principles treated in the Transcendental Analytic, he writes,

> are merely principles of the exposition of *appearances*, and the proud name of an *ontology*, which presumes to offer synthetic a priori cognitions of *things as such* in a systematic doctrine (e.g. the principle of causality), must give way to the modest one of a mere analytic of the pure understanding.[26]

This passage suggests that Kant considered transcendental philosophy and ontology to be highly different projects.[27] However, one discipline can only be said to replace another if they share common ground. Seen from Kant's vantage point, the discipline he calls 'analytic of the pure understanding' is similar to former ontology to the extent that both investigate the a priori concepts and principles that allow the human mind to turn something into an object of cognition at all. Whereas Kant does not share Wolff's assumption that these concepts can be attributed to all things, whether material or immaterial, he endorses the epistemological thrust of Wolffian ontology.

In sum, I take Kant to use the term 'transcendental philosophy' primarily to denote any first-order systematic treatment of the pure concepts and a priori principles constitutive of objects of cognition as such.[28] This formal definition fits both Wolffian ontology and the reformed transcendental philosophy Kant intended to elaborate on the basis of the *Critique of Pure Reason*.

If this is granted, then Kant's reference to the "transcendental philosophy of the ancients" makes perfect sense as well.[29] I contend that, for Kant, this expression simply denotes the scholastic elaboration of the discipline concerned with the first principles of human cognition. This early mode of

---

[26] A247/B303, emphasis mine, cf. Prol, 4:332.

[27] See Grier (2001: 85–86). As regards this point, my reading is in agreement with Lu-Adler (2019: 58).

[28] See Pinder (1986: esp. 14–20).

[29] There is, Kant writes, "yet another chapter in the transcendental philosophy of the ancients that contains pure concepts of the understanding, which, although they are not reckoned among the categories, ... should also count as a priori concepts of objects.... These are expounded in the proposition, so famous among the scholastics: *quodlibet ens est unum, verum, bonum.*" According to Kant, the only real problem with these concepts is that they "were used in a merely formal sense, as belonging to the logical requirements for every cognition" and at the same time "were carelessly made into properties of things in themselves" (B113, translation modified).

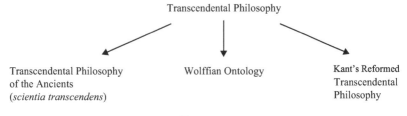

Figure 1

transcendental philosophy is distinguished from later versions by its emphasis on *transcendentalia* such as unity, truth, and perfection. Considered in this way, Kant's formal concept of transcendental philosophy contains at least three determinations (see Figure 1).

By operating with this formal conception of transcendental philosophy, Kant is able to subsequently determine the specific features – or failures – of the instances of transcendental philosophy preceding his own.

First, former instances of transcendental philosophy ignored that space and time are a priori intuitions rather than concepts (cf. A15–16/B29–30). Second, as Kant points out repeatedly, they treated pure concepts without relying on a rigorous principle and therefore attained mere aggregates rather than proper systems.[30] Third, transcendental philosophy always assumed that concepts such as substance and causality could be applied indiscriminately to sensible things such as billiard balls and supersensible things such as the soul, the world as such, and God.

As is well known, Kant seeks to remedy the second and third defect in the chapters of the Transcendental Analytic devoted to the metaphysical deduction, the transcendental deduction, and the schematism of the pure understanding. The analyses carried out in this context yield the result that transcendental philosophy – considered as the first part of metaphysics – must limit itself to a systematic treatment of the pure concepts and a priori principles involved in the cognition of objects of experience rather than that of things as such.[31]

Kant's use of terms such as 'transcendental cognition' and transcendental philosophy' must be strictly distinguished from what he calls the

---

[30] A64/B89, A831–32/B859–60.

[31] See Fulda (1988), Benoist (1996), and Cramer (2001) for interpretations that emphasize the shift from 'things' to 'objects' accomplished in the *Critique of Pure Reason*. Contrary to Fulda, Benoist downplays Kant's determination of objects as such in terms of objects *of experience* (cf. 153). Similarly, Sala (1988) claims that for Kant transcendental analytic and ontology basically refer to the same discipline.

'transcendental use' of pure concepts, a subject to which I now turn.[32] Put generally, this expression refers to a use of pure concepts that does not rely on sensible intuition and, hence, is not limited to the realm of appearances (cf. A139). Thus, Kant in this context uses the term 'transcendental' to refer to a mode of thought that is purely intellectual yet differs from general logic in that it does not abstract from all content. By using a category in a purely intellectual way, Kant writes, the understanding merely establishes "the thought of an object as such" without determining the latter.[33]

Kant's formal description of the term 'transcendental use' disregards the question as to whether this type of use is warranted or not. However, the *Critique* often uses the term in a pejorative sense, namely, to characterize the strand of Wolffian ontology according to which the act of predicating pure concepts of things as such amounts to cognition proper. An example of this is the use, in former ontology, of the concept of causality to assert that all things have a cause. Seen from Kant's perspective, the principle of causality merely articulates a way in which we can produce thoughts of an object as such. Ontology is justified in *treating* this principle, but not to actually *use* the concept of causality in a judgment that purports to extend our cognition of things. Used transcendentally, such concepts lack the content required to actually determine something. Seen from Kant's perspective, they therefore should not be used in this way:

> Pure categories, without formal conditions of sensibility, have merely transcendental significance, but are not of any transcendental use.[34]

According to Kant, categories are elements of cognition proper only to the extent that they are related to appearances. Rejecting the assumption he attributes to former ontology, he writes:

> The transcendental use of a concept in any sort of principle consists in its being related to things as such and in themselves; its empirical use, however, consists in its being related merely to appearances, i.e., objects of a possible experience.[35]

---

[32] Kant introduces the term 'transcendental use' at A56/B80–81. The term here denotes the unwarranted assumption that space and time are determinations of things in themselves. Principles treated in former ontology are sometimes called 'transcendental' in this pejorative sense as well (cf. A259/B315).

[33] A247/B304. Similarly, the Doctrine of Method identifies the transcendental use of reason with a use that proceeds by means of "mere concepts" (A711/B739, cf. A712–13/B740–41).

[34] A248/B305. According to this passage, categories that are not used with regard to appearances are not completely meaningless, but not sufficiently meaningful to provide cognition proper of all things. I treat this issue in more detail in Chapter 5.

[35] A238–39/B297–98, cf. Bxxvii, A246/B303, A258/B314, A296/B352–53, A720–21/B748–49.

This passage suggests that the term 'transcendental use' replaces, at least in part, what Kant in the *Dissertation* called the real use of the intellect (2:394) and at that point did not yet take issue with. More precisely, what Kant rejects in 1781 is a use of pure concepts that aims to obtain a priori cognitions not only of appearances but also of things as such. Thus, inviting confusion, Kant uses terms such as 'transcendental cognition' in a way that is in agreement with Wolff's epistemological understanding of the term 'transcendental,' whereas the term 'transcendental use' is often employed to denote a questionable assumption of former Wolffian ontology.

Insofar as pure concepts are used with regard to appearances alone, Kant calls their use 'empirical' (A238/B297–98) or 'immanent' (A296/B353). In my view, however, he attributes this empirical use not to transcendental philosophy but to the human mind insofar as it turns appearances into objects of empirical cognition, something that it does preeminently in the sciences. This is to say that transcendental philosophy qua first part of metaphysics, for its part, should not itself try to determine things independently of experience, but should merely provide a systematic account of the concepts and principles required to carry out that task.

In accordance with the distinction between general and special metaphysics, albeit without spelling this out, Kant refers to the unwarranted use of pure concepts in former *special* metaphysics as their 'transcendent use.' The latter differs from the transcendental use of pure concepts in that it reaches beyond appearances not in order to determine things as such, as was done in former ontology, but in order to determine things such as the soul, the world as such, and God. Drawing on ontological principles alleged to be valid of things as such, special metaphysics, Kant writes, produces principles that are transcendent in the sense that they "incite us to tear down all … boundary posts and to lay claim to a wholly new territory that recognizes no demarcations whatsoever."[36] Enticed by the

---

[36] A296/B352. In this passage and elsewhere, the term 'transcendent' qualifies the principles themselves rather than their use (cf. A308/B365). In other cases, the term denotes "the objective use of the concepts of pure reason," that is, of the ideas of the soul, the world as such, and God (A327/B383, cf. Prol, 4:374n), or these ideas themselves insofar as they are taken to refer to objects (A309/B366, A565/B593). Kant also calls the transcendent use of pure concepts "hyperphysical" (A63/B88). Seen in light of the distinction between general and special metaphysics, Kant's distinction between the transcendental and transcendent use of pure concepts is rather straightforward: in the former case the human mind assumes that these concepts are applicable to things rather than appearances; in the latter it deliberately moves beyond experience toward particular things such as the soul or God. If we consider, moreover, that the term 'transcendental use' sometimes denotes *any* use of pure concepts aimed at the cognition of things independently of

principle of sufficient reason, metaphysics in this case uses pure concepts to achieve cognition of things that by definition cannot be intuited.

In sum, I take Kant to hold that pure concepts can be employed in three different ways. Whenever the human mind unifies a manifold of sensible intuitions by relying on a concept such as substance, the latter is used empirically. If the concept of substance is used transcendentally, by contrast, it allows the human mind to posit, for instance, that all things consist of simple elements. This is actually done in ontology. Special metaphysics, finally, can apply this fallacious ontological principle to things that by definition cannot be sensibly intuited, and posit, for instance, that the soul is indivisible or that the world as such consists of indivisible elements.

Seen in this way, all Kant had to do in order to prevent the transcendent use of categories in special metaphysics was to reveal where former general metaphysics went wrong, a task that is carried out throughout the Transcendental Analytic. I have argued, however, that Kant did not wish to abandon the first-order tasks carried out in general and special metaphysics in all regards, but rather sought to achieve their self-limitation. But how does Kant account for the mode of cognition that carries out this twofold self-limitation itself? Answering this question requires that we zoom out to Kant's notion of transcendental critique and its relation to the first-order mode of transcendental cognition discussed so far.

5   Transcendental Critique

As was seen in the preceding section, Kant initially defines transcendental cognition as a mode of cognition that is "occupied ... with our a priori concepts of objects as such" (A11–12). Clearly, this formal definition applies to the various instances of transcendental philosophy considered as the first part of metaphysics. As I will argue in this section, this definition also applies to the second-order investigation into the very possibility of metaphysics that is called transcendental critique and constitutes the main task of the *Critique*. Thus, returning to the notion of critique discussed in the preceding chapter, this section examines the way Kant seeks to account for the critical strand of the *Critique* by means

experience, then it makes sense that Kant sometimes uses this term in the context of his discussion of former special metaphysics as well (cf. A329/B386, A348/B406). My reading is in line with Allison (2004: 326–28). Disregarding Kant's critique of Wolffian metaphysics, Knoepffler (2001: 58–59) assumes that Kant in this context confuses the terms 'transcendental' and transcendent.' See Ficara (2006: 45–46) for a similar criticism.

of terms derived from the metaphysical tradition. Before doing so, however, a few remarks on the Transcendental Analytic as a whole are in place.

In my view, we cannot make sense of the *Critique of Pure Reason* unless we see how each of its parts carries out both a first-order and a second-order investigation into a particular kind of a priori cognition. Whereas the former inquires into what these elements are, the latter assesses their actual employment.[37] Accordingly, I take the concept of transcendental logic to refer to two complementary modes of transcendental cognition, such that one of them enacts a critical assessment of the other. Thus, insofar as the Transcendental Analytic, to which I will limit my account, treats pure concepts and their corresponding a priori principles in a systematic fashion, it engages in the first-order mode of transcendental cognition that was carried out in a defective way in Wolffian ontology and is called transcendental philosophy in the *Critique of Pure Reason*. Insofar as the Transcendental Analytic seeks to determine to what extent the use of these concepts is warranted, by contrast, it engages in the second-order mode of transcendental cognition that Kant calls transcendental critique.

Various passages indicate that Kant planned to carry out the task he assigns to first-order transcendental cognition in an appropriate and comprehensive manner in the theoretical part of his projected metaphysical system.[38] He notes in the Introduction that, in *this* regard, the account put forward in the *Critique of Pure Reason* is preliminary and incomplete. This account identifies the "root concepts" of the a priori cognition the human mind can obtain (A13/B27), but does not provide a complete system of these cognitions themselves. Accordingly, Kant writes,

> the *Critique of Pure Reason* ... is the complete idea of transcendental philosophy, but it is not yet this science itself, since it goes only so far in the analysis as is required for the complete estimation of synthetic a priori cognition.[39]

---

[37] This distinction is clearly reflected in Kant's distinction between a metaphysical and transcendental exposition of space and time in the Transcendental Aesthetic (see B38, B40). In LM Volckmann (1784–85), the term 'transcendental philosophy' is used to refer to both the first-order investigation into basic concepts and principles and the "rational science that determines *how far* I can reach with my pure reason" (28:391–92, emphasis mine).

[38] The *Critique of Pure Reason*, Kant notes in the Introduction, outlines "the entire plan" of transcendental philosophy "architectonically, i.e., from principles, fully guaranteeing the completeness and certainty of all the components that comprise this edifice" (A13/B27). Contrary to the translators, I take Kant here to refer to the book titled *Critique of Pure Reason* rather than to the activity denoted as critique, for the latter is precisely *not* involved in presenting the outline of Kant's projected first-order transcendental philosophy.

[39] A14/B28, cf. Axxi, A12/B25, A81/B107.

Clearly, the metaphysical deduction of the categories and the chapter devoted to the principles of the pure understanding belong to the first-order mode of transcendental cognition partly carried out in the Transcendental Analytic. If brought to completion, it would deserve the name of transcendental philosophy.

Its second-order strand, conversely, prevails in the Transcendental Deduction, the Schematism Chapter, and the concluding chapter on the distinction between phenomena and noumena.[40] This strand seeks to demonstrate that and why the pure concepts and a priori principles that inform both the sciences and special metaphysics can be used with regard to objects of possible experience alone. As was mentioned above, this is the task that Kant attributes to transcendental critique. This discipline, he writes,

> does not aim at the amplification of the cognitions themselves, but only at their correction, and is to supply the touchstone of the worth or worthlessness of all cognitions a priori.... Such a critique is accordingly a preparation, if possible, for an organon and, if this cannot be accomplished, then at least for a canon, in accordance with which the complete system of the philosophy of pure reason ... can ... be exhibited.[41]

Given this description, Kant appears to conceive of transcendental critique and transcendental philosophy as two complementary modes of the inquiry into a priori concepts of objects that he calls transcendental cognition (cf. A11–12/B25).

However, it is not clear that his other remarks on transcendental cognition are in keeping with this account. So let us consider a passage in which Kant defines transcendental cognition in more detail:

> And here I make a remark the import of which extends to all of the following considerations, ... namely, that not every a priori cognition must be called transcendental, but only that cognition by means of which we comprehend *that and how* certain representations (intuitions or concepts) are applied entirely a priori. (A56/B80, emphasis mine)

---

[40] Kant's investigation into the various faculties involved in the production of a priori cognition in the Transcendental Deduction may seem to belong to the first-order mode of transcendental cognition. I will argue in Chapter 5, however, that this investigation is not an end in itself, but constitutes a specific step in Kant's second-order investigation into the possibility of metaphysics. Seen in this way, this investigation belongs to transcendental critique rather than transcendental philosophy proper.

[41] A12/B26. The Architectonic distinguishes between critique and system of pure reason along similar lines (A841/B869). The term 'transcendental critique' is not very prominent in the *Critique of Pure Reason*, but occurs throughout the work (cf. A297/B353, A498/B526, A609/B637, A712/B740, A783/B811) and is equivalent to terms that are used more frequently such as 'critique' or 'critique of pure reason.'

Since Kant makes this point in order to introduce transcendental logic qua science of "the origin, the domain, and the objective validity" of our a priori cognition of objects (A57/B81), it is clear that he conceives of transcendental logic as an instance of transcendental cognition. Kant's remark is intended to distinguish transcendental logic from the a priori cognitions that can be obtained by non-philosophers, for example, in mathematics or physics. Thus, an a priori intuition such as space can become the subject matter of a transcendental cognition insofar as the philosopher, first, conceives of it as an a priori representation and, second, investigates how it can be related to objects of experience.[42] The same, Kant adds, holds for the "acts of pure thought" that constitute the subject matter of transcendental logic (A57/B81). Transcendental logic merely differs from transcendental aesthetic in the sense that it is concerned with the a priori cognitions "through which we think objects completely a priori" (A57/B81).

A related passage considers transcendental philosophy to trace pure concepts to their unique origin in the understanding as well as to analyze their pure use (A65–66/B90–91). On my reading, the former task is carried out by first-order transcendental cognition, that is, transcendental philosophy in the strict sense, while the latter task is carried out by transcendental critique. However, Kant's use of the term 'transcendental philosophy' in a generic sense, here and elsewhere, obscures this distinction.[43] Since this generic meaning came to denote the *Critique of Pure Reason* as a whole, it became hard to distinguish between the propaedeutic function of the work and the reformed first-order transcendental philosophy that is only provisionally elaborated in the Transcendental Analytic.

Kant's unpublished notes and letters indicate that he used terms such as 'transcendental philosophy' in a variety of ways. There is no doubt that the ensuing ambivalence has left traces on the *Critique of Pure Reason*. I have argued, however, that Kant in this work seeks to solve the problem – though not very conspicuously – by conceiving of transcendental philosophy and transcendental critique as first-order and second-order species of transcendental cognition and, hence, by considering transcendental aesthetic and transcendental logic to contain both elements. This solution

---

[42] A56/B81. Obviously, this kind of transcendental cognition is achieved in the Transcendental Aesthetic. The example, somewhat simplified, is Kant's. I paraphrase the relevant passage because the German is convoluted and possibly corrupt.

[43] Cf. A135/B174, A424/B452 and, among many other passages, CJ, 5:289, 341. Similarly, the diagram in R4851 (dated 1776–78) considers ontology and critique as two branches of transcendental philosophy (see also R4455, dated around 1772, and R5127, dated 1776–78).

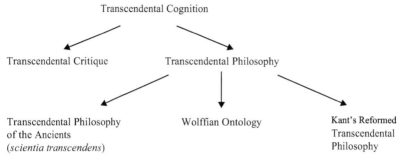

Figure 2

makes it possible, further, to conceive of transcendental philosophy qua first-order metaphysical discipline as the genus of its various historical instantiations. Seen in this way, the diagram presented above can be completed as in Figure 2.

As I see it, Kant had in mind his second-order reflection on the possibility of metaphysics – that is, transcendental critique – when he in various letters referred to the philosophy carried out in the first *Critique* as a completely new discipline or a metaphysics of metaphysics.[44] These references cannot be used, therefore, to maintain that the transcendental philosophy commonly attributed to Kant is new in all respects. Rather, I hold that Kant accepted many of the premises – if not the actual elaboration – of the transcendental philosophy exemplified by Wolff's ontology. The only crucial feature he considered to be lacking from the latter was transcendental critique, as is clearly stated in the following passage, already quoted in Chapter 1, from the Preface to the second edition:

> In someday carrying out the plan that criticism prescribes, i.e., in the future system of metaphysics, we will have to follow the strict method of the famous Wolff, the greatest under all dogmatic philosophers, who gave us the first example ... of the way in which the secure course of a science is to be taken ... ; he had the skills for moving a science such as metaphysics into this condition, if only *it had occurred to him to prepare the field for it by a critique of the organ, namely, of pure reason itself.* (Bxxxvi–xxxvii, emphasis mine)

---

[44] See Kant's letter to Herz dated May 11, 1781 (10:269). Baum (1993: 13) also takes this passage to refer to Kant's idea of a transcendental critique. Similarly, in R5644 (28:286, dated 1780–89), Kant notes that "metaphysics is itself the object" and refers to critique as "that which investigates its possibility." When Kant in his letter to Garve of August 7, 1783, refers to the *Critique of Pure Reason* as "not metaphysics at all, ... but a completely new and thus far a never attempted science," he seems to identify the term 'metaphysics' with first-order metaphysics alone.

Seen from this perspective, Kant's investigation into the a priori activities carried out by the human mind is intended to reform the defective version of transcendental philosophy he attributed to Wolff and his followers rather than to provide either empirical knowledge or metaphysics with a secure foundation.

6   Kant's Criticism of Wolff's and Tetens's Conceptions of Ontology

This section turns to Kant's lectures on metaphysics from the 1780s because they clarify a feature of his assessment of Wolff that remains largely implicit in the *Critique of Pure Reason*. According to some of the lecture transcripts, Kant took issue with Wolff's own understanding of the discipline he called ontology or fundamental science rather than with its content, even though he considered the latter to be flawed as well.[45] On my reading, Kant thought Wolff should have avoided the term 'ontology' because the discipline thus denoted is in fact nothing but an analytic of the concepts and principles produced by the human mind. The term 'ontology' is misleading, Kant states, because the reference to all things equals a reference to nothing at all:

> Thus, the science of all basic concepts and basic propositions upon which all of our pure cognitions of reason rests is ontology. But this science will not be properly called ontology. For to have a thing as such as an object is as much as to have no object and to treat only of cognition, as in logic. The name, however, sounds as if it had a determinate object. But this science . . . rather . . . considers understanding and reason itself, namely their basic concepts and basic propositions in their pure use . . . ; the most fitting name would be transcendental philosophy.[46]

This conception of transcendental philosophy – as a first-order metaphysical discipline – is completely in line with the passages from the *Critique of Pure Reason* discussed above. Unlike the latter, however, Kant's lectures allow us to see that his critique of Wolff's conception of ontology consists of two different elements. First, Kant held that Wolff should have realized that the "proud name of an ontology" (A247/B303) actually means

---

[45]   For the sake of simplicity I will refer to Wolff alone even though Kant lectured on Baumgarten's *Metaphysics*. In this regard their views are similar.

[46]   LM Mrongovius (1782–83), 29:786, cf. 755–56, 784–86; see also LM Volckmann (1784–85), 28:390–91 and LM L₂/Pölitz, 28:541–42 (around 1790). Similarly, Kant states in a note dated 1776–78 that "metaphysics deals not with objects, but with cognitions" (R4853). See also R3948 (dated 1769) and R4369 (dated 1771–75).

nothing else than transcendental philosophy, conceived as analytic of thought, and should therefore be replaced by the latter. Seen in this way, it is no coincidence that Kant in the *Critique of Pure Reason* urges that the "proud name" of the discipline be replaced rather than the discipline itself. Second, Kant considered Wolff's former ontology itself to be misguided, and this first and foremost because of its assumption that categories such as substance and causality can be employed in empirical sciences as well as in general cosmology, rational psychology, and natural theology. Contrary to the term 'ontology,' the term 'transcendental philosophy' leaves completely open to which kind of things pure concepts can be applied.

However, matters are somewhat more complicated, because in the lectures from 1782 to 1783 Kant also takes issue with the way his contemporaries understood the term 'transcendental philosophy.' Thus, he is reported to maintain that

> no one has had a *true* transcendental philosophy. The word has been used and understood as ontology, but (as it is easy to make out) this is not how we take it. In ontology one speaks of things in general, and thus actually of no thing – one is concerned with the nature of the understanding for thinking of things – here we have the concepts through which we think things, namely, the pure concepts of reason – hence it is the science of the principles of pure understanding and of reason.[47]

In this passage Kant does not target Wolff, but takes issue with contemporaries who had replaced the term 'ontology' by that of 'transcendental philosophy' without reforming the discipline along Kantian lines.

Indeed, as Krouglov and others have pointed out, prior to Kant both Lambert and Tetens had used German versions of the term to denote the first, general part of metaphysics. Thus, in the *Architectonic*, published in 1771, Lambert uses the term 'transcendent' with regard to theories that abstract from the various domains to which a concept can be applied.[48] As he acknowledges, the term 'transcendent' in this sense is akin to its scholastic meaning.[49] In 1775, Tetens used the term 'general transcendent philosophy' to denote the part of metaphysics devoted to the highest and most general principles of human cognition. These principles, he writes in his *On General Speculative Philosophy*,

---

[47] LM Mrongovius, 29:752, emphasis mine. Kant uses the term 'transcendental philosophy' here with regard to what I have called its first-order mode, that is, general metaphysics. See Prol, 4:279, for a similar passage.

[48] Lambert, Arch 29. See Krouglov (2005: 46–47), who points out that Lambert does not yet distinguish between 'transcendent' and 'transcendental.'

[49] Lambert, Arch 301.

consist in certain general judgments about the relations between things and their properties. The first, most general concepts are our representations of things or objects themselves as such.[50]

Tetens's conception of transcendental philosophy is close to Kant's insofar as he considers the discipline to be concerned with concepts rather than things.[51] According to Kant, however, Lambert and Tetens no less than Wolff assumed that the pure concepts treated in transcendental philosophy could be applied to material as well as to immaterial things.[52] What is lacking in both Wolffian ontology and the modern conceptions of transcendental philosophy known to Kant, in short, is a preliminary reflection on the limits within which pure concepts can be applied, a form of reflection to which his lectures too refer as critique:

> The critique of pure reason belongs necessarily to transcendental philosophy. But since one used to treat ontology without a critique – what was ontology then? An ontology that was not a transcendental philosophy.[53]

In this passage, I take it, Kant once more uses the term 'transcendental philosophy' in the formal sense of any investigation into the concepts and principles produced by pure understanding and pure reason. If this investigation is carried out without a preliminary critique, as was the case in the Wolffian tradition, it will conceive of itself as an ontology concerned with the basic determinations of sensible as well as supersensible things (and preeminently with the latter). In that case, it does not amount to transcendental philosophy proper qua first-order discipline.

Clearly, Kant considered it the task of transcendental philosophy in this sense to examine cognitions rather than things and, hence, to reflect on its

---

[50] Tetens, ASP 36. While Allison (2015: 144n) points to the lack of evidence that Kant had read this work, I take it to be very likely he had done so.

[51] "Transcendent philosophy," Tetens writes, "is nothing but a general theory that in itself is no more concerned with actual things than the analysis of the mathematicians. It has the same nature as the latter, and it might well be called a higher analysis of things, if it did not possess a sufficient number of names and titles already" (ASP 24, cf. 18).

[52] Tetens indeed maintains that "the fundamental science should contain the universal principles according to which we judge and infer about all things as such, about all genera of actual beings, about spirits and bodies, about the immaterial and the material, about the infinite and the finite" (ASP 51). In a note dated 1776–78, Kant contrasts his own transcendental philosophy with Tetens's investigation by arguing that the latter did not question the objective validity of pure concepts (R4900, cf. R4901). See Allison (2015: 143–63) and Blomme (2018) for recent discussions of Kant's relationship to Tetens. Krouglov (2005) suggests that Tetens may have influenced Kant's use of the term 'transcendental philosophy' in German. However, since Kant used the term already in his 1772 letter to Herz, it seems to me that Lambert's *Architectonic* is a more likely source of both Tetens's and Kant's adoption of the term.

[53] LM Mrongovius, 29:784–85.

proper nature and limits in a way precluded to its Wolffian instantiations. In other words, transcendental cognition must enact itself as a second-order critique in order to accomplish its first-order investigation into the a priori elements of all cognition in an adequate way. Moreover, insofar as first-order transcendental philosophy aims to identify and clarify the a priori elements of any cognition of objects, it already contains the seeds of the second-order mode that Kant calls transcendental critique. The latter, conversely, allows first-order transcendental philosophy to be turned into a proper science. Seen in this way, there is no gap between, on the one hand, the various instances of general metaphysics, ontology, or first-order transcendental philosophy elaborated in the history of philosophy and, on the other hand, the reflection of metaphysics on its proper sources and limits to which Kant refers as transcendental critique.

7   Conclusion

Kant's occasional use of the term 'transcendental philosophy' in a generic sense makes it hard to grasp the logic, if it can be called that, that governs the multiple meanings of the term 'transcendental' in the *Critique*. This chapter has tried to clarify at least part of this logic by distinguishing three main clusters.

First, insofar as the term 'transcendental' modifies a type of *philosophical cognition*, I have argued, it denotes a discipline that treats the constitution of a priori cognition from a perspective that is purely intellectual yet not logical. This formal notion of transcendental cognition allows Kant to conceive of transcendental philosophy – and its historical instantiations – as a first-order investigation into the concepts and principles constitutive of any cognition of objects and of transcendental critique as a second-order variety of the same. Given this distinction, the critique of metaphysics carried out in the *Critique* and the system of pure reason Kant intended to establish on its basis can be regarded as complementary modes of transcendental cognition.

Second, Kant transfers the term 'transcendental' from the philosophical discipline to the *contents* it treats, that is, to the various cognitive elements involved in the a priori cognition of objects. In this sense, a term such as 'transcendental imagination' refers to the imagination insofar as it is treated from a perspective on a priori cognition that is purely intellectual, but differs from general logic in that it does not abstract from all content.

Third, Kant uses the term 'transcendental' to denote the *use* of pure intuitions or concepts in judgments about things as such. As far as Kant's critical account of the pure understanding and pure reason is concerned, the term refers to a use of pure concepts that is purely intellectual yet not logical. Clearly, this meaning of 'transcendental' is in line with the core meaning of the term. However, Kant often employs the term 'transcendental use' pejoratively, namely, to denote the efforts on the part of former metaphysics to obtain knowledge of things by means of the intellect alone.

Seen in this way, the various ways in which Kant uses the adjective 'transcendental' can be traced back to, on the one hand, his effort to disentangle the gnoseological strand of Wolffian metaphysics from its dogmatist view on the power of the intellect and, on the other hand, his attempt to account for the status of this critique itself. My reading entails, obviously, that Kant did not refer to the project carried out in the *Critique of Pure Reason* as transcendental philosophy because it examines conditions of possibility of experience, as most commentators have it. Nevertheless, the meaning of the terms 'transcendental' and 'condition of possibility' can be said to converge to the extent that Wolff's pre-critical elaboration of transcendental philosophy, qua first philosophy, no less than Kant's reformed version of the latter investigates the concepts and principles that ground any cognition of objects. Unlike the Wolffians, however, Kant's *Critique* examines these a priori elements of any mode of cognition in view of the a priori activities carried out by the human mind. He does so, moreover, with an intention completely unknown to them, namely, to demonstrate that pure reason cannot obtain knowledge of things in themselves. Evidently, this contested issue requires a separate chapter.

CHAPTER 4

Things in Themselves, Transcendental Objects, and Monads

1 Introduction

The *Critique of Pure Reason* has probably been denounced most often because, put simply, Kant in this work seems to maintain both that things in themselves cannot be known and that they are the cause of representations. Following in the wake of Maimon and Fichte, many commentators have tried to overcome the alleged inconsistency of Kant's account by abolishing those passages that deal with the thing in itself qua cause of impressions.[1] Many others, including Allison, have proposed ways of reconciling Kant's apparently contradictory claims on the subject. Whatever their particular stance, however, scholars tend to divorce these claims from Kant's effort to demonstrate that purely intellectual cognition of quasi-objects such as the soul, the world as such, and God is impossible. Challenging this tradition, the present chapter aims to reframe Kant's remarks on the thing in itself and related concepts in terms of what I have called strand [2] of Kant's critique of metaphysics.[2]

Accordingly, I do not believe that the two-aspect approach Allison took over from Prauss and defends in *Kant's Transcendental Idealism* succeeds in solving the riddles Kant's text presents.[3] In line with Adickes, Allison and

---

[1] Following Jacobi, Fichte in 1797 derided his Kantian contemporaries because of the contradictory meanings of the thing in itself they embraced: "Their thing-in-itself, which is a mere thought, is supposed to operate upon the I! Have they again forgotten what they first said, and is their thing-in-itself, which a moment ago was a mere thought, now something other than that?" (Fichte, "Second Introduction to the *Wissenschaftslehre*," I 483). Fichte considers the passages that deal with the issue of affection to represent a merely empirical point of view, a point of view of which the system has to provide the true ground (cf. I 488). As I hope will become clear in what follows, I agree with the first part of Fichte's position, but not with the second. For reasons of space, I will not elaborate on the early reception of Kant's theory. I do so with regard to Jacobi in the article that contains an earlier and longer version of this chapter (De Boer 2014). I also refer the reader to this article for a more extensive discussion of interpretations of the problem at hand, including Prauss (1974), Langton (1998), and Allison (2004).

[2] See, in particular, Chapter 2, Sections 5 and 7.

[3] See Prauss (1974: 13–43); Allison (2004, 50–57).

many other commentators substitute the term 'thing in itself' for both the object that is said to affect the senses and the transcendental object that is said to be the ground or cause of appearances.[4] Instead of adding another artificial solution to the confusion this assumption entails, this chapter seeks to demonstrate that terms such as thing in itself, noumenon, and transcendental object acquire a different meaning in the various parts of the *Critique of Pure Reason*.

More specifically, I will contend that whatever is said to affect us cannot be said to be a thing in itself in the sense of a noumenon, because the latter term merely refers to our way of conceiving of something.[5] Once these two meanings of the concept 'thing in itself' have been dissociated, it becomes possible to shift the focus to the role of concepts such as thing in itself, noumenon, and transcendental object in Kant's critical engagement with Wolffian metaphysics. In this regard, I argue, first, that Kant uses these concepts primarily to dissect the various strands of the Wolffian concept of a thing and, second, that he does so in order to distinguish between, on the one hand, our purely intellectual thoughts about objects as such and quasi-objects such as the soul and God and, on the other hand, the efforts on the part of Wolffian metaphysics to obtain knowledge of the latter.

It is perhaps no coincidence that Kant, in the second Preface of the *Critique of Pure Reason*, introduces the distinction between appearances and things in themselves by referring to the soul as something that ought to be considered not only as "subject to natural necessity" but also as a "thing in itself."[6] In this context, the soul is conceived not as a thing that somehow affects our senses, but rather as an idea that can and must be thought by pure reason in order to safeguard the possibility of human freedom.[7]

I begin, in Section 2, by discussing Kant's remarks on affection. Section 3 considers the problem of the thing in itself in view of Kant's distinction

---

[4] Allison (2004: 64, cf. 50). I discuss this issue in Section 3.

[5] Contrary to most commentators, and in line with Fichte, Prauss (1974: 108–12) rightly considers the transcendental object to result from a projection by the subject and disconnects it from the issue of affection. Rescher (1981: 349) likewise stresses that the thing in itself is a product of the understanding. Yet he maintains that the understanding conceives of the thing in itself in order to posit that our representations "are grounded in extra-phenomenal reality" (352), thus confusing the two senses of the thing in itself that I propose to distinguish.

[6] Bxxvii, emphasis mine, cf. Bxviii–xix, note.

[7] It might be argued that the soul, considered as human mind, has the capacity to affect itself in the sense that the thoughts it generates necessarily present themselves to it in the form of inner sense (cf. B67–68, B155). However, in that case the human mind is considered precisely not as a thing but as a source of cognitive activity. In what follows I disregard Kant's remarks on the way in which the mind affects itself through inner sense.

between the psychological and metaphysical approaches represented by Locke and Leibniz. These sections pave the way for a detailed examination of Kant's use of the terms 'thing in itself' and 'noumenon' (Section 4) and 'transcendental object' (Section 5). Leaving behind the problem of affection, these sections interpret Kant's account in light of his critique and intended reform of Wolffian general and special metaphysics.

2 Affecting Objects

In the *Critique of Pure Reason*, Kant repeatedly notes that sensations result from objects that affect our senses, but he never treats the issue in any detail. Thus, he mentions at the very beginning of the Transcendental Aesthetic that objects can be given to us only if they affect us:

> The capacity . . . to acquire representations through the way in which we are affected by objects (*Gegenstände*) is called sensibility. Objects are therefore given to us by means of sensibility, and the latter alone provides us with intuitions.... The effect of an object on the capacity for representation, insofar as we are affected by it, is sensation. (A19–20/B33–34)

Generally, Kant uses the term 'object' (*Gegenstand*) to refer to the things that affect our sensibility.[8] In line with many other commentators, Allison assumes that the term 'object' in this context can refer only to things in themselves. He advances two arguments for this position. Following Jacobi, he rightly maintains, first, that this term cannot refer to appearances, which, qua representations, are themselves produced by the mind on the basis of impressions.[9] Drawing on Adickes's *Kant und das Ding an sich* (1924), he claims, second, that Kant in numerous passages regards the thing in itself or the transcendental object "as affecting the mind or as the non-sensible 'cause' or 'ground' of appearances."[10] Yet this purported

---

[8] B1, A26/B42, A35/B51, A51/B75, A372. Somewhat confusingly, Kant occasionally also uses the term *Objekt* to denote the things that affect the senses (B72, A358).

[9] Allison (2004: 65, cf. 67). This is in agreement with the following remark by Kant, according to which "it would never occur to anyone to take as an external cause what he has already recognized as a mere representation" (A390).

[10] Allison (2004: 64). Allison further maintains that "Kant does speak of the transcendental object (or its equivalent) as affecting the mind" (65) and "unambiguously" asserts "the affection by things in themselves" (460 n 24). Of the passages to which Allison in this note refers to support his reading – which he takes over from Adickes – some deal with that which affects the senses (B72), some with the transcendental object (A380, A393, A494/B522), and some with both (A44/B61, A190–91/B235–36, A358). Most other commentators likewise assume that Kant considers things in themselves to affect the senses without distinguishing between the various meanings of this term and/or without reference to specific passages. See, among many other examples, Herring (1953: 13–14, 78–82) and Rescher (1972: 175–83). Rescher rightly distinguishes between

textual evidence is based on Adickes's and Allison's tacit identification of the terms 'object,' 'thing in itself,' and 'transcendental object' in passages such as the following:

> The capacity . . . to acquire representations through the way in which we are affected by objects is called sensibility. (A19–20/B33–34)

> The transcendental object that grounds both outer appearances and inner intuition is neither matter nor a thinking being in itself, but rather an unknown ground of those appearances. (A379–80)

Kant here and elsewhere indeed conceives of the transcendental object as the ground or cause of appearances. But this does not necessarily entail that his remarks about affecting objects and the transcendental object pertain to the same issue. Moreover, we need not assume, as Allison does, that the term 'object' must refer to either appearances or things in themselves. In the remainder of the present section I leave aside Kant's use of the term 'transcendental object' and focus on the passages concerned with affection.

As I see it, Kant distinguishes appearances from things in themselves in order to take the former as the starting point of his investigation into the various cognitive activities carried out by the human mind. These activities are considered in view of how they contribute to the order and unification of sensations and, hence, to the production of objects of cognition. On this account, Kant does not mean to deny that things such as billiard balls exist independently of the human mind. He in the *Critique of Pure Reason* rather takes up a mind-immanent position in order to examine the cognitive activities through which the mind turns as yet undetermined appearances of things such as billiard balls into objects of empirical cognition.[11] What Kant seeks to investigate, in other words, is how "a cognition of objects is to come about which rests solely on the synthesis

---

causality in the common sense of the term and a form of grounding that concerns the relation between noumena and phenomena (176). In my view, however, there is no need to attribute what Rescher calls "noumenal causality" to affecting objects (cf. 178) or to assume, with Rosefeldt (2013), that Kant changed his view on this issue between the first and second editions of the *Critique*.

[11] Cf. A20/B34. Kant also considers an appearance to be an "object of empirical intuition" (A89). Thus, in my opinion, what Kant calls 'transcendental idealism' is not a first-order doctrine about the mind-dependence of things but a methodological principle according to which the cognitive activities carried out by the human mind are exclusively investigated from within, that is, as he puts it, "without going beyond mere self-consciousness and assuming something more than the certainty of representations in me" (A370, cf. A369). In the present section I as yet disregard Kant's aim to investigate the mind in view of the cognitive activities it carries out a priori, that is, independently of experience.

of the representations" (A155/B194). Whether or not the object of cognition thus produced corresponds to the ball considered as material thing is irrelevant to Kant's perspective (cf. A104).

Nevertheless, Kant does not hesitate to refer to things such as billiard balls as things that give rise to sensations. As was mentioned above, most of the passages use the term *Gegenstand* to refer to that which affects the senses.[12] I hold that Kant, in this context, uses the term simply to denote material things, that is to say, not the objects of experience brought about by the human mind (cf. A56/B81, A120). This reading is supported by the following passage from one of Kant's lectures:

> [T]he objects (*Gegenstände*) are that which affects me. Accordingly, thinking concerns things that affect my body; thus my thinking is directed toward the impressions of the brain which my body receives. These bodily impressions are the *ideae materiales*. Thus, it follows from this that the body is also affected by thinking. We can go no further here in the investigation.[13]

Kant had good reasons to avoid the term 'thing in itself' in the context of his remarks on affection, I contend, because strictly speaking these remarks belong to the domain of the sciences, or common sense, rather than transcendental critique. Thus, at one point in the Transcendental Aesthetic, Kant notes that colors are modifications of our eyesight, a sense "that is affected by light in a certain way."[14] Even if light is a phenomenon less easy to grasp than a rock or a rose, it seems quite far-fetched to regard light as an unknowable thing in itself. Kant, I would contend, here and elsewhere deliberately conforms to the language of the scientist, who considers the world to consist of causally interconnected material things.[15]

However, various passages related to the issue of affection do use the term 'thing in itself' rather than the term 'object.' While they seem to undermine the reading I propose, I believe they can be explained by referring to Kant's distinction between a physical and metaphysical sense of the term 'thing in itself.'

Seen from the perspective of transcendental critique, natural scientists deal with appearances, that is, with representations that can be turned into objects of experience. For the scientists themselves, however, it does not

---

[12] Cf. B1, A26/B42, A35/B51, A51/B75.   [13] LM L1, 28:259–60 (dated mid-1770s).
[14] A28, cf. A213/B260; cf. Allison (2004: 67, 461 n 37).
[15] Elsewhere in the *Critique of Pure Reason* Kant occasionally refers to things in a non-philosophical sense as well (cf. A42/B59, B275, A373).

make sense to treat something like a rose or a raindrop as an appearance rather than a thing in itself. According to Kant, scientists are perfectly justified to treat a raindrop as a thing in itself in the *physical* sense of the term, that is, as mind-independent. The following passages illustrate this point:

> Thus, whereas we would call a rainbow a mere appearance in a sunshower, we would call this rain the thing in itself, and this is correct, as long as we understand the latter concept in *a merely physical sense*, as that which in universal experience and all different positions relative to the senses is always determined thus and not otherwise in intuition. But if we consider this empirical object as such and . . . ask whether it . . . represents an object in itself, then the question of the relation of the representation to the object is *transcendental*, and not only these drops are mere appearances, but even their round form, indeed even the space in which they fall are nothing in themselves, but only mere modifications . . . of our sensible intuition.[16]

> For in this case that which is originally itself only appearance, e.g., a rose, counts *in an empirical sense as a thing in itself*, which yet can appear different to every eye in regard to color. The *transcendental concept of appearances* in space, on the contrary, is a critical reminder that . . . objects in themselves are not known to us at all, and that what we call outer objects are nothing other than mere representations of our sensibility. (A29–30/B45)

Scientists may investigate the exact way in which certain light frequencies produced by material things affect the optic nerve so as to cause mental images. By contrast, Kant abstracts from the fact that things exist outside of us in order to focus exclusively on the efforts on the part of the human mind to unify its sensible representations. Once the redness is considered as the content of a sensation, the question as to its cause is no longer pertinent.

In sum, I hold that Kant is perfectly justified in considering plain material things such as roses to affect our senses, because the process of affection falls outside the scope of transcendental critique. While he must refer to this process, he does not have to account for it in philosophical terms.

---

[16] A45–46/B63, emphasis mine. I take it that the first 'we' in this passage refers to the scientists and the second to the philosophers. The 'we' in the following passage also seems to concern the position of the scientists: "In all the tasks that may come before us in the field of experience, we treat those appearances as objects in themselves, without worrying ourselves about the primary ground of their possibility (as appearances)." (A393). Opposing Adickes, Prauss is one of the very few commentators to maintain that the process of affection belongs to the subject matter of the sciences rather than philosophy (see Prauss 1974: 207, 223). He also points out that Kant in this context occasionally uses the term 'thing in itself' in a merely empirical sense (44–45, 200).

If, accordingly, the objects that are said to affect the senses do not have to be identified with either appearances or things in themselves, then most of the passages on affection quoted by Adickes and Allison become unproblematic and do not require an artificial solution. Yet other passages may well be considered to challenge the interpretation I have put forward so far, because they mention affection and things in themselves or the transcendental object as if in one breath. In the next section, I aim to put these passages into relief by taking into account Kant's largely implicit engagement with Locke and Leibniz's philosophical conception of things in themselves.

3   Locke versus Leibniz

In the following passage from the Transcendental Aesthetic, Kant might seem to affirm that the human mind is affected by things in themselves:

> The representation of a body in intuition, on the contrary, contains nothing at all that could pertain to an object in itself, but merely the appearance of *something* and the *way in which we are affected by it*; and this receptivity of our cognitive capacity ... remains worlds apart from the cognition of the *object in itself* even if one might grasp this representation through and through.[17]

But perhaps the text calls for closer scrutiny. The immediate context makes it clear that Kant here takes issue with the "Leibnizian-Wolffian philosophy" (A44/B61), which, on his account, conflated appearances with things in themselves and alleged that the latter could be known. Kant contends that while we are necessarily affected by something, the representation that emerges from this affection by no means provides the understanding with

---

[17] A44/B61, emphasis mine, translation modified. The first three passages that I discuss in this section are among those that Allison takes to demonstrate that Kant considers things in themselves to affect our sensibility (Allison 2004: 460 n 24). While Allison follows Adickes's account of non-empirical affection, he does not take on board his view that the human mind is affected by two kinds of entities at once (66, 68). Drawing on Prauss (1974) in this regard, Allison rather understands the distinction between empirical and non-empirical affection as a distinction between two ways of considering the same empirical object (62, cf. 67). For reasons not clear to me, he holds on to the notion of transcendental affection by things in themselves. In my view, any attempt to reconcile the alleged contradictions in the *Critique of Pure* Reason by taking recourse to the idea of double affection, introduced by Adickes (1929), is unnecessary and lacks textual basis. See Wolff (1963: 169–73) for a relatively recent defense of the classical version of this doctrine. Gram's critique of this position hinges on the claim that the notion of a thing in itself does not exclude that it can be intuited (Gram 1975: 54). In my view, however, this claim is not warranted with regard to the things in themselves at stake in metaphysics and, accordingly, does not amount to a satisfactory solution.

the characteristics of – for instance – the rose qua thing in itself, that is, with the set of characteristics contained in the very concept of a rose.[18] As I see it, Kant in this passage attributes the capacity to affect the mind to an unspecified 'something' and uses the term 'object in itself' only to reject the claim of the Wolffians that things such as they are in themselves can be known. There is no reason, therefore, to identify the term 'something' with the term 'object in itself.'

Other passages also become less problematic if we take them to be concerned with Kant's account of how *philosophers have conceived of that which underlies appearances*. Clearly, the following passage from the Paralogisms of Pure Reason primarily addresses Leibniz's monadology:

> [T]he something that ... affects our sense in such a way that the latter receives the representations of space, matter, shape, etc. – this something, *considered as noumenon* (or better, as transcendental object) could at the same time also be the subject of thoughts, even though we receive no intuition of representations, volitions, etc. through the way in which our outer sense is affected by it [the something].... But this something is not extended, not impenetrable, not composite, because these predicates pertain only to sensibility and its intuition, insofar as we are affected by such objects (otherwise unknown to us).... Yet the predicates of inner sense, representation and thought, do not contradict the something.[19]

By referring, again, to a 'something' that affects our sensibility and, hence, produces representations, Kant follows in the footsteps of what he elsewhere terms Locke's physiology of the human understanding (Aix). Yet he goes on to note that we *need not* conceive of the 'something' that underlies appearances as a material object. If, by contrast, the 'something' that we one way or another need to posit is conceived as monad, as Leibniz had done, then nothing seems to prevent us from conceiving of this monad as something that is capable of representation and apperception. At least, doing so is not self-contradictory.

---

[18] Cf. A272/B328, where Kant notes that, for Leibniz, to know a drop of water as a thing in itself is to know it with regard to "all of its inner determinations," something that is achieved by abstracting from the way in which individual drops present themselves to the senses or, as Kant puts it elsewhere, "without regard to representations through which they affect us" (A190/B235). In his view, this alleged cognition is nothing but an attempt at defining concepts, while achieving real cognition of the properties of things such as water must rely on experiments (A728/756). I return to Kant's critique of Leibniz in Chapter 7.

[19] A358–59, emphasis mine, translation modified. I take it that the term 'dadurch' in the clause "die Art, wie unser äußerer Sinn dadurch affiziert wird" refers back to the 'something' mentioned at the beginning of the passage and not to the 'something' that is being considered as noumenon. See Locke, *Essay*, II.23.5.

I take Kant's point to be that, whether or not we accept the Leibnizian view that appearances are grounded in monads, there is an epistemological gap between the 'something' that is said to affect our sensibility and the noumenon that we can consider to possess the capacity to represent and think. However, attributing these characteristics to monads by no means amounts to cognition proper.

In the context of the Second Analogy, Kant likewise remarks that philosophers should not treat things like houses as something of which the inner characteristics can be known. Unlike the passages discussed so far, he here attributes the capacity to affect the mind not to an undetermined 'something' but to 'things' of which we do not know what they are in themselves:

> [H]ow *things in themselves* may be (without regard to representations through which they *affect* us) is entirely beyond our cognitive sphere.... Now, however, as soon as I raise my concept of an object to transcendental significance, the house is not a thing in itself at all but only an appearance, i.e., a representation, *the transcendental object of which* is unknown. (A190–191/B235–236, my emphasis)

This passage is clearly concerned with the shift from the standpoint of common sense to that of transcendental critique mentioned above. If we assume that the parenthetical clause, once again, concerns a Lockean account of cognition, then there is no reason to identify the things that are said to affect us with the transcendental object mentioned in the last sentence.

Seen from a Lockean perspective, the whiteness that I see originates in the thing by which I am affected, but the things that are "really operating upon us" can be known only with regard to the manifold of simple ideas to which they give rise.[20] In my view, Kant follows Locke by referring to the house that affects our sensibility as a thing in itself in the physical sense of the term.[21] Like Locke, however, Kant takes this explanation to be only part of the story. In order to establish unity among its representations, Locke writes,

---

[20] Locke, *Essay*, IV.4.4–5.
[21] Opposing Berkeleyan idealism, Kant writes in a similar vein: "There are things given to us as objects of our senses existing outside us, yet we know nothing of them as they may be in themselves, but are acquainted only with their appearances, that is, with the representations these things produce in us because they affect our senses" (Prol, 4:289). On my reading, this passage is concerned with the way our sensibility is affected by actual material things such as roses and houses. Whereas Kant accepts Locke's distinction between primary and secondary qualities, he does not consider it to be relevant to his own purposes (A45/B62). Seen from a transcendental perspective, *all* properties of objects must be said to belong to appearances alone (Prol, 4:289). For a recent 'Lockean' account of Kant's conception of the thing in itself, see Chignell (2011). While Chignell does not ignore the

the mind produces the idea of substance, an idea "which is nothing but the supposed, but unknown, support of those qualities we find existing."[22] Clearly, this idea cannot be identified with the affecting object. In the second part of the passage quoted above, Kant shifts the focus to this second aspect of Locke's account. If the house is treated from the mind-immanent perspective adopted in the *Critique*, I take him to argue, then the issue of affection is no longer relevant. The only thing that matters in this case is the transcendental object that the human mind must posit in order to turn the house, qua appearance, into an object of cognition.

Kant states elsewhere that we cannot *reduce* things such as houses to their appearance, because the very concept of appearance implies a reference to something that itself does not appear:

> [I]t follows naturally from the concept of an appearance as such that something must correspond to it that is not in itself appearance, for appearance can be nothing for itself and outside of our kind of representation; thus … the word 'appearance' must already indicate a relation to something the immediate representation of which is, to be sure, sensible, but which in itself, without this constitution of our sensibility … *must be something, i.e., an object independent of sensibility.*[23]

In this particular context, I hold, Kant abstracts from the various ways in which philosophers have distinguished between appearances and their corresponding non-sensible 'something' so as to address all of them.[24] His formal description leaves open whether the latter is conceived as idea (Plato), as material cause of ideas (Locke), as an unknowable support of qualities posited by the human mind (Locke), as monad (Leibniz), as

---

differences between Kant and Locke, I hold that important aspects of Kant's view cannot be understood in terms of a Lockean model of cognition.

[22] Locke, *Essay*, II.23.2, cf. II.23.15.   [23] A251–52, emphasis mine, cf. Bxxvi–xxvii.

[24] This is confirmed by the following, analogous passage from the *Prolegomena*, which explicitly refers to a distinction established "from the earliest days of philosophy." Kant writes here: "[I]f we view the objects of the senses as mere appearances, as is fitting, then we thereby admit at the same time that a thing in itself underlies them, although we are not acquainted with this thing as it may be constituted in itself, but only with its appearance, i.e., with the way in which our senses are affected by this unknown something. Therefore the understanding, by the very act of assuming appearances, also admits to the existence of things in themselves, and to that extent we can say that the representation of such beings as underlie the appearances, hence of mere intelligible beings, is not merely permitted but also inevitable" (4:314–15). On my reading, Kant here initially refers to things in themselves in the empirical sense of the term, because only these things can be said to affect the senses. Only if we consider Kant, here and elsewhere, to move from a common-sense account of knowledge to a philosophical one does it make sense, it seems to me, that he in the second part of the passage attributes to 'the understanding' the view that appearances are grounded in noumena. By contrast, Allison (2004: 53–54) takes the things in themselves mentioned in the first line to refer to "the transcendental causes or grounds of appearances."

essence that grounds the characteristics of a thing (Leibniz and Wolff), or in yet different ways. Thus, I hold that Kant in this passage does not provide his own account of the non-sensible 'something' that must be considered to underlie appearances. In the next sections, I will argue that he uses the term 'thing in itself' primarily to separate the worthwhile and worthless aspects of the Wolffian assumption that things can be known by the intellect alone.

4 Things in Themselves and Noumena

The aim of the present and following sections is to elucidate the account of things in themselves that Kant elaborates first and foremost in the chapter of the Transcendental Analytic devoted to the distinction between phenomena and noumena. In this chapter, Kant seeks to clarify the crucial difference between his own philosophy and what he took to be the Leibnizian roots of Wolffian general metaphysics.[25] In line with Wolff, he considers this discipline to treat of things as such (*Dinge überhaupt*), a term that pertains indiscriminately to material things such as roses and immaterial things such as the soul or God.[26]

But what is a thing? Seen from Kant's perspective, the concept of a thing assumed in this discipline is seriously underdetermined. I would suggest that Kant introduces concepts such as noumenon and transcendental object to critically dissect the various elements of the concept of a thing and specify their role in the context of general and special metaphysics, respectively. In this context, I contend, Kant uses the term 'thing in itself' in its metaphysical sense, which is to say that he completely disregards the role of affecting objects. Evidently, the outcome of this investigation is that the mind, for various reasons, can and must conceive of noumena, but that doing so does not yield cognition proper.

On Kant's account, Wolff, Crusius, and their followers did not limit the use of categories such as substance to appearances, but assumed that categories could be used to obtain knowledge of things as such, *regardless of the way they are given to us*. As we have seen in the preceding chapter, Kant refers to this use as the transcendental use of categories. The following passage leaves no doubt that he rejects this use insofar as it aims at the cognition of objects:

---

[25] This aim emerges explicitly in the Appendix that follows Kant's account of the distinction between phenomena and noumena. I consider this text in Chapter 7.

[26] A238/B298, cf. A242, A246/B303.

> That the understanding can therefore make only an empirical use of all its a
> priori principles, indeed of all its concepts, but never a transcendental use, is
> a proposition that ... points to important consequences. The transcenden-
> tal use of a concept in any principle consists in its being related *to things as
> such and in themselves*; its empirical use, however, in its being related merely
> to appearances, i.e., objects of a possible experience.[27]

But what does it mean to relate a category to things in themselves? Most
passages in the *Critique* that mention things in themselves state either that
appearances should not be treated as things in themselves or that the latter
cannot be known. In my view, these passages – no less than those about
things as such – pertain to the way in which things *used to be conceived* in
Wolffian metaphysics rather than to Kant's own first-order account of the
matter.

On my reading, Kant basically uses the concept 'thing in itself' in its
metaphysical sense to refer to any object that is conceived independently of
its spatial and temporal determinations, in other words, by means of the
pure understanding alone. These things, Kant notes, are

> things that the understanding must think without relating them to our kind
> of intuition, thus not merely as appearances. (B307)

This passage makes it clear that Kant, contrary to what is often assumed,
considers the thing in itself in the proper, metaphysical sense of the term to
refer not to something alleged to exist independently of the human mind
but to that which the philosopher conceives of *by abstracting from the way
in which it can be sensibly intuited*. This definition applies to a rose insofar
as it can be thought, that is, insofar as one identifies the marks contained in
its concept, but also to things such as monads, the soul, and God. As seen
in Chapter 2, the *Inaugural Dissertation* distinguishes between appearances
and things in themselves along the same lines (cf. 2:392).

In the Transcendental Aesthetic, Kant also defines things in themselves
in this way. All appearances, he writes here, possess

> two sides, one where the object is considered in itself (regardless of the way
> in which it is intuited ...), an other where the form of the intuition of this
> object is taken into consideration, a form that must not be sought in the
> object in itself but in the subject to which it appears.[28]

---

[27] A238–39/B297–98, cf. A247–48/B304, A279/B335. On this, see Chapter 3, Section 4.

[28] A38/B55. Similarly, Kant notes that space lacks objective validity, or reality, if it is used by reason
"with regard to things ... considered in themselves, i.e., without taking account of the constitution
of our sensibility" (A27–28/B44). Arguably, this passage primarily targets Crusius's conception of

Both ways of conceiving things are carried out by philosophers alone. Thus, by considering the characteristics contained in the very concept of a drop of water, they treat the latter as a thing in itself in the metaphysical sense of the term. In this case, they completely abstract from the sensible differences between various drops of water:

> Granted, if I know a drop of water as a thing in itself according to all of its inner determinations, then I cannot let any one drop count as different from another if the entire concept of the former is identical with that of the latter. (A272/B328)

Kant considers Leibniz, Wolff, and their followers to represent this position.[29] Thus, drawing on the Scholastic tradition, Baumgarten notes in his *Metaphysics* that something which is not considered in relation to something else is considered in itself (*spectatur in se*). Wolff and the early Kant use similar expressions.[30] In Kant's view, the Wolffians rightly claimed that things can be considered by means of the understanding alone, but wrongly assumed that this consideration could yield true cognition of objects.[31]

---

the soul and God (discussed in Chapters 1 and 2). Allison takes Kant to distinguish between things such as they present themselves to "discursive knowers with our forms of sensibility" and things that are considered "apart from their epistemic relation to these forms," in which case they are considered "qua objects for some pure intelligence" (Allison 2004: 16–17). While I agree with this account, I do not quite see how it can be squared with his view that Kant considers things to affect the mind transcendentally. In a similar vein, Westphal (1968) argues that for Kant the thing in itself is "the thing for God's creative intellect" (124). However, it seems unnecessary to refer to God if one considers Kant to be concerned with the model of philosophical cognition he attributed to the Leibnizian tradition.

[29] A271/B327. I deal with this issue in some detail in Chapter 7.

[30] See Baumgarten, M 15. This passage is quoted by Prauss (1974: 20–21), who rightly notes that the expression 'thing in itself' is an abbreviation of 'that which is considered such as it is in itself.' Similarly, according to Wolff's *Latin Ontology* "*a thing is considered in itself or absolutely* if we pay attention to nothing but its essence or, instead of it, to its definition" (LO 301). In the *Inaugural Dissertation*, Kant distinguishes between a connection of things in themselves (*in se*) and the world considered as phenomenon (*spectatur ut phaenomenon*). Kant suggests that the former connection – the *mundus intelligibilis* – is grasped by the intellect, whereas considering the world as phenomenon means considering it in relation to the way in which it is perceived (2:398). See also Kant's comments on Baumgarten's use of the expression 'spectatur in se' in lectures dated 1782–83 (LM Mrongovius, 29:813).

[31] Kant takes his account to prove "the nullity of all inferences about objects that one simply compares with each other in the understanding," because, "although appearances cannot be ranged among the objects of pure understanding as things in themselves, they are nevertheless the only objects by means of which our cognition can have objective reality, namely, where intuition corresponds to the concepts" (A278–79/B334–35, translation modified). Kant here seems to oppose not only the Wolffians but also the position he defended in the *Inaugural Dissertation*. See A249–50 and A255–56/B311 for further articulations of this self-criticism.

Yet it is not warranted, in my opinion, to maintain that Kant uses the term 'thing in itself' merely in order to distinguish two perspectives on things such as roses or drops of water, as has been done by Prauss, Allison, and others. These commentators assume that the things of which Kant states that they can be considered as they are in themselves are the very things that are said to affect the senses. I submit, however, that Kant not only distinguishes two complementary approaches to things that can be encountered by means of the senses, but also singles out a class of things that can be conceived by means of thought *alone*. This is to say that I do not accept the dichotomy between the 'two-aspect view' that Allison endorses and the 'two-object view' he opposes. Seen from Kant's perspective, material things such as roses can be treated either as appearances or as they are in themselves. The latter is done if we seek to obtain definitions of them. Yet metaphysics can also seek to achieve knowledge of things that cannot be treated as appearances at all, e.g., things such as monads, the soul, and God. In the following passages Kant distinguishes obliquely between these two classes of things:

> Nevertheless, if we call certain objects, as appearances, sensible beings (*phaenomena*), because we distinguish the way in which we intuit them from their constitution in itself, then our concept entails that we oppose them, as it were, *either* to these very objects considered in view of said constitution . . . *or* else to other possible things, which are not objects of our senses at all, and call them intellectual beings (*noumena*).[32]

> But we believe to be able to go beyond our concepts and to amplify our cognition a priori. We attempt to do this *either* through the pure understanding, with regard to that which can at least be an object of experience, *or* even through pure reason, with regard to such properties of things, or even with regard to the existence of such objects, that can never occur in experience.[33]

Once metaphysics assumes that things such as roses can be known by means of the intellect alone, I take Kant to argue, nothing seems to prevent it from assuming that it can achieve cognition proper of the soul and God as well. As I see it, Kant mainly uses the term 'thing in itself' to identify

---

[32] B306, emphasis mine, translation modified; cf. Prol, 4:350.

[33] A764–65/B792–93, emphasis mine, cf. A2–5/B6–7, A146–47/B186. In my view, these passages undermine Prauss's and Allison's reduction of the concept 'thing in itself' to its physical sense (see Prauss 1974: 200; Allison 2004: 3, 16–17). To my knowledge, Adams (1997) is one of the very few commentators who, with reference to B306, states that Kant "postulates both noumena that are definitely identical with some phenomena and noumena that definitely are not" (822). He adduces Kant's conception of God in the *Critique of Practical Reason* and elsewhere to support this point.

and reject this twofold assumption, which is what I have called strand [2] of his critique of metaphysics.

However, Kant clearly does not wish to reduce the scope of metaphysics to the realm of appearances. That is why he introduces various concepts that correspond to the concept of a thing in itself but, contrary to the latter, do not imply that things that are considered independently of sensibility amount to objects of cognition.

One of these concepts, already mentioned above, is that of a noumenon. Kant considers this concept merely to refer to "the thinking of something as such, in which I abstract from all form of sensible intuition" (A252). In this regard, the noumenon does not differ from the thing in itself. Contrary to the concept of the latter, however, the concept of noumenon is said to mark "the boundaries of our sensible cognition" and so to prevent both sensibility and the pure understanding from encroaching on the mere thought of something.[34] The 1787 edition clarifies this point by distinguishing the concept of a noumenon "in the negative sense" from the noumenon conceived as "object of a non-sensible intuition" (B307). For example, insofar as the soul is conceived as a noumenon in the negative sense, it can neither be subjected to natural laws (cf. Bxxvii) nor be treated as the subject of a priori judgments such as 'the soul is immortal.' Wolffian metaphysics erred, on Kant's account, by mistaking "the entirely undetermined concept of an intellectual being . . . for a determinate concept of a being that we could come to know through the understanding in some way," in other words, by substituting that which can only be thought with the notion of a thing that can be known independently of sensibility.[35]

Thus, I take it that, for Kant, both material things such as roses and immaterial things such as monads, the soul, and God can be treated as noumena, but that he uses the term primarily with regard to the latter, that is, in the context of his critique of former metaphysics.[36] As we will see in the next section, passages that invoke the concept of transcendental object are likewise part of Kant's effort to clarify the distinction between Wolffian

---

[34] A288–89/B345, cf. A254, A206. See Chapter 2, Section 7.

[35] B306–307, emphasis mine, translation modified. Already in the 1781 edition, Kant considers the concept of noumenon to be "a boundary concept" that serves "to limit the pretension of sensibility" and therefore has only a "negative use" (A255/B10–11).

[36] Cf. A541/B569; CPrR, 5:54. Kant here uses the terms 'noumenon' and 'thing in itself' indiscriminately with regard to the soul, qua ground of freedom, and God. According to Kant, noumena such as the soul and God can be determined only through practical reason (cf. CPrR, 5:5–6, 54–56, 68, 114).

metaphysics and the reformed version of it he envisioned, but have a much wider scope.

5　The Transcendental Object

Kant's discussions of the transcendental object are probably among the most elusive of the *Critique of Pure Reason*. Perhaps this is why he removed the term from the parts he reworked for the second edition.[37] Even so, I hold that the matter can be clarified by assuming that the concept of transcendental object, like that of noumenon, serves to identify and assess a particular feature of the underdetermined concept of a thing in the Wolffian tradition. As in other cases, moreover, it is helpful to distinguish between Kant's use of the term in a formal sense and his use of the term in the context of his critique and projected reform of general and special metaphysics. This will allow me, I hope, to support my claim that the passages in which Kant conceives of the transcendental object as ground or cause are not concerned with affecting objects.

Taken in a formal sense, the term 'transcendental object' denotes the something = X that must be posited in order to conceive of a manifold of representations as a unity at all. In this regard, Kant draws on Locke's account of empirical cognition. However, he departs from Locke, first, by exclusively considering the unificatory acts that the understanding carries out *a priori* and, second, by considering these acts to be articulated by categories.

For Kant, categories are purely intellectual articulations of a priori rules for the unification of representations, which is to say that they allow the mind to conceive of something as an object in a particular respect, for instance, as a substance of which attributes such as redness can be predicated.[38] For this reason, categories can be said to constitute determinations of the transcendental object or any object whatsoever insofar as it can be thought. I take this to be the gist of the following passage, which was partly discussed in the preceding chapter:

> Thinking is the act of relating given intuitions to an object. If the manner of this intuition is not given in any way, *then the object is merely transcendental*, and the concept of the understanding has none other than a transcendental

---

[37] However, Kant did not remove references to the transcendental object from the part of the chapter he did not rework (cf. B304) or from other parts of the *Critique*, including the Transcendental Dialectic (cf. A191/B236, A478/B506, A698/B726).

[38] Cf. A55/B80, A110, A142/B181. This point will be discussed in more detail in Chapters 5 and 6.

use, namely the unity of thought of a manifold as such. Thus, through a pure category, in which *abstraction is made* from any condition of sensible intuition, as the only one that is possible for us, no *object* is determined, but only the *thought of an object as such*, according to different modi, is expressed.[39]

While the a priori acts of thinking an object as such do not amount to cognition proper, they are first and foremost carried out with the aim of establishing unity among *empirical* representations, which we do, for example, by attributing redness to a rose or determining one event as the effect of another. Kant writes:

> The pure concept of this transcendental object (which in all of our cognitions is really always one and the same = X) is that which in all of our empirical concepts can provide relation to an object, i.e., objective reality, at all. (A109)

> The object to which I relate the appearance as such (*überhaupt*) is the transcendental object, i.e., the entirely undetermined thought of something as such. (A253)

As said, these passages are reminiscent of Locke's account of empirical cognition. Yet Kant borrows Locke's idea, I hold, in order to shed light on the concept of a thing assumed in Wolffian general metaphysics: what Kant in this context calls 'transcendental object' indicates the need of the mind to posit a something = X that can function as the bearer of a number of *a priori* determinations. Without doing so, it would be impossible to establish a priori, for instance, that all things have a cause. The transcendental object in *this* sense, Kant notes, is

> a something = X, of which we know nothing at all nor can know anything whatsoever . . . , but . . . that, as a correlate of the unity of apperception, *can serve only as the unity of the manifold in sensible intuition*, a unity that allows the understanding to unify said manifold in the concept of an object. . . . This transcendental object is . . . only the representation of appearances under the concept of *an object as such*, a representation that is determinable through the manifold of those appearances.[40]

---

[39] A247/B304, my emphasis, cf. A96–97.

[40] A250–51, emphasis mine, translation modified. Categories, Kant adds, "serve only *to determine the transcendental object* . . . through that which is given in sensibility, in order thereby to cognize appearances empirically under concepts of objects" (A251). Since the transcendental object *in this sense* merely allows the understanding to conceive of appearances as objects of possible experience, it cannot even be treated as a noumenon in the sense of a particular object that can be thought (such as the soul or God) (A253).

Kant even refers to the transcendental object in this sense as "object of a sensible intuition as such" (A253) and "transcendental object of experience" (A495/B523). In this capacity, it can be said to denote the worthwhile element of the concept of a thing assumed in former general metaphysics. Unlike the Wolffians, however, Kant restricts the legitimate function of the transcendental object to the process of unifying sensible representations. I take him to hold, in other words, that things such as the soul and God cannot function as the 'something = X' that must be posited in order to unify a sensible manifold and, hence, to produce objects of cognition proper.

Yet Kant also discusses the transcendental object in the Transcendental Dialectic, that is, in the context of his critical engagement with former special metaphysics. As was noted in Chapter 2, Kant here dissects the Wolffian assumption that the world as such, the soul, and God are things that can be known. Accordingly, the Transcendental Dialectic deals with a manifold of transcendental objects rather than the unique transcendental object presupposed in any empirical cognition of objects at stake in the Transcendental Analytic.

Thus, Kant considers the four cosmological ideas to constitute determinations of a single transcendental object, namely, the world as such:

> Such transcendent ideas have a *merely intelligible object*. Although it is certainly allowed to admit this object as a *transcendental object*, of which nothing more is known, we have on our side neither grounds of the possibility ... of *thinking it as a thing determinable by its distinguishing and inner predicates* nor the least justification to assume such an object.[41]

Arguably, Kant considers ideas such as the world as such to refer to transcendental objects insofar as they allow the understanding to unify its representations to the highest possible extent. This is the feature the concept of the world as such has in common with the 'something = X' at stake in the Transcendental Analytic. Unlike the latter, however, the world as such, qua subject matter of cosmology, is a transcendental object *that must be completely divorced from the element of sensibility*: it denotes a totality that itself "is no longer empirical, since it cannot be given in any experience" (A479). In this context, accordingly, the transcendental object is a something = X that must be posited in order to conceive of a manifold of purely intellectual determinations as a unity, but does not allow the human mind to turn this manifold into an object of cognition.

---

[41] A565–66/B593–94, emphasis mine, translation modified.

Similarly, Kant refers to the soul as the transcendental object of inner sense. On his account, rational psychology considers the activities carried out by the human mind to refer to an undetermined 'something' that itself does not appear:

> While it is true that one can purport to know that the thinking I, the soul (a name for *the transcendental object of inner sense*), is simple, this expression does not therefore have a use that pertains to real objects, and hence cannot extend our cognition in the least.[42]

Kant here suggests that we are allowed to conceive of the soul as simple as long as we keep in mind that we thereby do not determine an actual object. Nothing prevents us, in other words, from treating the soul as a noumenon in the negative sense of the term (cf. B307). Time and again, however, he emphasizes that the transcendental objects to which the ideas of reason refer should not be conceived as things of which the inner determinations can be known, which is precisely what he reproaches Leibniz and the Wolffians for.

Kant also considers the idea of God, traditionally conceived as the necessary cause of all things, to refer to a transcendental object:

> If the object is transcendental and thus in itself unknown, e.g., . . . whether there is a cause of all things taken together that is absolutely necessary, etc., then we should seek an object for our idea, which we can concede to be unknown to us, but not on that account impossible. (A478/B506)

In this case, Kant notes elsewhere, we have "only presupposed a something, of which we have no concept at all of what it is in itself (a merely transcendental object)." Yet we are allowed to conceive of this transcendental object as "intelligence" insofar as our study of nature requires that we presuppose "the systematic and purposive order" of the world (A697–98/B725–26).

As regards the passages discussed so far, Kant's use of the term 'transcendental object' is coherent and relatively straightforward. None of these passages presents the transcendental object as a thing capable of causing empirical representations, in other words, as an affecting object. However, it cannot be denied that Kant in a number of cases conceives of the transcendental object as *ground* or *cause* of that which appears. As was mentioned above, Allison adduces these passages to identify the transcendental object with the affecting object and, hence, to argue that Kant

---

[42] A360–61, emphasis mine, translation modified; cf. A478/B506, A682–83/B710–11.

affirms transcendental affection. The remainder of this section challenges the reading he represents by separating Kant's remarks on affecting objects from those that concern the intelligible ground or cause of appearances. On my reading, the latter only make sense in light of Kant's engagement with the Leibnizian tradition.

In the following passage from the Paralogisms, already quoted in Section 2, Kant regards the transcendental object as that which grounds appearances as well as the inner intuitions of ourselves:

> The transcendental object that grounds (*zum Grunde liegt*) both outer appearances and inner intuition is neither matter nor a thinking being in itself, but rather an unknown ground of those appearances. (A379–80)

As can be seen from the context, Kant's intention here is to deny metaphysics the right to posit the soul as a thinking thing and, hence, to conceive of all things on this model, that is, as monads capable of perception. Clearly, this is the position he attributes to Leibnizianism. At the same time, Kant denies materialism the right to posit that the human soul is a material thing and, more generally, that all things are material through and through. In this regard, the term 'transcendental object' has the same function as the term 'noumenon': it refers to the something = X that must be presupposed in the parts of metaphysics concerned with the object of outer and inner sense, but cannot itself be determined. As such, it acts as a gatekeeper rather than an actual cause of impressions (cf. A255/B310–11).

Kant's use of the term 'ground' in this context can be further clarified by examining some of his remarks on the soul qua object of rational psychology. Following Leibniz, Wolff's *German Metaphysics* attributes to the soul "a power to represent the world in accordance with the position of its body in the world" and conceives of this power as "the ground ... of all changeable states that occur in the soul."[43] Using similar terms, Kant notes that Leibniz considered "an internal power of representation" to ground the "outer relation" of monads as well as "the community of their states" (A267/B323).

In an already quoted passage, Kant stresses that it is by no means contradictory to attribute the capacity to produce representations to a something = X. Whereas it is possible to conceive of this 'something' as a material thing that affects our sensibility (A358), we might as well

---

[43] Wolff, GM 753–55, cf. Baumgarten, M 741–42. On this, see Blackwell (1961).

consider the something that grounds outer appearances as noumenon. This is, of course, what he took the Leibnizians to have done:

> [T]he something ... considered as noumenon (or better, as transcendental object) could at the same time also be the subject of thoughts.... But this something is not extended, not impenetrable, not composite, because these predicates pertain only to sensibility and its intuition.... Only the predicates of inner sense, representation and thought, do not contradict the something.[44]

This passage suggests that Kant did not oppose Leibniz's conception of monads as the non-sensible ground of their representations insofar as the human soul is concerned. We need to conceive of the soul in this way because otherwise it would be impossible, first, to conceive of the activities carried out by the human mind as a unity and, second, to safeguard the possibility of human freedom and morality.[45]

I take Kant to hold that this twofold requirement can only be met if it is possible to consider appearances *as such* to be grounded in a something = X that is not subject to the laws of nature. This is a task that Kant attributes to cosmology. A passage concerned with the thrust of the third cosmological conflict summarizes this point as follows:

> For if appearances are things in themselves, then freedom cannot be saved. In that case, nature is the complete and sufficiently determining cause of every occurrence.... If, on the other hand, appearances do not count for any more than ... mere representations ... , then they themselves must have grounds that are not appearances.... However, such an *intelligible cause* is not determined by appearances, even though its effects appear and so can be determined through other appearances.... The effect can therefore be considered as free in regard to its intelligible cause, and yet simultaneously, in regard to appearances, as their result according to the necessity of nature.[46]

---

[44] A358–59, emphasis mine, translation modified; cf. A265–66/B321–22.

[45] On this, see Ameriks (1982/2000: esp. 42–46, 189–233).

[46] A536–37/B564–65, emphasis mine, translation modified. Cf. Bxxviii–xxix, A538–39/B566–67, A541/B569, A613–14/B641–42; Prol, 4:345–46. Somewhat implicitly, Kant also uses the term "intelligible cause" with regard to the world as such qua transcendental object of cosmology. The latter, he writes, can be regarded as the "merely intelligible cause of appearances as such" to which we can attribute "the whole extent and connection of our possible perceptions" (A494–95/B522–23). In my view, the term 'cause' in this context refers to a ground that must be posited in thought rather than to something that actually has an effect on my sensibility. Without taking into account the context of this passage, Allison considers it to "stipulate how the affecting object must be conceived of in the transcendental account of affection" (72, cf. 460 n 24). Neither Allison nor Prauss addresses Kant's conception of particular transcendental objects in the Transcendental Dialectic.

Thus, on the condition that the something = X that used to be called the soul is not treated as an object of a priori cognition, Kant argues that we must hold on to it as the merely "intelligible ground" of "appearances and their connections."[47] In this context, he seeks to account for the capacity of human reason to act in accordance with the moral law. Clearly, as was pointed out at the beginning of this chapter, it does not make sense to treat the soul in this sense as a thing in itself that causes my sensibility to produce the representation of a rose or a house.

Kant notes that his remarks on the intelligible cause of appearances may seem "extremely subtle and obscure" but that this notion will be clarified by its application (A537/B565). Indeed, the first *Critique* can only carve out a space for the something = X, a space that must be provided with content, or objective reality, from a moral and ultimately teleological perspective. Insofar as we adopt the latter perspective, it is both warranted and necessary, according to Kant, to conceive of a supreme intelligence as cause of the world insofar as it can be grasped by the intellect, that is, of a *mundus intelligibilis*. One of Kant's unpublished notes, dated 1776–78, articulates this utterly Leibnizian view as follows:

> It is a necessary hypothesis of the theoretical and practical use of reason in the whole of our cognition, consequently in relation to all ends and an intelligible world, to assume that the sensible world is grounded on an intelligible world, a world of which the soul as intelligence is the subjective archetype, but of which an original intelligence is the cause; i.e., just as in us the *noumenon* is related to the appearances, so does this supreme intelligence relate to the *mundi intelligibilis*.[48]

Kant's remarks on the metaphysical discipline concerned with the object of outer sense, that is, nature, no less betray his debt to Leibniz. In the Architectonic, Kant deviates from Wolff's threefold division of special metaphysics by introducing a discipline, called rational physics, devoted to the purely rational principles of any investigation into nature qua object of outer sense (cf. A846/B874). Bridging the gap between general metaphysics and empirical physics, rational physics is said to deal with the determinations that must be attributed a priori to all material objects.[49] Although Kant hardly mentions this new part of his projected metaphysical system in the *Critique*, it seems to me that his shattered remarks on the concept of matter must be interpreted in this light.

---

[47] A545/B573, cf. A538/B566.   [48] R5109 (18:91).
[49] MFNS, 4:469–73. I elaborate on this issue in Chapter 8, especially Section 4.1.

As was to be expected, Kant rejects efforts on the part of metaphysics to specify the inner determinations of matter. Yet he affirms the necessity to distinguish matter, considered as appearance, from a something = X that must be assumed as its intelligible, yet indeterminable ground:

> [T]hat which the pure understanding conceives of as the inner core of matter (*das Innerliche der Materie*) in an absolute sense is a mere fancy . . . ; the transcendental object, however, which might be the ground of the appearance that we call matter, is a mere something, of which we would not understand what it is even if someone could tell us this. (A277/B333, cf. A366)

Kant holds that the understanding must limit sensibility to the realm of appearances in order to think "an object in itself, but only as a transcendental object, which is the cause of appearance (thus not itself appearance), and that cannot be thought of either as magnitude or as reality or as substance, etc." This thought, he adds, merely serves to represent "a space that we can fill neither through possible experience nor through the pure understanding" (A288/B344).

But why should we posit a merely intelligible transcendental object in the context of rational physics? Why should our investigations of nature not be concerned with appearances all the way down? The passages in the *Critique of Pure Reason* that refer to the merely intelligible cause of matter only make sense, it seems to me, if we assume – with Rae Langton – that Kant in this work does not reject Leibniz's monadology and his own early sketch of a physical monadology in all respects.[50]

---

[50] I agree with Langton (1998) that the *Critique of Pure Reason* departs from Leibniz by claiming that the relational properties of substances, that is, phenomena, cannot be reduced to the intrinsic properties of monads, not by abolishing the very idea of the latter (5, cf. 96, 109). Accordingly, she takes Kant to hold that we cannot get access to things in themselves by starting out from the way in which they appear to us in space and time (154–55, 161). Taking her bearings from Locke, on the other hand, Langton argues that, for Kant, the power of things to affect the human mind must be attributed to their external rather than intrinsic properties (139, 205). As I see it, her focus on Locke – as well as on early texts such as *Thoughts on the True Estimation of Living Forces* and the *Physical Monadology* – leads her to reduce Kant's discussions of the thing in itself in the *Critique of Pure Reason* to the view that matter is grounded in physical monads that affect us by means of their extrinsic properties but themselves cannot be known (99, cf. 77). This is to say that she ignores Kant's second-order reflection on the transcendental object at stake in the various parts of metaphysics. Unsurprisingly, Allison denounces Langton's "virtual identification of Kant's things in themselves with Leibnizian monads" (Allison 2004: 10). While I think she has a point, I concur with Allison that Kant does not attribute existence and causality to things in themselves considered as metaphysical entities, as Langton has it (18). Langton, for her part, challenges Allison's view that "Kant is not interested in making existence claims" and that "there are no unknowable entities in the picture" (Langton 1998: 8–9).

There is no doubt that Kant – following Wolff – rejected Leibniz's conception of matter as grounded in substances capable of perception. In his view, the ultimate subject matter of sense perception is the *substantia phaenomenon* that consists exclusively of relations (cf. A265/B321, A442/ B470). However, Kant does not reject the idea that outer appearances are grounded in a monad-like something = X at all. This can be gleaned from the *Metaphysical Foundations of Natural Science*, a treatise that Kant published in 1786 and that will be discussed in more detail in Chapter 8.

In line with the *Dissertation*, Kant in this work lauds Leibniz because of his distinction between appearances and things in themselves. His monadology, he writes,

> is a principally correct Platonic concept of the world ... , insofar as the latter is considered not as object of the senses, but as thing in itself, and is merely an object of the understanding, which, however, does indeed ground the appearances of the senses.[51]

In this context, Kant attributes to matter insofar as it can be thought not the capacity to represent the universe, but merely the interplay of complementary forces. These forces are said to be constitutive of the material object qua something that occupies a space and has the capacity to resist other material objects (4:511). The following passage neatly summarizes his position:

> The concept of matter is reduced to nothing but moving forces.. . . But who pretends to comprehend the possibility of the fundamental forces? They can be assumed only if they necessarily belong to a concept that is demonstrably fundamental ... (like that of the filling of space). These are repulsive forces and the attractive forces that counteract them as such.[52]

Taken together, these passages strongly suggest that Kant continued to accept a minimal and agnostic version of Leibniz's monadology: while he does not conceive of the primary forces constitutive of material objects on the model of the human mind, he seems to maintain that they are noumenal rather than phenomenal.[53] I agree with Ameriks, accordingly,

---

[51] MFNS, 4:507, cf. 504–5, 521.

[52] MFNS, 4:524. Kant here partly draws on the *Physical Monadology* from 1756. In this text, he attributes to monads the capacity to exert an activity that results in their occupation of a certain space (1:481, cf. 480). Even though Kant here already tries to disentangle the domains of geometry and metaphysics, his conception of physical monads introduces metaphysical considerations into the domain of physics in a way that he would later reject.

[53] As seen in Chapter 1, Section 5, Watkins (2006: 281–82, 288) attributes this agnosticism already to Wolff's account of monads. Hahmann (2008: 190) points out that Baumgarten considered the ultimate elements of matter to be themselves immaterial. Unlike Watkins, I hold that Kant's

that Kant's account of the forces constitutive of matter is on a par with his account of the cognitive and volitional powers of the human mind.[54]

Seen in this way, even Kant's remarks on the transcendental object considered as ground or cause of matter do not warrant the conclusion that he took things in themselves to affect the human mind. Rather, the purely formal notion of appearances grounded on something that itself does not appear allows Kant to consider each of the metaphysical disciplines outlined in the Architectonic to be concerned with a particular transcendental object, that is, with a noumenon that can and must be thought but cannot be turned into an object of cognition. More importantly, as seen, it allows him to account for the possibility of a merely intelligible cause and, hence, for the possibility of human freedom. Thus, whether the something = X assumed in the various parts of metaphysics is called a noumenon, a transcendental object, a thing in itself, or a monad, it remains "worlds apart" (A44/B61) from things considered as affecting objects.

6 Conclusion

This chapter has argued that the problems and inconsistencies attributed to Kant's account of the thing in itself arise on the flawed assumption that everything the *Critique of Pure Reason* has to say about objects, things in themselves, and transcendental objects belongs to a single, one-dimensional system. If one assumes, moreover, that this system ought to be able to deal with the issue of affection in a philosophical way, it becomes extremely difficult to resolve the alleged contradictions in the *Critique of Pure Reason*. Challenging past and present readings, I have tried to solve the problem by differentiating between the various contexts within which Kant treats of the thing in itself and, more specifically, by arguing that terms such as 'thing in itself,' 'transcendental object,' and 'noumenon' are pivotal to the second-order reflection on the condition of possibility of metaphysics at stake in the *Critique of Pure Reason* as a whole. However, while we have seen that and why Kant asserts that things in themselves

---

position is closer to that of his German predecessors in this regard than one might think. The fact that Kant used Newton's terms to refer to the primitive forces constitutive of matter as such does not necessarily entail that he considered these forces to be themselves physical. According to Edwards (2000), Kant's theory of matter in the *Physical Monadology* is not grounded in a concept of material substance or material force (122, cf. 51).

[54] See also B427–28. Drawing on this passage, Ameriks notes poignantly that, for Kant, "what underlies mind and what underlies matter can be said to be fundamentally alike in that they both must be immaterial" (Ameriks 1982/2000: 316).

cannot be known, I have not yet discussed the arguments he puts forward to reach his aim. As was mentioned in Chapter 2, Kant does so in the context of a thoroughgoing investigation into the a priori conditions that allow the human mind to establish something as an object of cognition at all. The two coming chapters analyze the complementary aspects of this investigation.

CHAPTER 5

The 1781 Transcendental Deduction of the Pure Concepts of the Understanding

1 Introduction

Kant presents the transcendental deduction as an investigation intended to establish how pure concepts such as substance and causality can "relate to objects a priori," in other words, to what extent their "pure use" is warranted.[1] He notes in the *Prolegomena* that he undertook this investigation "on behalf of metaphysics," and this in order to "settle" its very possibility (4:260).

However, it is not immediately clear how the various elements of the actual texts can be aligned with these descriptions of the overall aim of the transcendental deduction. Neither of its two versions mentions metaphysics. Moreover, many parts of the text seem to be concerned with a quite different issue, namely, the possibility of experience. These passages are clearly intended to argue, against Hume, that experience – considered as empirical cognition (B147) or a coherent whole of such cognitions (A237/B296) – would be impossible without the a priori rules contained in the categories.[2] Focusing on these passages, many commentators consider the core of the transcendental deduction to consist in Kant's account of the categories as conditions of possibility of experience. Among them is

---

[1] A85/B117. Similarly, Kant states that the main aim of the transcendental deduction consists in "establishing (*dartun*) and make comprehensible the objective validity" of the pure concepts of the understanding (Axvi, translation modified). As we will see, this aim is fully achieved only in the Schematism Chapter, which seeks to demonstrate that "the schemata of the concepts of pure understanding are the true and sole conditions under which the latter can be related to objects and, thus, acquire significance" (A145–46/B185). In the Transcendental Deduction and elsewhere, Kant tends to use the terms 'category' and 'pure concept of the understanding' interchangeably (cf. A85/B118). While I follow this usage, I hold that the latter term is often more adequate given Kant's own distinction between the two terms in the Schematism Chapter. This point will be discussed in Chapter 6, Section 4.

[2] Kant asks, for instance: "From whence could experience derive its certainty, if all the rules, according to which it proceeds, were always themselves empirical, and therefore contingent? Such rules could hardly be regarded as first principles" (B5, cf. A112).

Strawson, who claims in *The Bounds of Sense* that this chapter is above all concerned with "the necessity of a certain ... connectedness of experiences, just that connectedness which ... is involved by the employment of concepts of objects conceived of as together constituting an objective world."[3]

If Strawson is correct, then the transcendental deduction centers on the question as to how the human mind can produce a coherent system of empirical cognitions rather than on the question as to how it can obtain cognitions of objects at all. Yet accounts such as Strawson's have a hard time making sense of large swaths of the text, especially those that treat the various faculties involved in the cognition of objects. Strawson solves this problem by dismissing the allegedly psychological strand of the text as incoherent and superfluous, but this can hardly count as a satisfactory solution.[4]

The shortcomings of the approach represented by Strawson have been convincingly pointed out by various commentators and need not be discussed here.[5] Yet this is not to say that the alternatives put forward succeed in clarifying how each of the strands of the transcendental deduction contributes to its overarching aim – if the latter is discussed at all.[6] Even if the categories are put center stage, most commentators take the chapter to be concerned with the way the human mind produces empirical knowledge rather than with the limits within which metaphysics is possible.

Notable exceptions include Manfred Baum and Manfred Kuehn.[7] In various articles, Kuehn distinguishes between a positive and a negative

---

[3] Strawson (1966: 121, cf. 18).   [4] Strawson (1966: 13, 51).

[5] See, for example, Baum (1986: 175–81), Kuehn (1988), Carl (1989a: 125–26), Ameriks (2003), Wunsch (2007: 43–83). Whereas Baum denies that the *Critique* contains transcendental arguments, Ameriks takes issue with accounts of the transcendental deduction, by Strawson and others, that consider it to be a progressive transcendental argument intended to establish that the mind is capable of objective empirical knowledge or even "that there is an objective world" (280, cf. 286). Ameriks opposes this approach by claiming that Kant's aim is to prove the objective validity of the categories, a task that requires an account of categories as conditions of possibility of experience (281). I completely agree with Ameriks on this point. However, he takes the Transcendental Deduction to prove, by means of a regressive argument, that empirical knowledge "requires the universal validity of a number of a priori concepts" (281). No less than his opponents, he thus seems to assume that the chapter investigates the conditions of possibility of experience for their own sake.

[6] From the publication of Henrich's 1969 article on the structure of the transcendental deduction onward, most attention has gone to the formal aspects of Kant's text and argumentation, especially as regards the B-Deduction (see, for example, Thöle 1991; Barker 2001). Notwithstanding Kant's occasional use of the term 'proof' (A97), efforts such as Henrich's to reconstruct Kant's argument in logical terms are, in my opinion, not very fruitful, especially if based on unwarranted assumptions about its larger context.

[7] Baum (1986) considers the Transcendental Deduction to demonstrate "the possibility of synthetic a priori cognition of objects" and, by doing so, to decide the fate of metaphysics (8). Yet in his actual

strand of the text and takes most interpretations to focus one-sidedly on the former, namely, Kant's account of categories as conditions of possibility of experience. Critical of this trend, Kuehn prioritizes the negative strand – said to "usually drop out of sight very quickly" – which he takes to demonstrate, in accordance with Hume, that the use of reason is *restricted* to the realm of possible experience.[8] Thus, on Kuehn's account, Kant investigates the possibility of experience not for its own sake, but in order to support his criticism of Wolffian special metaphysics.

While I agree with the main tenet of his approach, Kuehn does not explain in any detail why Kant thought that the various strands of the transcendental deduction are necessary to achieve this negative aim. Moreover, what seems to drop out of sight in his own account is Kant's effort to establish, contra Hume, that the human mind is capable of a priori cognition of objects, albeit within certain limits.[9] What is still lacking, in my view, is an interpretation that satisfactorily relates the various strands of the text to the aim of the chapter as a whole.

The interpretation of the A-Deduction put forward in the present chapter seeks to achieve this task.[10] More specifically, it aims to clarify

---

commentary on the B-Deduction Baum takes the text to aim at justifying the use of categories with regard to *empirical* objects (64–65), a reductive reading shared by most commentators (see Zöller 1984: 158; Carl 1992: 41; Klemme 1996: 140; Allison 2015: 200). My view is more in line with Thöle (1991: 17–18), who considers the Transcendental Deduction to investigate the limits within which we can use categories at all, although I do not quite share his highly formal approach. Caimi (2001), focusing on the B-Deduction, rightly takes Kant's account of the categories as conditions of possibility of experience to be a subordinate step in the argument as a whole (48).

[8] Kuehn (1988: 48, cf. 55–56, 63), see also Kuehn (1983). Opposing Strawsonian readings, Kuehn considers the Transcendental Deduction to continue Hume's fight against dogmatism rather than to carry out an anti-skeptical attack on Hume (1988: 63, cf. 59–60). Hatfield (2003) frames the Transcendental Deduction along similar lines. However, while my reading agrees with his on a number of points, Hatfield does not closely examine the actual arguments of the A-Deduction and their mutual relations.

[9] Unlike in his 1988 article, Kuehn (1997) interprets the Transcendental Deduction from the viewpoint of Kant's engagement with Wolffianism. By arguing that the chapter is "also an argument against Hume, who denied the possibility of any a priori concepts" (246), Kuehn seems to want to correct his earlier emphasis on the continuity between Hume and Kant. His article contains an interesting discussion of elements of the Transcendental Deduction that are indebted to Wolff, Lambert, and Tetens, but it is unclear how he thinks his two approaches can be combined. In line with Kuehn, Dyck (2011) helpfully shows how the Transcendental Deduction deals with problems versions of which had already been addressed by Wolff and Tetens. I concur with Dyck's criticism of the anti-skeptical reading, but hold that the question as to how empirical concepts can possess objective reality on which he focuses is not very relevant to the Transcendental Deduction.

[10] Unless indicated otherwise, I will refer to the A-Deduction as the Transcendental Deduction. My decision to prioritize the first version stems from my attempt to read the *Critique of Pure Reason* in view of its origin rather than in view of the modifications the project underwent after 1781. I also hold that the subjective deduction, which is more prominent in the first version, is pivotal to the

how Kant's accounts of possible experience, the faculties involved in the cognition of objects, and the categories contribute to identifying the conditions under which synthetic a priori cognitions of objects can be obtained at all. Since this is the type of cognition that metaphysics purported to be capable of, the transcendental deduction is part and parcel of strand [2] of Kant's critique of metaphysics.

Yet shifting the focus from experience to the categories can be only a first step, for it has often been argued that Kant seeks to demonstrate the objective validity of the categories in order to overcome a Cartesian skepticism of sorts. Kant indeed invokes the hypothetical possibility of "empty" pure concepts, noting, for instance, that "appearances could . . . be so constituted that the understanding would not find them in accord with the conditions of its unity."[11] Referring to this passage, Allison claims that both versions of the transcendental deduction "are centrally concerned with eliminating this specter."[12] It is certainly true that Kant seeks to demonstrate that appearances can and must be subjected to the a priori rules contained in the categories and, thus, that the latter are not empty insofar as they are used for this purpose. Yet I hold that Kant's evocation of this "difficulty," as he calls it (A89/B122), plays a subordinate role in the

critical strand of the transcendental deduction as a whole. While I will refer to the B-Deduction occasionally, a comparison of the two versions falls outside the scope of this chapter. Evidently, the structure of the A-Deduction is not crystal clear, and, as many commentators have pointed out, various elements can be traced back to earlier stages in Kant's development. Yet this does not entail that the way they are brought together amounts to 'patchwork.' To use a different metaphor: a new machine can very well reuse and assemble elements developed earlier to solve certain aspects of a problem. Rather than stressing the disparity of the elements or labeling part of them as 'uncritical' to resolve alleged contradictions, I hold that the text is coherent, though partly repetitive, and that each of its strands can be shown to contribute to reaching the overall end of the chapter. See Carl (1989a) for a helpful discussion of ideas and analyses that Kant developed from 1772 onward and that found their way to the Transcendental Deduction. For an early criticism of the patchwork theory defended by Vaihinger and Kemp Smith, see Paton (1936a: 38–43, 328–32). In line with earlier proponents of the theory, Wolff (1963) mistakenly identifies some introductory passages as pre-critical, for instance, Kant's assertion at A85/B117 and elsewhere that categories "relate to objects completely a priori." Ignoring Kant's critical distinction between thinking and knowing, he takes this assertion to testify to the pre-critical doctrine that "we can know independent reality" (92). Yet asserting that the use of categories does not depend *on* experience by no means excludes, as Kant goes on to demonstrate, that this use (1) is required to conceive of something as an object and (2) is valid *with regard to* possible objects of experience alone.

[11] A90/B123. This passage stems from the first of the two preliminary sections of the Transcendental Deduction; cf. A111–12, A121. At a later stage, Kant explains that pure concepts are not empty insofar as they contain a synthesis that constitutes a condition of the form of experience (A220/B267).

[12] Allison (2015: 9, cf. 191, 200, 203–4, 434); see Dyck (2011). While Allison's commentary contains valuable analyses, I disagree with his assumption that the problem tackled in the Transcendental Deduction concerns the objective validity of empirical propositions (8). The passage at A90/B123 he cites is clearly concerned with the objective validity of the categories themselves.

transcendental deduction proper. For categories are *also* empty if used to acquire a priori cognitions of the world as such, the soul, and God, as Kant took the Wolffians to have done.[13] I hold that it is primarily because of *this* possibility – which was all but hypothetical in Kant's time – that the transcendental deduction seeks to determine to what extent the use of categories is warranted.

Accordingly, the second shift I propose is one from categories considered *as* conditions of possibility of experience to categories considered *as* elements of the a priori cognition of objects to which metaphysics aspired. In this regard, I will argue that Kant's discussion of the categories qua a priori rules for the constitution of objects of experience is embedded, as a means, in his less perspicuous investigation into categories qua a priori rules for the constitution of objects per se.

I will support this reading by reviewing, in Section 2, Kant's own account of the aims of the transcendental deduction in the *Critique of Pure Reason*. Drawing on Henrich and Proops, this section brings Kant's juridical metaphors to bear on his attempt to solve the dispute between Hume's attack on the possibility of purely intellectual cognition of objects and Wolff's defense of the latter. After discussing Kant's account of pure concepts in Section 3, Section 4 elaborates on what I take to be the negative and positive focal points of the transcendental deduction, namely, Kant's critical response to Wolff and Hume, respectively.[14] These sections pave the way for Sections 5 and 6, which treat the subjective and objective deductions in light of the question as to the conditions under which the use of categories is warranted. Finally, I argue that the outcome of the transcendental deduction denies the human mind the capacity to obtain synthetic a priori cognitions of particular objects but does not for that reason preclude metaphysics from being turned into a science.

2   The Aims of the Transcendental Deduction according to Kant

Kant's presentation of the main aim of the transcendental deduction concurs with his account of the aim of transcendental logic as a whole, namely, to determine "the origin, extension (*Umfang*), and objective validity" of the

---

[13] Thus, Kant writes in the Paralogisms that concepts such as substance or simplicity are "completely empty" if used in order to achieve knowledge of the soul (A400, cf. A486/514).

[14] Evidently, Kant's response to Hume is critical as well. Yet I will refer to this second strand of the transcendental deduction as positive – in line with one of Kant's own descriptions – because it defends the use of the categories against Hume's skepticism.

cognitions "by means of which we think objects completely a priori."[15] In the first Preface, Kant refers to the investigations carried out in the Transcendental Deduction as the most important ones known to him as regards our insight into the faculty "we call the understanding" and the "determination of the rules and boundaries of its use" (Axvi). Somewhat implicitly, he here distinguishes three tasks: (1) to analyze the understanding, (2) to identify the a priori rules by which its use is governed, and (3) to determine the domain within which these rules can rightfully be carried out. While task (2) is dealt with in the metaphysical deduction, tasks (1) and (3) can be said to be pursued in the transcendental deduction, more precisely in the strands to which Kant refers as the subjective and objective deductions (Axvii).

Kant considers the objective deduction, task (3), to belong essentially to his ends (Axvi) and to be his "primary concern" (Axvii). This strand of the transcendental deduction seeks to establish "the objective validity" of the concepts employed by the pure understanding (Axvi) and so to determine the limits within which these concepts can be used to obtain cognitions of objects.[16] Reiterating the question addressed to Herz in 1772, Kant introduces the chapter by noting that pure concepts

> always require a deduction of their entitlement (*Befugnis*), since ... one must know how these concepts can be related to objects that they do not obtain from any experience. I therefore call the explanation (*Erklärung*) of the way in which concepts can relate to objects a priori their transcendental deduction.[17]

---

[15] A57/B81, translation modified, cf. the section title at B6 and A10/B23. Because of Kant's reference to 'objective validity,' I take it that the term 'cognitions' here refers to 'concepts.' By and large, Kant distinguishes between *Umfang*, on the one hand, and *Grenze* or *Gültigkeit*, on the other (cf. Axii, A3/B7). I agree with Zöller (1984: 89) that the term *Umfang* refers to the *number* of cognitions by means of which we think objects completely a priori (cf. A72–73/B97). The only criterion that Kant uses to determine this extension is purity, that is, their origin in thought itself.

[16] In some contexts, the terms 'objective reality' and 'objective validity' are used interchangeably. According to the scholastic tradition, which Kant seems to accept in this regard, concepts possess objective reality insofar as they represent something (see Zöller 1984: 77–79). Kant also seems to draw on Wolff's distinction between definitions that concern the merely logical possibility of a concept and definitions that concern its real possibility (cf. A242n; Wolff, GL 35, 40). On this, see Kuehn (1997: 232–40). Unlike Kuehn, however, I hold that Kant introduces the term 'objective validity' because it allows him to deal more adequately with a question unheard of in the Wolffian tradition. Thus, he attributes 'objective validity' to cognitions if they refer "to objects that can be given to us in intuition" (B150–51, cf. A109, A155–56/B194–95). The term is most prominent in the context of Kant's deductions of pure intuitions, concepts, and ideas (cf. A28/B44, A35/B52, A87/B119–20, A111, A669/B697), and is the only one Kant uses when describing the task of transcendental philosophy (cf. A57/B81, A782/B810).

[17] A85/B117. Cf. Kant to Herz, February 21, 1772 (10:130). As was argued in Chapter 2, Section 5, this question can be traced back to Kant's reflection on the position defended in the *Inaugural Dissertation*.

Similarly, Kant notes with regard to these concepts that the transcendental deduction seeks to prove that "by means of them alone an object can be thought" (A97). Not by accident, these passages do not contain a reference to objects of experience.[18]

Kant takes for granted neither the accepted conception of categories nor that of the intellect. Somewhat inconspicuously, he argues that latter faculty requires a transcendental deduction as well: what needs to be clarified, he writes, is the capacity of the pure understanding to relate to objects at all (A97). Thus, it is clear that Kant conceived of the subjective and objective deductions as analogous at least with regard to their aims.

According to the first Preface, carrying out the subjective deduction requires that the pure understanding be treated as a faculty that itself rests on various other "cognitive powers" (Axvi–xvii). Arguably, this strand of the deduction consists in dissecting the Wolffian conception of the intellect into the complementary activities involved in it. While Kant notes that this analysis of the understanding is "of great importance" with regard to the "chief end" of the transcendental deduction (Axvii), he, unlike Tetens, did not regard it as an end in itself.[19] As I see it, Kant rather considered the subjective deduction to be important as a means toward settling the overall question as to "what and how much the understanding and reason can know free of all experience" (Axvii). Accordingly, as will be argued in Section 5, Kant's analysis of the empirical acts of apprehension, reproduction, and recognition should be given less weight than it has received in the literature.[20]

In a well-known essay, Dieter Henrich has argued that Kant's understanding of the task at stake in the transcendental deduction relies on the juridical meaning of the term 'deduction' common at the time.

[18] In line with mainstream approaches, Allais adduces the passage in which Kant characterizes the transcendental deduction as an "explanation of the way in which concepts can relate to objects a priori" (A85/B117) to support her claim that the transcendental deduction explains "how a priori concepts relate to *empirical objects* that are given in *empirical intuition*" (Allais 2015: 261, emphasis mine). She also surreptitiously replaces 'object' by 'empirical object' in relation to the passage at A97 quoted above (263).

[19] See R4900 and R4901 (dated 1776–78). Kant may well have exaggerated the differences, especially as regards Tetens's *On General Speculative Philosophy*, which was briefly discussed in Chapter 3, Section 6.

[20] This view is supported by the fact that Kant's account of the threefold synthesis is largely omitted from the B-Deduction. Given my focus on the problem of a priori cognition, I do not share Wolff's view that the subjective deduction seeks to prove the possibility of genuine empirical knowledge (see Wolff 1963: 111). As regards Kant's presentation of the subjective deduction in the first Preface, Wolff simply claims that Kant was wrong in considering this part to be less than essential, a view that obviously is not very convincing (80). See Bauer (2010: 440–41) for a discussion of this point.

A deduction in this sense is intended to justify potentially contested claims, especially concerning the possession or use of land. As Henrich explains, such a deduction requires that the alleged rights be traced back to *facta* by virtue of which they have been acquired.[21]

Intimating this model, Kant indeed presents the transcendental deduction as an investigation intended to determine whether the understanding's actual use of pure concepts is legitimate or not, that is, to answer the question *quid juris*.[22] While it is not always clear whether Kant uses the term 'deduction' to denote a proof or, in a weaker sense, a justification, I take the latter meaning to better convey the thrust of the text as a whole.[23]

In any case, a juridical deduction must rely on facts that may have been covered over. Although Kant does not spell out the role played by the question *quid facti* in the transcendental deduction, I assume that he took the latter to trace the purported right of the understanding to use pure concepts to indubitable *facta*, albeit, of course, not by empirical means.[24] What these facts are will be clarified in the sections that follow.

Kant's quasi-juridical framing of the transcendental deduction ties in rather well with his presentation of the *Critique of Pure Reason* as a court of justice in the first Preface, which was briefly discussed in Chapter 2.[25]

---

[21] Henrich (1989: 35, 39). Similarly, Kant notes with regard to pure reason's unfounded amplification of our cognition that we should not "accept even the clearest dogmatic proof of this sort of proposition without documents that could provide a well-grounded deduction" (A209–10/B255).

[22] "Jurists, when they speak of entitlements and claims, distinguish in a legal matter between the questions about what is lawful (*quid juris*) and that which concerns the fact (*quid facti*), and since they demand proof of both, they call the former, that which is to establish the entitlement or the legal claim, the deduction" (A84/B116).

[23] See A96–97. Kant refers to the transcendental deduction as a "clarification" at A85/B117 (cf. Axvii, B145, A233/B286). The *Critique of Practical Reason* presents this type of deduction as a "justification ... of the objective and universal validity" of a synthetic judgment a priori (5:46). I agree with the gist of Henrich's 1989 article, according to which "Kant's notion of a deduction is compatible with any kind of argumentation suitable for reaching the goal – namely, the justification of our claims to a priori knowledge" (Henrich 1989: 39).

[24] A86/B118, see Henrich (1989: 37) and especially Proops (2003: 211–19). Focusing on the question *quid juris* and the distinction between a transcendental and an empirical deduction, Kant does not offer a proper explanation of the question *quid facti* taken in a transcendental sense. Proops's article develops Henrich's account in various ways, especially by disentangling the various notions of a deduction that Kant appeals to, elaborating on the role played by *facta* in the first and second *Critique*, and clarifying the Metaphysical Deduction by pointing to the juridical undertones of terms such as 'birth certificate' and 'pedigree.' Henrich's and Proops's approach has the additional advantage of clarifying why so much of the actual text is taken up by analyses that do not seem to pertain to the *quid juris* question announced at the beginning: they work their way toward *facta* that any answer to the juridical question requires.

[25] See Chapter 2, Section 6. Henrich does not discuss this point. Proops (2003: 211) does, but without mentioning that the act of providing a deduction is different from, and subordinate to, the ruling carried out by a judge. Moreover, Kant's appeal to the juridical notion of a deduction does not entail that he conceived of the transcendental deduction on this model alone.

Adopting the position of an impartial judge, pure reason carries out the critique at stake in the *Critique of Pure Reason* as a whole. It does so in order to assess its first-order use of categories in metaphysics, an inquiry that according to Kant had become necessary because of Hume's thoroughgoing attack on the objective validity of the concept of causality.[26]

Put briefly, Hume had argued that what is commonly called causality is nothing but a way in which the human mind, drawing on experience and imagination rather than the intellect, establishes connections between things or events that succeed one another. It follows from this analysis that the a priori cognition of objects at stake in metaphysics is impossible.[27] For Kant, however, Hume's position is not an endpoint (cf. A760–61/B787–88). With reference to Hume, he notes in the *Prolegomena* that the idea of a transcendental deduction, undertaken "to settle the possibility of metaphysics," had never "occurred to anyone but him, even though everyone confidently made use of these concepts without asking what their objective validity is based on."[28] Thus, Kant takes Hume's charge to entail the demand that metaphysics justify its use of pure concepts by means of a deduction, in other words, that it answer the question as to "how subjective conditions of thinking should have objective validity" (A89–90/B122).

Evidently, the verdict reached in the Transcendental Deduction is more nuanced than Hume's. On the one hand, Kant grants the Humean complainant that categories lack objective validity if they are used to determine things such as the soul or God. On the other hand, he grants the Wolffian defendant that synthetic a priori cognition of objects is possible under certain conditions.[29]

---

[26] Kant notes in the *Prolegomena* that Hume's question "was not, whether the concept of cause is right, useful, and, with respect to all cognition of nature, indispensable," but "rather whether it is thought through reason a priori, and in this way has an inner truth independent of all experience, and therefore *also a much more widely extended use which is not limited merely to objects of experience*" (4:258–59, emphasis mine, cf. CPrR, 5:50). In a similar vein, but without mentioning Hume, Henrich (1989: 38) considers the Transcendental Deduction to respond to the skeptic's attack on "the claim of reason to be in possession of a priori knowledge of objects." In his *Discursus praeliminaris*, Christian Wolff compares philosophers to judges who seek to determine who is right and wrong in philosophical controversies (DP 52–53). In the specific controversy that concerns Kant, obviously, Wolff occupies one of the contrary positions rather than that of an impartial judge.

[27] Cf. A760/B788; Prol, 4:257–58. On this, see De Boer (2019a). Like Kuehn (1988), Thöle (1991) notes that Kant took Hume first and foremost to be skeptical of metaphysics (27, cf. 28–35).

[28] Prol, 4:260; cf. A764/B792.

[29] Similarly, Kant writes with regard to the B-Deduction that it aims to steer human reason between two cliffs, namely, "attempts at cognitions that go far beyond the boundary of all experience" and, on the other hand, a thoroughgoing skepticism according to which "what is generally held to be

Kant's various presentations of the aim of the transcendental deduction can easily be aligned with the juridical metaphor thus understood. At an important juncture of the text, Kant takes himself to have shown "what we really wanted to know," namely, that categories have a priori objective validity because they "allow thought to refer appearances to objects at all" (A111). Summarizing the result of the transcendental deduction, finally, Kant writes that it

> did not have to accomplish more ... than to make comprehensible this relation of the understanding to sensibility and, by means of the latter, to all objects of experience, hence to make comprehensible *the objective validity of its pure a priori concepts*, and thereby determine *their origin and truth*. (A128, emphasis mine)

These passages strongly suggest that Kant considered the investigation into the conditions of possibility of experience as a means required to answer the question concerning the warranted use of the categories rather than as an end in itself. The same holds true of the subjective deduction: in order to establish to what extent the pure understanding can relate to objects at all, we must consider the faculty not just in view of the "cognitive powers" on which it rests (Axvi–xvii), but more specifically in view of the "subjective sources" that make experience possible (A97–98).

This reading is somewhat complicated by Kant's remarks on the subject in a long note appended to the Preface of the *Metaphysical Foundations of Natural Science* (1786). Responding to his critics, Kant here considers the transcendental deduction to have demonstrated that categories "obtain objects and become cognitions" only insofar as they are applied to intuitions.[30] This description is in line with the passages discussed so far. He points out, however, that the chapter also pursued a second aim, namely, to answer "the question as to *how* categories make ... experience possible."[31] This task is said to be "merely useful" rather than "necessary."[32]

---

reason" is "a deception of our faculty of cognition" (B128). In the *Critique of Practical Reason*, Kant likewise considers the Transcendental Deduction to block "extravagant pretensions and theories of the supersensible to which we can see no end" (5:141).

30 MFNS, 4:474n. Kant here specifically responds to Schultz's anonymous review of Ulrich's *Institutiones Logicae et Metaphysicae*, both of which had raised doubts about the Transcendental Deduction. A detailed discussion of these remarks falls outside the scope of this chapter. On this, see Thöle (1991: 274–80) and Kuehn (2001: 321–22).

31 MFNS, 4:474n, emphasis in the original.

32 "[A]lthough the answer to the question how the categories make such experience possible is important enough for completing the deduction where possible, with respect to the principal end of the system, namely, the determination of the limits of pure reason, it is in no way necessary, but merely useful" (MFNS, 4:474n, translation modified).

In my view, this subordinate aim is not clearly identified and elaborated in the transcendental deduction itself. Undoubtedly, Kant's remark on the subordinate nature of this aim stems from his attempt to rebut his critics. Thus, he suggests, critics who are unsatisfied with his account of how exactly categories make empirical cognitions possible need not for that matter reject the deduction's main achievement.

My discussion so far has brought out that Kant considered the transcendental deduction to pursue various coordinated aims at once (see Figure 3). For now, I believe we can infer from Kant's remarks that he considered the main aim of the chapter to consist in answering the question concerning the objective validity or warranted use of the categories (1). This aim has a positive and a negative side: the text seeks to establish, against Hume, that categories possess objective validity insofar as they are used with regard to possible objects of experience (1a) and, against Wolffian special metaphysics, that their use in judgments about the soul and God is unwarranted (1b).

Achieving aim (1a) requires that one demonstrate, as a means, *that* experience would be impossible without the categories. This task is basically achieved in the *objective deduction*. Insofar as the categories are concerned, however, the transcendental deduction also purports to clarify *how* categories allow the human mind to obtain empirical knowledge. This task might be considered its subordinate aim (2).

Finally, dissecting the faculty that used to be called the intellect, the *subjective deduction* contributes to the positive aim of the chapter by demonstrating that the pure understanding can produce objects of cognition if the unity it produces rests on the synthetic activity carried out by pure imagination, which is the case insofar as this activity is geared toward appearances. The subjective deduction contributes to the negative aim of the transcendental deduction, on the other hand, by demonstrating that, *for this very reason*, the pure understanding is not warranted to use categories with regard to anything whatsoever (1b). Kant seems to consider this negative result to follow immediately from the arguments by means of which the qualified use of categories is justified. Despite the parallels between the objective and subjective deductions mentioned above, it seems to me that Kant assigns this negative task primarily and perhaps even exclusively to the latter.

One of the reasons that the Transcendental Deduction is such a daunting text is that Kant does not make it very clear how each of its elements is supposed to contribute to the overall solution. But at least we can now frame the text in view of Kant's multifaceted effort to determine

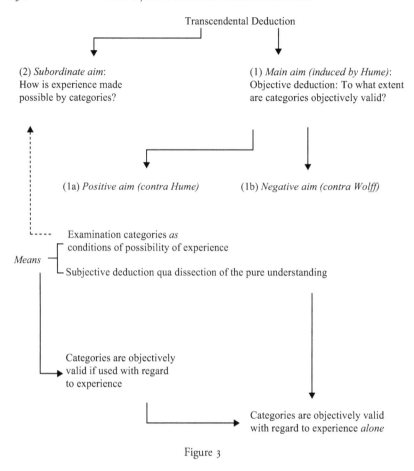

Figure 3

the conditions under which the a priori cognition of objects aspired to by metaphysics is possible. Abstracting as much as possible from the subordinate aim of the transcendental deduction, the sections that follow consider the various strands of the text in this light. The first strand to be examined is Kant's innovative understanding of pure concepts.

3   Pure Concepts of the Understanding

Kant's discussion of the categories in the Transcendental Deduction presupposes the result of the metaphysical deduction, which can be said to establish the first relevant *factum*, namely, the "birth certificate" that proves the a priori origin of the categories.[33] However, this pedigree does not tell us whether the understanding is justified in using categories to obtain a priori knowledge of objects. As was noted in the previous section, Kant calls the transcendental deduction an "explanation of the way in which concepts can relate to objects a priori" (A85/B117). It is crucial, in my opinion, that he leaves open whether these objects are objects of experience or objects of purely intellectual cognition, because the task is precisely to determine whether, or to which extent, the use of pure concepts is justified at all.[34]

Carrying out this task requires, among other things, a new and critical account of what a concept is. According to Wolffian general logic, concepts are representations of things or events in thought.[35] This is to say that general logic, on Kant's account, treats the understanding by abstracting from the "difference between the objects to which it may be directed" (A52/B76). While Kant does not take issue with this approach as such, he holds that it does not allow metaphysics adequately to reflect on its use of concepts such as substance and causality and, hence, to limit said use to the realm of experience.

Kant himself sometimes refers to categories as ontological predicates, thus highlighting the common ground of his approach and that of the Wolffians.[36] Yet in most cases he avoids the term, and this for good reasons: considering categories as determinations of things precludes two of the questions that Kant, following Hume, raises in the Transcendental Analytic, namely, first, what it means to use a category at all and, second, under which conditions that use results in the cognition of an object.

If categories are not to be understood as ontological predicates, how *are* they to be understood? A crucial step in Kant's argument consists in conceiving of the understanding as a faculty of rules (A126) and of a concept, as far as its form is concerned, as "something . . . that serves as a rule."[37] Thus, Kant proposes that we regard the concept of a triangle as a rule that tells us to unify a manifold of lines in a particular manner and, in this way, lets us "think of a triangle as an object" (A105). Similarly, the empirical concept of a dog can be considered a rule that tells us to conceive

---

[33] A86/B119; see Proops (2003: 220).   [34] See Chapter 2, Section 5.
[35] Wolff, GL 1.4. See Kuehn (1997). In his illuminating article, mentioned above, Kuehn examines Kant's employment of Wolffian concepts and ideas in the Transcendental Deduction, including the view that a concept is possible if it refers to a possible object (241). Evidently, this is not to say that the arguments Kant puts forward in this chapter are themslves indebted to Wolff.
[36] Prol, 4:358; CJ, 5:181.
[37] A106, cf. A55/B80, A135, B145. On this, see Longuenesse (1998: 48–52).

of a particular manifold of representations – including 'barking' and 'tail-wagging' – as a unity and, hence, to conceive of this unity *as* a unity.[38] Without such rules it would be impossible to refer our intuitions to an object (A106).

Implicitly drawing on such examples, Kant maintains that pure concepts of the understanding, or categories, are nothing but a priori rules for the unification of a manifold of representations. These concepts are said to represent a priori syntheses, that is, acts "of putting different representations together and comprehending their manifoldness in one cognition."[39] Seen in this way, the concept of causality represents the a priori rule that tells the mind, as it were, to unify a sequence of representations in such a way that one of them is posited as necessarily preceding another. By dint of this rule, the mind can conceive of any object whatsoever – the transcendental object – as cause and effect of something else (cf. A198/B243) and, hence, become conscious of a given manifold of representations *as a unity*. Accordingly, Kant conceives of pure concepts as "concepts of an object as such."[40] The concept of causality, he notes,

> is nothing other than a synthesis (of that which follows in the temporal series with other appearances) according to concepts; and without such unity, which has its rule a priori, and which subjects appearances to itself, thoroughgoing and universal, hence necessary unity of consciousness would not be encountered in the manifold perceptions. (A112, cf. A113)

Clearly, this feature of pure concepts cannot be revealed from the standpoint of general logic, according to which cognition is a matter of connecting a subject and predicate or of subsuming representations under concepts (cf. A79/B105, B140–41). Seen from the standpoint of transcendental logic, by contrast, cognition is rather a matter of establishing unity among a manifold of representations so as to turn them into objects of cognition.[41] As seen, Kant holds that cognition in this sense relies on the a

---

[38] Kant uses the example of the dog in the context of the Schematism Chapter (A141/B180). Both examples will be considered in more detail in the following chapter.

[39] A77/B103, cf. A78/B104. Kant considers the empirical act of synthesis to consist in going through, taking up, and combining a manifold of representations in a particular way (A77/B103). Contrary to Martin (2006: 44–47), I hold that Kant on the whole uses the term 'synthesis' to denote this threefold act rather than the formal act of combining subject and predicate in a judgment per se.

[40] A93/B126, cf. A88/B120, A109, B166n.

[41] B141. While Kant's account of how we bring about empirical concepts and judgments in his logic lectures is certainly illuminating in some respects, I hold that the approach he adopts there should be sharply distinguished from the perspective of transcendental logic adopted in the *Critique*. Accordingly, I consider his discussion of the logical forms of judgment in the Metaphysical Deduction to be merely a first stepping-stone toward his account of the categories qua a priori

priori rules represented by pure concepts such as causality. However, it does not seem to follow from this account that such concepts possess objective validity by dint of being used with regard to a manifold of intuitions. This is where experience comes in.

4   Possible Experience

In the section that prepares the transcendental deduction proper, Kant notes that the transcendental deduction of all a priori concepts "has a principle toward which the entire investigation must be directed, namely, that they must be conceived *as* a priori conditions of the possibility of experience" (A94/B126, emphasis mine). Evidently, this point is well known. Yet I would contend that Kant's motive for conceiving of pure concepts in this way extends far beyond the question as to how the human mind produces empirical cognitions. Even though the text is not always clear in this respect, I hold that Kant primarily adopts this stance because examining the empirical use of pure concepts allows him to reveal *what it means to use pure concepts at all.* Accordingly, I consider the passage just cited to refer to a proposal or starting point rather than to the result of an argument.

This meaning of the passage is obscured, however, by passages in its vicinity that anticipate the actual result of the transcendental deduction. As seen, Kant takes this inquiry to establish that the use of pure concepts is justified insofar as they, in their capacity of a priori rules, allow the human mind to turn sensible representations into objects of cognition at all. Insofar as pure concepts are employed for this purpose, they refer to objects and, thus, are not empty (cf. A220/B267). In this regard, Kant states that

> the objective validity of the categories, as a priori concepts, rests on the fact (*wird darauf beruhen*) that *through them alone* experience is possible (as far as the form of thinking is concerned).[42]

In terms of Kant's juridical metaphor, the possibility of experience might be considered a *factum*, or indisputable fact, on the basis of which the

---

rules for the unification of representations. It is true that this reading seems to be undermined by Kant's identification of the categories with the logical forms of judgment in the B-Deduction (B143). However, Kant's account of what a judgment achieves in this context – objective unity of apperception (B141) – is part and parcel of transcendental logic. In this regard, my reading differs substantially from Longuenesse's (cf. Longuenesse 1998: 9, 11, 59).

[42] A93/B126, emphasis mine, cf. A111, A128. The latter passages suggests that establishing the objective validity of the categories is the sole aim of the transcendental deduction. On my reading, as said, this is somewhat misleading on Kant's part and at odds with passages that focus on the *limits* of this validity.

judge can reject the Humean claim that pure concepts lack any objective validity whatsoever.[43]

However, establishing this second *factum* – the positive aim of the transcendental deduction – represents just one side of the medal, for Kant in the same section also anticipates the conclusion that pure concepts possess objective validity in this case *alone*:

> [P]ure a priori concepts ... must ... be strictly a priori conditions for a possible experience, as that *alone* on which their objective reality can rest.[44]

While these two passages nicely capture the positive and negative sides of the main aim of the transcendental deduction, in the sections that follow the negative aim is overshadowed by the positive one and, as a result, has received little attention.[45]

Yet Kant refers to this negative aim on various occasions. Somewhat implicitly, he notes, for example, that categories are "nothing other than the conditions of thinking in a possible experience" (A111). The Schematism Chapter, for its part, summarizes the result of the transcendental deduction as follows:

> After what has been shown in the deduction of the categories, hopefully no one will be in doubt about how to decide the question, whether these pure concepts ... , as conditions of a possible experience, relate a priori solely to appearances, or whether, as conditions of the possibility of things in general, they can be extended to objects in themselves. (A139/B178, cf. A253)

In the B-Deduction, Kant makes a claim that he calls "of the greatest importance," since it "determines the boundaries of the use of the pure concepts of the understanding in regard to objects" (B148). The claim is that

---

[43] Proops (2003) identifies the a priori origin of the categories established in the Metaphysical Deduction as *factum* (220–24). I agree that the latter is part of the deduction in a broad sense (cf. CPrR, 5:141), but I do not think it provides a sufficient ground of the ruling in which the transcendental deduction results.

[44] A95, emphasis mine, translation modified. Tellingly, Guyer and Wood take 'ihre objektive Realität' to refer to experience. By, accordingly, translating 'ihre' as 'it,' the passage appears to concern the nature of experience. However, 'objective reality' can refer only to 'concepts' here: throughout the transcendental deduction, it is their reality that is at stake.

[45] As was mentioned above, this is pointed out by Kuehn (1988). Kant's first explicit discussion of the objective validity of pure concepts is in a note dated 1772–73, which is around the time of his letter to Herz of February 21, 1772. This discussion seems to target the Wolffians: "If certain concepts in us do not contain anything other than that by means of which all experiences are possible on our part, then they can be asserted a priori prior to experience and yet with complete validity for everything that may ever come before us. In that case, to be sure, *they are not valid of things as such*, but yet of everything that can ever be given to us through experience" (R4634, 17:618, emphasis mine; cited in Carl 1989b: 7–8).

categories do not afford us cognition of things ... *except through* their possible application to empirical intuition.... [They] consequently have no other use for the cognition of things *except insofar* as the latter are taken as objects of possible experience.[46]

The latter two passages make it particularly clear that the transcendental deduction also targets the assumption of the Wolffians that things can be known by means of the intellect alone, in other words, that the use of pure concepts is warranted in all cases.

Yet the A-Deduction poses two related problems to this reading. First, Kant here does not explicitly distinguish what I have called the positive and negative elements of the main aim of the transcendental deduction. Second, he does not seem to offer a separate argument as to why the use of pure concepts ought to be *restricted* to the realm of possible experience: it seems that the Wolffians could easily maintain that the pure understanding – apart from its role in experience – can carry out the unification of representations all by itself and, accordingly, that metaphysics is licensed to determine purely intellectual objects such as the soul or God as well.

In order to clarify Kant's argument against the Wolffians, the next section examines the subjective deduction – concerned with the cognitive activities carried out by the human mind a priori – in some detail. In accordance with its subject matter, this section abstracts from Kant's account of the categories. Turning to the objective deduction, Section 6 will examine the way in which Kant brings the result of the subjective deduction to bear on the question concerning the validity of the categories and, thus, on the main task of the transcendental deduction as a whole.

5   Kant's Dissection of the Pure Understanding

Kant's distinction between a subjective and objective deduction in the first Preface to the *Critique of Pure Reason* is hard to nail down and has generated much debate.[47] Yet the task he attributes to the subjective deduction is relatively straightforward. As seen, this strand of the chapter is said to investigate "the powers of cognition" on which "the pure understanding ... itself rests" (Axvii). It is much less clear, however, what can be gained from this investigation as regards the main aim of the transcendental deduction. Why does the objective deduction not suffice to reach this aim? Indeed, Kant states at one point that

---

[46] B147–48, emphasis mine, cf. B166, B288–89, B294; MFNS, 4: 474n.
[47] See Carl (1992: 47–54). I discuss some of the literature below.

> [i]t is already a sufficient deduction of [the categories], and justification of their objective validity, if we can prove that by means of them alone an object can be thought.[48]

Thus, strictly speaking, the deduction of the categories merely consists in establishing that the latter can and must be used to conceive of something as an object at all.

I take Kant to hold, however, that this objective deduction cannot be achieved without scrutinizing the faculty that uses pure concepts with the aim of obtaining knowledge of objects. Thus, the following passage, implicitly concerned with the subjective deduction, maintains that

> the understanding itself, as a faculty of cognition that purports to be related to objects (*das sich auf Objekte beziehen soll*), requires that the possibility of this relation be elucidated as well. (A97, translation modified)

At first sight, the subjective deduction seems to be aimed at Hume rather than the Wolffians. As I hope to show in what follows, however, Kant considered his investigation into the pure understanding to entail that the latter can carry out its unifying activity with regard to possible objects of experience *alone*. Given this result, the subjective deduction contributes importantly to what I have called the negative aim of the transcendental deduction as a whole.

Kant's dissection of the pure understanding is no less guided by the juridical model discussed above than his examination of the categories. More specifically, I hold that the subjective deduction seeks to identify a third *factum*, namely, the birth certificate that establishes the pedigree of the pure understanding itself. This investigation reveals that this faculty, while pure, partly originates in transcendental imagination and therefore is not purely intellectual.[49] This *factum* provides the ground of the ruling that grants the pure understanding the right to think objects by means of categories, yet only insofar as these objects are possible objects of experience.

But how does Kant proceed to reveal this *factum*? As is well known, he distinguishes three original "capacities or faculties of the soul" (A94) or "sources of cognition" (A97, cf. A125–26), arguing that they "make

---

[48] A96–97, cf. A93/B125. This remark ties in with Kant's understanding of pure concepts as "concepts of an object as such" mentioned above (A93/B126). Kant here abstracts from the question as to whether conceiving of something as an object requires more than the use of categories. According to a later passage, doing so requires that the latter are related to intuitions (A95).

[49] See Prol, 4: 257–58. Kant can be said to follow Hume by revealing the role of the imagination in cognitive activities considered to be purely intellectual, but to depart from Hume by abstracting from their empirical guises.

possible even the understanding and, through the latter, all experience" (A97–98). Thus, just as he did in the case of the categories, Kant starts by examining the pure understanding in view of its involvement in the production of empirical cognitions.

However, as was mentioned above, this examination is a means rather than an end in itself. In order to expose which original faculties are involved in the pure thought of an object, Kant, I take it, proceeds in three steps, none of which is clearly delineated in the text and for that reason should perhaps rather be referred to as elements. Any which way, I would contend that these steps correspond to the three following questions:

[1]   Which empirical faculties are required to produce objects of experience?
[2]   Which pure faculties are required to produce objects of experience?
[3]   Which pure faculties are required to produce objects of thought as such?

Put briefly, in step [1], Kant draws on the empirical psychology of Locke, Wolff, Hume, and Tetens.[50] However, unlike them, as was pointed out above, Kant seeks to examine the faculties of the human mind insofar as they are involved in the *pure* thought of an object. In step [2], he identifies these pure faculties and considers them in view of their a priori contribution to empirical cognition. In step [3], finally, he considers these very faculties in view of their a priori contribution to the production of objects of thought as such, concluding that this production rests necessarily on the transcendental imagination.

Insofar as step [3] deals with the faculties rather than the categories, it belongs to the subjective deduction. However, insofar as this step is part of Kant's effort to determine "what and how much" the understanding can know independently of experience (Axvii), it is geared toward the question at stake in the objective deduction, namely, to determine under which conditions the use of categories is warranted. For this reason, the two lines of argument arguably begin to converge in step [3].[51] The remainder of the present section discusses steps [1]–[3].

---

[50]   See Chapter 1, Section 3, for an indication of the topics covered by Wolff's empirical psychology.
[51]   Since parts of the text combine various steps, it is difficult to assign all passages or sections to one of them. But it seems clear to me, at least, that A84–97 is merely preparatory. Kant announces the task of the subjective deduction at A97 and seems to carry it out at A98–110. However, since the largest part of the section on recognition (A104–10) provides an introductory account of transcendental apperception, the transcendental unity of apperception, and the transcendental object, the

[1] Kant begins the subjective deduction by considering the various syntheses carried out by the human mind insofar as they contribute to empirical cognition, namely, the apprehension of a manifold of successive representations, the reproduction of the unity produced by apprehension, and the recognition of the represented unity *as* unity by means of concepts (A97, cf. A98–103). Even though Kant's actual treatment of the three syntheses abstracts from the difference between a priori and empirical cognition, the text strongly suggests that he took the latter as his model. This is confirmed by the remark that "the synthesis of apprehension must also be exercised a priori, i.e., in regard to representations that are not empirical."[52]

Kant's investigation reveals that these three syntheses stem from two basic capacities, faculties, or modes of spontaneity, namely, imagination, involved in apprehension and reproduction, and apperception considered as the capacity to explicitly conceive of a unity *as* unity. This result comes out clearly only in the section that according to Kant summarizes his preceding analyses. He here writes that the possibility of experience

subjective approach here seems to slide quickly into the objective one (see Paton 1936a: 356; Klemme 1996: 153). At A110, Kant turns to a discussion of the categories, i.e., to the objective deduction. The title of this subsection – "Provisional Explanation of the Possibility of the Categories as A Priori Cognitions" – suggests that it contains only part of the objective deduction. It differs from the second part by presenting the categories as concepts constitutive of the form of experience (A111). What I refer to as step [3] is carried out in essence at A115–18, where Kant deals with transcendental apperception and imagination. Although this discussion is devoted to faculties, it considers the understanding in view of its capacity to obtain a priori cognition of objects and so might be considered to feed into the objective deduction. At A119, without starting a new section, Kant starts bringing together his analysis of the understanding with that of the categories, but apart from referring to rules a few times he does not explicitly do so until A125. From A125 to A128, elements of Kant's earlier account of the faculties are inserted into a discussion of the categories (and rules and laws more generally) and so subordinated to what I take to be the second part of the objective deduction proper, which ends toward the end of A128. As regards debates on this issue, some authors take the subjective deduction to span from A98 to A114 (cf. Thöle 1991: 41), which is highly implausible given the title of section 4. Carl (1992: 53–54), among others, mistakes A92–93 for the objective deduction itself and infers that the remainder is largely devoted to the subjective deduction. I take my own proposal to solve the problem to which these commentators respond in different ways by arguing that not everything Kant states about the faculties is part of the subjective deduction. More convincingly than the authors mentioned so far, Klemme (1996: 153–56) takes the subjective deduction to end at A104 and the objective deduction to take up the remainder of the text (without being very specific). While Allison (2015) rightly considers the subjective deduction to be indispensible to the objective deduction (199), his actual discussion of the A-Deduction, following Kant, does not specify which parts he takes to be concerned with the former. I would like to thank Fernando Moledo for his helpful comments on an earlier version of my interpretation on this point.

[52] A99. While Kant here refers to the "pure synthesis" constitutive of space and time (A100), I take it that he considers this pure version to underlie empirical apprehension as well. In relation to the empirical synthesis of reproduction, Kant states explicitly that it is grounded in a transcendental synthesis carried out by the imagination (A101–2).

rests on three subjective sources of cognition: sense, imagination, and apperception. . . . *Sense* represents the appearances empirically in perception, the *imagination* represents them in association (and reproduction), and *apperception* represents them in the empirical consciousness of the identity of these reproductive representations with the appearances through which they were given, hence in recognition. (A115)

Since the act of apprehension presupposes intuition, Kant here identifies sense as a third basic faculty. However, the transcendental deduction is concerned with the contribution of *thought* to the constitution of objects. For that reason, he mentions sense occasionally – causing some confusion – but without treating it properly (cf. A94–95).

Sensibility apart, the three syntheses are assigned to only two faculties. In the passage just quoted, Kant does this by considering the imagination to be involved in both the association of representations called apprehension and the reproduction of representations thus apprehended (cf. A102). The act of recognition, for its part, consists in identifying something that I actually see (say, a dog-like figure) with similar representations (other dog-like figures) by means of a concept or judgment. Carrying out this act establishes the sensible manifold as a unity of which I am aware *as* a unity, that is, *as* an object.

[2] In this step, Kant shifts the focus from the imagination and apperception as such to their pure or transcendental instances. From this point onward, he disregards their involvement in empirical syntheses, because all we need to retain from step [1] is the discussion of the faculties required to carry them out.[53] Actually, this shift is carried out, or referred to, at various points throughout the text. Yet for the sake of clarity I will treat it as a separate systematic step.

---

[53] In the B-Deduction, Kant writes that "the reproductive imagination, whose synthesis is subject solely to empirical laws, namely those of association, . . . contributes nothing to the explanation of the possibility of cognition a priori, and on that account belongs not in transcendental philosophy but in psychology" (B152). On my reading, the A-Deduction does not discuss the empirical syntheses for their own sake either, but only to direct our attention to the a priori faculties on which they rest, that is, to pure imagination and apperception. By contrast, Longuenesse (1998) considers the A-Deduction to be most relevant because of its initial account of the threefold synthesis and, confusingly, considers the latter to contain Kant's examination of the pure understanding itself. Accordingly, she takes the two versions of the transcendental deduction to differ substantially (cf. 57–58). Offering a detailed interpretation of Kant's account of the imagination in the A-Deduction, Wunsch (2007) likewise takes the threefold synthesis as his guiding thread. Even though he distinguishes between the empirical syntheses and the transcendental capacities underlying them (124–30), his account deals exclusively with the contribution of these capacities to empirical cognition (cf. 129). Bauer (2010) not only completely ignores Kant's distinction between the empirical and pure use of the faculties, but largely draws on passages where Kant purports to worry about the plausibility of his own claims.

Kant introduces this step by noting that the threefold synthesis discussed above offers "a clue (*eine Leitung*) that leads toward three subjective sources of cognition" (A97). We can discover the latter because, for Kant, any empirical act is made possible by a pure act that possesses similar features. In a part of the passage at A115 not quoted above, Kant refers to the principle of this step in the following way:

> Each of these [sources of cognition] can be considered empirically, namely in application to given appearances, but they are also elements or grounds a priori that make this empirical use itself possible. (A115, cf. 97)

Similarly, Kant writes that empirical cognition rests on three pure sources of cognition, namely, pure intuition, imagination, and apperception:

> Now pure intuition grounds the totality of perception a priori . . . , the pure synthesis of the imagination grounds association a priori; and pure apperception, that is, the thoroughgoing identity of oneself in all possible representations, grounds empirical consciousness a priori. (A115–16, cf. A94, A123)

Thus, step [2] identifies pure intuition, pure imagination, and pure apperception as subjective conditions of the possibility of experience. As was noted above, Kant sometimes includes intuition in his discussion, and sometimes disregards it in favor of the two complementary modes of spontaneity that are involved in *thinking* objects and constitute the focus of the Transcendental Analytic as a whole. Insofar as step [2] reveals that the pure understanding can refer appearances to objects by dint of the synthesis carried out by the pure imagination, it makes "comprehensible this relation of the understanding to . . . all objects of experience" (A128) and so can be said to achieve the positive aim of the subjective deduction.

By conceiving of the synthetic activities carried out by transcendental imagination and transcendental apperception as analogous to those carried out by their empirical counterparts, Kant frames the way in which the human mind operates on given intuitions in an unprecedented manner. However, as was mentioned above, step [2] is not concerned with the subjective sources of experience for their own sake, but rather considers transcendental imagination and transcendental apperception in view of their complementary contribution to any cognition of objects whatsoever. Before turning to this part of the transcendental deduction, I will briefly dwell on what I have called the *subordinate aim* of Kant's investigation.

In this regard, Kant notes that experience presupposes not only the unifying activity of transcendental imagination and transcendental apperception but also the categories: the latter are said to be responsible for the specific form in which we apprehend, associate, and recognize appearances *all the way down*. The categories, Kant writes,

> ground all formal unity in the synthesis of the imagination, and by means of the latter also all of its empirical use (in recognition, reproduction, association, and apprehension) down to the appearances, since the latter can belong (*angehören können*) to cognition and our consciousness as such and, hence, ourselves, only by means of these elements.[54]

I assume that the details of this account concern what the *Metaphysical Foundations* refers to as the "merely useful" strand of the transcendental deduction, of which Kant admitted that the details are not spelled out.[55] And rightly so: Kant's main question is not how the categories guide the synthetic activities that result in empirical judgments, but how they guide the effort of the understanding to achieve a priori knowledge of objects per se. Indeed, the title of the section is "On the Relation of the Understanding to Objects as Such and the Possibility of Obtaining A Priori Knowledge of Them" (A115). In order to clarify *this* possibility, as I take Kant to be doing so in step [3], we should not redescend to the plane of empirical cognition, but remain on the plateau of pure cognition.[56]

[3] The third step consists in determining to what extent the human mind is capable of producing objects of thought independently of experience. It relies on step [2] insofar as the latter reveals that *any* a priori unification of representations requires not only a purely intellectual synthesis, that is, transcendental apperception, but also a synthesis carried

---

[54] A125, translation modified, cf. B164–65. The term 'der' in 'der Erkenntnis' is not a genitive case, but a dative case required by the verb 'angehören.'

[55] Kant notes repeatedly that the question as to how categories make experience possible (B167) or how they can be applied to appearances as such (A138/B177) is answered in the Schematism Chapter. While Kant here indeed details how the rules contained in the categories allow the mind to unify its successive representations, he does not relate the transcendental schemata to the various empirical syntheses discussed in the Transcendental Deduction, which is to say that the strand of his analysis devoted to the chapter's subordinate aim remains unachieved.

[56] Based on a remark at A119, the objective deduction is commonly divided into an argument 'from above' (A115 or A116 to A119) and 'from below' (A119–28) even though the former term is not mentioned by Kant. See Carl (1992: 95–110, 198), Wunsch (2007: 187–88), and Allison (2015: 243), to mention a few examples. While Kant here and earlier on indeed can be said to move in two different directions, I do not think that the so-called argument 'from above' is meant to descend to the level of appearances. The text at hand largely overlaps with what I have called step [2], which, on my reading, rather aims to show that the pure understanding rests on pure apperception and the pure imagination. Seen in this way, the assumption that both arguments intend to reach the same aim by different means is unwarranted. More generally, I think that the role of the distinction is overrated and obscures Kant's actual line of thought.

out by the transcendental imagination. As I hope to show in what follows, the negative aim of the transcendental deduction hinges on this step.

Pure apperception, Kant writes, "yields a principle of the synthetic unity of the manifold in all possible intuition" (A117). But his point is that pure apperception cannot achieve this unity all by itself, in other words, that the activity commonly called the understanding can be pure but cannot produce objects of thought, let alone of cognition, insofar as it is purely intellectual. For we are supposed to have discovered in step [2] that only the imagination is able to relate the purely intellectual synthesis rooted in apperception to a sensible manifold and, hence, to refer representations to objects.[57] According to Kant, the pure or transcendental synthesis carried out by the imagination is no less "an a priori condition of the possibility of all composition of the manifold in a cognition" (A118). Thus, the purely intellectual synthesis carried out by pure apperception constitutes one principle out of two: it constitutes the necessary ground of any form of thought (cf. B150), but it does not amount to thinking *an object* or achieving synthetic unity proper. The latter also requires the "productive synthesis" carried out by transcendental imagination. Synthetic unity proper, Kant notes rather elliptically,

> presupposes a synthesis, or contains it (*schließt sie ein*), and if the former unity is to be necessary a priori then the latter synthesis must also be a synthesis a priori.[58]

Kant's dissection of the faculty "we call the understanding" (Axvi) thus reveals that the latter – qua capacity to think objects at all – rests on two complementary activities, namely, transcendental apperception and transcendental imagination.[59]

The B-Deduction explains how these original faculties must cooperate in order to produce synthetic unity proper in perhaps somewhat clearer

---

[57] "We therefore have a pure imagination, as a fundamental faculty of the human soul, that grounds all cognition a priori. By means of it we bring together the manifold of intuition on the one side and the condition of the necessary unity of apperception on the other" (A124). In the B-Deduction Kant refers to the synthesis carried out by pure apperception as "not only transcendental, but also merely purely intellectual" (B150).

[58] A118. The imagination, Kant notes elsewhere, "is therefore also a faculty of a synthesis a priori . . . and, insofar as its aim in regard to all the manifold of appearance is nothing but the necessary unity in the synthesis of this appearance, this synthesis can be called the transcendental function of the imagination" (A123).

[59] Allison (2015: 203) points this out as well, but does not elaborate on it. I take Kant to carry out the same dissection in the following passage: "The unity of apperception in relation to the synthesis of the imagination is the understanding, and this very same unity, in relation to the transcendental synthesis of the imagination, is the pure understanding" (A119). See also B137.

terms.[60] The understanding, now conceived as spontaneity at large rather than, say, the capacity to judge, is said not only to produce the form of thought as such but also to determine the form of "inner sense," that is, time, so as to "think a priori synthetic unity of the apperception of the manifold of sensible intuition."[61] The latter mode of synthetic unity is the result of the synthesis carried out by the transcendental imagination, which Kant here calls "figurative synthesis" (B151) and distinguishes from the purely intellectual synthesis carried out by transcendental apperception qua "source of all combination" (B154). Thus, unlike transcendental apperception, transcendental imagination is capable of determining time, qua "formal condition of inner sense," from within. Since time is that in which all representations "must be ordered, connected, and brought into relations" (A99), only transcendental imagination allows the human mind to actually carry out the a priori rules contained in the categories.[62]

Adopting a more genealogical perspective, Kant maintains in § 24 of the B-Deduction that the pure spontaneity of which the human mind is capable – the understanding taken in a broad sense – enacts itself primarily as transcendental imagination, that is, as the a priori capacity to unify a sensible manifold. The synthesis it carries out, he writes, is the "first application" of the understanding "to such objects of intuition as are possible for us."[63] Already at this level, the transcendental imagination operates on sensible intuitions in a way that is informed by the a priori rules contained in the categories.[64] In order to establish true objectivity, however, the human mind must explicitly subject its successive

---

[60] For the sake of clarity I as yet abstract from the role of the categories in producing synthetic unity (unlike Kant).

[61] B150, cf. B153–54, B155. At B130, Kant likewise identifies the understanding in a broad sense with spontaneity or the capacity to unify a manifold as such. This latter capacity can be further distinguished into imagination and the understanding in a narrow sense: "It is one and the same spontaneity that introduces unity into the manifold of intuition: in the former case [empirical apprehension], it does so under the name of the imagination, in the latter [pure apperception] it does so under the name of the understanding" (B162n, translation modified; cf. B153–54).

[62] I take it that Kant here refers to the way in which transcendental imagination establishes the schemata that present the rules contained in the categories in an intuitable way. Since transcendental schemata 'format' time from within, as it were, Kant calls them 'determinations of time' (A138/B177). On this, see Chapter 6, Section 4.

[63] B152, cf. B153–54. Already in the Metaphysical Deduction, Kant refers to the imagination as a "blind though indispensable function of the soul, without which we would have no cognition at all," but which does not suffice to produce cognitions of objects proper (A78). Clearly, this is not to say that the pure understanding cannot act independently of the pure imagination. In this case, however, its use of categories does not result in cognition proper.

[64] Kant notes that the activity of the transcendental imagination is from the outset "in accordance with the categories" (B152). This claim need not exclude that, at this level, the *empirical* imagination relates representations in a merely subjective manner, for example, by means of the principles of

representations to these very rules. For Kant, establishing objectivity is a matter of consciously positing a manifold of representations as a unity. Since the categories articulate the various ways in which transcendental unity of apperception can be brought about,[65] he can maintain that transcendental apperception "must be added to the pure imagination in order to make its function intellectual" (A124, cf. A78/B103).

In my view, this intellectualized mode of transcendental imagination is nothing but the faculty that Kant calls the pure understanding – in a narrow sense – and implicitly distinguishes from the traditional conception of this faculty. This interpretation does justice to the primacy of transcendental imagination without therefore identifying it as the 'common root' of pure sensibility and pure thought, as Heidegger does.[66] Accordingly, I contend that both editions are primarily concerned with identifying two complementary strands of spontaneity. It is not contradictory to maintain the basic difference between pure intuitions and pure concepts and, on the other hand, to argue that transcendental imagination, qua particular mode of spontaneity, is involved in the production of both.

Differences between the two editions apart, Kant clearly retains the idea that any a priori thought of objects of which human beings are capable stems from *two sources*: it requires not only the purely intellectual capacity to grasp a manifold as unity, but also the less than purely intellectual capacity to determine the form of inner sense and, hence, to produce unity among a manifold of (successive) sensible intuitions.

This result confronts the Wolffians with their one-sided conception of the intellect. Drawing on general logic, they identified the capacity that Kant calls the pure understanding with its purely intellectual origin. By thus overlooking, as it were, the mixed pedigree of the capacity to judge, they could assume that a priori knowledge of objects can be achieved by the intellect alone. On their account, more specifically, the intellect obtains knowledge of things by clarifying the confused content of representations, that is, by moving from a given whole to its distinctive parts. Seen from Kant's transcendental perspective, by contrast, even *thinking* an object is a matter of unifying a given manifold, that is, of moving from given parts to a whole:

---

association treated by Hume. In this regard, I take it, Kant in § 19 distinguishes between an empirical judgment considered as a relation between representations "that is objectively valid" and "the relation of these same representations in which there would be only subjective validity." In the latter case, the relation is said to rest, "for example, on laws of association" (B142, cf. Prol, 4:297–98, 312).

[65] I discuss this further in relation to step [4] below.   [66] See Heidegger (1929/1997: 137–38/96).

> The synthesis of a manifold ... first brings forth a cognition, which to be sure may initially still be raw and confused, and thus in need of *analysis*; yet it is the *synthesis* that properly gathers the elements for cognitions and unifies them into a certain content.[67]

Only by drawing on this model can it be argued, as Kant does, that the pure understanding must rely on pure imagination to achieve its aim, namely, synthetic unity of apperception or the a priori consciousness of something *as an object*. By establishing this third *factum*, Kant can rule that the pure understanding's claim on the capacity to produce a priori cognitions of objects is legitimate only insofar as it relies on the a priori synthesis of the imagination and, hence, pure intuition. Clearly, this result is pivotal to the negative aim of the transcendental deduction. But we are not yet there, since the role of the categories in the production of a priori cognition of objects has not yet been discussed.

6 The Objective Deduction

The aim of the objective deduction, as said, is to determine to what extent the use of categories is warranted. It is here – in step [4] – that Kant returns to his starting point and reaches the verdict addressed to both Hume and the Wolffians, that is, achieves the aim of the transcendental deduction as a whole. In what follows I hope to show that Kant achieves this main aim by combining the results of step [3] outlined above, his earlier analysis of the categories, and his conception of the transcendental unity of apperception.

So far I have mentioned this keystone without elaborating on it. Given the purpose of the present chapter, it suffices to note that Kant, first, reinterprets the rationalist conception of cognition as the act of constituting an object of cognition and, second, conceives of this act as the conscious representation of a sensible manifold *as a unity*. This unity of apperception, as he calls it, is established by means of concepts or judgments.[68] I take Kant to hold that the human mind cannot but seek to produce such unity to the highest possible extent, which is to say that this unity constitutes the *telos* of any synthetic activity the human mind carries out. He argues, moreover, that the unity of apperception produced by means of empirical judgments relies on the *a priori* capacity to bring about

---

[67] A77–78/B103, emphasis mine, cf. B130. The activity of the understanding, Kant notes elsewhere, is not primarily "to make the representation of the objects distinct, but rather to make the representation of an object possible at all" (A199/B244).

[68] A judgment, Kant writes, "is nothing other than the way to bring given cognitions to the objective unity of apperception" (B141, cf. B145).

such unity, that is, on the capacity to bring about *transcendental* unity of apperception. The human mind, Kant writes, "could not possibly think of the identity of itself in the manifoldness of its representations" without subjecting the empirical synthesis of apprehension "to a transcendental unity," that is, without unifying its perceptions "according to a priori rules."[69] This a priori synthetic activity rests on the intellectualization of the pure imagination mentioned above and underlies any objectification of given contents.[70]

Along the same lines, Kant writes in the B-Deduction that all representations – given in the forms of space and time – stand under "the original synthetic unity of apperception," which I take to mean that the human mind from the very outset conceives of its representations as a manifold to be unified one way or another. But, Kant continues, this unity is something under which these representations "must also be brought."[71] This is to say that actually producing unity of apperception requires the mind to engage in the a priori synthetic activity guided by the categories. Insofar as it does so, the function of the pure imagination is made intellectual.

Kant's account of the transcendental unity of apperception arguably constitutes the hinge between the subjective and objective strands of the transcendental deduction: whereas the subjective deduction traces this unity to transcendental imagination and transcendental apperception, the objective deduction traces it to the categories. Combining the results of these two parts, Kant draws the objective deduction to a close by arguing that transcendental unity of apperception can be produced only if the mind unifies a given manifold according to rules that *are nothing but the categories*.[72] As the B-Deduction puts it, the understanding "is able to

---

[69] A108. Kant notes that "appearances can certainly be given in intuition without functions of the understanding" (A90). Insofar as the mind is set to obtain knowledge of something, however, it will seek to subject appearances to empirical rules as much as it can. I take Kant to hold that the rules of association identified by Hume do not suffice to account for the result of this process. If the mind failed to produce transcendental unity among its representations, he writes, "the manifold perceptions ... would be nothing but a blind play of representations, i.e., less than a dream" (A112, cf. A156, A159). Insofar as the synthetic activities of the mind are geared toward objectivity, they will be steered by the same set of a priori rules from beginning to end. As Kant famously puts it, the function, or rule, that "gives unity to the different representations in a judgment" also "gives unity to the mere synthesis of different representations in an intuition" (A79/B104).

[70] The transcendental unity of apperception, Kant writes in the B-Deduction, "is that unity through which all of the manifold given in an intuition is united in a concept of the object" (B139, cf. A103–5).

[71] B135–36, cf. A99, B144, A177/B220.

[72] Cf. A125. I hold that this final step is prepared by A105–7 and actually elaborated at A125–28. However, Kant does not properly explain the import of these paragraphs. That is why I will take

bring about the unity of apperception a priori only by means of the categories and only through precisely this kind and number of them."[73]

It follows from this account of the transcendental unity of apperception that the human mind, in order to sustain itself in the face of a potentially overwhelming "swarm of appearances," *needs* to subject the latter to the a priori rules laid down in the categories (A111). It follows from the Transcendental Aesthetic, on the other hand, that the human mind actually *can* do so, for since the appearances given in space and time are nothing *but* representations, they necessarily expose themselves to their unification from the moment they are being perceived and, as Kant puts it, "insofar as *objects are to be given to us* through them."[74] More is not required, I take it, to rule, against Hume, that categories *can and must* be used with regard to appearances as such and, hence, possess objectively validity.

But could not this result have been achieved much more economically? Does not Strawson in *The Bounds of Sense* rightly consider Kant's account of synthesis an aberration and, more broadly, reject what he calls the latter's transcendental psychology? I hold, by contrast, that Kant's reply to Hume requires at least the notions of synthesis and transcendental unity of apperception and that he needs his account of the codependent sources of spontaneity at least to target Wolffian metaphysics.

Kant, as seen, takes himself to have shown that producing objects of thought requires not just the purely intellectual rules contained in the categories that stem from transcendental apperception but also the transcendental imagination: only the latter allows the human mind to project

---

into consideration Kant's anticipation of the results at A93–94 and A95 as well as passages from the B-Deduction.

[73] B145–46. The A-Deduction does not make this point very clear (but see A119). In the B-Deduction, by contrast, Kant refers to the categories as "rules for an understanding whose entire capacity consists in thinking, i.e., in the act of bringing the synthesis of the manifold that is given to it . . . *to the unity of apperception*" (B145, emphasis mine). The "synthesis of apperception" is said to be "intellectual and contained in the category entirely a priori." Accordingly, it does not involve the imagination (B162n). Thus, the categories merely determine *how* a given manifold can consciously be posited as a unity, that is, as object of cognition.

[74] A110, emphasis mine, cf. A113, A120, B162. This is to say that I take Kant to adopt a teleological perspective even if he does not use the term in this context. I hold, in other words, that Kant's alleged proof hinges on the view that the human mind *needs* to subject its representations to their lawful unification to the largest possible extent in order to establish itself as unity. In this sense, Kant refers to the "indispensability" of the concept of causality "for the possibility of experience" (B5). Seen in this way, he does not overcome Hume's subjectivism, and he indeed notes his agreement with Hume on this point (Prol, 4:258). Yet by arguing, against Hume, that the human mind is capable of truly objectifying its representations by means of the categories, Kant thinks he can account for a qualitative difference between the objectivity established in the sciences and merely subjective processes of association.

these rules onto the form in which intuitions necessarily present themselves, that is, onto time. In this capacity, transcendental imagination is one of the faculties that makes possible experience. This is the strand of the subjective deduction that belongs to step [2] and, as regards the details, constitutes a subordinate aim of the transcendental deduction at large.

As regards the negative strand of his main aim, on the other hand, I take it that Kant infers from the subjective deduction that transcendental imagination is required to carry out the rules contained in the categories not just in the case of experience but *in all cases*. His investigation into the categories *qua* conditions of possibility of experience reveals, first, that they are *nothing but* a priori rules for the unification of successive representations and, second, that these rules are empty, or meaningless, unless geared toward intuition by means of the transcendental imagination. Absent the latter condition, Kant notes, categories would be nothing but "the logical form for a concept, but not the concept itself through which something would be thought" (A95). In this case, they would not be able to pertain to any object whatsoever:

> Without this original relation to possible experience, in which all objects of cognition are found, their relation *to any object whatsoever* (*irgendein Objekt*) could not be comprehended at all. (A94/B126–27, emphasis mine)

Thus, Kant's ruling against the Wolffians seems to come down to the claim that *any* use of pure concepts, or *any* effort to produce objects of cognition independently of experience, is a matter of establishing synthetic unity of apperception. The "unity of consciousness," he writes in the B-Deduction,

> is that which alone constitutes the relation of representations to an object, thus their objective validity, and consequently that which makes them into cognitions, which is what even the possibility of the understanding rests on.[75]

On this account, the transcendental object is not a thing that can be known by the intellect alone, because it is nothing but the *correlate* of this synthetic unity (A250) and, for this reason, presupposes the synthetic activity carried out by transcendental imagination in relation to the form of inner sense. Considered in this light, the *factum* that concerns the mixed

---

[75] B137. By contrast, Allais (2015), who chooses to "say very little" about the transcendental unity of apperception (260), takes the transcendental deduction to show that thought can relate to objects only if "there are things that are given in intuition: things with which we have an acquaintance" (289).

pedigree of the pure understanding, as it were, allows Kant to rule that, notwithstanding its purity, the pure understanding is not warranted to use categories for the purpose of determining things as they are in themselves. In other words: categories are objectively valid with regard to possible objects of experience *alone*. As said, I take this to be the negative side of the aim on behalf of which the transcendental deduction was undertaken.

But is this result in agreement with the available textual evidence? Does not the first Preface assert that the subjective deduction is not essential to the main aim of the transcendental deduction, even though it is "of great importance" in respect of the latter (Axvii)? I have tried to make sense of these remarks by arguing that the crucial part of Kant's analysis of the pure understanding – step [3] – does not fall squarely within the scope of the subjective deduction even though it deals with the faculties rather than the categories. As was suggested above, more-over, Kant may well have downplayed the role of the subjective deduc-tion to dissociate his work from Tetens's, because even steps [1] and [2] are taken in view of step [3]. I take the Preface to stress, in sum, that the subjective deduction is nothing but a means toward achieving the aim of the transcendental deduction as a whole, namely, to establish that the categories are objectively valid if used with regard to possible objects of experience and in this case alone.

Yet if the transcendental deduction was undertaken "on behalf of" metaphysics, as the *Prolegomena* has it, then the verdict it pronounces cannot entail the impossibility of metaphysics as such. The next and final section relates the result obtained so far to Kant's conception of the synthetic a priori cognitions at stake in this discipline.

7   Synthetic A Priori Cognition of Objects

In line with the A-Deduction itself, the preceding sections were focused on what it takes to *think* objects a priori, that is, on the way in which transcendental imagination and transcendental apperception, guided by the categories, contribute to the a priori unification of a sensible manifold. The question that remains to be answered is what it takes to *know* an object independently of experience, for metaphysics "stands or falls" with the answer to this question.[76] Kant leaves no doubt that synthetic a priori judgments are possible and even actual:

[76] B19, cf. Prol, 4: 276.

> We are really in possession of synthetic a priori cognition, as is established
> by the principles of the understanding that anticipate experience.[77]

But how can Kant account for the possibility of these synthetic a priori
cognitions? Why should they amount to cognitions of an object?

According to the *Stufenleiter*, both concepts and intuitions are cognitions taken in a broad sense, that is, representations pertaining to objects.
This also holds true of pure concepts.[78] But neither of these representations amounts to a *cognition of an object*, that is, to cognition proper. As is
well known, Kant holds that the latter requires an intuition through which
the object is given as well as a concept "through which an object is thought
that corresponds to this intuition."[79] Drawing a parallel with mathematical
concepts, Kant notes in the B-Deduction that pure concepts, "even if
applied to a priori intuitions . . . , provide cognition only insofar as these a
priori intuitions . . . can be applied to empirical intuitions."[80] Once more,
Kant here asserts that categories can be used only with regard to possible
objects of experience (B147–48), thus frustrating the ambitions of former
special metaphysics.

However, pure concepts are not just means in the service of empirical
cognition: as was noted above, they can be considered cognitions themselves as well. But can they be combined with pure intuition in such a way
that they produce synthetic a priori cognition proper? Pure concepts
possess objective reality, Kant writes, insofar as the synthetic unity of
apperception they contain is applied to intuition and, thus, can "determine
an object" (B148–49). For example, the concept of causality has objective
reality insofar as it is used to determine the form of inner sense – that is,
time – and, hence, to unify empirical intuitions such as two colliding
billiard balls. The classical version of the judgment that articulates this use
is the synthetic a priori judgment 'every event has a cause' (cf. A9, B4–5).
Seen in this way, such synthetic a priori judgments – the principles of the
pure understanding – are nothing but further articulations of the a priori

---

[77] A762/B790, cf. B4–5, Prol, 4:275. Kant considers all principles of the pure understanding to be
valid instances of synthetic a priori judgments (A216/B263). I discuss this point in more detail in
Chapter 6, Section 5.

[78] A320/B376–77. The title of section 2.4 of the A-Deduction seems to refer to categories as
"cognitions a priori" in this broad sense (A110; see also A57/B81).

[79] A92–93/B125, cf. A78/B103, B146.

[80] B147, cf. B165–66. Kant notes that while geometrical principles "are generated in the mind
completely a priori, they would still not signify anything at all if we could not always exhibit
their significance in appearances" (A223–40/B299, cf. B147, A157/B196).

rules for the synthesis of intuitions contained in the categories (A148/
B187–88).

Yet Kant insists that cognitions "consist in the *determinate* relation of
given representations to an object" (B137, emphasis mine). Does the
judgment 'every event has a cause' also meet the second criterion for
cognition proper, that is, can it be said to relate a representation to an object
in a determinate way? Kant's answer to this question seems to be the
following. As was mentioned in Section 3, he conceives of pure concepts
as "concepts of an object as such" (A93/B126). Actually, however, these
concepts contribute to the cognition of an object as such only insofar as the
rule they contain is carried out – by means of the transcendental imagination – with regard to pure intuition. Only in this case do pure concepts
constitute determinations of the transcendental object that any of our
empirical cognitions presupposes: they determine the various ways in which
appearances, represented by empirical concepts, can be assigned to objects at
all (A109). According to Kant, however, these a priori determinations do not
amount to cognitions of this transcendental object itself.[81] Unlike empirical
concepts such as 'black,' pure concepts such as substance or causality do not
refer to a determinate intuition. A pure concept, Kant writes,

> cannot contain any determinate intuition at all, and therefore concerns
> nothing but that unity which must be encountered in a manifold of
> cognition insofar as the latter is related to an object. (A109, cf. A719–20/
> B747–48)

Thus, the judgment 'every event has a cause' brings an a priori representation – the rule – to bear not on a *particular* intuition (a black cat) but on
any *possible* intuition and, hence, on any *possible* object of experience.
Insofar as the judgment does this, the pure concept it contains (1) pertains
to a pure intuition, namely, time, and (2) determines *how* a sensible
manifold can be related to an object. For this reason, Kant considers
synthetic a priori judgments to qualify as valid synthetic a priori cognitions
of objects insofar as they are geared toward possible objects of experience:

> If a cognition is to have objective reality, i.e., to be related to an object . . . ,
> the object must be able to be given in some way. . . . To give an object . . . is
> nothing other than to relate its representation to experience (whether this
> be actual *or at least possible*). . . . The possibility of experience is therefore
> that which gives all of our cognitions a priori objective reality. (A155–56,
> emphasis mine)

---

[81] See Chapter 4, Section 5.

However, proving that synthetic a priori cognition of objects is possible under these conditions does not amount to proving that *metaphysics* is possible under the same conditions, so let us turn to some of Kant's remarks on this discipline.

According to Kant, the human mind carries out the rules contained in the categories whenever it seeks to unify a manifold of sensible representations (cf. A119). Now I take it that Kant, following Wolff and Baumgarten, considers these rules to be part and parcel of the "natural metaphysics" that the mind enacts whenever it is involved in the cognitive activities constitutive of both non-scientific and scientific judgments. I consider him to hold, in other words, that synthetic a priori cognition proper is possible at least insofar as it is carried out in metaphysics qua natural predisposition.[82]

But what about the mode of metaphysics called 'artificial' by Baumgarten, that is, the mode of metaphysics that may or may not be turned into a science? In order to answer this question, we must take into account that the Doctrine of Method – the final part of the *Critique* – considers metaphysics, like any other branch of philosophy, to be "rational cognition from concepts," that is, to be discursive from beginning to end.[83] If combined with the result of the transcendental deduction, this point seems to entail that metaphysics, qua theoretical discipline, may treat the intellectual conditions of synthetic a priori cognitions of objects but cannot obtain such cognitions itself. However, as was to be expected, Kant holds that this result does not necessarily obtain of the discipline that used to be called general metaphysics or ontology.

According to the passage quoted above, a pure concept such as causality possesses objective reality if it is related to *possible* experience (A156/B195). For Kant, general metaphysics consists in an explicit and systematic treatment of the a priori concepts and principles employed in natural

---

[82] See B21–22. Although Kant in this context focuses on the natural version of special metaphysics, I hold that he, like the Wolffians, considered general metaphysics to possess a natural and artificial mode as well. Thus, the Transcendental Analytic is said to examine "nothing more than what we should in any case have practiced in the merely empirical use of the understanding" (A237/B296, cf. Bxxxi). The *Prolegomena* as a whole is said to exhibit "metaphysics as actually given in the natural predisposition of human reason" (4:363, cf. 365). Distinguishing between natural and artificial ontology, Wolff's *Latin Ontology* considers the former to contain the confused concepts that correspond to the explicit judgments about beings as such treated in artificial ontology (LO 21, 23). See also Baumgarten, M 3.

[83] A713/B741. Kant notes that the "transcendental synthesis from concepts alone" carried out by the philosopher "never concerns more than a thing as such, with regard to the conditions under which its perception could belong to possible experience" (A719/B747, cf. Axx, A722/B750, A732–33/B760–61).

metaphysics. Like its natural counterpart, general metaphysics relates the concept of causality to possible experience. It differs from natural metaphysics, however, in that it explicitly predicates causality of any possible object of experience by means of the synthetic a priori judgment 'all events have a cause.' On the condition that the judgment determines how appearances can become objects of empirical cognition, it constitutes a warranted instance of synthetic a priori cognition. Indeed, Kant asserts in the Doctrine of Method that synthetic a priori judgments amount to "secure principles" only on the condition that the concept that functions as the predicate of the judgment is related "to something entirely contingent, namely possible experience" (A736–37/B764–65). Seen in this way, the transcendental deduction merely denies general metaphysics the right to predicate pure concepts of any thing whatsoever. As Kant puts it in the second Preface, this discipline can be turned into a science insofar as it concerns itself "with concepts a priori to which the corresponding objects appropriate to them can be given in experience" (Bxviii–xix).

As regards its negative aim, Kant takes the transcendental deduction to have demonstrated that pure concepts are empty unless they function as rules for the unification of a manifold of sensible representations. Clearly, this result is "very disadvantageous" to special metaphysics (cf. Bxix), for this discipline claimed to be capable of synthetic a priori cognitions of objects such as the soul and God. Yet this negative judgment need not entail the end of special metaphysics: the transcendental deduction does not rule out that this part of metaphysics devotes itself to a systematic treatment of the purely intellectual conditions of synthetic a priori cognitions of the world as such, the soul, and God, in other words, that it limits its scope to these transcendental objects insofar as they can be thought.

8   Conclusion

This chapter has tried to disentangle the various strands of the transcendental deduction by starting from the premise that Kant's account of the conditions of possibility of experience is nested in a complex argument intended to reveal the conditions of possibility of the use of pure concepts per se. If abstraction is made from the tortuous structure of the text, the transcendental deduction can be considered to have a two-pronged result. According to its first prong, the text establishes that the use of pure concepts is warranted insofar as these concepts are employed to turn something into an object of empirical cognition at all. In this regard, *pure concepts* are considered as conditions of possibility of cognition. According to its second prong, the text establishes that the use of pure concepts is warranted if it involves the synthesis carried out by the transcendental imagination. In this regard, it is a *faculty* that is considered a condition of possibility of cognition. Combining the results of these two deductions, Kant judges, contra Hume, that synthetic a priori judgments are warranted if they predicate pure concepts of all appearances and, contra the Wolffians, that synthetic a priori judgments are unwarranted if they predicate pure concepts of things as such and, hence, of the world as such, the soul, and God. Whatever we are to make of the details, I hold that Kant's exposition of both the categories and transcendental imagination as conditions of the possibility of synthetic unity of apperception and, hence, objectivity, is pivotal to strand [2] of his transcendental critique of Wolffian metaphysics. His account of the schematism of the pure understanding – to which I now turn – is in line with the transcendental deduction thus understood and arguably nothing but one more way to achieve the end that animates the *Critique of Pure Reason* as a whole.

CHAPTER 6

The Schematism of the Pure Understanding

1 Introduction

According to the A-Deduction, all cognitions "are in the end subjected to the formal condition of inner sense, namely time, as that in which they must all be ordered, connected, and brought into relations."[1] We have seen in the preceding chapter that Kant considers this unification of successive representations to be guided by pure concepts such as substance, causality, and necessity. However, the A-Deduction dwells neither on what it takes to actually carry out the rules contained in these concepts nor on the role played by the form of inner sense in this regard.

These questions take center stage in the chapter titled "On the Schematism of the Pure Concepts of the Understanding."[2] Kant introduces this short and dense chapter by noting that it "deals with the sensible condition under which alone pure concepts of the understanding can be employed" (A136/B175). As regards this issue, it dovetails with the A-Deduction and is motivated by the same end. The Schematism Chapter complements the latter, however, in at least two respects. First, it focuses on the a priori rules articulated by pure concepts rather than the faculties involved in their production and use. Second, in line with its focus on the sensible condition mentioned above, the chapter first and foremost seeks to demonstrate that these a priori rules cannot be used to obtain the purely intellectual cognition of objects to which the Wolffians laid claim. As I hope will become clear over the course of this chapter, it is only in the Schematism Chapter that Kant fully develops the argument that supports his critique of post-Leibnizian metaphysics in the Transcendental Analytic.

---

[1] A99, cf. A139–40/B178–79.

[2] A137/B176. Kant sometimes uses the term 'schema' in contexts other than that of the Schematism Chapter and in a somewhat looser sense (cf. A665/B693, A833/B861). A discussion of these passages falls outside the scope of this chapter.

Considered in this way, it makes sense that Kant, in a late note, refers to the schematism of the pure understanding as one of the most difficult as well as one of the most important issues treated in the *Critique of Pure Reason*.[3] Yet the chapter has not received the attention and credit it deserves.[4] In my opinion, its apparent obscurity is partly due to the peculiar strategy Kant employs: while he frames his analysis in terms that he could expect his readers to be familiar with, he gradually develops ideas that breach any traditional account of cognition. This is true of his references to the power of judgment and the related view that cognition is a matter of subsuming intuitions under concepts as well as of the suggestion that schemata bridge an initial gap between categories and appearances (A138/B177).

In what follows I aim to cast light on the Schematism Chapter by shifting the focus from these introductory moves to what I take to be the core of Kant's analysis, namely, his effort to reveal that any priori cognition of objects rests on non-intellectual conditions he calls schemata. I will argue, moreover, that Kant considers this a priori schematization to occur wherever the human mind unifies a given manifold, except in the purported a priori judgments about things as such, the soul, the world as such, and God to which former metaphysics aspired. Unlike most commentators, I take Kant to hold, accordingly, that the categories employed for this purpose are nothing but deschematized pure concepts.[5]

---

[3] R6359 (18:686). See also Kant's letter to Tieftrunk, December 11, 1797 (12:224–25). The *Prolegomena* considers the Schematism Chapter to be "indispensable" to the critique of metaphysics carried out in the *Critique* (4:316–17).

[4] At least from Adickes onward, the Schematism Chapter has often been considered obscure or even superfluous (Adickes 1889: 171n; Wilkerson 1976: 94). Commentators who pay considerable attention to the chapter, yet without relating it to Kant's criticism of Wolffian metaphysics, include Paton (1936b), Allison (1981, 2004) and Guyer (1987). The latter considers the chapter "to show exactly how these categories can be instantiated ... in our sensible intuitions of objects" (158). As is well known, Heidegger (1929/1997) both takes the *Critique of Pure Reason* to spring from Kant's critical engagement with the Wolffian tradition and puts the Schematism Chapter central stage. However, his actual interpretation is shaped by his own reflections on the finite nature of the human understanding rather than by his understanding of Kant's criticism of his predecessors. Daval (1951) considers Kant's account of the transcendental schemata to be the "key" to Kant's latent metaphysics (8, cf. 24) but does not dwell on Kant's engagement with the Wolffians. Walsh (1957/1958) notes that this chapter serves Kant's case against what he calls "the empty character" of traditional metaphysics and, accordingly, supports his corresponding reform of the metaphysical tradition (105). However, he does not elaborate on this point. Symington (2011) brings Kant's account to bear on contemporary metaphysics, but ignores Kant's own engagement with metaphysics in the *Critique of Pure Reason* and assumes that Kant did not realize "the full ramifications for metaphysics" of his doctrine.

[5] In this regard, my reading converges with that of Rosales (2000: 260–77). I became aware of his insightful work only while editing the present chapter. Further literature on this issue will be discussed in Section 4 below.

This insight did not fall from the sky. As was argued in Chapter 2, Kant already in the *Inaugural Dissertation* denounced the encroachment of sensibility on the allegedly intellectual principles employed in Wolffian and post-Wolffian metaphysics. In accordance with this earlier analysis, the present chapter considers Kant's account of the schematism of the pure understanding no less to target Wolffian metaphysics.

In order to substantiate this reading, the various elements of the text need to be unpacked one by one. Since the way in which Kant frames his account of transcendental schemata implicitly relies on the theory of judgment presented in Wolff's *German Logic* (1713) and Meier's *Excerpts from the Doctrine of Reason* (1752), Section 2 introduces the topic in view of the relevant elements of these works. In Section 3, I turn to Kant's initial presentation of the schematism of the pure understanding, which is the part that has caused most misunderstandings. Section 4 focuses on Kant's account of transcendental schemata as sensible conditions of any a priori cognition of objects and its various ramifications. In this context, I also expound what I propose to call Kant's 'two-aspect' theory of pure concepts. Drawing on the results of this section, the final section takes stock of the increasingly concrete accounts of the a priori rules constitutive of any cognition of objects that Kant elaborates throughout the Transcendental Analytic.

2   The Wolffian Background of Kant's Account of Transcendental Schemata

Following the Aristotelian tradition, Wolff's *German Logic* takes a judgment (*Urteil*), expressed by a proposition (*Satz*), to consist in the connection of two or more concepts (GL 3.2). He maintains, moreover, that predicating something of a thing must have a ground or reason (*Grund*). In the case of the judgment 'the stone is hot,' the actual heat of the stone is the ground or condition that allows me to connect 'hot' and 'stone.' But the heat of the stone, qua ground, is itself not a part of the assertion in the strict sense. That is why Wolff writes that any proposition

> can be easily analyzed into two parts. The first part is the condition (*Bedingung*) under which something can or cannot be attributed to a thing, namely, either because there is something or other that belongs to the thing, or because the thing is determined by certain circumstances. The second part is the assertion (*Aussage*), which contains that which either can or cannot be attributed to a matter of fact (*Sache*). (GL 3.6)

According to Wolff, the ground or condition that allows me to predicate something of a thing can lie either outside of the thing itself, as in the example mentioned above, or in its essence, as is the case when I predicate 'being heavy' of a stone (GL 3.5). It is not difficult to recognize Kant's distinction between analytic and synthetic judgments here (cf. A6–7/B10).

I take Wolff to hold that the condition is not necessarily articulated in the proposition itself but that we can always modify the latter in such a way that it does. He seems to use the proposition 'the hot stone heats' as an example to this effect. In this case, the condition of the proposition consists in the hot stone, whereas the assertion consists in predicating 'heating' of the stone. Wolff admits that it is more usual to think of these two parts by referring to the structure of a hypothetical judgment.[6] But Wolff's point is that *each* judgment can be analyzed in this way. Even an apparently unconditional judgment such as 'a triangle has three angles' could not take place, he submits, without the triangle itself being enclosed within three lines, which for that reason can be called its condition (GL 3.7). In short, Wolff calls 'condition' the ground that allows us to predicate something of something, yet is not part of the assertion itself.

Meier's *Excerpts from the Doctrine of Reason* discusses the same issue in terms of the truth of judgments.[7] Whereas Meier focuses on the judgments themselves rather than on the things to which they pertain, his distinction between inner and outer, or necessary and contingent, conditions is similar to Wolff's.

Commenting on Meier's work in the *Vienna Logic*, dated around 1780, Kant, in his turn, conceives of the condition of judgments as the determination of the subject that contains the ground of the truth of categorical judgments.[8] Like Meier, Kant here focuses on the judgment itself. He gives the example of the judgment 'a vicious man is deserving of punishment.' In this judgment, 'being vicious' is the determination of the subject that grounds the truth of the judgment. If this condition is removed, the judgment ceases to be true (24:932).

---

[6] Wolff, GL 3.6. In the *Latin Logic*, Wolff refers to the extrinsic condition that needs to be added to the subject for a predicate such as 'hot' to be attributed to it as *determinatio subiecti* (LL 228). Commenting on this text, Longuenesse notes that Kant departs from Wolff because the latter "never looked for the condition of predication outside concepts, especially where a priori ... predication was concerned" (1998: 97). However, I take it that Wolff in his *German Logic* does consider things as conditions and, more generally, that Kant's account of the condition of synthetic a priori judgment is indebted to his reading of Wolff to a greater extent than Longuenesse maintains.

[7] Meier, EDR 297–99, 303; cf. Wolff, LL 509.   [8] Kant, *Vienna Logic*, 24:932.

A similar example can be found in the Transcendental Aesthetic. Alluding to Crusius's principle, Kant argues here that the judgment 'all things are in time' is true on the condition that the subject 'all things' is restricted to 'all appearances':

> We cannot say: all things are in time, because the concept of things as such abstracts from the various ways in which these things might be intuited, whereas *this intuition is the real condition* under which time belongs to the representation of objects. Now *if the condition is added to the concept*, and the principle says that all things *as appearances* . . . are in time, then the principle has its sound objective correctness and a priori universality.[9]

Thus, only on the condition that the subject of the judgment refers to things that can be intuited is it warranted to posit that these things are in time. In this case, the principle does not allow us to conceive of the soul or God as being in time.

These examples shed light on Kant's account of the schematism of the pure understanding. As was mentioned in the introduction to this chapter, he considers this schematism to constitute "the sensible condition under which alone pure concepts of the understanding can be employed" (A136/B175). Evidently, we need not conceive of the assumption underlying the a priori synthetic activity carried out by the human mind in logical terms. Yet one of the ways in which Kant tries to clarify the nature of this assumption is by conceiving of a transcendental schema as a condition of synthetic a priori judgments. As was seen in Chapter 3, this is the approach Kant adopts in the Introduction to the *Critique of Pure Reason*. The relevant passages can be further clarified by assuming that Kant in this context draws on Wolff's logical distinction between the judgment itself and the condition under which it is warranted.

Echoing the question put forward in his 1772 letter to Herz, Kant in the Introduction refers to the condition at stake as the X that allows the mind to predicate pure concepts of anything at all:

> Take the proposition: 'Everything that happens has its cause.' In the concept of something that happens, I think, to be sure, of an existence which was preceded by a time, etc., and from that analytic judgments can be drawn. But the concept of a cause indicates something different from the concept of something that happens and *is not contained* in the latter

---

[9] A35/B51–52, emphasis mine. See Chapter 1, Section 3. In my view, Kant's argument against Crusius in the *Dissertation* (see Chapter 2, Section 4) is similar to that in the *Critique of Pure Reason*, even though it is presented in different terms: the point is in each case that the principle rests on a sensible condition and, for that reason, can be used with regard to appearances alone.

representation at all. How then do I come to say something about that which happens as such (*von dem, was überhaupt geschieht*) that is completely different from it and to grasp the concept of cause as belonging to everything that happens even though it is not contained in it? What is the X here on which the understanding relies (*sich stützt*) when it believes to discover beyond the concept of A a predicate that is foreign to it and *that is yet connected with it*?[10]

In this passage, Kant clearly takes recourse to the Wolffian idea that the act of predication rests on a condition that is not part of the judgment itself. Following Wolff, he explains that, in the case of synthetic a posteriori judgments, the X that functions as the condition of the judgment can be found in the experience of the thing that is being judged (A8/B12), for example, I add, in the experience of the hot stone. But the question Kant raises concerns the condition under which it is warranted to predicate causality to everything that happens in a synthetic *a priori* judgment. In this case, I take him to mean, we should be looking for a condition *that is necessary rather than contingent* (since the judgment is a priori) yet *not contained in the subject* (since the judgment is synthetic). Evidently, the Wolffian opposition between the being-heavy and the being-hot of a stone is unhelpful in this regard: whereas Kant's question concerning the possibility of synthetic a priori judgments can be framed in Wolffian terms, his answer cannot.

Somewhat frustratingly, Kant in the Introduction does not provide the solution to the riddle, but merely affirms that it consists in "uncovering the ground of the possibility of synthetic a priori judgments" (A10). I will argue in Section 4 that the Schematism Chapter presents three candidates for this ground or condition: time qua form of pure intuition, possible experience, and the transcendental schemata. Each of these answers points into the same direction, namely, the claim that the warranted employment of pure concepts rests on an a priori condition that is sensible rather than intellectual. However, Kant's analysis of the transcendental schemata offers the most detailed account of this sensible condition and accordingly deserves pride of place.

---

[10] A9, first emphasis mine, translation modified, cf. B13, A155/B194. Kant asks the same – Humean – question with regard to geometrical propositions. In this case he answers it by referring to space considered as pure intuition (A47–48/B64–65). In the second edition of the Introduction, all but one of the references to the X are removed, such that Kant's use of the term at B13 becomes difficult to understand without referring to the first edition. The X in the quoted passage can be said to refer to the sufficient ground or reason of a synthetic a priori judgment (cf. A9). Contrary to Leibniz, however, the Schematism Chapter aims to prove that this ground is not purely intellectual.

As was mentioned in the introduction to the present chapter, I consider Kant's account of the schematism of the pure understanding to be pivotal to his critique of Wolffian metaphysics. According to Wolff's logic, the judgment 'the hot stone heats' is no longer true if the condition 'being hot' is omitted. Drawing on this element of Wolffian logic, Kant rejects a core assumption of Wolffian metaphysics, namely, the assumption that the intellect can obtain a priori cognitions of things all by itself. If metaphysicians abstract from the sensible condition under which alone the pure understanding can predicate, for instance, causality of anything whatsoever, then the act of predication has no object anymore. Kant writes:

> Now if we leave out (*weglassen*) a restricting condition, it may seem as if we amplify the previously limited concept; thus the categories in their pure significance, without any conditions of sensibility, might be considered to obtain of things as such, *as they are*, instead of their schemata merely representing them *how they appear*.[11]

However, I hold that Kant's discussion of schemata as conditions or grounds of synthetic a priori judgments serves as an introduction to the problem rather than a real argument: it does not explain *why* the cognitive activity commonly attributed to the pure understanding necessarily relies on schemata rather than categories. The same can be said of Kant's potentially misleading remarks on the subject in the opening pages of the chapter. Drawing on the result obtained so far, the next section aims to put these remarks into perspective.

3 Kant's Initial Presentation of the Schematism of Pure Concepts

Kant prefaces his presentation of the transcendental schemata by distinguishing between, on the one hand, the pure understanding qua source of a priori rules and, on the other hand, its capacity to carry out these rules in an appropriate way.[12] The latter capacity, called transcendental power of judgment, requires a critique, he maintains, because of its tendency to make "missteps" in its use of "the few concepts of the pure understanding that we possess" (A135/B174). In order to curb this tendency, transcendental logic must point out to which "case" the rules that are represented by pure concepts can be applied (A135/B174). According to Kant,

---

[11] A146–47/B186, translation modified, cf. B305–6. I return to this point in Section 4 of this chapter.
[12] A132/B171, A135–36/B174–75.

carrying out this task requires that one examine "the possibility of applying pure concepts of the understanding to appearances as such."[13]

At first sight, Kant here seems to refer to the application of pure concepts to particular appearances such as colliding billiard balls.[14] This seems to be the only way of interpreting Kant's suggestion that *something* has to be singled out. Yet these passages make more sense, it seems to me, if we take them to pertain to the tendency of Wolffian metaphysics to disregard the difference between appearances and things in themselves and, hence, to employ pure concepts such as substance or causality for the purpose of attaining a priori cognition of things such as the soul, the world as such, and God. Thus, just as a doctor has to determine whether the concept 'flu' applies to a certain patient, so metaphysics has to determine whether the pure concepts that it possesses apply to anything whatsoever or rather to appearances alone. If illuminated by critique, Kant suggests, metaphysics will realize once and for all that the latter is the case (A135/ B174–75). This is, at least, how I propose to interpret Kant's rather abstract remarks on the necessity to curb the cognitive activity carried out by the pure understanding.

I am not sure if Kant's reference to the transcendental power of judgment is a very helpful way of introducing the schematism of the pure understanding. This also holds for his effort to clarify the problem at hand by taking recourse to the logical concept of subsumption. In this regard, Kant asks how it is possible to subsume empirical intuitions under pure concepts, in other words, to apply the category to appearances (A137–38/ B177). Such a subsumption, he adds, requires that categories and appearances have something in common, which does not seem to be the case. I can consider an actual billiard ball to fall under the concept of a billiard ball because my intuition and the concept share a number of marks.[15] But if there is no mark common to a concept such as causality and appearances such as billiard balls, how can we ever consider the latter to range under the former?

---

[13] A138/B177, translation modified. In somewhat less specific terms, Kant considers the chapter to teach the power of judgment "to apply the concepts of the understanding ... to appearances" (A132/B171). For the expression 'appearances as such,' see A31, A34/B51, A93, A156/B195, A170/ B212. Obviously, according to this passage there is a considerable overlap with the task, or one of the tasks, carried out in the Transcendental Deduction (cf. A85/B117). Yet in the context of the Schematism Chapter, Kant approaches the problem from a direction that up to this point had remained largely unexplored.

[14] See Freuler (1991: 404).   [15] Cf. Wolff, GL 1.26–27; Meier, EDR 261.

Since the model of concept subordination leads nowhere in this case, Kant more or less implicitly turns to the way in which *syllogisms* connect various conceptual elements. A rule such as 'all billiard balls are round' can be applied to an individual billiard ball by means of the minor premise 'this thing is a billiard ball,' which means that the syllogism subsumes the individual case under the rule given in the major premise. While a syllogism may connect empirical or non-empirical concepts, the procedure by means of which syllogisms apply rules to particular cases is a priori. This may well have been one of Kant's reasons to couch his presentation of the problem of the schemata in terms derived from syllogistic logic. As we will see, this holds in particular for the view that a third element is required to connect two apparently heterogeneous elements.

Clearly, the act of subsuming a certain case under a rule requires the power of judgment. However, in the case of pure concepts it is not immediately clear why the power of judgment can attribute, for example, causality to all events prior to experience. In the Transcendental Dialectic, Kant discusses an example that I take to be highly illuminating in this regard. In order to understand the judgment 'Caius is mortal' as resulting from an a priori procedure, he writes, "I seek a concept containing the condition under which the predicate ... of this judgment is given." This concept is the concept of a human being. The latter is said to 'contain,' as a condition, the predicate 'mortal,' which is thought "in its whole domain" in the major premise 'all humans are mortal.' It is this premise that makes it possible to attribute mortality to an individual human being such as Caius – which means that the conclusion "restricts" the predicate 'mortal' to a certain object.[16] In other words, the predicate 'mortal' that is implied by the concept 'human being' constitutes the condition that allows me to subsume Caius under the concept of mortal human being.[17]

If we transfer this account to the question concerning the applicability of pure concepts, then the Schematism Chapter can be said to carry out an inquiry into the condition, implied by the pure concept of causality, that allows the pure understanding to subsume all events, qua appearances,

---

[16] A322/B378–79, cf. A330/B386–87. On this, see Longuenesse (1998: 94–95). Instead of regarding the condition as that which makes possible the subsumption, she seems to hold that it is the condition itself that must be subsumed.

[17] Thus, both judgments and syllogisms can be analyzed in view of the condition of their truth. In syllogisms this condition takes the form of a judgment rather than a predicate (cf. *Jäsche Logic*, 9:120–23).

under the a priori rule represented by this concept. Kant appears to have had this question in mind when he states that the subsumption of appearances under pure concepts requires a mediating representation:

> Now it is clear that there must be a third element (*ein Drittes*), which must be homogeneous with, on the one hand, the category and, on the other, the appearance, and makes possible the application of the former to the latter. This mediating representation must be pure (without anything empirical) and yet intellectual on the one hand and sensible on the other. Such a representation is the transcendental schema. (A138/B177, translation modified)

Kant's effort, in this passage, to clarify the condition under which categories can be applied to appearances suggests that categories are prior to schemata and, accordingly, that the latter are required to bridge an initial gap. Yet the passage need not be read in this way. I take Kant to mean, rather, that philosophy needs to identify the X that allows the human mind to carry out the rules contained in the categories at all. Seen in this way, the passage draws an analogy – albeit without signaling so – between the act of subsuming a particular case under a rule carried out in syllogisms (treated in general logic) and the transcendental act of subsumption carried out whenever the human mind unifies its successive representations according to a priori rules (treated in transcendental logic).[18]

Yet there is one important difference: in the case of pure concepts, the condition that allows me to attribute causality to all events is itself not a concept but a schema. This is to say that in order to subsume 'all events' under the category of causality, for example, the human mind has to represent the a priori rule contained in this category as "the succession of the manifold insofar as it is subject to a rule" (A144/B183). Unlike the category itself, this representation involves time qua form of inner sense and is the product of pure imagination (A142/B181). Kant indeed concludes at a later point that "appearances must not be subsumed under the categories *per se*, but only under their schemata."[19] Only the latter provide

---

[18] Kant explicitly distinguishes logical and transcendental subsumption in his 1797 letter to Tieftrunk (12:224–25).

[19] A181/B223. In his lectures on logic, Kant generally uses the concept of subsumption to refer to the act of ranging an individual case under a universal rule, an act that is formalized in the syllogism (cf. *Blomberg Logic*, 24:24; *Pölitz Logic*, 24:586; *Dohna-Wundlacken Logic*, 24:771–72; *Jäsche Logic*, 9:120–21, 123). See also A304/B360, A330/B386. On this, see Longuenesse (1998: 92–97). While Longuenesse rightly points out that Kant generally uses 'subsumption' when referring to syllogisms, her own interpretation makes much more of what she calls the subsumption of objects under concepts, enacted by judgments, than in my view is warranted by Kant's text (cf. 92 n 23). Moreover, she does not relate the issue of subsumption to the Schematism Chapter. See Curtius

the condition under which the subsumption of appearances under concepts such as causality or substance can actually be carried out.

Considered in this way, Kant's presentation of the schematism of the pure understanding and his account of synthetic a priori judgments in the Introduction are concerned with the very same issue. In both cases, Kant aims to draw our attention to the non-intellectual X that functions as the condition under which the pure understanding is able to conceive of any object of cognition as measurable in terms of its extension or degree, as substance, as cause or effect, as possible or actual, and so on.[20] Since this condition presupposes time qua form of intuition, the pure understanding can employ these concepts with regard to appearances alone.

As was seen above, Kant introduces his account of transcendental schemata by comparing them to the condition that in the case of syllogisms allows us to subsume a case under a general rule. He may well have thought of this analogy as a guiding thread, or clue, intended to direct the reader to the problem at hand, similarly to the guiding thread that is supposed to direct the reader from the sphere of general logic to that of transcendental logic in the case of the metaphysical deduction (cf. A67–69/B92–94). On this account, there is no reason to assume that Kant considered there to be an initial gap between categories and appearances that should somehow be bridged by a third element.[21] As I see it, he rather draws on the analogy to argue – against the Wolffians – that the purely intellectual rules contained in the categories do not suffice to turn a manifold of representations into an object of cognition.

In order to clarify this crucial point, we should take a closer look at the distinctions Kant draws between categories, pure concepts, and transcendental schemata. Constituting the core of the Schematism

---

(1914: 348–50) and Allison (1981: 64–65) for accounts that consider Kant's comments on subsumption and the mediating element to draw on syllogistic logic.

[20] On this point my reading is likewise in agreement with Allison (1981: 65). However, I disagree with his view that synthetic a priori judgments predicate concepts of pure intuitions (67). Maintaining that Kant does not properly explain the "deep" structure of synthetic a priori judgments that he attributes to him (75), Allison argues that Kant considered schemata as pure intuitions (73) and, accordingly, that synthetic a priori judgments predicate pure concepts of schemata (73–75). Even apart from the lack of textual basis, I find it hard to make sense of this assertion. See also Allison (2004: 216).

[21] For criticisms of Kant's failure to bridge this alleged gap, see, for instance, Gardner (1999: 170). Curtius (1914: 358, cf. 363–65) rejects Kant's presentation of the problem in terms of subsumption altogether. Walsh (1957/58) likewise distinguishes between what he considers to be Kant's unsatisfactory presentation of the issue in terms of a third thing and his account of schemata as rules (99).

Chapter, these distinctions were so far left in the background so as not to encumber the exposition.

4 Naked Categories, Pure Concepts, and Transcendental Schemata

Kant famously maintains that concepts possess a content insofar as an object is added to them in intuition (A51/B75). This must hold true of empirical and pure concepts alike. Determining whether pure concepts such as causality meet this requirement is a task that is foreign to general logic. Contrary to the latter, Kant tells us, transcendental logic does not abstract "from all content of cognition," because it is concerned with "the rules of the pure thinking of an object" (A55/B80). As was seen in Chapter 5, he considers such rules to be contained in the pure concepts of the understanding. Already in the Metaphysical Deduction, Kant asserts that pure concepts possess a "transcendental content" insofar as the rules they contain "pertain to objects a priori" (A79/B105). In this case, we can infer, they are not empty. But in which case are they empty?

Clearly, this question cannot be answered by conceiving of the content of pure concepts on the model of marks, or characteristics, derived from sensation. For this reason, Kant once more departs from Wolffian logic: in order to examine pure concepts in view of the condition by dint of which they acquire a transcendental content, he shifts the focus from the marks that all concepts contain to the capacity of the latter to relate to objects.[22] Only from this perspective does it become possible to demonstrate that the human mind must rely on transcendental schemata and, hence, on time, in order to generate synthetic a priori cognitions of objects.

In order to actually prove this point, I contend, Kant basically takes two steps. The first step, carried out in the Transcendental Deduction, consists in reinterpreting concepts as a priori rules that the human mind must employ to unify any manifold of representations. The second step is implied by Kant's account, in the same chapter, of how the transcendental imagination, guided by these rules, actually produces the a priori synthesis of successive representations.[23] It is only in the Schematism Chapter, however, that this task is carried out in detail. As was seen above, moreover, Kant now frames the problem at hand in terms of the sensible

---

[22] Cf. A62–63/B87, A239/B298. By contrast, Longuenesse (1998: 333) regards permanence as "a necessary mark of the concept of substance" and by so doing erases the difference between general and transcendental logic.

[23] See Chapter 5, Section 5.

condition under which the a priori rules contained in pure concepts can actually be carried out.

As is usual, he begins the task by considering examples derived from other domains. In this case, he does so by examining the condition under which empirical and mathematical concepts can refer to objects. Seen from Kant's perspective, even an empirical concept such as 'dog' cannot be adequately explained in terms of the marks its contains. Wolffian general logic can clarify why the concept of a dog can be ranged under the concept of a mammal, but it cannot explain why we can relate the content of the concept *to an object*. To do the latter, the concept of a dog must be conceived as a rule that tells us how to unify the features proper to dogs as such, yet independently of any individual dog that we may see or imagine (cf. A141/B180). When I hear barking, for example, I associate this representation with a number of other representations that I do not actually perceive so as to attribute them to a single object, and I carry out this rule-governed activity each time I have a reason to conceive of something as a dog.[24] As Kant puts it, the empirical concept "signifies" the rule by means of which the imagination outlines that which is common to all dogs in an intuitable way.[25] He by no means suggests that the schema bridges an initial gap between the concept of a dog and the intuited singular dog. The question as to whether the concept precedes its schema therefore seems to miss the point.

---

[24] Kant's various efforts at clarifying what a schema is are somewhat ambiguous. He asserts that a schema, though produced by the imagination, is not itself an image, but rather the representation of a procedure that allows the mind to represent a concept such as the number 1,000 "in an image" (A140/B179–80). What allows me to grasp the meaning of this number is the representation of the act of adding one unit after another a certain number of times rather than something that looks like the number 1,000. If we take him to mean that the procedure represented by a schema *may* result in images (as it does in the case of empirical and mathematical concepts), but does not do so *in all cases*, then Kant does not contradict himself by stating that "the schema of a pure concept of the understanding," produced by transcendental imagination, "is something that can never be brought to an image at all" (A142/B181).

[25] "The concept of a dog signifies a rule according to which my imagination can outline (*verzeichnen*) the shape of a four-footed animal in general" (A142/B181, translation modified). Somewhat puzzling, this passage does not contain the term 'schema.' Contrary to Allison (2004: 208), I do not think it needs to be corrected. I agree with La Rocca (1989: 135) that the act Kant here attributes to the imagination consists in the schematization of the very rule that the concept, for its part, articulates in an intellectual manner. Pippin (1976) takes Kant's alleged identification of empirical concepts and schemata to pose a problem (165–66), arguing that it precludes an account of how exactly empirical concepts are being schematized (171). However, this problem disappears if we take Kant to hold that empirical concepts are from the outset geared toward the schematic representation of the rules they contain. This is also the position of Guyer (1987: 163–64), who, however, does not hold that the rule contained in a concept can be viewed from two different perspectives.

Similarly, Kant takes the concept of a triangle to consist in a rule that tells me how to unify three lines and, in this way, produce a spatial figure. On his account, this act must take recourse to space qua pure intuition (A141/B180). Whereas the rule itself is not sensible, it manifests itself in a sensible way in the triangle that I produce by carrying out the rule, that is, by constructing it. If we abstract from the differences between particular triangles, the resulting figure can be considered the sensible representation, or the schema, of the rule that tells me to unify a manifold of lines in a particular way.[26]

Kant's conception of transcendental schemata appears to rest on the assumption that what is true of geometrical concepts is true of all non-empirical concepts. Thus, whereas the schemata of geometrical concepts represent rules that allow the mind to determine *spatial relations* in a particular way, the schemata of pure concepts allow the mind to unify representations that present themselves in *inner sense* one after the other. Put differently, these schemata determine time, considered as the form of inner sense, prior to any impression received from without. A transcendental schema, Kant writes, is

> only the pure synthesis, in accord with a rule ... expressed by the category, and is a transcendental product ... which concerns the determination of inner sense as such ... in regard to all representations. (A142/B181)

We can infer from this passage that Kant distinguishes between, on the one hand, the a priori rule contained in the category and, on the other, the act of carrying out this rule so as to unify a manifold of successive representations. As was noted above, this unification requires that the rule be represented in a way that involves time, in other words, a schema. As we will see, Kant conceives of schemata as conditions without which these rules could not be enacted at all.

This point can be clarified by considering a passage in which Kant implicitly targets the use of the category of substance in Wolffian special metaphysics and the metaphysical tradition as such. On his account, metaphysicians employed this concept by abstracting from the schema that represents the a priori rule at hand in a sensible manner, namely, persistence:

---

[26] Kant writes that "we *think* of a triangle as an object by being conscious of the composition of three straight lines according to a rule, such that an intuition of this object can always be exhibited" (A105, emphasis mine). He states elsewhere that we can think the concept of a two-sided figure, because it does not contain a contradiction, but that the rule it contains cannot be carried out to construct a figure in space (A220/B268, cf. A24, A240/B299, A713/B741).

> Now if I say through mere category: 'the soul is a simple substance,' then it
> is clear that, since the understanding's naked concept of substance contains
> nothing beyond the requirement that the thing be represented as a subject
> in itself without in turn being the predicate of another subject, nothing
> about persistence follows from this concept. (A401)

Seen from the perspective of transcendental logic, the naked rule contained
in the category of substance allows the mind to determine something as a
logical subject, but not to conceive of an object as persisting.[27] By contrast,
the schema of the pure concept of substance, which Kant describes as the
"persistence of the real in time" (A144/B183), represents the a priori rule
contained in the category of substance as a rule that tells the mind to unify
successive representations in view of something that persists.[28] Only by
carrying out this rule can the mind establish unity among its representations and so refer the latter to an object.

Similarly, as was noted above, Kant describes the schema of causality as
"the succession of the manifold insofar as it is subject to a rule" (A144/
B183). Thus, whenever I conceive of something as cause, I assume that it
necessarily precedes something else. This element of temporal succession is
lacking from the category of causality itself. If this category is employed
with regard to things as such rather than appearances, accordingly, the
purely intellectual rule it contains is nothing more than the logical distinction between ground and consequence (cf. A95).

Relying on this account of transcendental schemata, Kant argues that
Wolffian metaphysics went wrong by assuming that the 'naked' category of
substance sufficed to determine the soul as that which persists and, on that
basis, as immortal. If the act of determining the soul as substance were to
amount to the cognition of an object, I take him to mean, it ought to
involve the schema of persistence. However, since in this case the act
would merely consist in the subjective unification of successive

---

[27] A254/B309, cf. A96, A89/B122.

[28] A144/B183. Kant does not clearly point out whether schemata are themselves rules or whether they
merely result from the intellectual rules articulated by the categories. On the one hand, he states
that the schema of a triangle "signifies" a rule (A141/B180) and he calls a schema a "rule for the
determination of our intuition" (A141/B180). On the other hand, he notes that the schema of a
pure concept of the understanding is "the pure synthesis, in accord with (*gemäß*) a rule of unity . . .
expressed by the category" (A142/B181) and that it is an a priori determination of time "according
to (*nach*) a rule" (A145/B184). The ambiguity can be resolved, it seems to me, if we take Kant to
hold that schemata represent the very rules that the categories, for their part, express in a purely
intellectual way. Here I agree with Daval (1951: 175), who considers the schemata to 'project' the
objectifying forms produced by the understanding onto the element of intuition. Seen in this way,
Kant is justified in writing of both the *concept* of a dog and the *schema* of a triangle that they 'signify'
rules (A142/B181, A141/B180): they do so in different ways.

representations, it would not yield the "pure and sense-free" determination of a thing such as the soul to which metaphysics aspires (A259/B315). It follows that Wolffian metaphysics cannot make use of categories at all.[29]

I take Kant to hold, accordingly, that the human mind can *either* rely on time so as to produce synthetic a priori cognitions of any possible object of experience *or* determine the soul by means of the intellect alone without thereby establishing the latter as an object of cognition. In other words: pure concepts possess a transcendental content if their use involves schemata, but are empty if used by the intellect to determine things as such.[30] Evidently, this result can be traced back to the analysis carried out in the *Dissertation* and its aftermath.[31]

In line with the distinction between categories and schemata discussed above, Kant refers to the latter as transcendental determinations of time (A138/B177). Produced by the pure imagination, these schemata determine the form of inner sense from within, as it were, by representing the a priori rules produced by the pure understanding as specific ways of

---

[29] Kant writes succinctly that since pure categories "ought not to be used empirically and cannot be used transcendentally, they cannot be used at all if separated from all sensibility" (A248/B305, translation modified).

[30] Kant stresses this point on numerous occasions, most famously in the passage, mentioned above, according to which thoughts without content are empty (A51/B75). This statement is tautological except if he had in mind a specific kind of content, namely, intuition. That this is the case is corroborated by the next sentence, which states that intuitions without concepts are blind (cf. A240/B299). It is obvious that empirical cognition requires both intuitions and concepts. Kant's point is, however, that this must be true of a priori cognition as well. In this case, the intuitive element is contributed by the schemata, which accordingly turn our a priori thoughts into cognitions of possible objects of experience. Kant generally emphasizes that categories by themselves do not possess content, which means, on his account, that they do not pertain to objects and lack significance (A155–56/B194–95, A240/B299, B306). However, categories can be said to possess a content in a weak sense insofar as they contain the logical functions that tell the mind how to unify a manifold in a purely intellectual way: "Every concept requires, first, the logical form of a concept (of thinking) as such, and then, second, also the possibility of giving it an object to which it can be related. Without this possibility the concept has no sense, and is entirely empty of content, even though it may still contain the logical function for making a concept out of whatever sort of *data* there are" (A239/B298, translation modified, cf. A55/B80, A95). If categories are not related to pure intuition, their significance is "merely logical" (A147/B186) or "merely transcendental" (A248/B305). While categories in this sense are involved in the thought of "an object as such" (A247/B304, cf. A254/B309, B128–29), they do not suffice to think or determine any object (A248/B305). Accordingly, Kant took the Wolffians to have attributed more "significance and content" to categories than they actually possess (Prol, 4:315–16).

[31] A note dated 1769 suggests that Kant already prior to the publication of the *Dissertation* considered the concept of substance to be composed of a purely intellectual element and an element that pertains to temporal succession: "In the case of that which succeeds something else, the concept of substance involves (*hat bei sich*) not only the idea of subject, but also the concept of permanence and the identity in these successive states (*Folge*), which for this reason are called the changes of one and the same thing. Since, however, all accidents are variable and the substantial is not known at all, the permanence of the latter is assumed without certainty (*precario*)" (R4054, my translation).

unifying successive representations.[32] Thus, the transcendental schemata can be said to 'format' time prior to its empirical determination by representations such as thoughts or impressions.[33]

Seen in this way, it makes sense to maintain, as Kant does, that the schemata of pure concepts themselves are both sensible and intellectual (A138/B177). Insofar as the schema of persistence, for example, represents the rule contained in the category of substance in a way that presupposes time, it can be called sensible. The schema can be called intellectual, on the other hand, insofar as the rule it represents can be traced back to the logical function contained in the category.[34]

---

[32] A140/B179–80, cf. A142/B181. Kant refers to these schemata as sensible concepts (A146/B186), schemata of sensibility (A146/B185, A664/B692), sensible conditions (A147/B186), conditions of sensibility (A139–40/B197, A147/B186), and sensible determinations (A147/B186). Kant is very brief – and not very clear – about the way in which the various schemata actually determine the form of the inner sense. He writes that the schema that concretely represents the rule, or rules, articulated in the categories of quantity is 'number.' This schema, qua representation of the act of counting, brings forth time itself (A142–43/B182, cf. B155) and determines time qua *time-series* (A145/B184). I take this to mean that it is by representing the act of counting that we can conceive of time as that in which events occur one after another. The schema that concretely represents the rule, or rules, articulated in the categories of quality is 'degree' (A143/B183). It allows us to determine appearances in view of their degree, for instance, by measuring their temperature. This schema is said to determine time in view of its *content* (A145/B184) because each temporal moment can be considered to be relatively 'full' or 'empty' as regards a quality such as heat. In the case of the categories of relation and modality, Kant distinguishes schemata for each category. The schemata that concretely represent the rules articulated in the categories of relation (substance, causality, and community) allow us to determine appearances as such as persisting, successive, or simultaneous and therefore to determine time in view of the *order of time* (A145/B184–85). The schemata that concretely represent the rules articulated in the categories of modality, finally, allow us to determine appearances as taking place at some point in time, at a determinate point in time, or at every point in time (A144–45/B184). These schemata can therefore be said to determine time as that in which every possible object takes up a determinate position (A145/B185). For more detailed expositions, see Paton (1936b: 42–65) and Daval (1951: 168–74).

[33] This view is supported by the following note from the *Duisburg Nachlass* (1773–75): "Thus we represent the object to ourselves through *an analogue of construction*, namely that it can be constructed *in inner sense*, namely that . . . when something happens it always follows something else, or that this representation is one of the universal actions through which appearances are being determined, actions which thus give a rule, just as a triangle is constructed only in view of a rule and serves as a rule for all triangles" (R4684, 27:670–71, emphasis mine). In the 1787 edition of the *Critique of Pure Reason*, Kant argues that categories become meaningful insofar as we take recourse to space as well (B291–93), which is a problem I will disregard.

[34] The apparent ease with which Kant maintains that schemata are both sensible and intellectual can also be clarified by considering the puzzling example of the plate (A137/B176). Although Kant does not quite put it this way, I take it that the example is intended to clarify what it means to range the plate under the concept of round things. On his account, the concept of a circle basically consists in a rule that tells one how to draw a circle. We grasp what a circle is by means of intuition rather than thought. On the other hand, the empirical concept of a plate, qua concept, contains a number of marks, including 'roundness,' that can be grasped by thought. The act of ranging the plate under the concept of round things presupposes that I move from the roundness that I think in the concept to the roundness that I intuit by representing to myself the rule that tells me how to draw a circle.

Thus, if considered in view of Kant's critique of Wolffian metaphysics, the distinction between categories and transcendental schemata is less mysterious than one might think. However, Kant's account is somewhat complicated by another, related, distinction, namely, that between categories and pure concepts of the understanding. Since the preceding parts of the Transcendental Analytic largely abstract from the difference between both products of the mind's spontaneity, it has largely been ignored. In what follows, I will explain what might be called Kant's 'two-aspect theory of pure concepts' in some detail.

Briefly put, I maintain that Kant in the Schematism Chapter distinguishes between pure concepts of the understanding and categories by asserting that pure concepts contain or presuppose transcendental schemata, whereas categories articulate the a priori rules at hand in a purely intellectual way. Thus, he writes that the synthesis of appearances

> is thought only in the *schema of the pure concept of the understanding*, such that of the unity of this synthesis ... the category contains the function that is unrestricted by any sensible condition.[35]

According to this passage, Kant regards pure concepts not as 'naked' but as clothed, or enveloped, by an element that is as pure as these concepts themselves, but differs from the latter in that they represent a priori rules in an intuitable way.

Put differently, what emerges if pure concepts are considered under their intellectual aspect alone are the categories. This is the perspective that Kant attributes to the Wolffian tradition and that he adopts in those parts of the Transcendental Analytic, including the Metaphysical Deduction, that focus on this particular aspect. As was mentioned in the preceding chapter, in these parts the two terms are often used interchangeably.[36]

This means that, depending on the form of my representation, the roundness can be intuited as well as thought.

[35] A181/B224, translation modified, emphasis mine.

[36] See, for instance, A76/B102, A85/B118, A93/B126, A96, A111, A119, B128, A146/B185. In some cases, Kant uses the term 'category' simply because he treats the classical conception of pure concepts (cf. B147–48, A184/B227). In the Metaphysical Deduction, Kant does not yet distinguish his own position from the Wolffian one, because he here deals exclusively with the purely intellectual element of all a priori cognition of objects, regardless of the purposes for which pure concepts may be used. By defining categories as "fundamental concepts for thinking objects as such" (A111), he leaves open the possibility that they do not *suffice* to produce a priori cognitions of objects. Like most scholars, Kemp Smith (1923: 339–40) ignores Kant's distinction between categories and pure concepts and blames him for his "characteristic carelessness in the use of his technical terms" (339). However, in the passages where Kant does distinguish categories and pure concepts, he does so in a consistent manner. Already in the Metaphysical Deduction, he discusses the term 'pure concept of the understanding' in view of the capacity of such concepts to unify the

Conversely, what emerges if pure concepts are considered under their sensible aspect, as Kant thinks a critique of metaphysics ought to do, are the schemata. Seen from this perspective, a pure concept turns out to 'contain' its schema:

> [P]ure concepts a priori, in addition to the function of the understanding in the category, *must also contain* a priori formal conditions of sensibility (in particular of the inner sense), conditions that contain the general condition under which alone the category can be applied to any object. We will call this formal and pure condition of sensibility, to which the use of the concept of the understanding is restricted, the *schema* of this concept of the understanding.[37]

It seems to me that, in this dense passage, the term 'conditions of sensibility' refers to the schemata, each of which in turn contains, or presupposes, time considered as the general condition under which a priori rules can be applied to a given manifold.

The passage reveals that Kant considers a pure concept to possess two strands, namely, the purely intellectual function of the understanding articulated in the category and the non-intellectual counterpart of the latter represented by the schema. If this is correct, then Kant turns out to conceive of pure concepts such as causality in exactly the same way as he conceives of the faculty that produces such concepts in the context of the Transcendental Deduction. As was argued in Chapter 5, Kant here considers the pure understanding to be nothing else than transcendental apperception – qua purely intellectual faculty – insofar as it is related to the synthesis carried out by the transcendental imagination (A118–19). In this case as well, he maintains that the transcendental unity of apperception "presupposes" or "contains" the synthesis carried out by the transcendental imagination (A118) and, thus, that the faculty commonly called the pure understanding actually has a mixed pedigree. This means, we have seen, that it cannot establish transcendental unity of

---

"the mere synthesis of different representations in an *intuition*" (A79/B104–5, emphasis mine). At one point in the A-Deduction, Kant implicitly distinguishes categories from pure concepts by stating that the latter express the "formal and objective condition of experience *universally and sufficiently*" (A95–96, emphasis mine). In the same context, he writes that in the "pure thought" that a pure concept contains "there is more at work than the sole capacity to think" (A96–97), a remark that in my view can refer only to the schemata. Kant elsewhere defines the concept of notion (*notio*) as "the pure concept, insofar as it has its origin solely in the understanding (not in a pure image of sensibility)" (A320/B378, cf. B150, B167). This passage confirms the view that Kant considered pure concepts to stem from two origins.

[37] A139–40/B178–79, first emphasis mine, cf. A132/B171.

apperception – or objectivity – unless it relies on a mode of spontaneity that itself is not purely intellectual.

Similarly, the Schematism Chapter maintains that without relying on the schemata produced by the transcendental imagination, the human mind would not be able to carry out the rules that the categories articulate in merely intellectual terms and, hence, to establish something as an object of cognition. As Kant puts it:

> [T]he schemata of the concepts of the pure understanding are the true and sole conditions for providing these concepts with a relation to objects, and hence with significance. For this reason, the categories are in the end of none but a possible empirical use, since they merely serve to subject appearances to general rules of synthesis through grounds of an a priori necessary unity ... and thereby to make them fit for a thoroughgoing connection in one experience.[38]

Even though the text sometimes suggests otherwise, I hold that Kant nowhere means to say that schemata have to be added to unschematized categories in order to relate the latter to appearances. Rather, he considers transcendental schematism to occur spontaneously whenever the human mind unifies its successive representations with the aim of establishing transcendental unity of apperception.[39] It would be more apt, accordingly, to think of categories as *deschematized pure concepts* and to consider this deschematization to have occurred in the metaphysical tradition alone.[40]

---

[38] A145–46/B185, cf. A62–63/B87, B148, A139/B179, A239/B298.

[39] The understanding, Kant writes, "originally and spontaneously" imparts unity to the synthesis of the imagination (A237/B296). I take him to hold that his act precedes the isolation of the purely intellectual aspect of this synthesis that results in the categories and is carried out in philosophy alone. Guyer (1987) emphasizes the priority of the schemata from a genealogical perspective. Drawing on the *Duisburg Nachlass*, he distinguishes what he takes to be Kant's original doctrine from the official version included in the *Critique*, which he calls a "late accretion to his thought" (182). Whereas the latter version maintains, in his words, that "the categories are first derived from the logical functions of judgments and only subsequently associated with their transcendental schemata" (172, cf. 161), the original doctrine is said to set out from the schemata, qua determinations of time, and to derive the categories from the latter (175–76). While I agree with the latter part of his claim, it seems to me that Guyer does not sufficiently distinguish between the content of Kant's account in the *Critique* and the order in which its various aspects are presented. It is not contradictory to maintain that the a priori rules that the human mind employs for the sake of empirical cognition are from the very outset schematized and to analyze these rules by first focusing on their purely intellectual origin. On this, see Rosales (2000: 261, 268).

[40] As was mentioned in the introduction to this chapter, I entirely agree with Rosales (2000) on this point. As he puts it, Kant must assume "that the understanding thinks deschematized categories (*entschematisierte Kategorien*) in order to clarify the fact of dogmatic metaphysics and to take issue with its alleged transcendental use of these concepts" (272, my translation). However, unlike Rosales I attribute this process to pure concepts rather than categories. While admitting that the term 'schematized category' does not occur in Kant's work, Paton (1936b) nevertheless uses the term to discuss what Kant himself calls schemata (cf. 19, cf. 41–60, 69). Many other commentators

If, moreover, categories and schemata merely represent two different instantiations of the rules that tell the mind how to unify a manifold prior to experience, then questioning the fact that they run parallel, as Allison does, does not make much sense.[41]

Arrived at this point, we can return to Kant's initial presentation of the question at hand in terms of the possibility of synthetic a priori judgments. As seen, he argues in the Introduction of the *Critique of Pure Reason* that the pure understanding, in order to connect subject and predicate in synthetic a priori judgments, must rely on an X that neither is contained in the subject nor stems from experience (A9). Given my interpretation so far, this passage strongly suggests that Kant considers the *predicate* of the judgment, that is, a pure concept such as causality, to presuppose, or contain, a condition that makes it possible to attribute it to all events prior to experience, namely, its schema. For without relying on the latter, the human mind would not be able concretely to present to itself the rule that tells it to determine its successive representations in terms of cause and effect. Thus, the question concerning the X raised in the Introduction is answered by Kant's account of the transcendental schemata. Since the latter presuppose time, as seen, time might also be regarded as an answer to Kant's question, albeit a less specific one.

Finally, Kant repeatedly refers to the possibility of experience as the "third element" or "medium" that allows us to connect subject and predicate in synthetic a priori judgments.[42] An a priori cognition, he writes, possesses objective reality only insofar as it is related to possible experience, and this requires a synthesis, guided by concepts "of the object of appearances as such" (A156/B195). Although Kant does not mention the schemata in this context, it seems to me that the synthesis at stake is the a priori unification of successive representations that the preceding chapter had attributed to the schematism of the pure understanding.[43] Thus, both time, schemata, and the possibility of experience can be

---

use the term as well (cf. Detel 1978: 40; Symington 2011: 295). Even though Paton rightly points out that schemata are more fundamental than categories (67–68), he thus creates part of the confusion that he attributes to Kant (cf. 62, 76).

[41] Allison (2004) asks how Kant can assert that "a certain schema corresponds uniquely to a particular category" and then introduces "schema judgments" in order to solve this alleged problem (218–19). Despite his earlier description of schemata as phenomenal counterparts of categories (102), Walsh (1957/1958) raises the same question (104–5).

[42] A155–56/B194–95, cf. A95–96, A259/B315, A766/B794.

[43] Kant implicitly refers to the schematism as something that can be found "in" the possibility of experience at A217/B264.

considered the third element that allows the human mind to apply the rules contained in pure concepts to anything at all (cf. A138/B177).

In line with my discussion so far, I would contend that Kant, whenever he mentions the issue of the X or the third element, implicitly or explicitly targets his Wolffian predecessors. This is brought out very clearly in the course of his concluding reflection on the difference between *phenomena* and *noumena*. Addressing the philosopher who purported to possess purely intellectual knowledge of the soul and God, he asks:

> Whence will he derive these synthetic propositions, since the concepts are not to hold of possible experience but rather of things in themselves (*noumena*)? Where is in this case the third element (*das Dritte*) that any synthetic proposition requires in order to connect concepts that have no logical (analytical) affinity? He will ... not even be able to justify the possibility of such a pure assertion, without taking account of the empirical use of the understanding, thereby fully renouncing the pure and sense-free judgment.[44]

I hope to have shown that the full answer to this question is offered in Kant's account of the schemata of the pure understanding. Just as Wolffian logic takes into account the condition under which a predicate can rightfully be assigned to a subject, so Kant's transcendental logic takes into account the non-intellectual condition under which the purely intellectual function articulated in the categories can rightfully be assigned to any object whatsoever. If, as Kant argues, a synthetic a priori principle such as 'every event has a cause' is nothing but a specific articulation of the rule contained in the pure concept 'causality,' and if this rule *makes sense* only if carried out with regard to representations that succeed one another in time, then it follows that synthetic a priori principles can be used only with regard to possible objects of experience and not with regard to purported things such as the soul or God. As he puts it,

> everything that the understanding draws out of itself ... it nevertheless possesses solely for the sake of using it with regard to experience. The principles of the pure understanding ... contain nothing but the pure schema, as it were, for possible experience.[45]

As was mentioned above, Kant considers Wolffian ontology to ignore the sensible condition under which the intellect can obtain a priori cognitions of objects. In my view, however, he attributed this blind spot not

---

[44] A259/B315, cf. A216–17/B263–64, A733/B761. See also *On a Discovery* (8:242).
[45] A236–37/B295–96, translation modified, cf. A181/B223–24.

only to the Wolffians but to the history of metaphysics as such. I take him to hold, more specifically, that Aristotle and his followers identified the ultimate principles of cognition in a one-sided manner, namely, by stripping the rules articulated in the categories of the condition of their applicability, as it were, so as to use their denuded versions for lofty purposes such as proofs of the existence of God or the immortality of the soul. I take this to be the thrust of the following passage, which was partly quoted in Section 2 above:

> Now if we leave out (*weglassen*) a restricting condition, it may seem as if . . . the categories in their pure significance, without any conditions of sensibility, obtained of things as such, *as they are*, instead of their schemata merely representing them *how they appear*, and they would therefore have a significance independent of all schemata and extending far beyond them. In fact, even after abstraction from all sensible condition, the pure concepts of the understanding retain significance, but only a logical significance of the mere unity of representations, but in this case no object and thus no significance is given to them that could yield a concept of the object. Thus, if one would leave out the sensible determination of persistence, substance would signify nothing more than a something that can be thought as a subject (without being a predicate of something else). Now out of this representation I can make nothing, as it shows me nothing at all about what determinations the thing that is to count as such a first subject is to have. Without schemata, therefore, the categories are only functions of the understanding for concepts, but do not represent any object.[46]

This passage succinctly captures not only Kant's critique of former metaphysics, but also his critique of the position he himself defended in the *Dissertation*. On my reading, however, the latter treatise also contains the "key to the whole secret of metaphysics" mentioned in the 1772 letter to Herz. Drawing on his nuclear insight into the impact of sensibility on allegedly intellectual principles, Kant arguably came to conceive of the schematism of the pure understanding as this very key. It is the element to which the letter refers as the "ground of the relation of that in us which we call representation to the object" (10:129) and to which the *Critique* refers

---

[46] A146–47, cf. A240–44/B300–302, A244–45, A247/B304, A286/B342, A679/B707; Prol, 4:332. The B-Deduction maintains that the category of causality is obtained "if I abstract from the constant form of my inner intuition, time," which is to say that the presentation of this unity "in time, qua inner intuition, in which I ground the appearance" is primary (B163, translation modified). I cannot elaborate on the relevant elements of Kant's account of the paralogisms of pure reason (cf. A401–3).

to as the X on which the human mind must rely in order to generate valid synthetic a priori cognitions.[47]

5   The Trajectory of the Transcendental Analytic

Zooming out from Kant's account of transcendental schemata, the present section seeks to summarize the main results of the Transcendental Analytic as a whole in light of Kant's critique of the Wolffian tradition. In line with the Schematism Chapter, I will do so by focusing on the set of rules, or functions, that originate in the pure understanding, taken in its broad sense, and dictate the ways in which the mind can unify its successive representations. As I see it, Kant throughout the Transcendental Analytic considers these rules from a number of angles, ranging from the logical forms of judgment to the principles of the pure understanding, that is, from their most abstract to their most concrete instantiations.

The *logical forms of judgment* treated in the Metaphysical Deduction articulate these a priori rules by abstracting completely from the question as to how representations can be turned into objects of cognition.[48] Since these rules do not involve the transcendental imagination, Kant arguably considered them to stem from transcendental apperception alone. The Metaphysical Deduction departs from Wolffian logic not only by calling these forms logical functions and presenting them in a table but also, more importantly, by considering them to exhibit, in an abstract manner, the very rules that former ontology treated under the heading of ontological predicates or categories (cf. A79/B104–5).

Like the logical functions, *categories* abstract from the sensible condition of any cognition of objects: they are purely intellectual. Unlike the former,

---

[47] A9. Taking into account the overlap between the Transcendental Deduction and the Schematism Chapter, I disagree with commentators who take the cited passage from the letter to Herz to anticipate the former alone (cf. Carl 1989a: 52–53; Carl 1989b: 5; Mensch 2007). Watkins (2001: 77) argues that the passage does not "map neatly onto any particular doctrine or section within the first *Critique*" without considering the Schematism Chapter.

[48] See A79/B105, A136/B175, A321/B377. The Metaphysical Deduction primarily uses the term 'logical function' to refer to these forms (A70/B95), something that can be explained by the fact that Kant here aims to lay bare the functions of the understanding as such. Granting a pivotal role to the logical forms of judgments, Longuenesse (1998) blames Kant for abandoning the issue of the logical forms of judgment after the Metaphysical Deduction (52–53). As I see it, by contrast, Kant examines these forms exclusively with the aim of singling out the functions they exhibit. His subsequent transcendental account of these functions leaves the framework of general logic behind. By projecting the content of Kant's lectures on logic onto the *Critique of Pure Reason*, Longuenesse tends to erase the distinction between general and transcendental logic and, thus, to obscure the thrust of the analyses carried out in this work.

however, they articulate the a priori rules at hand insofar as they purport to pertain to objects, whether material or immaterial. For this reason, they can be said to be "concepts of an object as such" (B128). I take it that Kant considers this latter conception to be common to Wolffian ontology and his own version of the discipline.

As was discussed above, however, Kant turns against Wolff by arguing that categories merely articulate the *intellectual* condition of the synthetic a priori cognitions that the human mind is capable of. Seen from his perspective, categories actually amount to concepts of an object only insofar as they allow the human mind to unify its sensible intuitions, an activity that is carried out by the transcendental imagination but that is commonly and erroneously attributed to the pure understanding alone. For Kant, categories constitute "concepts of an object as such" only to the extent that by means of them the "intuition" of an object "is regarded as determined with regard to one of the logical functions for judgments" (B128). It is only in *this* capacity that categories make it possible to conceive of something as extended, as determinable in terms of degree, as persisting, as necessarily following one another, and so on. In all other cases, the categories are nothing but logical forms of judgment (Prol, 4:324), something that Kant took Wolffian metaphysics to have ignored. As seen, insofar as Kant explicitly takes into consideration the non-intellectual aspect of the concepts that used to be called categories he refers to them as *pure concepts of the understanding.*

Kant refers to this non-intellectual aspect of pure concepts itself as their *schema. Transcendental schemata* articulate the sensible condition under which the a priori rules articulated in the categories can be applied at all, which means that they restrict the realm of these rules to possible objects of experience.

Finally, the *principles of the pure understanding* – not discussed so far – represent these very a priori rules in the form of judgments (cf. A161/B200). A proper treatment of the chapter in which Kant, drawing on the grid of the table of categories, elaborates on these principles is beyond the limits of this chapter. For present purposes it suffices to note that, unlike the schemata, the principles of the pure understanding present the a priori rules contained in the categories in the form of "synthetic judgments ... that the understanding actually brings about a priori" (A148/B187). Kant asserts that these judgments "flow a priori from pure concepts of the understanding" under the condition of the transcendental schemata (A136/B175). For example, whereas the schema of substance is "the persistence of the real in time" (A144/B183), the corresponding principle states that "all appearances contain that which persists (substance) as the object itself, and that which can change as its mere determination" (A182). Similarly, Kant considers the schema of causality – "the succession of the manifold insofar as it is subject to a rule" (A144/B183) – to be further articulated in the principle according to which "everything that happens ... presupposes something which it follows according to a rule" (A189).

This a priori principle, in turn, makes it possible to determine the sequence of all appearances in a way that is independent of the order in which they initially present themselves in inner sense (cf. A215/B262). For this reason, it constitutes one of the basic principles of the natural sciences or, as Kant puts it, a law of nature that originates in the understanding (A127). This means that the human mind, insofar as it engages in the objectification of its successive representations, must presuppose that the sequence of objects it seeks to establish is determined by rules that, for their part, can be discovered by empirical means alone.[49]

Given my discussion so far, there can be no doubt that the principles of the pure understanding instantiate the synthetic a priori judgments the possibility of which is at stake throughout the *Critique of Pure Reason*. Thus, framed in logical terms, the principle that replaces the classical guise of the principle of causality attributes the predicate 'being determined by something that precedes in a rule-bound manner' to the subject 'all appearances' or 'possible objects of experience.' This judgment is synthetic because the predicate is not contained in the subject and a priori because it makes possible experience. It is warranted, finally, because the predicate relies on the schema of causality and, hence, on time, rather than on the category per se (cf. A184–85/B227–28). As Kant puts it, "although the schemata of sensibility first realize the categories, they likewise restrict them, i.e., limit them to conditions that lie outside the understanding (namely, in sensibility)" (A146/B186–87). Accordingly, the analogies of experience, and by extension all principles of the pure understanding, are said to have "their sole significance and validity ... as principles of the empirical use of the understanding."[50] As such, they make up the natural metaphysics that informs both experience and the natural sciences.[51]

Notwithstanding the restriction imposed on their use, however, these principles themselves no less than their classical counterparts belong to the discipline that used to be called ontology. Kant, I hope has become clear,

---

[49] Cf. A195/B240, A206–7/B252, A766/B794.   [50] A180–81/B223, cf. A240–41/B299–300.
[51] On this, see Chapter 5, Section 7.

examines them not primarily in order to provide physics with a foundation, but in order to pave the way for his intended reform of ontology and, hence, of metaphysics as such. Leaving no doubt as to his intentions, the *Prolegomena* states in this regard that neither mathematics or physics would "have needed, for the purpose of their own security and certainty, a deduction of the sort we have hitherto accomplished" and that only metaphysics "needs such a deduction for its own sake."[52]

6 Conclusion

The architectonic of the *Critique of Pure Reason* as well as Kant's initial presentation of the issue at hand suggest that categories are primary and that schemata are somehow added to them. I have argued, by contrast, that Kant considers any cognition of objects to rely from the very outset on transcendental schemata and that he takes the categories used in former metaphysics to abstract from the sensible condition of their application. If we accept that the order in which Kant treats the various elements of human cognition does not necessarily coincide with what he regarded as the actual production of a priori cognition, then there is no need to assume an initial gap between categories and appearances to be bridged by obscure entities called 'schemata.' On this reading, the terms 'category' and 'schema' rather represent two different perspectives on the a priori rules that allow the mind to unify a manifold of representations. Whereas the former perspective treats the *purely intellectual* strand of the rules produced by the human mind, the latter perspective reveals the necessary condition of any a priori cognition of *objects*.

Seen in this light, Kant's critical reflection on the limits within which metaphysics is possible and, hence, the *Critique of Pure Reason* as a whole, hinges importantly on his account of the schematism of the pure understanding. Far from being obscure or redundant, it reveals that any a priori cognition of objects rests on a non-intellectual condition and, hence, that the categories can be employed with regard to possible objects of experience alone.

However, Kant's understanding of categories is not merely negative: whenever the use of categories is not geared toward the objectification of successive representations, as is the case in practical philosophy, the use of deschematized versions of pure concepts is both possible and required.[53] As will be argued in Chapter 8, moreover, Kant's critique does not

[52] Prol, 4:327, cf. A237/B296, A710–11/B738–39. [53] See CPrR, 5:5–6, 65, 136.

preclude a purely intellectual determination of ideas of reason by means of categories.

Regardless of the new insights Kant achieved after 1772, there is no doubt that the core of his critical distinction between categories and schemata originates in the *Inaugural Dissertation*. As seen, Kant already in this text distinguishes two ways in which pure concepts can be used, namely, either by relying on time or by abstracting from it. Already in this context, he considered time to serve "as a means for forming the concept of the predicate" and, hence, as a condition on which we must rely to arrive at the "intellectual concept of the subject."[54] In the *Dissertation*, this analysis is part and parcel of Kant's effort to establish metaphysics as a purely intellectual discipline, that is, of strand [1] of his critique of Wolffianism. The *Critique of Pure Reason* extends this critique by arguing that naked categories do not suffice to obtain cognitions of objects, which is what I have called strand [2] of Kant's critique. Despite this shift, the key argument of the Schematism Chapter is remarkably continuous with the *Dissertation*.

Kant's account of the principles of the pure understanding concludes the Transcendental Analytic insofar as the first-order strand of his reform of ontology is concerned (cf. A235/B294). I have argued that Kant, especially in the Transcendental Deduction and the Schematism Chapter, intertwines this strand with a second-order critique of former ontology. The Appendix to the final chapter of the Transcendental Analytic can be said to contain yet another strand, namely, Kant's effort to clarify the conceptual distinctions from which his second-order critique of metaphysics itself takes its bearings. The following chapter is devoted to this inconspicuous and enigmatic part of the work.

---

[54] Diss, 2:415. See Chapter 2, Section 4.

CHAPTER 7

Transcendental Reflection

1 Introduction

The short Appendix to the final chapter of the Transcendental Analytic, titled "On the Amphiboly of the Concepts of Reflection," appears to be mainly devoted to a rather schematic critique of Leibnizian monadology.[1] On closer scrutiny, however, the various elements of the text turn out to be steps toward a less conspicuous and more daunting goal. Kant takes each of these steps, I will argue in this chapter, in order to uncover the root of the fallacious ontologies of his predecessors as well as the measures required to turn this discipline into a science.

Like the preceding parts of the Transcendental Analytic, the Appendix hinges on the question as to the very possibility of synthetic a priori judgments. Yet Kant here pushes further in that he seeks to account for this possibility in terms of a decision – or lack of the same – concerning the very vantage point from which possible objects of cognition are to be treated. Unlike most commentators, accordingly, I hold that Kant uses his account of Leibniz as a foil to clarify why ontology as such, including systems such as Wolff's, tends to misinterpret the distinction between phenomena and noumena.[2] Since the Appendix critically examines the

---

[1] Two different, but equally schematic versions of this critique are presented in the very condensed first part of the Appendix itself and a somewhat longer Remark.

[2] I will disregard the question as to whether Kant's criticism of Leibniz is pertinent, something that many commentators, including Parkinson (1981), have doubted. Pereboom (1991) regards Kant's "attack on intrinsicality" to be rightly aimed against Leibniz himself. According to Malter (1981), Jauernig (2008), and Fichant (2014), among others, Kant's criticism rather targets Wolff's philosophy. It seems to me that Kant cannot have intended Wolff in all respects, since Wolff, unlike Baumgarten, did not accept Leibniz's monadology (see Honnefelder 1990: 297). Graubner (1972: 15–24) argues convincingly that Kant primarily targeted Baumgarten's metaphysics. I hold, however, that Kant deals with Leibniz to identify a strand or tendency of metaphysics instantiated, in various degrees, by Plato, Leibniz, Baumgarten, Wolff, and others.

diverging ways in which ontology can conceive of its very subject matter, it fittingly concludes the Transcendental Analytic.[3]

As we will see, Kant introduces the notion of transcendental reflection to broach this meta-metaphysical question. Whereas it is often assumed that this notion refers to a feature of Kant's critical philosophy alone,[4] I contend that he considers the ontology of his predecessors and the discipline outlined in the Transcendental Analytic to rest on a dogmatic and critical species, or instantiation, of this act.

Kant's actual argument, if it can be called that, relies in part on his account of logical reflection and, hence, on Wolffian logic. As I see it, however, this account is subservient to his effort to get clear on the two different vantage points from which ontology can treat its subject matter at all. Thus, while I agree with Longuenesse's contextualization of the act that Kant calls logical reflection, I hold that the problem of empirical concept formation on which she focuses is foreign to the problem that the Appendix addresses and seeks to solve.[5]

In what follows, I will identify and discuss the various strands of the Appendix in a way that deviates considerably from Kant's own tangled treatment of the matter. I begin by considering the Wolffian background of Kant's account of logical reflection, including Wolff's discussion of the concepts of sameness and difference in the *German Metaphysics* (Section 2). Turning to the Appendix, Section 3 examines Kant's discussion of logical reflection and the table of concepts he considers to guide it. Section 4 shifts the attention to what I call the 'real' use of the concepts of reflection and, hence, analyzes Kant's conception of transcendental reflection. Sections 5 and 6 seek to reconstruct Kant's account of the way in which transcendental reflection takes its bearings from the concepts of reflection discussed in

---

[3] Disregarding the critique of former general metaphysics carried out in the Transcendental Analytic, Kemp Smith (1923) alleges that the Appendix "discusses problems of metaphysics and ought therefore to have found its place in the Dialectic" (419). Others have followed in his track, which is rightly challenged by, among others, Broecken (1970: 199–207) and Graubner (1972: 243–44).

[4] See, for instance, Malter (1981), Longuenesse (1998: 126), Smit (1999), Allison (2004: 325–26), and Merritt (2015). While I am sympathetic to a number of elements of Smit's article, I do not believe that, for Kant, transcendental reflection simply consists in a particular type of reflection of the mind on its own operations. Smit ties transcendental reflection very closely to the transcendental critique carried out by Kant and disregards both the role of the concepts of reflection in transcendental reflection and Kant's engagement with Leibnizian ontology.

[5] See Longuenesse (1998: 131–66). To be sure: I do not take issue with her effort to reconstruct Kant's view on empirical concept formation by drawing on the account of the concepts of reflection put forward in the Appendix. I also agree with much of her discussion of Kant's critique of Leibniz. My worry is, rather, that she merges said reconstruction with an interpretation of elements of the text that serve a very different purpose. Tellingly, she hardly addresses the issue of transcendental reflection (cf. 114 and 127n).

Section 3. Whereas Section 5 does so by focusing on the myopic mode of transcendental reflection Kant attributes to Leibniz's ontology, Section 6 seeks to shed light on the mode of transcendental reflection that informs the Transcendental Analytic itself.

2 The Wolffian Background of Kant's Account of Logical Reflection

In order to contextualize Kant's account of transcendental reflection, this section examines the relevant elements of Wolff's account of the act that Kant calls logical reflection (A262/B318). These elements are discussed from two different angles in the *German Logic* and the *German Metaphysics*.

In the *German Logic*, Wolff explains that we produce relatively general concepts by comparing the concepts of different things in view of "what they have in common, or in which respect they are similar." By considering what the concepts of a triangle and a square have in common, for example, we can produce the concept of a figure enclosed by straight lines (GL 1.26). The same procedure, which can be repeated as much as one wishes, allows one to classify all things in view of their species and genus (1.27). Conversely, we can also produce more specific concepts out of more general ones by adding, for instance, the determination 'equilateral' to the concept of a triangle (1.30). By means of the same procedure, Wolff notes, metaphysicians can start from the concept of the soul and specify the "species of non-corporeal things that are similar to the soul" (1.30). The section of the *German Metaphysics* to which he refers at this point indeed uses this procedure to conceive of monads, animal souls, finite spirits, and God as such species (GM 900–904).

A more detailed treatment of these issues can be found in Meier's *Excerpt from the Doctrine of Reason* (1752), which is the textbook Kant used in his lectures on logic throughout his career.[6] In line with this work, in turn, the *Jäsche Logic* – based on lecture notes Kant added to it over the years – maintains that the production of concepts requires that one *compare* the relevant representations among one another, *reflect* or consider how these representations "can be conceived in one consciousness," and *abstract* from the elements by dint of which the representations differ from

---

[6] According to Meier's *Excerpt*, we produce relatively general concepts by *identifying* the marks proper to the more specific concepts from which we start, by *abstracting* from the marks by dint of which they differ from one another, and by *unifying* the remaining ones in a concept (259; 16:549–50).

one another.[7] Clearly, in this context the term 'reflection' means focusing on that which the initial concepts have in common, whereas the term 'abstraction' denotes the act of disregarding the respects in which they differ from one another.

Wolff's *German Metaphysics* is more relevant in this context because a section of the ontology contained in this work treats the concepts that ultimately inform the acts involved in any production of concepts, namely, sameness and difference.[8] Wolff clarifies the meaning of these and related terms by offering a definition as well as examples taken from common experience. In accordance with the task carried out in this work, he considers the various ways in which we can compare things rather than concepts.

One of Wolff's examples concerns the act of weighing things. When I compare a leaden and an iron ball in view of their weight, they can turn out to be 'the same' insofar as their weight is concerned. In this case, he writes, "we consider merely the weight, not the size, the kind of matter, and what else might be found in such cases" (GM 17). Clearly, doing so requires that we single out one aspect and disregard all the others, that is, carry out the very acts that according to the *German Logic* are required to produce relatively general concepts. What Wolff does not spell out, however, is that the act of determining *in which respect* the comparison is to be drawn precedes the actual production of the intended concept or the intended judgment about things.

Wolff appears to regard 'similarity' (*Ähnlichkeit*) as a special case of 'sameness.' By approaching things in terms of their similarity, he explains, I compare them not in view of contingent marks, but in terms of that by which they are *known*. Thus, two houses are said to be similar if their only distinction concerns their location (19–20). Even if only the size of the houses were different they would be completely similar, according to Wolff, because they would still be *defined* in the same way (18). On his account, similarity does not pertain to the size of things,

> because size as such (*vor sich*) cannot be comprehended by the understanding, but can only be given and, accordingly, can be grasped by the senses alone. (20)

---

[7] *Jäsche Logic*, 16:94. On this, see Longuenesse (1998: 111–22).

[8] Wolff, GM 17. The section is concerned with "that which is the same (*einerlei*) and different (*unterschieden*)." Since Wolff mainly discusses the comparison of things in a particular respect, the term 'identity' seems to be less apt than the term 'sameness.'

This passage shows that Wolff – contrary to the position Kant attributes to him[9] – at least in this context assigns a different epistemological function to sensibility and the understanding: insofar as we compare things by means of the understanding, we disregard spatial features such as the location and size of things and focus exclusively on their essential marks, that is, those marks by means of which they are defined. Accordingly, the very houses we consider to be dissimilar insofar as the comparison involves the role of sensibility might be considered similar insofar as the comparison is carried out by the understanding alone. Even though Wolff does not put it this way, the passage cited above suggests that he was well aware that the comparison of two things has a different outcome depending on whether its vantage point is or is not purely intellectual.

It is clear, however, that Wolff does not give much weight to this observation: his analysis is first and foremost concerned with the way in which the *understanding* determines the extent to which things are similar and dissimilar, because this allows the human mind to provide proper definitions of things and to classify all things in terms of their genus and species (182). Seen from his point of view, the features of things that only sensibility can account for are insignificant.

Unlike Wolff, Baumgarten explicitly relates his discussion of the concepts of sameness and difference to Leibniz's principle of the identity of indiscernibles. A short section of his *Metaphysics* provides definitions of "relative predicates" such as similarity, sameness, equality, identity, and their counterparts along Wolffian lines (265–79). Baumgarten states, for example, that two things are similar if they have one or more qualities in common, equal if they have at least one quantity in common (265), and congruent if they have both qualities and quantities in common (266).

Explaining what we mean by numerical identity, Baumgarten states that "singular things that are totally the same are the same in number" and takes this to be the broad meaning of Leibniz's principle of the identity of indiscernibles (269). He infers from this principle that those things that exist outside of other things – in space – must be partially different, incongruous, dissimilar, and unequal (273).

Kant's unpublished notes and lecture transcripts include various critical comments on § 269 of Baumgarten's treatise, comments that perhaps target Leibniz's purported position rather than the letter of Baumgarten's text. Thus, a note dated 1776–78 advances that Leibniz's principle is false insofar as it pertains to judgments about things that are in a different

---

[9] See A44/B61–62, A844/B872, Diss, 2:395.

location, but true insofar as the relevant judgments are purely intellectual. As Kant puts it, "by means of the intellect I can only account for different things if the inner determinations differ from one another."[10] Regardless of whether Kant understood the principle correctly, his critique may well have put him on the track of the activity that the Appendix calls transcendental reflection. Since Kant's account of this issue draws on his analysis of logical reflection, I will first examine the Appendix in this respect.

3 Logical Reflection and the Table of Concepts of Reflection

While the Appendix clearly draws on the relevant sections of Wolff's logic and ontology, Kant seems to have been the first to subsume the cognitive activity treated in them under the concept of logical reflection. On his account, this act consists in comparing the content of various representations on behalf of actual judgments, which means that it necessarily precedes the latter (A262/B318). To use Wolff's example: in order to determine that two balls are the same or not I first need to compare their representations from a particular angle, that is, in view of features such as weight, size, or color.

At first sight, it is perhaps not very clear why Kant discusses this topic at all. I take him to hold, however, that some of the characteristics of logical reflection can provide a 'clue' to the analysis of the activity at stake in the Appendix, namely, transcendental reflection. In other words: he considers logical and transcendental reflection as different instantiations or determinations of reflection as such. In this regard, Kant's strategy is similar to the one employed in the Metaphysical Deduction and various other parts of the *Critique*.

Logical reflection and transcendental reflection have at least two features in common: both acts precede the act of judging proper and both require that one adopt a particular vantage point. As Longuenesse points out, moreover, Kant no less than Wolff seems to consider logical reflection to precede the formation of both concepts and judgments: we can compare two different things either with the aim of producing new concepts or with the aim of determining, in a judgment, in which respect they are the same

---

[10] R5342, my translation, cf. R5552 (dated 1778–79) and R5907 (dated 1780–89). Kant makes the same point at A271–72/B327–28 and A281–82/B337–38. Already in 1755, he challenges the "metaphysical universality" of Leibniz's principle (NE, 1:410), albeit not yet in terms of his later distinction between sensibility and the understanding. See also LM Mrongovius (1782–83) (29:838–39).

or different.[11] In both cases, we carry out the comparison by relying on the concepts of sameness and difference.

However, Kant's analysis, while very sketchy, goes beyond Wolff's in various respects. Unlike Wolff, to begin with, Kant seems to assume that we logically reflect on concepts also in the case of judgments that themselves do not take the form of a comparison: what we compare are the concepts that function as subject and predicate in any judgment whatsoever rather than two different balls or the concepts of a triangle and a square. I take Kant to hold, in other words, that the judgment 'this ball is white' no less than the judgment 'this ball is heavier than that one' requires a preliminary act of reflection guided by sameness and difference.

A second, more important way in which Kant moves beyond Wolff consists in identifying *four* ways in which logical reflection, broadly conceived, can be carried out. Seen from Kant's perspective, the cognitive activity that precedes our actual judgments is guided not only by the concepts of sameness and difference but also by those of agreement and conflict, the inner and the outer, and matter and form. He considers these four pairs of concepts, called concepts of reflection (A270/B326), to exhaustively represent the vantage points from which the concepts that are to be combined in a judgment can be compared.[12]

Without offering examples, Kant explains the role of the first two pairs by relating them to the first two classes of the logical forms of judgment treated in the Metaphysical Deduction, namely, quantity and quality:

---

[11] See Longuenesse (1998: 133–34). On this point I disagree with Hessbrüggen-Walter (2004), who considers logical reflection to be irrelevant to the act of concept formation (165) and takes it to consist in the act of *assessing* one's potential judgments (168). In line with Kant's own account in the Appendix, I will focus on how the concepts of reflection underlie the very production of judgments (cf. Malter 1982: 134–35).

[12] Kant discusses these four pairs of concepts in some detail at A263–68/B319–24. A note dated 1772 (R4476) draws a link between the four pairs of concepts of reflection and the activity that the *Critique* calls logical reflection, but is too sketchy to warrant conclusions. The first note that mentions "concepts of reflection," dated 1776–78, conceives of them as concepts that, "qua grounds of the possibility to make judgments, contain the mere act of the understanding, which in the judgment is applied to the relation, in an absolute manner" (R5051, my translation). I assume that Kant here refers to the relation between subject and predicate that any judgment establishes. Apart from sameness and difference, the other pairs of concepts of reflection were also discussed in Wolffian treatises, though not in the strict manner of the Appendix. On this, see Broecken (1970: 59–68). Baumgarten's *Metaphysics* deals with matter, considered either as that which is determinable or as that which is actually determined in a judgment, that is, as subject, toward the end of the section on the relative predicates (344). Form is mentioned only in its capacity as formal cause (345). The *Prolegomena* criticizes Wolff and his followers for disregarding the difference between concepts of reflection and categories (4:326), but given my present purpose this point can be disregarded.

> Prior to all objective judgments we compare the concepts in order to arrive (1) at the *sameness* (of many representations under one concept) on behalf of *universal* judgments, or at their *difference* so as to generate *particular* judgments, (2) at *agreement*, from which *affirmative* judgments can be produced, and at *conflict*, from which *negative* ones can be produced, etc.[13]

We can infer from this passage that, for Kant, a judgment such as 'all balls are round' requires that I compare the balls at hand not only in view of sameness and difference but also in view of agreement and conflict. In the former case, the emphasis is on the subject concept. In the latter case, conversely, I consider the predicate 'round' and the subject 'ball' together so as to determine whether the former can be attributed to the latter at all. Since the predicate 'square,' for example, conflicts with the mark 'round' contained in the subject concept, my comparison in this case results in the negative judgment that 'no balls are square' (cf. A151/B190–91). I also carry out the comparison of the concepts at hand in view of agreement and conflict in the case of judgments such as 'some balls are white' or 'this ball is not red.' In the latter case, the redness merely conflicts with the representation of the white ball I actually perceive.

A later passage allows us to get clearer on Kant's understanding of the third and fourth pairs of concepts of reflection, that is, the inner and the outer, and matter and form. In logical reflection, Kant writes, we compare concepts in order to determine

> (1) whether two of them have the same content, (2) whether or not they contradict each other, (3) whether something is contained in the concept internally or is added to it, and (4) which of these concepts should count as given and which merely as a way to think the given concept. (A279/B335)

As regards the third vantage point, Kant suggests that, prior to my actual judgment, I need to single out a mark that is either contained in the very concept of the thing or can be attributed to the latter by drawing on sense perception: I can assert either that 'all balls are round' or that 'some balls are white.' In other words, I can choose to approach the subject concept in view of marks that are internal or external to it.

---

[13] A262/B317–18, translation modified. Here and below I add the numbers 1 to 4 for the sake of clarity. Kant's use of 'etc.' suggests that he considered the third and fourth pairs to run parallel to the third and fourth classes of the logical forms of judgment. On this, see Wolff (1995: 152–54) and Longuenesse (1998: 140–42, 147–49). In my opinion, both authors needlessly complicate the problem by drawing in elements of general logic, such as the analytic/synthetic distinction, that in this context are irrelevant. I will not delve into this much-debated issue, but keep focused on Kant's understanding of the concepts of reflection themselves.

The fourth and final vantage point Kant lists, matter and form, is concerned with the question as to which of the concepts involved I take to be 'determinable' and 'determining' (A261/B317). Thus, in the case of the two concepts 'ball' and 'round,' I must single out one concept as the subject and the other as the predicate prior to any comparison of their content. By dint of this aspect of logical reflection, I can consider the concept 'ball' either as something that can be determined by means of the predicate 'round' or as a determination of 'round things.' Kant notes that the concepts of matter and form "ground all other reflection, so inseparably are they bound up with every use of the understanding" (A266/B322).

Kant presents these four pairs of concepts as his "table of concepts of reflection" (A270/B3260). Clearly, this table is analogous to the table of the forms of judgments and, hence, to the table of the categories (A80/B106). These analogies – not explicitly mentioned in the text – suggest that Kant considered the concepts of reflection to instantiate the very functions of the pure understanding that the Metaphysical Deduction treats from a different point of view.[14]

However, these intriguing analogies need not concern us here. What should rather be retained from Kant's account is, first, that logical reflection requires that we determine from which vantage point the concepts at hand are to be compared and, second, that these vantage points are specified by concepts of reflection. As we will see, Kant considers transcendental reflection to take its bearings from these very concepts: since it is nothing but a different instantiation of reflection as such, it could not be otherwise. Thus, just as Kant uses the table of the forms of judgment as a stepping-stone toward the metaphysical deduction of the categories (cf. A78–79/B104–105), so he uses the table of the concepts of reflection as a stepping-stone toward his account of the concepts that guide transcendental reflection.

A final feature that ought to be mentioned at this point is that, for Kant, the "mere comparison" carried out by logical reflection "completely abstracts from the cognitive power to which the given representations belong" (A262–63/B318, cf. A54/B78). I will argue in Section 5 below that Kant considers this feature to have been unduly carried over to transcendental reflection, that is, to the act that necessarily precedes our a priori judgments about things and has produced amphibolous principles such as the principle of the identity of indiscernibles.

---

[14] See Kant's remark to this effect in the *Prolegomena* (4:326).

4 Transcendental Reflection and the Real Use of the Concepts of Reflection

Before turning to Kant's actual account of transcendental reflection, this section examines his allusive remarks on a type of reflective activity that precedes any judgment *about objects* – whether empirical or transcendental. These remarks are relevant because they provide Kant with a stepping-stone toward the account of transcendental reflection that is complementary to his analysis of logical reflection: contrary to the latter, this unspecified reflective activity is geared toward the cognition of objects and does not necessarily obliterate the distinction between sensibility and thought. For these reasons, one might consider this type of reflection to consist in the 'real' use of the concepts of reflection – even though Kant does not use the term 'real' or any other qualification in this context.[15]

At the beginning of the Appendix, Kant merely notes that *any* judgment requires an act of reflection that consists in distinguishing "the cognitive power to which the given concepts belong" (A261/B317) and, hence, of determining whether the representations to be connected must be considered from the vantage point of sensibility or that of the understanding:

> The first question prior to all further treatment of our representations is this: in which cognitive faculty do they belong together? Is it the understanding or is it the senses before (*vor*) which they are connected or compared? Many a judgment is accepted out of habit or connected through inclination. But since no reflection preceded or at least critically succeeded it, it counts as one that has its origin in the understanding. (A260–61/ B316–17)

While Kant does not provide examples, he clearly hints at cases where someone, on reflection, concedes she was carried away by strong feelings or prejudices.[16] In this context, Kant draws out one element of the accepted meaning of the concept of reflection, namely, the act of distinguishing which of one's representations stem from the understanding and which stem from the senses. Another example that could be adduced here is that

---

[15] See Diss, 2:393. Willaschek (1998: 341) also draws this connection. Strangely enough, however, he attributes the use of concepts of reflection not to transcendental reflection itself but to the "objective comparison" of representations made possible by the latter (343).

[16] See Hessbrüggen-Walter (2004) and Merritt (2015) for helpful contextualizations of this theme, including a discussion of relevant passages from Kant's lectures on logic. While Merritt rightly deflects the prevailing focus on empirical concept formation to Kant's critique of metaphysics, I hold that she, like Longuenesse, downplays the specifics of Kant's account of transcendental reflection.

of optical illusions: we can realize, on reflection, that we unduly connected the concepts 'stick' and 'bent' from a vantage point determined by the senses instead of the understanding.

Kant introduces his analysis of transcendental illusion in the Transcendental Dialectic by alluding to similar cases (cf. A294/B350–51). In the context of the Appendix, however, he focuses his attention on the very capacity of the understanding to frame things either in terms of the way they are given to the senses or by abstracting from the way they appear, that is, as phenomena or noumena. I will refer to these contrary possibilities as the vantage points of sensibility and the pure understanding, respectively.

While Kant's remarks to this effect might be considered obscure or contrived, it is clear which purpose they serve. Kant tacitly – but in accordance with a by now familiar strategy – transfers the capacity to consider one's empirical judgments in view of the subjective sources from which they stem to *any* mode of reflection and, hence, to the mode of reflection that is concerned with *objects as such* rather than representations of balls or houses. This transferral leads Kant to the concept of transcendental reflection, which he defines as follows:

> I call transcendental reflection (*Überlegung*) the act by means of which I hold together (*zusammenhalte*) the comparison of representations *as such* with the cognitive power in which (*darin*) the comparison is carried out, and by means of which I distinguish whether they are to be compared to one another as belonging to the pure understanding or to sensible intuition.[17]

Thus, the question Kant addresses in this context concerns neither the source of predicates such as substance or causality nor the conditions of their actual use. The question is rather whether the intended *objects* are to be treated as phenomena or noumena. Whereas, in the former case, the concepts to be connected are to be approached from the vantage point of sensibility, in the latter case they are to be connected from the vantage point of the pure understanding.[18]

---

[17] A261/B317, translation modified, emphasis mine, cf. A295/B351. The Cambridge translation takes the passage to mean that the representations themselves are situated in one or the other cognitive power even though Kant uses a singular noun (the comparison). Moreover, the German version refers not to pure intuition but to sensible intuition. In the *First Introduction to the Critique of the Power of Judgment*, Kant defines reflection as such as the act "of comparing and holding together given representations either with other representations or with one's power of cognition" (20:211, cf. CPJ, 5:180–81). A comparison of the Appendix with these and other passages is beyond the scope of the present chapter.

[18] In this regard, my reading shares common ground with Malter (1982: 138–44). To avoid confusion, it should be noted that a pure concept is treated from the vantage point of sensibility if its use is geared toward appearances. Thus, treating representations from the vantage point of

According to Kant, this preliminary consideration is irrelevant to the merely logical comparison of concepts in view of sameness and difference. However, it is only by dint of this consideration that "the surreptitious acts of the pure understanding" (A268/B324) can be avoided:

> The concepts can be compared logically without worrying about where their objects belong, whether as noumena to the understanding or as phenomena to sensibility. But if we would get to *objects* with these concepts, then what is first and foremost required is transcendental reflection about the specific cognitive power they are to be objects for (*für welche Erkenntniskraft sie Gegenstände sein sollen*), whether for the pure understanding or for sensibility. Without this reflection I can make only a very insecure use of these concepts, and there arise allegedly synthetic principles ... that rest solely on a transcendental amphiboly, i.e., a confusion (*Verwechslung*) of the pure object of the understanding with the appearance.[19]

There can be no doubt, I think, that Kant has in mind principles such as Leibniz's principle of the identity of indiscernibles, to which the Appendix refers repeatedly.[20] If Leibniz had considered whether the principle establishes a connection between 'thing' and 'identity' from the vantage point of sensibility or, rather, that of the pure understanding alone, he would have realized that the latter is the case and, consequently, that the principle holds true of noumena but not, for example, of leaves one can pick up in a garden.[21]

Given the *Inaugural Dissertation*, Kant must have considered his critique to apply to Crusius as well: the latter would not have asserted that "everything that exists is somewhere" if he had realized that this principle establishes a connection between 'thing' and 'existence' from the vantage point of sensibility and, hence, holds true of appearances alone.[22]

What is lacking in each of these cases, in sum, is a preliminary consideration as to whether the conception of the intended object does or does not rest on sensibility and, thus, whether it ought to be treated as phenomenon or noumenon. Depending on the outcome of this reflection, the pure understanding ought to use the pure concepts that function as the

---

sensibility does not mean that the understanding is not involved in their subsequent connection in a judgment. Willaschek (1998: 341–42) seems to overlook these distinctions.

[19] A269–70/B325–26, translation modified, emphasis mine, cf. A279/B355.

[20] See A271–72/B327–28 and A281/B337.

[21] Kant also uses the example, already discussed in Chapter 4, Section 4, of two water droplets (A272/B328).

[22] See Diss, 2:412n, and my comments on this topic in Chapter 2, Section 4.

predicates of its a priori judgments *either* empirically *or* in a purely intellectual manner.

Obviously, carrying out this reflection in an adequate manner requires that one conceive of sensibility and thought as two separate sources of representations in the first place. Kant precisely blames his predecessors, regardless of whether they prioritized sensibility (Locke) or the intellect (Leibniz), with assuming the continuity of these cognitive powers.[23] Since their alleged synthetic a priori judgments rested on this unwarranted assumption, it falls to critical philosophy to correct it after the fact.

As we will see in the next section, Kant's more specific critique of the continuism he attributes to Leibniz and his followers takes its bearings from the table of concepts of reflection discussed in Section 3. This is to say that he more or less implicitly transfers the result of his analysis of the concepts underlying logical reflection to his examination of the misguided assumption underlying former ontology.

5   Kant's Critique of Leibniz

As was seen above, Kant follows Wolff by arguing that logical reflection rests on the concepts of sameness and difference. By dint of the concept of sameness I can either identify the marks that two different concepts have in common or posit that two balls are the same as regards their weight. In the latter case, I implicitly treat these balls from the vantage point of sensibility.

Given his example of the two houses, moreover, Wolff seems to have held that philosophy deliberately abstracts from features such as location and size so as to determine what things have in common from the vantage point of the intellect. Along the same line, I will argue below, Kant points out that the human mind necessarily relies on the concept of sameness to make a priori judgments about things, in which case it abstracts from the vantage point of sensibility.

However, Kant's assessment of this insight is very different from Wolff's, for he uses it as the starting point of his critique of Leibniz and the metaphysical tradition preeminently represented by him. On Kant's

---

[23] See Chapter 1, Sections 3 and 5. For Leibniz, Kant writes in an oft-quoted passage, "sensibility was only a confused kind of representation ... and not a special source of representations; for him appearance was the representation of the thing in itself, although distinguished from cognition through the understanding in its logical form.... In a word, Leibniz intellectualized the appearances" (A270–71/B326–27). At A44/B61–62 Kant attributes this position to Wolff as well. See also A853–54/B881–82.

account, Leibniz's principle of the identity of indiscernibles rests on a fateful combination of the logical use of the concept of sameness and what I have called the real use of this very concept. Enticed by the capacity of logical reflection to manipulate concepts, Leibniz relied on the concept of sameness to make purely intellectual judgments about things as such as well.[24]

Yet Kant's critique of Leibnizianism does not target the principle of the identity of indiscernibles alone. Drawing on his earlier account of the four pairs of concepts of reflection, Kant implicitly infers that Leibniz's system must also rest on an amphibolous use of the concepts of agreement, the inner, and form. As he puts it, the table of the concepts of reflection

> has the unexpected advantage of laying before our eyes that which is distinctive in his theory *in all its parts* as well as the leading ground of this peculiar way of thinking, which rested on nothing but a misunderstanding. (A270/B327, emphasis mine)

Accordingly, Kant analyzes Leibniz's ontology by adopting the table of the concepts of reflection as his guiding thread. As was mentioned above, he argues that Leibniz's ontology relied on the concept of *sameness* to assert that things are identical if all of their intrinsic determinations are identical (A263/B319). In his view, moreover, Leibniz relied on the concept of *agreement* to assert that the qualities affirmed of things cannot conflict with one another (A264/B320) and on the concept of *the inner* to assert that all things possess intrinsic characteristics (A265/B321). Last, he claims that Leibniz considered things to *precede* and *determine* their spatiotemporal form rather than being determined by the latter, which means that he conceived of them as monads.[25]

I take Kant to maintain, in short, that Leibniz, as regards his ontological principles, was "deceived by the amphiboly of the concepts of reflection" (A270/B326) because he unduly considered the connection between things as such and their determinations from the vantage point of the pure understanding alone and this, more specifically, in view of the concepts of sameness, agreement, the inner, and determination rather than their counterparts.

---

[24] Cf. A280/B336. Focusing on the distinction between analytic and synthetic judgments, Lanier Anderson (2015) is devoted to this aspect of Kant's critique of former metaphysics.

[25] A267/B323. Kant covers the same ground in somewhat more specific terms at A272/B328, A273/B329, A274/B330, and A276/B332. I draw on elements of both versions. See Hess (1981) and Jauernig (2008) for more detailed discussions of this aspect of the Appendix.

However, Kant does not blame Leibniz for positing noumena such as monads per se.[26] His principles are misguided, he writes, only insofar as he "extended" their scope beyond "concepts of things as such" to "the objects of the senses."[27] By thus assuming the continuity between pure thought and sensibility, I add, Leibniz allegedly paved the way for the confusions and controversies that plagued the Wolffians and their early opponents alike. Leibniz himself is said to have erred insofar as he, no less than the anonymous "monadists" mentioned in the Transcendental Dialectic (A439/B467), "believed himself to have made no little advance in the cognition of nature."[28] Seen from Kant's perspective, by contrast, the natural sciences rest on principles that allow the human mind to treat objects that differ from one another as regards their location and extrinsic determinations.[29] In order to determine the relation between a leaden and an iron ball in terms of size, weight, or causality, Leibniz's purely "intellectual system of the world" (A270/B326) is of no avail.

Arrived at this point, one might ask: What if it turned out, on reflection, that the concepts to be connected for the sake of a priori judgments about noumena such as the soul and God must be considered from the vantage point of pure thought, whereas a priori judgments about phenomena require that the relevant concepts are considered from the vantage point of sensibility? Clearly, this question took center stage in the *Dissertation*. As was argued in Chapter 2, Kant must have realized in the early 1770s that only the latter kind of a priori judgments can actually lay claim to objectivity. Somewhere during the 1770s he must have asked himself, finally, whether these judgments – the principles of the pure understanding – no less than their purely intellectual counterparts ultimately take their bearings from concepts of reflection. Whereas the first two issues are dealt with from various angles throughout the *Critique of Pure Reason*, the latter question, I hope to show in what follows, is addressed in the Appendix alone.

---

[26] A283/B340, cf. Broecken (1970: 246). Jauernig (2008) also puts into perspective Kant's critique of Leibniz and/or Wolff. This approach is supported by Kant's well-known reply to Eberhard in *On a Discovery* (1790) that the *Critique of Pure Reason* is a "true apology for Leibniz" (8:250; cf. Jauernig 2008: 44). For reasons of space I cannot elaborate on Kant's engagement with Leibniz and his followers in this work.

[27] A272/B328, cf. A264/B319.

[28] A271–72/B327–28, cf. A42–44/B59–62, A60–61/B85. According to Kant's lectures, Leibniz aimed "to prove that two things *in the world* are not and cannot be identical and similar" (LM Mrongovius, 29:839, emphasis mine).

[29] B320, cf. B321. As was mentioned in Chapter 5, Section 4, Langton (1998: 96) stresses that Kant rejected Leibniz's reduction of physical relations to the intrinsic properties of monads.

6 Transcendental Reflection Proper

So far we have seen that, for Kant, transcendental reflection determines whether the representations to be connected in an a priori judgment are to be considered from the vantage point of the pure understanding or from that of sensibility. Clearly, this act undergirds the transcendental critique carried out in the *Critique of Pure Reason*. Moreover, since Kant refers to transcendental reflection as a "duty" that must be assumed (A263/B319), he seems to use the term to refer to transcendental critique alone. Yet some passages point in a different direction. Thus, Kant notes at one point that Leibniz's intellectualization of space and time "arose solely from ... the mistake (*Täuschung*) of transcendental reflection."[30] Such a mistake cannot occur if someone is merely involved in logical reflection and presupposes at least the real use of concepts of reflection.

While the text remains ambiguous on this point, the problem might be solved by assuming that Kant took Leibniz to have carried out a defective version of transcendental reflection. Kant's definition of transcendental reflection, cited in Section 4, is applicable to Leibniz in the sense that the latter, first, distinguished between sensibility and the pure understanding and, second, decided to compare the relevant concepts from the vantage point of the pure understanding alone. As was argued in Chapter 3, Kant often uses the term 'transcendental' to denote any mode of cognition that is "occupied ... with our a priori concepts of objects as such."[31] If this broad sense of the term is taken into account, it is plausible that Kant considered the critical enactment of transcendental reflection to differ from its Leibnizian counterpart in that it does not suppress the sensible conditions under which something can become an object of cognition.

Clearly, it is only by attributing a misguided version of transcendental reflection to Leibniz's ontology that Kant can illuminate its "various parts" in terms of the four pairs of concepts of reflection alleged to be constitutive of the discipline as such. Now if Kant's own transcendental critique rests on a mode of transcendental reflection as well, as is clearly the case, then it must likewise rely on these four pairs of concepts. But how do the various parts or aspects of this critique differ from Leibniz's conception of things as such?

---

[30] A275/B331, cf. A271/B327. The context suggests that Kant took the three preceding mistakes he attributes to Leibniz to stem from transcendental reflection as well. Moreover, Kant writes that Leibniz was "deceived by the amphiboly of the concepts of reflection" (A270/B326).

[31] A11–12. On this, see Chapter 3, Section 4.

As was seen above, Kant suggests that Leibniz's ontology rests on an undue extension of logical reflection in that it treats all representations as "homogeneous."[32] In the case of a priori judgments concerning monads, for example, both the subject and predicate are purely intellectual concepts, which is to say that their connection takes place from the vantage point of the pure understanding. In the *Dissertation*, Kant writes in this regard:

> As far as intellectual thoughts (*intellectualia*) as such are concerned, in respect to which *the use of the intellect is real*, the concepts of objects as well as of their relations are given by the nature of the intellect itself.[33]

Evidently, this homogeneity does not obtain necessarily. Kant continues the dense sentence that deals with this issue by noting that transcendental reflection, geared toward the cognition of objects, "contains the ground of the possibility of the objective comparison of the representations."[34] At this point, he appears to shift the focus to the act of transcendental reflection such as it *ought* to be carried out prior to the elaboration of any ontological system, that is, to the "duty" that the Leibnizians – including, to some extent, the author of the *Dissertation* – had forsaken and that therefore has to be carried out after the fact (cf. A263/B319).

If transcendental reflection is to retrieve the ground, or vantage point, from which the a priori comparison and connection of representations can actually produce *objects of cognition*, I take Kant to mean, then it must rid itself of the assumption that the representations to be compared must be homogeneous, that is, stem from the same source. As he puts it, transcendental reflection is "very different" from the comparison proper to logical reflection because it assumes that "the cognitive power to which the representations belong *is not the same*" (A262–63/B319, emphasis mine).

An example might help to clarify this crucial point. Thus, if we use the pure concept of causality to posit that all events – qua appearances – succeed one another in a rule-bound manner, then the concepts to be connected in the a priori judgment stem from *two different sources*: whereas the predicate 'causality' originates from the pure understanding, the subject concept 'appearances as such' originates from sensibility as far as its

---

[32] A262/B318. The German term is 'gleichartig.'
[33] Diss, 2:394, translation modified. On this, see Chapter 2, Section 4.
[34] A262/B319. Since Kant's text is very condensed and somewhat cryptic here, I take the liberty to fill some of the gaps.

content is concerned.[35] Thus, according to Kant, synthetic a priori principles that purport to be cognitions of objects are warranted only if the concepts that function as subject and predicate of the judgment are *heterogeneous*. Obviously, this is true of the principles of the pure understanding treated in the Transcendental Analytic, but not of their Leibnizian counterparts.

Framed in this way, the Appendix merely summarizes the result of the preceding parts of the Transcendental Analytic, namely, that synthetic a priori principles can be employed with regard to possible objects of experience alone (cf. A236/B295–96). Actually, however, Kant explores a more radical avenue. As I see it, every step he takes in the Appendix is intended to grasp the exact point at which Leibnizian ontology and his own reformed version of the discipline part ways.

Let me return once more to the table of concepts of reflection to explain what I take to be Kant's crucial insight in this regard. As seen, he considers Leibniz's ontology ultimately to prioritize the concepts of sameness, agreement, the inner, and determination at the expense of their contraries. But if the table of these concepts can be used to identify the main flaws of Leibnizian and post-Leibnizian ontology, I take Kant to hold, then it might as well be used to identify the main features of the reformed ontology he himself envisioned and partly carried out. The passages in which Kant elaborates this self-reflective strand of his analysis are not very easy to identify, because they are embedded within the fourfold critique of Leibniz discussed above. However, they can be 'abstracted' from this context and presented independently of the latter as follows:

(1) *Multiplicity and numerical difference* are already given by space itself as the condition of outer appearances. (A264/B320)

(2) That which is real in appearances (*realitas phenomenon*) ... can certainly be in *conflict* and, united in the same subject, something real can partly or wholly destroy the effect of the other, like two forces moving in the same straight line that either push or pull a point in opposite directions.[36]

(3) The inner determinations of a *substantia phaenomenon* in space ... are nothing but *relations*, and this substance itself is nothing but a sum total of mere relations. (A265/B321)

---

[35] The Schematism Chapter mentions that "pure concepts of the understanding ... , in comparison with empirical ... intuitions, are entirely heterogeneous (*ungleichartig*)" (A137–38/B176–77).

[36] A265/B320–21. The first text in which Kant makes this point is *Attempt to Introduce the Concept of Negative Magnitudes into Philosophy* (1763).

(4)   If [space and time] are merely sensible intuitions, in which we determine all objects merely as appearances, then the *form* of intuition ... precedes all *matter* (the sensations) ... and first makes the latter possible. (A267/B323)

Thus, if the human mind adopts the vantage point of sensibility, as it does first and foremost, it will consider things such as leaden and iron balls (1) to *differ* from one another at least in terms of location, (2) to be subject to *conflicting* forces, and (3) to be determined by *extrinsic* properties such as color and weight. Finally, the concept of determinable allows the human mind (4) to conceive of a thing as appearance, that is, as something that is *preceded* by the forms of space and time and *depends* on the latter to become an object at all.

These passages suggest, in other words, that the human mind, insofar as it conceives of the potential object of its synthetic a priori judgments from the vantage point of sensibility, does so by taking its bearings from the concepts of reflection of difference, the outer, conflict, and the determinable. In this case, its real use of the concepts of reflection is geared toward appearances and, hence, entails the warranted synthetic a priori judgments that Kant treats under the heading of 'principles of the pure understanding.'

Former ontology, for its part, substituted the concepts of reflection constitutive of the vantage point of sensibility by their counterparts to conceive of things by means of the pure understanding alone. It is this amphibolous use of the concepts of reflection, I take Kant to hold, that paved the way for the deceptive inferences concerning the soul, the world as such, and God treated at great length in the Transcendental Dialectic. In order to block this path, the second-order critique carried out in the *Critique* urges ontology to assume the original vantage point of sensibility and, accordingly, restrict the pure understanding's use of pure concepts to the realm of appearances. As was argued in Chapters 2 and 6 especially, however, this transcendental critique does not prevent former special metaphysics from assuming the vantage point of the pure intellect. Metaphysicians can do so, on Kant's view, on the condition that they refrain from conceiving of the ideas of reason as quasi-objects and, hence, from determining the latter by pure concepts the meaning of which is infected by pure sensibility.

7   Conclusion

Kant's critique of Leibnizian ontology in the Appendix can be seen as an attempt to comprehend the history of metaphysics in view of those few options available to it that follow from its very concept and, thus, define its actual course at least to some extent. Insofar as this strand of the text adopts a vantage point that is a priori rather than historical, it ties in with the extremely sketchy concluding chapter of the *Critique of Pure Reason* (A852/B880).

In line with the work as a whole, the Appendix targets the prevailing assumption of pre-critical metaphysics that the intellect can obtain cognitions of objects independently of the way they appear. Unlike any other part of the *Critique*, however, the text seeks to account for this propensity by suggesting that pre-critical ontologies, blinded by the power of logical reflection, extended the activity of the latter from the production and ordering of concepts to the cognition of things as such, that is, to anything whatsoever.

This means, on the reading put forward in this chapter, that these ontologies failed to carry out the act Kant calls transcendental reflection in the right way. Ignoring the radical distinction between phenomena and noumena, they approached the subject and predicate to be connected in synthetic a priori judgments from the vantage point of the pure understanding and, hence, let themselves be guided by the concepts of sameness, agreement, the inner, and determination.

There is no doubt that Kant attributed this myopic mode of transcendental reflection to Wolff and Baumgarten as well. As was mentioned in Chapter 1, one of Kant's notes portrays the latter as "a Cyclops among metaphysicians, who was missing one eye, namely critique."[37] Locke and Crusius, for their part, can be said to have carried out transcendental reflection in a myopic way too, namely, by one-sidedly assuming the vantage point of sensibility and, thus, conceiving of anything whatsoever as different from other things, potentially conflicting, constituted by outer determinations, and determinable. The third option Kant outlines, finally, consists in radically distinguishing the use of pure concepts with regard to noumena from their use with regard to phenomena so as to ensure that the one approach does not encroach on the other.

Considered in this way, the transcendental critique that is carried out throughout the Transcendental Analytic and comes into its own in the Appendix rests on the view that former ontology transgressed its limits by substituting difference with sameness, conflict with agreement, the outer with the inner, and the determinable with determination. While the ensuing homogeneity of the concepts to be connected is required to

---

[37] R5081 (dated 1776–78). See Chapter 1, Section 2.

conceive of noumena in purely intellectual terms, it must be avoided at all cost to obtain synthetic a priori cognitions of objects.

Kant's critique of special metaphysics in the Transcendental Dialectic apart, we now seem to have reached the position of someone who has solved all elements of a complex mathematical problem and is about to draw a final conclusion. Yet there is one element that has receded into the background over the course of my analysis of the Transcendental Analytic, namely, Kant's intention to elaborate a full-fledged system of pure reason. The questions that are still open, accordingly, concern Kant's views as to the form and content of a metaphysical system that, preceded by transcendental critique, can preclude the delusions produced by its Wolffian counterparts. Turning to the Architectonic, among other texts, the next chapter addresses these questions.

CHAPTER 8

Kant's Projected System of Pure Reason

1 Introduction

Already in the short outline of his 1765–66 lectures on metaphysics, logic, and ethics, Kant notes that a critique of metaphysics ought to contribute to the elaboration of "a precise ground-plan, on the basis of which ... an edifice of reason (*Gebäude der Vernunft*) can be erected in a lasting and rule-bound way."[1] In whatever ways Kant may have changed his mind on the structure and content of the building he envisioned, the view that a critical, meta-metaphysical investigation should prepare the ground for a scientific metaphysical system runs through his writings from the mid-1760s to the *Critique of Pure Reason* and a number of documents from the 1780s and 1790s. As we know, however, Kant not only spent most of the 1770s on the critical part of his project, but came to prioritize other projects after the publication of the first *Critique*. As a result, the "dogmatic" or "doctrinal" part of his metaphysical project remained largely unwritten and, consequently, receded into the shadows of Kant scholarship.[2]

Various passages on this issue, some of which have been quoted already, indicate that Kant did not regard the completion of the theoretical part of his projected metaphysics as particularly challenging. He even suggests in the *Critique* that elaborating "the system of pure (speculative) reason" (Axxi), as he calls it, could be carried out by his pupils and colleagues:

---

[1] *Announcement*, 2:310, translation modified. On this, see Chapter 2, Section 3.
[2] Kant confidently closes the Preface to the *Critique of the Power of Judgment* (1790) by announcing that, having completed his "entire critical enterprise," he will proceed "without hindrance to the doctrinal part" (5:170). As was noted in the Introduction to this book, the *Critique of Pure Reason* asserts that "metaphysics ... must necessarily be carried out dogmatically and ... in the manner of the schools (*schulgerecht*)" (Bxxxvi, translation modified). Further passages on this issue will be discussed in Section 6 below.

It can be no small inducement for the reader, it seems to me, to unite his effort with that of the author, when he has the prospect of carrying out, according to the outline given here (*das vorgelegte Entwurf*), a great and important piece of work, and that in a complete and lasting way. Now metaphysics, according to the concepts we will give of it here, is the only science that can rightly hope (*sich versprechen darf*) to be able to reach such a completion, and this shortly and with little but unified effort.... For this work is nothing but the inventory of everything we possess through pure reason, ordered systematically. Nothing here can escape us, because what reason brings forth entirely out of itself cannot be hidden, but is brought to light by reason itself as soon as the common principle of this inventory has been discovered.[3]

However, Kant's remarks on the subject were largely ignored, misinterpreted, or considered to provide too little guidance. Thus, in an essay published in 2001, Ameriks notes that "it is still very unclear what Kant had in mind by the demand for a system," and since then few commentators have tackled the issue.[4] While I do not pretend to completely clear the fog around this part of Kant's project, the aim of the present chapter is to reconstruct the theoretical part of the metaphysical system such as Kant envisioned it at least during the years he was working on the *Critique*. Drawing on the Architectonic, the Transcendental Dialectic, the *Metaphysical Foundations of Natural Science*, lecture transcripts, and letters, I hope to determine as precisely as possible which elements of Wolffian metaphysics Kant intended to take over, at which points he intended to depart from his predecessors, and which problems his intended reform of Wolffian metaphysics would have encountered.

I do not want to suggest that Kant's projected system would have been very appealing. Unlike the *Critique*, it would not have instructed us – or his contemporaries – about the workings of the human mind and the limits imposed on it. I hold, however, that the logic that animates the *Critique of Pure Reason* cannot be adequately grasped unless we take into account the idea on behalf of which it was undertaken, namely, the idea of a comprehensive treatment of the pure concepts and a priori principles

---

[3] Axix–xx, translation modified, cf. Bxxiii–xxiv, A13–14/B27–28. On my reading, Kant here considers the *Critique* itself to offer the outline of the theoretical part of his system of pure reason (which is mentioned at Axxi). In what follows I will largely abstract from the practical part of Kant's projected system, and use terms such as 'system of pure reason' and 'metaphysical system' to refer to its theoretical part alone.

[4] Ameriks (2001): 73. See Zöller (2001) for a contextualization of Kant's notion of a system and an account of the organicist elements of Kant's theory in this regard. While Wellmann (2018: 51–93) partly covers the same ground, she, unlike Zöller, relates them to the idea of a system of pure reason outlined in the Architectonic.

constitutive of any cognition of objects. Evidently, reading the *Critique* from this vantage point is a way of further supporting the interpretation defended in this book as a whole.

Some of Kant's remarks on the subject suggest that he hesitated or changed his mind on certain aspects, and I do not think he was able to resolve all problems he encountered. Nevertheless, I hope to show that Kant's various accounts of the theoretical branch of his system-to-be cohere to a fairly large extent. My analysis of the scattered material will be guided by a twofold hypothesis. I hold, first, that Kant's projected system would have resembled Baumgarten's *Metaphysics* in terms of both structure and content and, second, that its main differences from the latter can be inferred from the results of the *Critique*.

As regards its method, Kant's system would definitely have differed from Baumgarten's by taking its bearings from the table of categories, that is, from the constructive strand of the Transcendental Analytic. It follows from strand [2] of Kant's critique of metaphysics, further, that the system would not have contained synthetic a priori judgments about objects except such that pertain to possible objects of experience.[5] Seen from the perspective of the system, however, the critical question concerning the warranted or unwarranted application of pure concepts falls away, since metaphysics itself ought not to engage in the actual application of concepts at all. What remains, rather, is the task of generating, within each particular metaphysical discipline, the a priori concepts and principles that are presupposed and actually employed in disciplines such as empirical physics or moral theology.

More specifically, I will argue that Kant intended his system to differ from preceding versions by being completely devoid of empirical elements and, in part, even of sensibility as such. As we know, the criterion of intellectual purity follows from strand [1] of Kant's critique of metaphysics, which goes back to the *Inaugural Dissertation* and is in line with his conception of philosophy as "rational cognition from concepts"[6] and of the system as "the whole of . . . philosophical cognition obtained by pure reason" (A841/B869).

---

[5] On the distinction between the two strands, see, in particular, Chapter 2, Section 7. With reference to his projected system, Kant writes that the "completeness of the analysis as well as the derivation from the a priori concepts which are to be provided in the future will nevertheless be easy to complete once these concepts have been established as exhaustive principles of synthesis," that is, I add, as a priori rules that tell the mind how to unify its representations (A14/B28, translation modified).

[6] A713/B741, cf. A14/B28, MFNS, 4:469.

Apart from the criterion of purity, intellectual or otherwise, important clues about the content of the system can be found in the *Critique of Pure Reason* itself. I have argued in Chapter 3 that transcendental logic consists of a first-order and a second-order strand and that the *Critique* develops the former only insofar as this is required for the purpose of the latter. Thus, Kant writes with regard to his projected ontology – that is, transcendental philosophy qua first-order metaphysical discipline – that the *Critique* "is not yet this science itself, since it goes only so far in the analysis as is required for the complete estimation of synthetic a priori cognition."[7] Now I take it that Kant in the Transcendental Dialectic proceeds in a similar manner. I claim, more specifically, that he here elaborates his second-order critique of Wolffian rational psychology, general cosmology, and natural theology *in tandem* with a first-order treatment of the rational core of these disciplines, yet does so only insofar as this is required by the critical aim of the text. If this is the case, then it should be possible to let the second-order strand of Kant's account fade out so as to foreground the first-order elements of the projected system and, hence, to present them independently of the context in which they initially took root. As I will argue below, this is also done in Kant's division of metaphysical disciplines in the Architectonic.

Unlike Wood, Ameriks, and Dyck, among others, I grant much weight to this penultimate chapter of the *Critique*, which is discussed in Section 2.[8] Since Kant not only used Baumgarten's *Metaphysics* as his main textbook, but also told his readers to draw on it for the purpose of establishing a system of metaphysics, I will refer to this work rather than the works of Wolff or other Wolffians. Sections 3 and 4 seek to clarify the structure and content of Kant's projected ontology, rational physics, rational psychology, rational cosmology, and rational theology. Kant held that his reformed metaphysical system ultimately ought to further the moral ends of humanity. This issue is briefly addressed in Section 5.

---

[7] A14/B28. See Chapter 3, Section 5.

[8] Most readers, including Pollok (2001: 78), shy away from the Architectonic because it does not seem to fit the image of Kant as a critical philosopher. Tonelli (1994: 296–97) notes that Kant's division of metaphysics in this chapter "is not intended to correspond to the reality of Kant's philosophy." While this cannot be denied, I disagree with his claim that Kant did not *intend* to elaborate a system along the lines of this division. Insofar as I underline Kant's effort to preserve core elements of Wolffian special metaphysics, my interpretation concurs with Wood (1978), Ameriks (1982/2000), and Dyck (2014). Yet Ameriks's study of the paralogisms does not take into account the Architectonic and, thus, cannot but try to identify elements of Kant's "modest rationalism" in the Transcendental Dialectic itself (cf. xxii). Wood and Dyck likewise defend the indebtedness of the Transcendental Dialectic to branches of former special metaphysics without appealing to the Architectonic or Kant's projected system.

In Section 6, finally, I argue, against the common opinion, that Kant's explicit references to his projected system during the 1780s and 1790s are largely consistent.

2   The Building Plan

How is metaphysics possible as a science? Answering the question that figures most prominently in the *Prolegomena* requires first of all that we know what is meant by the term 'science.'[9] According to the *Metaphysical Foundations*, a science is "a whole of cognitions ordered according to principles" (4:467). On this rather minimal definition, a metaphysical system counts as a science if its content is ordered in a systematic manner. It appears that Kant would also conceive of his projected metaphysics as a science in the strict sense of the term, because the latter is said to treat its object, or subject matter, according to a priori principles alone.[10] But what is required to actually establish metaphysics as a science? Answering this question requires that we get clearer on the structure of Kant's projected system as well as on the method by means of which the 'inventory' of each of its parts can be generated. The present section engages in the first of these tasks.

Kant notes in the Introduction to the *Critique* that metaphysics ought to interrupt its work on the building of purported a priori cognitions in order to first investigate their "extension, validity, and value" (A3/B7). This act of critique is said to prepare the ground for a "complete system of the philosophy of pure reason" that should not be "so extended as to defy the hope that it can be entirely completed."[11] Reiterating this comparison, the Doctrine of Method considers the preceding parts of the *Critique* to have provided the materials required to erect the building as well as to have determined its "height and strength" in proportion to these materials. Much more modest than its pre-critical counterparts, the system Kant has in mind should be "suited to our needs" (A707/B735).

Kant considers the Doctrine of Method as a whole to determine "the formal conditions of a complete system of pure reason" (A707–8/ B735–36). Regardless of whether its four chapters can be fully subsumed

---

[9] Prol, 4:279–80, cf. A14/B18, B22.

[10] MFNS, 4:468–69, cf. A645/B673, A832–33/B860–61. Kant's various definitions do not include the requirement that a science produce cognitions of objects. Contra Willaschek (2018: 43), among others, I therefore hold that the question as to whether the branches of former special metaphysics can be turned into sciences cannot be settled – in the negative – by referring to Kant's criterion for the cognition of objects.

[11] A12/B26, translation modified, cf. A13/B27.

under this heading, this description fits the Architectonic very well. In this short and dense chapter, Kant actually outlines the "plan" or "schema" according to which the system of pure reason ought to be established.[12]

Kant maintains in the Architectonic that philosophy is pure if it does not rest on empirical principles.[13] This is true of both the transcendental critique carried out in the preceding parts of the *Critique of Pure Reason* and the "system of pure reason" for which it prepares the ground.[14] Although, as Kant notes, both critique and system could be considered branches of metaphysics, he proposes to use the term 'metaphysics' to denote the system of pure reason alone.[15] Considered in this way, metaphysics is the branch of pure philosophy that presents "all pure a priori cognition" in a systematic manner (A845/B873) and is divided into a metaphysics of nature and a metaphysics of morals (A841/B869). Its former part, to which Kant also refers as metaphysics in the narrow sense, is said to treat the principles that stem from concepts alone and make possible the theoretical cognition of things (A841/B869).

Remarkably, Kant notes that the system of pure reason, that is, the metaphysics of nature and morals taken together, consists in the "systematic interconnection" of the "true as well as apparent" philosophical cognitions produced by pure reason (A841/B869). As I see it, the term 'apparent' need not refer to the illusions produced in former special metaphysics.[16] A more plausible explanation consists in assuming that a metaphysics of morals cannot obtain theoretical cognitions of objects. However, the passage might also allude to the parts of the metaphysics of nature that treat the purely intellectual determinations of the world as such, the soul, and God. Seen from a critical perspective, attributing simplicity to the soul, for instance, does not amount to cognition proper, but doing so is nevertheless warranted under the condition that one refrains from treating the soul as an object.

As was explained in Chapter 3, Kant's further division of the metaphysics of nature into general metaphysics, or ontology, and special

---

[12] See A707/B735 and A833/B861.   [13] A840/B868, cf. A14/B28.

[14] A841/B869, cf. CPJ, 20: 195.

[15] A841/B869. A drafted diagram of the divisions of metaphysics, dated 1776–78, corresponds to the one presented in the Architectonic except insofar as it conceives of critique and ontology as two branches of transcendental philosophy (R4851). According to this diagram, critique constitutes the first part of the metaphysics of nature alone. This division is more in line with Kant's decision, in the years after 1781, to elaborate a separate critique of practical reason.

[16] Authors who assume the contrary, in accordance with the standard view, include Ferrarin (2015: 246) and Willaschek (2018: 42–43).

metaphysics follows the Wolffian tradition.[17] Unlike Wolff, however, Kant does not assume that metaphysics is concerned with things. Avoiding this term, he in the Architectonic conceives of the first part of the metaphysics of nature as a discipline that considers "the understanding and reason itself in a system of all concepts and principles that are related to objects as such" and that can be called either ontology or transcendental philosophy.[18] The latter term is used here in the same sense as in the Introduction to the *Critique of Pure Reason*. As seen, Kant here defines transcendental philosophy proper as the system of "our a priori concepts of objects as such," a system that is not carried out in an exhaustive manner in the *Critique* itself.[19] Kant's identification of ontology with transcendental philosophy in this sense in the Architectonic suggests that he in this context deliberately abstracts from the difference between pre-critical and critical instantiations of metaphysics: the "formal conditions" treated here concern the rational core of each of these instantiations, albeit that the latter may not reflect them in an adequate manner.

The Architectonic explains the relation between the disciplines that used to be called ontology and special metaphysics as follows:

> Metaphysics in this narrower sense consists of transcendental philosophy and the physiology of pure reason. The former considers only the understanding and reason themselves in a system of all concepts and principles that are related to objects as such, *without objects that would be given* (*Ontologia*); the latter considers nature, i.e., the sum total of *given* objects . . . and is therefore physiology (though only *rationalis*).[20]

According to this passage, the first part of the system, namely, transcendental philosophy, is concerned with the concepts and principles produced by the intellect, that is, with the elements treated to some extent in the Transcendental Analytic. Obviously, this raises the question as to whether Kant held that space and time ought to be treated in transcendental philosophy. The part of Baumgarten's *Metaphysics* devoted to ontology provides definitions of concepts such as space and time (239), extension

---

[17] Cf. Bxviii–xix. Kant uses the terms 'general metaphysics' and 'special metaphysics' explicitly in the diagram drafted in R4851 (dated 1776–78). On the divergent divisions of philosophy, including metaphysics, that Kant drafted between 1769 and 1795, see Tonelli (1994: 225–40, 325–41).

[18] A845/B873. On this, see Chapter 3, in particular Section 6.

[19] A11–12. See Chapter 3, Section 4.

[20] A845/B873, emphasis mine. See LM Mrongovius, 29:752. Possibly, the Architectonic considers transcendental philosophy to involve not only the pure understanding, but also pure reason because the discipline, qua part of metaphysics, seeks to comprehend the sum total of the cognitive elements that fall within its domain.

(241), place (281), and duration (299), but they are not treated in a separate chapter. Given Kant's later comments on the content of his projected transcendental philosophy, to be discussed in the next section, I do not think he intended to exclude space and time from his system. Unless Kant made a mistake in the passage just quoted, he might have meant that whereas space and time itself constitute the forms of intuition that allow the human mind to relate to objects as such, it is the pure understanding that produces the *concepts* of space and time. In other words: insofar as metaphysics treats space and time *as* a priori principles of human cognition, it treats them *as concepts* produced by thought. It is in this sense, I hold, that the 1787 version of the Transcendental Aesthetic refers to the concepts of space and time.[21]

On this account, Kant's definition of philosophy as rational cognition from concepts (A713/B741) can be harmonized with the purely intellectual consideration of the products of the pure understanding and pure reason carried out in the *Critique* and – presumably – the future system. However, while the mode of cognition that Kant calls metaphysical can be purely intellectual, this cannot be true of all concepts treated *in* metaphysics: concepts such as space and time, for instance, necessarily presuppose pure intuition. For this reason, arguably only those parts of the system that do not presuppose space and time can be purely intellectual in terms of both form and content.[22]

In the passage quoted above, Kant refers to the disciplines formerly subsumed under the title 'special metaphysics' as 'rational physiology' or 'physiology of pure reason.' This second main part of metaphysics is further divided into a rational physics, rational psychology, rational cosmology, and rational theology. This division does not correspond to the threefold structure of the Transcendental Dialectic, because Kant divides Wolffian general cosmology into rational physics and rational cosmology (A845–46/B873–74). The *Metaphysical Foundations* suggests a reason for this division. Kant here takes issue with the tendency of former elaborations of "the pure part of natural science" to run together metaphysical and

---

[21] See B37–38, 40, 46, and 48. See Willaschek (2018: 37–38) for a similar view. Rivero (2014: 211) points out that Kant in LM Dohna (1791–92) asserts within one page that the ontology should and should not include a discussion of space and time (28:622). In my view, however, Kant here intended to exclude mathematical principles (qua principles of pure intuition) from ontology, but, in agreement with other texts, maintains that the discipline must include a discussion of space and time qua necessary conditions of synthetic judgments.

[22] Seen in this way, ontology and rational physics can be purely a priori, whereas rational psychology, cosmology, and theology can also be purely intellectual. I am not aware of passages that suggest a solution along these lines.

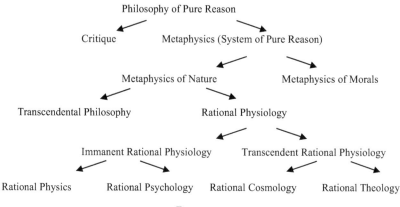

Figure 4

mathematical elements.[23] The rational physics that is carried out at least to some extent in the *Metaphysical Foundations* deals exclusively with the metaphysical principles that make it possible to treat objects of outer sense in mathematical terms (cf. MFNS 4:470). By contrast, Kant conceives of rational cosmology as a branch of metaphysics that treats the sum total of these objects in purely intellectual terms, which is to say that it abstracts even from space and time.

Accordingly, the division of Kant's projected system as a whole differs from Wolff's only by providing a separate rational physics and excluding empirical psychology (cf. A848/B876). Arguably, however, the main achievement of the Architectonic is its *derivation* of the divisions canonized by Wolff (see Figure 4).[24] Kant accounts for the various branches of rational physiology by means of a number of binary divisions, each of which seems to be guided by the distinction between the inner and the outer. He begins by dividing rational physiology into branches concerned with the immanent and transcendent employment of reason, respectively. The former branch is further divided into disciplines concerned with the object of outer sense (rational physics) and the object of inner sense (rational psychology). The branch of rational physiology concerned with

---

[23] MFNS, 4:473. Kant may well have thought of Baumgarten's cosmology, which, for instance, mixes a discussion of monads with discussions of motion, rest, and inertia (M 417–18).

[24] A846–47/B874–75. See Plaass (1965: 208–10). Kant's use of the term 'rational physiology' in these passages is not completely consistent. The text can be made coherent by assuming that his concluding list should have presented the second item as the immanent branch of rational physiology rather than the discipline as a whole.

the transcendent employment of reason, finally, is divided into disciplines concerned with the world as such (rational cosmology) and God (rational theology) (A845–47/B873–75).

As in the case of ontology, however, Kant does not define the two branches of transcendent rational physiology in terms of their alleged objects. Insofar as their role in theoretical cognition is concerned, he rather considers rational cosmology and rational theology to indirectly contribute to our cognition of nature qua object of outer and inner sense. These disciplines are considered transcendent because they deal with "a connection among the objects of experience that surpasses all experience" (A845–46/B873–74). This is to say that they seek to conceive of these objects as elements of a totality by taking recourse to the ideas of the world as such and God (cf. A672–73/B700–701). According to Kant, rational cosmology does so by treating the sum total of connections among objects of experience as *inner* connections, whereas rational theology relates the sum total of these connections to a being that itself is *not* part of nature (A846–47/B874–75).

Commentators have been troubled by the fact that the Architectonic assigns rational psychology to the immanent part of rational physiology and does not reject its transcendent part (rational cosmology and theology).[25] In my opinion, however, the confusion arises from projecting Kant's earlier distinction between the immanent and transcendent use of the pure understanding onto the division of metaphysics presented in the Architectonic (cf. A636/B664). On my reading, as was mentioned above, the Architectonic completely abstracts from the question as to whether the concepts at hand are used to obtain knowledge of objects. Kant's division in this chapter is concerned not with the objectifying act carried out by the *pure understanding* but with the attempt of *pure reason* to conceive of a manifold of cognitive elements as a totality. In this context, the terms 'immanent' and 'transcendent' do not pertain to the warranted and

---

[25] See, for example, Ferrarin (2015: 245–46) and Willaschek (2018: 39–43). In my view, Willaschek obfuscates the aim of the Architectonic's division by assuming that it ought to have included the 'transcendent' instantiation of rational psychology that Kant opposes in the Paralogisms. His effort at correcting Kant's division in this regard (41) does not take into account that the Architectonic abstracts from the historical instantiations of the disciplines at stake. Moreover, Willaschek seems to confuse rational psychology qua immanent branch of rational physiology with empirical psychology (40), a discipline that Kant intended to exclude from metaphysics altogether. In line with the commentators mentioned above, finally, he does not relate what he sees as the constructive elements of the Transcendental Dialectic to Kant's remarks on the system of pure reason. Baum (2015: 1537) seeks to solve the issue by assuming – without clear textual evidence – that Kant rejected the two transcendent parts of physiology on the ground that theoretical cognition of their objects is impossible.

unwarranted use of a faculty, but specify whether the cognitions treated in a particular metaphysical discipline relate to possible objects of experience in a direct or indirect manner.

It should be noted, further, that Kant's division abstracts from the question as to how a particular discipline depends on other disciplines for its principles. For instance, Kant mentions neither that transcendental philosophy treats the concepts and principles that all other disciplines presuppose nor that the metaphysics of morals rests on disciplines such as rational psychology and rational theology. For this reason, his account of the relationship between the various branches of metaphysics cannot be compared to Wolff's rather opaque account of the same in the *Discursus praeliminaris*.

Because Kant in the Architectonic uses the term 'transcendental philosophy' to refer to the first part of his projected system, it may seem natural to identify this part with the first-order strand of the Transcendental Analytic. However, I consider this identification to obscure the extent to which the first part of Kant's projected system would have resembled Baumgarten's ontology. In order to determine this proximity as well as the exact point at which Kant departs from Baumgarten, we need to turn to Kant's remarks on the concepts to be treated in this part. Since commentators commonly use the term 'transcendental philosophy' to denote the the *Critique* as a whole, I will use the term 'ontology' to refer to the first part of Kant's projected system of pure reason.

3   Kant's Intended Overhaul of Baumgarten's Ontology

In lectures on Baumgarten's *Metaphysics* delivered in 1782–83, Kant is reported to have noted that the author, "like everyone else, intended to develop a system" but lacked "the principle required to order the manifold." Consequently, this metaphysics "was not a system, but an aggregate" in the sense that the concepts he treated lacked "the order of the categories."[26] Similarly, but without mentioning Wolff or Baumgarten, Kant begins the Architectonic by contrasting cognitions that together make up a "mere aggregate" with those that are elements of an organic system, which is the case insofar as they are ordered in view of a single idea.[27]

---

[26] LM Mrongovius, 29:805–6.

[27] A832/B860. The Metaphysical Deduction criticizes Aristotle on the same ground (A80–81/B106–7). See also Prol, 4:322–25. As Gava (2018) points out, Wolff already compared the elements of a system to the way that "the limbs are connected in the human body" (AN 78). Seen from Kant's point of view, however, Wolff and his followers failed to meet the criterion of true systematicity they had identified.

In order to gauge the distance between Kant and his predecessors in this regard, a brief glance at the ontology contained in Baumgarten's *Metaphysics* suffices. Baumgarten's treatment of the "general predicates of things" (4) is not devoid of order per se: the three chapters of the discipline deal with predicates that can be assigned to anything whatsoever (universal predicates), pairs of predicates of which only one can be assigned to a particular thing (internal disjunctive predicates), and predicates that are used to determine the relation between things (relative predicates). The first section of the first chapter is devoted to 'the possible' and treats concepts such as nothing, something, possible, contradiction, and ground (7–18). Unlike Kant, Baumgarten treats 'necessity' and 'contingency' in a different chapter, namely, the chapter on the internal disjunctive predicates (101–23). Whereas 'substance' and 'accident' are also treated in this chapter, Baumgarten discusses 'the cause' and 'the caused' in the chapter devoted to the relative predicates (307–46). The species of causes he distinguishes in this context include efficient, deficient, instrumental, and occasional causes (319–23). Thus, Baumgarten treats the concepts of substance and causality in different chapters because they are used with regard to single things and the relations between things, respectively. The concepts related to space and time are treated partly in the second and partly in the third chapter. Unlike Kant, moreover, Baumgarten does not clearly distinguish between elementary and derived concepts.

According to various passages from the *Critique of Pure Reason*, Kant thought he could remedy the perceived lack of systematicity of Wolffian metaphysics by means of the table of categories. In the Metaphysical Deduction, he presents this table as a "systematic grid" that allows us to identify "the place where every concept properly belongs."[28] An addition to the second edition is more explicit in this regard:

> For that, in the theoretical part of philosophy, this table is highly useful, indeed indispensable to completely outline the *plan for the whole of a science* insofar as it rests on a priori concepts, ... emerges already from the fact that said table completely contains all the elementary concepts of the understanding, indeed even the form of a system of them in the human understanding, consequently that it gives instruction about all the moments, indeed even about their order, of a planned speculative science. (B109–10)

Clearly, Kant held that the internal division and content of all metaphysical disciplines ought to rest on the fourfold table of categories. However,

---

[28] A83/B109. I will use the term 'grid' to translate *Topik*.

for now I will focus on Kant's effort to overhaul former ontology. This effort can be said to involve three steps.

The first step does not presuppose the table of categories, but simply follows from Kant's division of sensibility and thought. Relying on this division, Kant argues that Aristotle should have excluded concepts that presuppose space and time from his list of categories (A81/B107). Obviously, this also holds for Baumgarten's ontology. As we will see, however, Kant planned to treat space and time in a first, separate section of his ontology.

Of those concepts treated in Baumgarten's ontology that stem from pure thought, Kant would certainly have assigned the ones he calls categories to the twelve sections defined by the table presented in the *Critique*.

However, once these two steps are taken, a great number of concepts treated in Baumgarten's ontology are not yet accounted for, something of which Kant was well aware. The third step, which is clearly the most challenging, consists in ordering these remaining concepts. As he puts it in the Metaphysical Deduction:

> [T]he categories, as the true root concepts of the pure understanding, have their equally pure derivative concepts, which could by no means be passed over in a complete system of transcendental philosophy. (A81–82/B107)

Among these pure derivative concepts, also called "predicables of the pure understanding," Kant counts force, action, presence, and change (A82/B108). They must be treated in ontology, or transcendental philosophy, because they do not stem from the senses and are presupposed in all other disciplines.[29]

Kant purports that ordering all predicables along these lines is "easy and more entertainment than labor" (Axxi). Similarly optimistic, the Metaphysical Deduction describes this task as follows:

> If one has the original and primitive concepts, one can easily add the derivative and subalternate ones and fully lay out (*völlig ausmalen*) the family tree of the pure understanding.... [O]ne could readily reach this aim if one took the ontological textbooks in hand, and, e.g. under the

---

[29] See LM Mrongovius, 29:803. In order to clarify his innovative distinction between the two kinds, Kant appeals to Aristotle's distinction between root concepts (categories or predicaments) and derivative ones (post-predicaments) (A81/B107). However, he departs from the meaning of the term 'predicable' in Aristotelian philosophy and simply uses the term to denote pure concepts that, unlike the categories, presuppose more than one cognitive element and therefore admit of analysis.

category of causality, subordinated the predicables of force, action, and passion, . . . and so on.[30]

At a later point, Kant reiterates his plan to carry out a detailed analysis of the predicables in "a future system of reason" by drawing from "familiar textbooks of this sort" (A204/B249). A note in the *Prolegomena* makes it clear he had primarily Baumgarten's *Metaphysics* in mind:

> If . . . all the predicables, which can be extracted fairly completely from any good ontology (e.g., Baumgarten's), are enumerated, and if they are ordered in classes under the categories and, moreover, if one does not omit as complete an analysis as possible of all these concepts, *then a solely analytical part of metaphysics will arise*, which, . . . through its determinateness and completeness, might not only have utility, but beyond that, in virtue of its systematicity, a certain beauty.[31]

However, it is not quite clear how Kant thought this gratifying task should be carried out. As regards this question, the *Critique* notes that

> the categories combined either with the *modis* of sensibility or with each other yield a great multitude of derivative a priori concepts, to take note of which and, as far as possible, completely catalogue, would be a useful and not unpleasant but here dispensable effort.[32]

While lecturing on Baumgarten's ontology in 1794–95, Kant reiterated this idea, which suggests that he at that point had not abandoned the project delineated in the *Critique*. More importantly, these lectures provide some examples, including one that concerns the predicable of duration.

Baumgarten defined 'duration' as "the continuation of existence" (M 299), which is to say that the concept of duration presupposes at least the concept of existence. Since the concept also presupposes that we know what time is, the concept of duration might be traced back to the concept of existence and the form of time. Kant discusses the concept of duration as follows:

---

[30] A82/B108. Kant here lists the concepts of generation, destruction, and alteration under the heading of modality (not under a particular category). See R5055 (dated 1776–78) for an early version of the thought that predicables, qua "mixed concepts," ought to be subsumed under each of the categories.

[31] Prol, 4:325–26n, emphasis mine. See Pollok (2001: 82).

[32] A82/B108. Similarly, Kant notes in the *Prolegomena* that he in the *Critique* postponed "appending in full, under the name of predicables, all the concepts derivable from [the categories] – either by connecting them with one another, or with the pure form of appearance (space and time), or with the matter of appearance, provided the latter is not yet determined empirically (the object of sensation as such)" (4:324). See also LM Vigilantius, 29:988 (1794–95).

> With regard to quality (*in Rücksicht der Qualität*) the concept of duration rests on reality or existence. Duration also possesses magnitude (*Grösse*) ... with respect to the existence in time (*in Ansehung der Existenz in der Zeit*).... This magnitude differs from the material quantity.[33]

Although the example is far from clear, I take Kant to hint at the idea that a given predicable can be analyzed by considering it *from the perspective* of one or more categories and/or forms of intuition Thus, if we consider that which endures in view of quality, we necessarily conceive of it as real or existing. If we consider the same enduring something in view of quantity, we necessarily conceive of it as taking up a certain amount of time.

Kant's second example, in the same lecture, concerns the predicable of movement. On his account, this predicable "presupposes actuality (*Dasein*) ... and involves the thought of the change of actuality as regards (*mit*) the contrary determinations of time and space.[34] Thus, Kant suggests that attributing movement to something presupposes that it is actual (modality) and is capable of change in respect of both space and time. On this account, the concept of movement presupposes, or contains, a category as well as forms of intuition.

As seen, the *Critique of Pure Reason* also lists 'force' among the predicables (A82/B108). Unlike 'movement,' this predicable does not presuppose space and time. It rather denotes, as Kant writes later on, "the causality of a substance."[35] This suggests that Kant took the concept of force to emerge from the combination of the categories of substance and causality alone. Evidently, this makes the concept suited to be used with regard to material as well as immaterial forces.

These examples are surely rudimentary and perhaps unconvincing. It is not surprising that those of Kant's disciples who could draw on the *Critique* and the *Prolegomena* alone had a hard time making sense of Kant's sparse and minimal instructions and, hence, to carry out the task he apparently wanted them to take on themselves. Since some of Kant's

---

[33] LM Vigilantius, 29:988. In this passage and the next I leave out a few elements that do not seem to make sense (may be due to mistakes on the part of the note taker). Due to their obscurity, my translations of these passages are not very literal.

[34] LM Vigilantius, 29:988, cf. LM K₂/Heinze extracts, 28:721 (1790–91). In the Transcendental Aesthetic, Kant writes that the concept of alteration rests on connecting of "contradictorily opposed predicates," for instance, attributing 'being in place A' and 'not-being in place A' to one and the same thing. This is possible only if we conceive of these contrary determinations as successive, that is, by relying on the representation of time (B48).

[35] A648/B676. In LM Mrongovius (1782–83), Kant considers the concept of force to denote the relation of a substance to its accidents, insofar as it contains the ground of their actuality (29:771). See also LM Pölitz PM 56, LM K₂/Heinze extracts, 28:718. On this point, see Howard (2017: 123).

letters supplement his published remarks on the subject, I will briefly consider the relevant passages.

Responding to Jakob's request to provide more guidance, Kant wrote in 1787:

> The ontology would begin, without any critical introduction, with the concepts of space and time, only insofar as these (as pure intuitions) ground all experiences. After that, four main chapters follow, containing [1] the concepts of the understanding, divided according to the four classes of categories, such that each of these [categories] constitutes a section: all of them to be treated merely analytically, in accordance with Baumgarten, and this together with [2] the predicables, indeed (*ja*), [2a] the connection [of the categories] with time and space and, similarly, in accordance with their order (*so wie sie fortgehen*), [2b] [their connections] among themselves, just as they can be found in Baumgarten. In each case, the synthetic principle that belongs to a category ... is presented (*vorgetragen*) only insofar as experience always and necessarily accords with it, and in this way ontology as a whole is carried out.[36]

The passage is clearly written in haste and the wording is somewhat elliptic. Yet I take Kant to mean – and have modified the translation accordingly – that each of the four main parts of the ontology should treat a class of categories and the predicables belonging to that class, both the predicables that emerge from the combination of categories with the forms of intuition and those that emerge from the combination of categories among themselves, and that one should proceed according to the order in which the categories are presented in the *Critique*.

Kant further notes that the categories and predicables should be treated merely analytically, which is to say that they should be clarified by exposing the elements they contain or presuppose. This point is in accordance with Kant's remark in the *Critique of Pure Reason* that "a system of pure reason" ought to provide definitions of the categories.[37] However, Kant also uses the term 'analytic' to warn against the actual use

---

[36] Kant to Jakob, September 11 (?), 1787 (10:494), translation modified, numbers added. At the end of the passage, Kant explicitly identifies the synthetic principles he mentions with the principles of the pure understanding.

[37] A82–83/B108–9. The Transcendental Aesthetic defines a metaphysical exposition as "the distinct (even if not complete) representation of that which belongs to a concept" a priori (B38). Kant remarks in the *Critique* that metaphysics consists to a large extent in the analysis or clarification of concepts (A5–6/B9) and that he defers a detailed analysis of the "root concepts" as well as "all those derived from them" (A13–14/B27–28). Similarly, the *Prolegomena* (4:273) maintains that definitions such as 'substance is that which exists only as subject' can be obtained by means of analysis and necessarily belong to metaphysics. This suggests that Kant intended to use versions of Baumgarten's definitions of categories such as substance and causality in his ontology.

of categories in judgments that purport to extend our a priori cognition of things. The only synthetic a priori cognitions that according to Kant can be included in ontology are the principles of the pure understanding that, as we known, rest on schemata rather than the categories per se.[38]

Apart from the reference to the division into chapters and sections, Kant's advice does not offer us much more than the *Critique* and *Prolegomena*. According to his plan, it can be surmised, the part of the ontology devoted to the pure understanding should contain four parts, each of which should be divided into three sections, each of which in turn should treat a category, a number of predicables falling under it, and the principle of the pure understanding corresponding to the category. As regards the predicables, each section should treat, first, the predicables that involve forms of intuition and, second, the purely intellectual predicables that result from the combination of categories among themselves.

A letter to Beck written in 1792 is in agreement with the one sent to Jakob. Referring to a sketch for a system of metaphysics he made a while ago, Kant mentions that his completely immanent ontology would first expound "the pure intuitions of space and time" and then treat

> the categories, in their proper order ... ; and ... demonstrate, at the conclusion of the exposition of each category (for example, the category of quantity and all predicables included under it, along with examples of their use), that no experience of sensible objects is possible except insofar as I presuppose a priori *that every such object must be thought of as a magnitude*, and similarly with all the other categories.[39]

This passage is problematic because quantity is not itself a category. If we use the category of plurality as an example instead, then the section devoted to this concept should begin with the category itself and end with the principle of all axioms of intuition, namely, the principle according to which all appearances must be treated as extensive magnitudes (A162). In between, the section should discuss those pure concepts that – I surmise – specify what we mean by 'quantity' in various respects or, what amounts to the same, that are used to conceive of something in quantitative terms. According to a summary of a transcript of lectures delivered in 1790–91, the so-called Heinze extracts, Kant here appears to have treated the

---

[38] Cf. A148/B187. See Chapter 6, Section 5.
[39] Kant to Beck, January 20, 1792 (11:313–14), emphasis mine.

predicables of number, multitude, measure, and infinity under the heading of plurality.[40]

If one were to proceed by relying on this grid, I take Kant to have held, it should be possible to assign all concepts treated in Baumgarten's ontology to the proper rubric and define them accordingly. It is in this sense that we should understand his concluding remarks on the predicables in the Transcendental Analytic:

> [A] complete lexicon (*Wörterbuch*) with all the requisite clarifications (*Erklärungen*) should not only be possible but even easy to produce. The sections (*Fächer*) already exist; it is merely necessary to fill them out, and a systematic grid (*Topik*), such as the present one, makes it easy not to miss the place where every concept properly belongs as well as to notice the one that is still empty. (A83/B109)

However, the path toward the execution of Kant's plan might well be more thorny than its author suggests. Let me pinpoint three potential obstacles.

First, as seen, one might hold that space and time ought to be excluded from metaphysics because Kant considers the discipline to deal with the pure understanding and pure reason alone.[41] As was suggested above, however, this problem might be solved if we take metaphysics, unlike the natural metaphysics carried out by the human mind as such, to treat space and time and the determinations dependent on them *as concepts*, that is, as products of the pure understanding.

Second, the *Critique* discusses a number of concepts of which it is not immediately clear in which part of the projected system they ought to be treated. Thus, Kant notes that transcendental philosophy ought to include

---

[40] See LM K₂/Heinze extracts, 28:715; cf. LM Mrongovius, 19:802. These predicables might be said to constitute the 'sphere' of the category of plurality (cf. MFNS, 4:470). The Heinze extracts are based on LM K₂ (1790–91), of which we no longer possess a transcript. Heinze notes that Kant in these lectures, unlike earlier ones, tried to do what he in his critical works had merely described, namely, "to lecture on the ontology according to the order of the categories." He rightly points out, however, that Kant did so in a way that is neither strict nor complete, and seems to have improvised (28:714, cf. 724). Deviating from the *Critique*, Kant seems to have ranged the concept of force under substance rather than causality (28:718, cf. A82/B108). Attraction and repulsion are treated under the category of community (28:720). Throughout, Kant provides many examples taken from daily life and the sciences. Evidently, what is done in the lecture series may have been connected only loosely to Kant's views – insofar as he had worked them out – on the first part of his projected system. See Blomme (2011: 152–61) for a helpful clarification of Kant's idea of an analysis of the predicables in relation to Baumgarten's treatment of the latter.

[41] This is the position of Cramer (1985: 122), who disregards Kant's letters on the issue. The Introduction to the *Critique of Pure Reason* notes that sensibility must belong to transcendental philosophy insofar as it contains a priori representations (A15–16/B29–30). I take the vague wording to imply that this holds true of the transcendental aesthetic elaborated in the *Critique* as well as the first part of the projected system.

the determinations of the concept of nothing that ensue if we treat the concept in view of the four classes of categories.[42] He might have intended to treat the concepts of nothing and something at the beginning of the ontology, but this is hard to corroborate.[43] In line with the tradition, Baumgarten also discusses the so-called *transcendentalia* of unity, truth, and perfection.[44] Kant suggests that they be treated in general logic rather than transcendental philosophy because they articulate nothing but criteria of thought as such, but this is at odds with comments in the lectures.[45] Further, the *Prolegomena* makes it clear that Kant, unlike Baumgarten, intended to disentangle the concepts of reflection from the categories so as to treat the latter separately, but it is unclear where the former would go.[46]

Third, it might be very hard, in practice, to allocate certain predicables to the proper rubric. If, for instance, force is conceived as the causality of a substance, should it be listed under the heading of causality or that of substance? If more than one category is involved in the meaning of a predicable, which one ought to determine the allocation? And does not the supply of predicables gathered in the metaphysical tradition resist the kind of analysis Kant proposes? It is hard to tell to what extent Kant himself came to perceive obstacles such as these. Before addressing this point, however, the next sections consider Kant's thoughts on the disciplines contained in former special metaphysics.

4   Kant's Projected Rational Physiology

In the introductory part of the Transcendental Dialectic, Kant refers to the disciplines that used to make up special metaphysics as transcendental disciplines. Each of these disciplines is said to be devoted to an idea of reason and a number of conceptual determinations of the latter that Kant calls 'modes':

> Pure reason provides the ideas for a transcendental doctrine of the soul (*psychologia rationalis*), a transcendental science of the world (*cosmologia rationalis*), and finally also a transcendental cognition of God (*theologia transcendentalis*).... What modi (*modi*) of pure concepts of reason (*reine Vernunftbegriffe*) stand under these three titles of all transcendental ideas

---

[42] A290–92/B346–480, cf. Prol, 4:325.
[43] This would be in line with both Baumgarten's *Metaphysics* (7–8) and the Heinze extracts (28:711).
[44] Baumgarten, M 72–100. On this, see Chapter 3, Section 4.
[45] B113–16. The Heinze extracts have it that Kant treated them under the heading of unity in LM K₂ (28:714).
[46] Prol, 4:326. According to the Heinze extracts, Kant discussed the concepts of reflection toward the end of the ontology of LM K₂ (28:726).

will be presented exhaustively in the following chapters. These modi run along the thread of the categories.[47]

Kant's use of the term 'transcendental' in this context appears to be in line with Wolff's use of the term 'transcendental cosmology.'[48] Used in this sense, the term basically indicates that the predicates treated in the various branches of rational physiology do not depend on outer or inner experience and, as such, provide the applied parts of the relevant disciplines with their a priori principles (cf. A848/B876). For this reason, Kant both here and in the Architectonic refers to the branches of former special metaphysics by using the terms 'rational' and 'transcendental' indiscriminately (cf. A846/B874).

If we take our bearings from the passage just quoted, it is hard to maintain that Kant intended to abolish former special metaphysics in all respects.[49] As was mentioned in the introduction to this chapter, I rather hold that the Transcendental Dialectic contains a consideration of the rational core of the disciplines that used to be called rational psychology, general cosmology, and natural theology. Seen in this way, the passage is in accordance with the division of metaphysics presented in the Architectonic, except for the discipline called 'rational physics,' that is, the branch of rational physiology devoted to the sum total of objects to which mathematics can be applied (A845–46/B873–74). Unlike the Architectonic, the Transcendental Dialectic does not deal with this discipline because it had not been identified as such prior to Kant. Thus, Kant seems to have held that one of the ideas of reason, the idea of the world, ought to be treated by two complementary branches of special metaphysics.

As can be seen from the passage quoted above, Kant held that all branches of metaphysics ought be elaborated by using the table of categories as a guiding thread. The *Prolegomena* reiterates unambiguously that one ought to proceed in this manner not only in ontology but in all metaphysical disciplines:

> Now this system of categories ... yields an undoubted instruction or guiding thread (*Leitfaden*) as to how and through what points of inquiry any metaphysical examination must be directed if it is to be complete. For

---

[47] A335/B392, cf. B109–10 (quoted in Section 3 above). Since Kant identifies pure concepts of reason with transcendental ideas or ideas of reason (A334/B391), the term 'modi' must refer to the conceptual determinations of these ideas.

[48] See Chapter 3, Section 3.

[49] Kant's intention can also be inferred from the second Preface of the *Critique*, where he mentions his intention to remove misunderstandings about "the paralogisms that are placed prior to the rational psychology" (Bxxxviii, translation modified). In my view, this remark can refer only to his projected system of pure reason.

this system exhausts all those moments of the understanding under which every other concept must be brought.... [E]ven in the division of concepts that are supposed to go beyond the physiological use of the understanding ... it is always the same guiding thread that ... forms a closed circle every time. (Prol, 4:325)

Kant here refers the reader to the fourfold division of rational psychology (A344/B402) and rational cosmology (A415/B443) presented in the Transcendental Dialectic. In the remainder of this section I aim to shed light on his intended reform of each of the branches of rational physiology by focusing on the role he assigns to the table of categories. I discuss these branches in the order in which they are presented in the Architectonic.

4.1   Rational Physics

As we have seen, the Architectonic presents rational physics and rational psychology as disciplines devoted to the objects of outer and inner sense, respectively (A848/B876). Since the Transcendental Dialectic does not deal with rational physics, clarifying Kant's thoughts on this part of his projected system of pure reason requires that we briefly consider the *Metaphysical Foundations of Natural Science*, which was published in 1786.

In the second edition of the *Critique*, Kant refers to this treatise as an example of how the table of categories makes it possible to elaborate "the whole of a science insofar as it rests on a priori concepts" in a comprehensive and systematic manner (B110). Does this mean that the *Metaphysical Foundations* coincides with the rational physics that the Architectonic presents as the first part of rational physiology? At a first glance, this inference seems to be denied by a letter Kant wrote to Schütz shortly after having completed the manuscript:

> Before I elaborate the promised metaphysics of nature, I had to write that which, to be sure, is a mere application of it, but nevertheless presupposes an empirical concept, namely, the metaphysical foundations of the doctrine of bodies.... For if said metaphysics is to be completely homogeneous (*ganz gleichartig*), it must be pure; moreover, I wanted to have something at hand, by way of concrete examples, to which I could refer in this metaphysics, so as to make the presentation comprehensible without bloating the system by including these examples in it. I finished these metaphysical foundations, titled *Metaphysical Foundations of Natural Science*, this summer.[50]

---

[50] Kant to Schütz, September 13, 1785 (10:406), translation modified. Similar remarks will be discussed in Section 6 below. As Plaass (1965: 206) points out, Kant expressed the same concern already in a letter to Lambert on December 31, 1765. He here tells Lambert of his plan – not

If the title 'metaphysics of nature' here denotes the complete theoretical part of the system, as it does in the Architectonic, then the letter entails that the *Metaphysical Foundations* does not coincide with the rational physics qua part of that system. On this reading, it lacks the purity required of the system as a whole. However, it is also possible that Kant in the letter uses the title 'metaphysics of nature' in a highly unusual way, namely, to denote the ontology alone. On this reading, Kant would simply refer to what ought to be left out from the full-blown ontology qua first part of his system of pure reason.[51] As we have seen in Section 3, this discipline would have included not only the categories, but also predicables such as force, movement, duration, and number. In this case, the letter suggests that Kant took the *Metaphysical Foundations* to at least partly instantiate his projected rational physics. Given the Preface to the *Metaphysical Foundations*, discussed below, the second option seems the most plausible one. Even so, however, the tension between the two options suggests that Kant was unsure as to how exactly to delimit the discipline that the Architectonic calls rational physics.

The Preface to the *Metaphysical Foundations* divides metaphysics of nature as such into (1) a pure or transcendental part and (2) two parts that apply the principles treated in the latter to objects of which we possess empirical concepts, namely, matter and the thinking being (MFNS 4: 469–70). These applied or special parts of the metaphysics of nature are said to be concerned with "the sphere of the cognitions that reason can obtain of these objects a priori" (4:470). Kant refers to the applied part concerned with matter qua object of outer sense as "metaphysics of corporeal nature" (4:472). Since the Architectonic identifies this discipline with rational physics (A846/B874), we can assume that the distinction

realized until the 1780s – to first publish "a few smaller works," including the metaphysical foundations of natural philosophy and the metaphysical foundations of practical philosophy, the content of which he had already worked out. In this way, the main work, on "the proper method of metaphysics," would not be "burdened excessively with detailed and yet inadequate examples." He considers these smaller works to "show in concreto" what the proper procedure of metaphysics should be (10:56). It is impossible to determine to what extent the text published in 1786 draws on this early draft. The letter makes it clear that Kant had read the manuscript of Lambert's *Architectonic*, which was actually published only in 1771. On Lambert's impact on Kant in this regard as well as Kant's criticism of Lambert, see Friedman (2013: 121–30, 236) and Wellmann (2018: 57–61). Wellmann also elaborates on Lambert's own attempted reform of Wolffian metaphysics in the *Architectonic* and other works (9–50). Prior to Lambert and Kant, the idea that scientific principles rest on particular combinations of simple concepts had already been already explored by Crusius (see Chapter 1, Section 4).

[51] The Preface of the *Metaphysical Foundations* seems to support this interpretation: Kant here notes that he did not want to burden his "general metaphysics" with examples belonging to the pure part of physics (MFNS 4: 477–78).

between the pure part of the metaphysics of nature and the applied part that deals with the object of outer sense corresponds to that between (1) ontology and (2) rational physics in the Architectonic.[52] Given this division, as well as the assertion in the letter to Schütz that the content of the *Metaphysical Foundations* rests on a treatise not yet published, there can be no doubt that Kant considered the *Metaphysical Foundations* to presuppose at least his projected ontology.[53]

Clearly, the empirical concept Kant mentions in the letter to Schütz is the concept of matter. As seen, the Architectonic conceives of rational physics as a discipline that treats the a priori cognitions of the object of outer sense insofar as they "can be applied in experience" (A845/B873). This is possible, Kant asserts, if it borrows from experience nothing but the concept of matter qua "impenetrable inanimate extension" (A847–48/B875–76, cf. A381). However, mathematical physics requires more than mathematical principles, the concept of matter, and experience. According to Kant, physicists must be able to conceive of the object of outer sense in more specific terms. As he puts it, they must necessarily rely on "metaphysical principles . . . that make the concept of . . . matter a priori suitable for its application to outer experience," principles that include "the concept of motion, the fullness of space, inertia, and so on."[54] It is only by dint of such a priori determinations of the concept of matter, I take Kant to mean, that the concept of matter can actually be referred to objects and, hence, acquire objective reality.

---

[52] In line with the Architectonic, the *Metaphysical Foundations* assumes an analogy between rational physics and rational psychology qua applied parts of metaphysics of nature (MFNS, 4:470). Kant specifies that neither of these parts rests on mathematics, but contrasts the two by arguing that an a priori *science* of the object of inner or outer sense must conceive of its object in mathematical terms (470). On this basis, he denies empirical psychology the status of a natural science (4:471). Yet I agree with Pollok (2001: 93–105) that Kant did not therefore intend to exclude *rational* psychology from his projected system of pure reason. According to the Transcendental Dialectic, rational psychology cannot be carried out as a doctrine (as theoretical synthetic a priori cognition of an object), but only as a discipline (B421). As will be argued below, however, in this capacity it must definitely encompass more than just the idea of the soul per se.

[53] This reading is in line with Plaass (1965: 209–10, 264–70) and Pollok (2001: 79–80). However, neither of them discusses Kant's remarks on the predicables in detail. Commentators who, instead, consider the applied part of the metaphysics of nature carried out in the *Metaphysical Foundations* to rest on the *Critique of Pure Reason* include Wundt (1924: 299), Watkins (1998), and Friedman (2013: 20). Whereas the Transcendental Analytic and the projected ontology obviously overlap in terms of content, only the latter, as seen, would have treated the predicables. The discussion of forces in the *Metaphysical Foundations* clearly presupposes the treatment of the predicable of force as such in the pure part of the metaphysics of nature, that is, Kant's projected ontology. However, I agree with Watkins (1998) that the *Metaphysical Foundations* draws on the table of categories rather than the principles of the pure understanding.

[54] MFNS 4: 472, cf. Prol, 4:295.

But how can rational physics be both pure and presuppose an empirical concept? The concept of matter need not affect the purity of rational physics, I hold, since this discipline *itself* does not apply the concepts it treats to material things: it merely treats the pure concepts and a priori principles *by means of which scientists can actually do so.*[55] In accordance with the Architectonic, Kant considers the metaphysics of corporeal nature elaborated in the *Metaphysical Foundations* to treat "all determinations of the general *concept* of matter as such."[56] While these determinations are suitable to be used with regard to material things, their content is obtained – ideally – by considering the concept of matter in view of the conceptual determinations treated in the ontology alone, that is, by deriving them in a scientific manner. If rational physics differs from ontology only by treating the pure concepts and principles that allow the human mind to obtain knowledge of material bodies rather than objects as such, as I take to be the case, then there is no need to exclude the discipline from the system of pure reason.

Now that the object and task of rational physics have been clarified, we can turn to the question of its actual elaboration. In accordance with the passages quoted above, Kant notes in the *Metaphysical Foundations* that one should proceed by relying on the table of categories:

> [T]he schema for the completeness of a metaphysical system, whether it be of nature as such or of corporeal nature in particular, is the table of categories. For there are no more pure concepts of the understanding that can be concerned with the nature of things. *All determinations of the general concept of matter as such* must be able to be brought under the four classes of these concepts, those of quantity, of quality, of relation, and finally of modality, and the same holds of everything that may be either thought a priori of matter, or presented in mathematical construction, or given in experience as a determinate object of the latter.[57]

Kant specifies his point by noting that in the four chapters of the treatise the concept of matter was "carried through" the four classes of categories, such that "in each of them a new determination of this concept was added" (4:476). Thus, Kant holds, first, that rational physics must treat

---

[55] See Plaass (1965: 285–90) for an alternative, much less straightforward proposal. While I hold that his interpretation of the *Metaphysical Foundations* has great merits, I do not think it necessary to assume that the treatise is "built on" the concept of matter (288).

[56] MFNS 4:475–76, emphasis mine, cf. 472.

[57] MFNS, 4:475–76, emphasis mine. On this, see Plaass (1965: 276). Thus, the fourfold grid is supposed to structure not only rational physics itself, but also the mathematical and experimental physics of which it isolates the a priori, yet non-mathematical elements.

the a priori determinations of matter presupposed in mathematical and experimental physics and, second, that it can do so systematically and exhaustively.

Arguably, this procedure deviates from Wolff's 'dogmatic' method in at least three respects: it presupposes the prior limitation to appearances of the concepts and principles to be treated in ontology; it relies on the grid provided by the table of categories; and it is not deductive in the classical sense of the term. Nevertheless, Kant may well have had in mind the method employed in the *Metaphysical Foundations* – published the year before – when he notes in the 1787 Preface to the *Critique* that the "future system of metaphysics" ought to follow "the strict method of the famous Wolff."[58]

Since something cannot be an object of outer sense unless it is considered to be capable of motion, the first determination discussed in the *Metaphysical Foundations* is the concept of motion.[59] Accordingly, the first chapter defines matter in purely quantitative terms, namely, as "the movable in space."[60] Further definitions in this chapter include those of rest and permanence (4:485). The second chapter, supposedly treating matter from the angle of quality, conceives of matter as that which fills a space (4:496) and offers definitions of, among others, attractive and repulsive force (4:498), penetration (4:501), material substance (4:502), and contact (4:511). The third chapter determines matter in view of the moving force it possesses (4:536) and presents the three laws of mechanics by drawing, to some extent, on the analogies of experience. Significantly, Kant considers the latter principles themselves to be part of "general metaphysics." As Pollok notes, this strongly suggests that the background of Kant's account is not the Transcendental Analytic, but his projected ontology.[61] The fourth chapter, finally, determines matter as the movable insofar as it can be an object of experience (4:554). As was mentioned above, Kant suggests that only definitions such as these allow the scientist to apply the very concept of matter to the object of outer sense and, hence,

---

[58] Bxxxvi. See Chapter 1, Section 2. Gava (2018) makes a similar point.

[59] MFNS 4:476. See Plaass (1965: 298–300) and Blomme (2015: 498). Blomme argues convincingly that if we conceive of change, qua predicable, as something that occurs in space and time, the predicable of motion ensues. This predicable, in turn, can be conceived either in geometrical terms, that is, by abstracting from experience, or as a determination of empirical objects. This explains how a single predicable can be considered to be both pure and empirical.

[60] MFNS, 4:480. Kant uses the terms 'clarification' and 'definition' interchangeably in this context (cf. 4:482, 536).

[61] MFNS, 4:541–44. See Pollok (2001: 81).

to determine the lawful relationship between material objects in mathematical terms.

It seems to me that at least the definitions provided in the *Metaphysical Foundations* fit Kant's idea of a rational physics in the Architectonic. Clearly, these definitions draw on the account of space and time Kant planned to elaborate in the first part of this ontology. They also presuppose, or explicitly draw on, a number of predicables to be treated in the latter, including change, motion, magnitude, and force. Thus, insofar as the *Metaphysical Foundations* specifies what these concepts mean insofar as they are used with regard to the object of outer sense, it arguably instantiates, albeit in a provisional manner, Kant's projected rational physics qua one of the applied parts of the metaphysics of nature.

Kant conceives of the procedure that generates increasingly concrete determinations of the concept of matter as the "complete analysis" of what is contained in the concept of matter as such, that is, of the a priori determinations that any investigation into the object of outer sense necessarily presupposes. Arguably, this analysis is carried out in view of, on the one hand, the concepts and principles treated in the ontology (cf. 4:472) and, on the other hand, the concepts and principles employed in the empirical part of physics. It is not clear to me whether this procedure is analytic, synthetic, or not to be classified in terms of this distinction. For instance, the first definition is said to "attribute" movability to matter (4:480). We can and must conceive of matter as movable, I surmise, because otherwise the concept of matter would not be applicable to actual objects of outer sense. But it does not seem to follow from this that 'movability' is contained in the very concept of matter. Seen in this way, even the definitions presented in the *Metaphysical Foundations* would result from a procedure that is not analytic in the usual sense of the term.

The metaphysical principles treated in the various chapters, for their part, appear to be – warranted – synthetic a priori judgments even though Kant does not use the term in this context: these principles arguably determine, independently of experience, how something can be an object of mathematical physics in the first place.[62] Thus, Kant notes that the scientist must necessarily conceive of matter as "divisible to infinity" (4:503) and that 'attraction' must be attributed to matter even though it is not contained in its concept.[63]

---

[62] The *Critique* considers the pure part of physics to contain synthetic a priori judgments (B17–18). See Watkins (1998: 582–87) for a similar approach.

[63] MFNS, 4:509. See Cramer (1985: 160–61).

I am not in a position to judge whether the *Metaphysical Foundations* meets the criterion imposed on rational physics qua purely rational discipline in all regards. Kant's 1785 letter to Schütz suggests that he considered the treatise to contain elements that are at home neither in ontology nor in rational physics and, thus, belong to empirical physics rather than metaphysics. Moreover, as will be discussed in Section 6 below, in both the second Preface to the *Critique of Pure Reason* (Bxliii) and a number of letters written after 1785, Kant refers to the metaphysics of nature as a work that remained to be published.

Regardless of Kant's own thoughts on the *Metaphysical Foundations*, however, the text arguably testifies to a tension he may not have been able to resolve: a pull toward concreteness required even in the foundational part of physics – as well as by most of his readers – and a pull toward purity required to remedy the defects of previous metaphysical systems.[64]

4.2   Rational Psychology

As was mentioned above, Kant in the *Prolegomena* adduces his treatment of the idea of the soul in the Transcendental Dialectic to illustrate how even rational psychology can be elaborated by using the table of categories as a guiding thread (4:325). The aim of this section is to identify those elements of Kant's projected rational psychology that, on his view, were already contained in its pre-critical instantiations but had been neither explicitly grasped nor presented in a systematic form.

In the Paralogisms, Kant maintains that rational psychology, qua "science transcending all powers of human reason" is impossible[65] and that studies of the soul should rather follow "the guiding thread of experience" (A382). Evidently, this suggests that he considered only empirical psychology to be a legitimate discipline. Yet Kant also states that a purely rational treatment of the soul is needed in order to ward off materialism (A383, cf. B421). These statements need not be contradictory if we assume – as I will do in what follows – that Kant considered rational psychology to be a

---

[64] This tension – which arguably pervades Kant's *Opus postumum* as well – recurs in the literature on the *Metaphysical Foundations* and explains the gap between the 'metaphysical' reading represented by Plaass (1965) and the 'Newtonian' reading put forward by Friedman (2013). Hardly mentioning the division of metaphysics in the Architectonic, Friedman sees it as a "strength" that Kant's "evolving explanation of the application of mathematics in pure natural science" increasingly emphasizes the role of empirical intuition (32).

[65] A382, cf. A361. See also LM Volckmann, 28:443.

warranted part of metaphysics on the condition that it treat the soul not as object of cognition but as noumenon in the negative sense of the term.

As was argued in Chapter 4, Section 5, Kant considered each branch of former special metaphysics to have its own transcendental object. In the case of rational psychology, this transcendental object, commonly called 'soul,' presents itself to us as the act of thinking or "the inner representation 'I think.'"[66] Accordingly, Kant holds in the Architectonic that rational psychology must draw its object from inner sense. In this regard, the discipline is similar to rational physics. However, the two disciplines do not run parallel in all respects: whereas the concept of matter cannot be completely severed of its empirical origin, the concept of the soul at stake in rational psychology is produced by completely abstracting from any sensible determination, that is, by isolating the mere act of apperception. In this case, therefore, the source from which the concept is drawn does not impinge on the purely intellectual nature of the discipline as a whole.[67]

Obviously, since the soul is not an appearance, the categories cannot be used to obtain cognitions of it (A479–80n/B506–507n). Nevertheless, Kant maintains that rational psychology can and must treat those transcendental predicates that one would have to use *if one were to treat the soul as an object*, something that can be done, I add, in the context of practical philosophy (cf. B430–31). As he famously puts it:

> 'I think' is thus the sole text of rational psychology, from which it is to develop its entire wisdom. One easily sees that this thought, if it is to be related to an object (myself), can contain nothing other than *transcendental predicates of this object*; because the least empirical predicate would corrupt the rational purity . . . of the science.[68]

---

[66] See A341–42/B399–400, A478/B506, A848/B876.

[67] A848/B876, cf. A343/B401, A354. On this, see Ameriks (1982/2000: 55). According to LM L₁ (mid-1770s), rational psychology takes "nothing more from experience than the mere concept of the soul, *that* we have a soul. The rest must be cognized from pure reason," which is to say that one here must "abandon the guiding thread of experience" (28:263). I agree with Dyck (2014: 72–81) that Kant's conception of rational psychology as a purely intellectual discipline targets the continuism typical of the Wolffian version of the discipline. While Dyck rightly points out that Ameriks (1982/2000) uses the term 'rationalism' in an overly general sense, it is clear – as Dyck admits – that Kant's critique also targets non-Wolffian, narrowly rationalist versions of rational psychology. However, if one distinguishes between cognition in the broad sense (possible) and cognition of objects (impossible), then Kant's conception of rational psychology in the 1770s is even more continuous with the one put forward in the *Critique* than Dyck takes it to be (cf. 78). Moreover, I do not quite see what, on Dyck's account of the "strict limits" imposed on the discipline (cf. 199), can be the content of Kant's rational psychology except the purely intellectual idea of the soul itself.

[68] A343/B401, cf. A346/B404, A354.

In order to identify these transcendental predicates, modes, or determinations of the soul, Kant adds, we can simply follow "the guiding thread of the categories." Doing so yields "the grid of rational psychology, from which everything else that it may contain has to be derived."[69]

The main transcendental predicates Kant goes on to attribute to the soul are substance (relation), simplicity (quality), unity (quantity), and 'in relation to possible objects in space' (modality) (A344/B402). Given the account of ontology presented above, we can assume that he conceived of these predicates as the headings of the four main sections or chapters of rational psychology.[70] As in the case of the ontological predicables, Kant claims that the further content of each of these sections, that is, "all concepts of rational psychology," can be obtained through the "combination" of these four transcendental predicates. The more specific predicates he purports to derive in this way – without claiming to be exhaustive – are immateriality, incorruptibility, personality, spirituality, 'interaction with bodies,' 'principle of life in matter,' and immortality.[71] This is to say that Kant in this context identifies eleven transcendental predicates or modes that allow the human mind to conceive of itself qua soul in a determinate manner.

Evidently, while these purely intellectual predicates allow us to specify the idea of the soul in the element of thought, they do not allow us to generate *cognitions* of the soul. However, while Kant opposes their fallacious use in former versions of rational psychology, he does not reject their systematic treatment per se.[72] These predicates are purposive, moreover,

---

[69] A344/B402, translation modified.

[70] These predicates also constitute the headings of the paralogisms of rational psychology, which takes up most of the chapter (cf. A345/B403). The way Kant frames his critique of the discipline is similar to the one that frames his critique of Leibnizian ontology, albeit that he relies on the four classes of categories rather than on the four pairs of concepts of reflection (see Chapter 7, Sections 5 and 6).

[71] A345/B403. Although Kant's account is extremely brief here, he appears to have thought of the generation of these composite predicates as a progressive determination of the concept of soul guided by the table of categories. The listed predicates are among those treated in Baumgarten's rational psychology, among many others (cf. M 740–60), but I will not compare Baumgarten's version with Kant's in this regard. At one point, Kant suggests that the four main transcendental predicates are the only "predicaments of rational psychology," using a term for 'category' drawn from the Aristotelian tradition. This is not to say, however, that the seven more specific predicates are therefore to be discarded. Kant's lectures on rational psychology are largely devoted to a critique of proofs of the immortality of the soul and of classical theories about the relationship between soul and body. However, LM L₁ briefly discusses substance, simplicity, singularity, and spontaneity as "transcendental concepts according to which we consider the soul" (28:265–69). See also LM Mrongovius, 29:904–5.

[72] Kant notes that the paralogisms are *concerned with* the predicates he has just listed, not that the very production of the latter is fallacious (A345/B403). By contrast, Grier (2001) and Thiel (2006), for example, identify the rational psychology at stake in the Transcendental Dialectic with the fallacious

because some of them must be assumed in order to unify the results obtained in empirical psychology (A672/B700, A682–84/B710–12) and all of them, I take it, to provide practical philosophy with the means to root out vain speculations, fight doctrines such as materialism, conceive of the human being as free, and further the ends of mankind at large.[73] Thus, Kant must have conceived of his reformed rational psychology as a purely intellectual discipline of very modest proportions and "suited to our needs" (cf. A707/B735). While this discipline can and must treat the transcendental predicates of the soul, it cannot contain synthetic a priori judgments about the latter (cf. A381, B410) and therefore does not amount to a doctrine (B421). Yet this restriction does not entail that rational psychology should be banned from metaphysics as such.

4.3   Rational Cosmology

This section is included to indicate a task that ought to be carried out elsewhere. As was mentioned in Section 2, Kant held that metaphysics ought to treat the world, qua sum total of objects of outer sense, from two complementary perspectives: it can consider this sum total to constitute a realm to which mathematics can be applied, but it can also conceive of this very sum total in purely intellectual terms, that is, by abstracting from the fact that appearances are necessarily spatiotemporal. Whereas the former is done in rational physics, the latter is done in rational cosmology. Thus, the latter discipline is similar to rational physics as regards its transcendental object, but similar to rational psychology and rational theology as regards the nature of the concepts it treats. If rational cosmology conceives of its transcendental object – the world as such – in purely intellectual terms, it will not get entangled in the conflicts that afflicted pre-critical versions of the discipline and that are treated in the Antinomy of Pure Reason.[74]

---

knowledge claims of its pre-critical versions. I hold that the problem should be framed not merely in terms of the possibility or impossibility of cognition of the soul but also in terms of how we can and ought to conceive of the soul in a determinate manner.

[73] I take Kant to hold at B421 that rational psychology, qua discipline, cannot fight materialism unless it contains not merely the idea of the soul but also the thought of its immateriality. In order to fight dogmatic spiritualism, on the other hand, rational psychology must abandon its efforts to treat the soul as object of cognition. See also Bxxviii–xxxiv, A365–66, A383, B421, A541/B569. The Architectonic stresses that the cognitions to be united in a system must be purposive (cf. A832/B860, A839–40/B867–68). The example of immateriality suggests that Kant considered this concept to be purposive as well as conducive to the end of humanity as such.

[74] On this, see Chapter 4, Section 5, and De Boer (2020).

As in the case of the other branches of former special metaphysics, the contours of the reformed version of rational cosmology can be discerned by examining the Antinomy of Pure Reason, because Kant here develops his critique of former general cosmology by starting from the concepts that are constitutive of the discipline as such. Adopting the table of categories as his guiding thread, Kant maintains – I take it – that any version of rational cosmology must treat four concepts, called ideas, that are "nothing except categories extended to the unconditioned" (A409/B436) and, hence, preclude infinite regress. These concepts can be used – in other disciplines – to conceive of the world qua sum total of objects of outer sense or appearances in particular respects (cf. A416/B443).

This means, more specifically, according to Kant's table, that rational cosmology, as regards its most basic principles, advances the idea (1) that all appearances taken together constitute an absolute totality, (2) that matter, qua appearance, is composed of indivisible elements, (3) that the series of causes that account for the generation of a given appearance is complete, and (4) that everything that exists, qua appearance, is ultimately grounded in something that itself is not grounded in something else.[75] It seems likely that Kant, like Baumgarten, planned to treat a number of derivative concepts under these four headings.

Unlike, for example, the cosmology outlined in the *Inaugural Dissertation*, Kant's projected rational cosmology does not contain synthetic a priori judgments, but merely treats the purely intellectual determinations of the unconditioned insofar as these are relevant to our cognitions of the object of outer sense.[76] While these determinations themselves do not amount to cognition proper, they function as warranted regulative principles insofar as they, first, motivate scientists to produce ever greater unity among their cognitions and search for ever simpler elements and, second, allow moral philosophers to conceive of appearances as grounded in something that itself does not appear and, hence, is not subjected to the laws of nature (cf. A671/B699, A684–85/B712–13).

4.4   Rational Theology

According to the Architectonic, we have seen, both rational cosmology and rational theology are disciplines that establish unity among objects of

---

[75] A415/B443. I have simplified Kant's presentation of the cosmological ideas.

[76] As in the case of rational physics, one might wonder whether Kant considered the act of conceiving of the soul or God in terms of their transcendental predicates as analytic or synthetic. My guess would be that the question is misguided, since these thoughts do not amount to actual judgments.

experience in a way that transcends the bounds of experience (A845–46/ B873–74). In the case of rational theology, on Kant's account, pure reason takes recourse to the idea of God to conceive of any possible object of experience as element of a comprehensive whole (A678/B706). His detailed critique of former natural theology in the Ideal of Pure Reason targets not so much the assumption of a highest being itself as the propensity of pure reason to treat this being as an object of cognition.[77] As in the case of the other parts of the Transcendental Dialectic, Kant's criticisms to this effect tend to obscure the elements of former natural theology that he aimed to take up in the final part of his projected system. What he saw as the rational core of this discipline can be gleaned from the concluding section of the Ideal.

In this section, Kant divides rational theology, qua branch of theology not based on revelation, into transcendental theology and natural theology (A631/B659). Unlike natural theology, transcendental theology does not assume the idea of a highest intelligence but "thinks its object ... merely through pure reason, by means of transcendental concepts alone (*ens originarium, realissimum, ens entium*)" (A631/ B659). The two disciplines Kant distinguishes correspond to the two first sections of the natural theology contained in Baumgarten's *Metaphysics*, which is to say that Baumgarten uses the term 'natural theology' in a much broader sense. Departing from Baumgarten, Kant considers only transcendental theology to be a properly metaphysical discipline. We can infer from this that Kant uses the term 'rational theology' in the Architectonic in a narrow sense, namely, to refer to the purely intellectual core of the discipline that the Ideal and some lecture courses term 'transcendental theology.' Kant further identifies this discipline with deism, which means that, on his account, a deist cannot even attribute intelligence to God.[78]

In accordance with the Ideal, a transcript of lectures from 1783–84 notes that transcendental theology cannot appeal

> to a divine understanding or will, for the concept of will can only be derived from the experience of our soul.... Transcendental theology is not tainted by any experience: in it, we represent and think substance,

---

[77] See A580–82/B608–10, A636/B664, A677–78/B705–7. The act of conceiving of the idea of God "as an actual object, and this object in turn as ... necessary," is said to rest on a transcendental subreption (A619–20/B647–48).

[78] A631/B659, cf. A675/B703. I will disregard Kant's further division of theological disciplines in the Ideal and elsewhere.

power, presence, etc. by means of pure reason alone (*aus lauterer Vernunft*).... If we want to conceive of a completely pure theology, we have to choose transcendental theology.[79]

In line with the Discipline of Pure Reason, the concluding section of the Ideal emphasizes the negative use of transcendental theology. Kant calls it a "censor" that ought to purge theology from anthropomorphisms as well as defend the discipline against attacks from without.[80] Transcendental theology can carry out the latter task because its conception of God, considered as ideal, can be neither proven nor refuted:

> [T]he highest being remains for the merely speculative use of reason a mere but nevertheless faultless ideal, a concept which concludes and crowns the whole of human cognition. Even though its objective reality cannot be proved on this path, it can neither be refuted; and if there should be a moral theology that can make good this lack, then transcendental theology ... will prove to be indispensable. (A641/B669)

Apart from its task as censor, however, Kant also assigns transcendental theology the task of determining the concept of God as precisely as possible so as to prepare the ground for the purely moral theology mentioned above:

> If in some other, perhaps practical relation, the presupposition of a highest and all-sufficient being, as supreme intelligence, were to assert its validity without any objection, then it would be of the greatest importance *precisely to determine this concept on its transcendental side*, as the concept of a necessary and most real being.[81]

As in the case of the other parts of metaphysics, Kant here distinguishes the purely intellectual act of determining the concept of the transcendental object – in this case, the highest being – from the unwarranted determination of the transcendental object itself by means of a priori judgments. As we have seen, he considers transcendental theology to conceive of God as *ens originarium*, *ens realissimum*, and *ens entium*. The Ideal concludes by listing a number of other concepts, called transcendental predicates, all of which are familiar from Wolffian textbooks. According to Kant, transcendental theology ought to treat purified versions of these concepts:

> Necessity, infinity, unity, existence outside the world (not as world soul), eternity without conditions of time, omnipresence without conditions of

---

[79] LPR Volckmann (1783–84), 28:1139–40, cf. 1163; see also LM L₂, 28:596 (1790–91).
[80] A640/B668, cf. A641/B669, A711/B739, LM Dohna, 28:695 (1792–93).
[81] A640/B668, emphasis mine, cf. A641/B669.

space, omnipotence, etc. are merely *transcendental predicates*, and hence
a *purified concept* of them, which every theology needs so very badly, can
be drawn from transcendental theology alone. (A642–43/B67–71,
emphasis mine)

In lectures delivered 1783–84, Kant calls the predicates one "can a priori
attribute to the *ens realissimum*" "ontological predicates," because they
pertain to God qua mere being rather than intelligence.[82] More specifically, he here maintains that transcendental theology must conceive of
God as possible, in view of his essence, as existing, necessary, a single
substance, distinct from the world, immaterial, distinct from the world
soul, cause, eternal, omnipresent, and omnipotent.[83]

While this list of predicates might indeed be required to ward off a
variety of attacks and to ground the applied parts of theology, it cannot be
said to be very neat. It contains part of the categories, but not all of them.
It treats two concepts that appear to presuppose time and space as well as a
concept derived from the predicable of force. By and large, Kant's exposition follows Baumgarten's, which is to say that he does not treat the
transcendental predicates of God according to the table of categories.[84] We
can surmise that the purification he mentions would have resulted in
concepts devoid of sensible elements, but it is hard to determine exactly
which concepts Kant's reformed transcendental theology would have
contained.[85]

In any case, it is clear that this theology – unlike its pre-critical
counterparts – would not have contained proofs of God's existence and
properties. Given the passages quoted above, however, there can be no
doubt that he intended the final part of his metaphysical system to treat
not just the idea of a highest being but also the predicates that make up the
purely intellectual and non-anthropomorphic determinations of this idea.

---

[82] LPR Volckmann, 28:1141.
[83] LPR Volckmann, 28:1160–61, cf. 1163. Kant's various lists differ somewhat (cf. LRT Mrongovius,
28:1252 and LM L₂, 28:600–602). A note from the same period has it that some of these predicates
can be used to oppose atheists and skeptics, whereas others can be used to oppose
anthropomorphism or positions attributed to the Stoics or Spinoza (R6214, 18:501–2). See
Baumgarten, M 846, 848, 855, for a similar discussion.
[84] See Baumgarten, M 800–862. Unlike Kant, Baumgarten frames his account of the divine properties
as an account of God's perfections.
[85] The passage from the Ideal quoted above (A642–43/B67–71) suggests that transcendental theology
can include the concepts of eternity and omnipresence on the condition that they are purged of all
elements stemming from intuition. However, according to one of the lecture transcripts, Kant held
that "the concept of eternity is … necessarily affected by time" and, hence, that "divine eternity"
can mean nothing else than "the necessity of God's existence" (LRT Mrongovius, 28:1263–64, cf.
LM L₂, 28:602–3). The lectures seem inconclusive on this point.

But why would such a discipline be useful? According to the Ideal, the predicates treated within transcendental theology itself are nothing but "empty titles for concepts."[86] In one of Kant's lectures, the discipline is said to be nothing but "a silhouette of a theology" (LM L$_2$, 28:605). Another lecture considers the purely intellectual branch of theology to be useless considered on its own:

> The transcendental concepts are completely pure, do not contain any sensibility. I therefore do not have to fear that I attribute properties to God that put him on a par with human beings.... The deistic concept of the highest being, if considered in isolation, amounts to no concept of God whatsoever. Although we must start from this concept, on its own it is useless. It constitutes the starting point insofar as it represents the property *in abstracto*.[87]

However, Kant also asserts that transcendental theology, though "very restricted," is "of utmost necessity,"[88] namely, insofar as it provides the concepts by dint of which other disciplines can represent the divine properties *in concreto* (LM L$_2$, 28: 605). Branches of theology that on Kant's account do not belong to metaphysics – including physico-theology – are permitted, he writes, to "conceive a being that I distinguish from the world by means of properties which belong solely to the world of sense," that is, to employ concepts such as cause and intelligence analogously.[89] Moreover, thus filling the 'empty titles' provided by transcendental theology with content is warranted not only for the purposes of practical reason, but also to conceive of nature in teleological terms. As Kant puts it in the Ideal:

> [T]he speculative interest of reason makes it necessary to regard every ordinance in the world as if it had sprouted from the intention of a highest reason, for such a principle provides our reason ... with entirely new

---

[86] A679/B707, cf. A696/B724. Kant makes an analogous remark on the categories treated in ontology: without schemata, they are nothing but "functions of the understanding for concepts, but do not represent any object" (A147/B187).

[87] LRT Mrongovius, 28:1163–64, cf. 1141.   [88] LM Dohna, 28:695 (1792–93).

[89] A678/B706, translation modified, emphasis mine. According to Kant, we are licensed to conceive of God in analogical terms insofar as we do so to conceive of the world as a purposive whole. In this case, he writes, we do not determine this being itself, but merely "attribute to the latter just those properties that, according to the conditions of our reason, could contain the ground for such a systematic unity" (A698/B726, cf. Prol, 4:357–60). On this, see Wood (1978: 83–92) and Chance and Pasternak (2019). The latter provide a helpful account of the difference between Kant and Baumgarten in this regard. Whereas they emphasize the shortcomings of transcendental theology, I focus on Kant's account of the discipline qua part of metaphysics. Wood's pioneering study, in turn, focuses on Kant's critique of former natural theology and appears to reduce the elements Kant intended to preserve to moral theology.

prospects of connecting things in the world according to teleological laws and thereby attaining the greatest systematic unity among them. The presupposition of a supreme intelligence, as the sole cause of the world-whole, but of course merely in the idea, can therefore always be useful to reason and never harmful to it.[90]

Thus, insofar as transcendental theology provides other disciplines with a limited number of purely intellectual predicates, it indirectly supports the attempts carried out within these disciplines to conceive of possible objects of experience as elements of a well-ordered totality.[91] However, since disciplines such as physico-theology, unlike transcendental theology, employ concepts derived from inner experience, they are necessarily "polluted" by anthropomorphisms (LM L_2, 28:605) and therefore ought to be excluded from metaphysics. Clearly, this also obtains of all but the first section of Baumgarten's natural theology.

Read in this way, Kant's critique of Wolffian natural theology illuminates the idea behind his critique of former special metaphysics as such. As I hope to have shown, this critique consists essentially in dividing the pure and applied parts of a discipline more rigorously than the Wolffians had done. More specifically, the *Critique of Pure Reason* seeks to purify the various branches of former special metaphysics by, first, restricting their pure or a priori parts to the treatment of a limited number of purely intellectual, quasi-empty determinations of a particular idea of reason and, second, assigning the tasks of the applied parts to disciplines defined by moral or teleological concerns.[92] These disciplines, in turn, can draw on sources other than sensibility to provide the concepts treated in the

---

[90] A686–87/B714–15, cf. A297–98/B353–54, A678/B706, A697/B725.

[91] On this, see Wood (1978: 82). According to LM L_2, only transcendental theology can "provide a pure concept of God that keeps all anthropomorphisms at bay. For this reason, all theologies must be grounded on it" (28:600).

[92] Since Kant's reformed version of former special metaphysics would have treated the ideas of reason and their purely intellectual predicates alone, the task carried out in its various branches would have been very similar to the one carried out in his projected ontology or transcendental philosophy. I believe that Kant became aware of this continuity at least after the publication of the *Critique*. Various passages suggest that he came to use the term 'transcendental philosophy' to denote not just the first branch of the theoretical part of his projected system, but this part as a whole. In LM Mrongovius (1782–83), Kant is said to have asserted that transcendental philosophy deals both with pure concepts that are used immanently and with pure concepts, such as God, the use of which is transcendent (29:768). In his open letter to Fichte (1799), discussed in Section 6 below, the term 'transcendental philosophy' also seems to refer to the theoretical part of his projected system as a whole. However, it is also possible that Kant was aware of said continuity prior to 1781, but did not want to draw attention to it. This might explain the tension between, on the one hand, his explanation of transcendental philosophy in a way that would remind the reader of former ontology (cf. A11–12/B25, A845/B873) and, on the other hand, his use of the term with regard to the theoretical part of his projected system as such (A13/B27). Theis (2012: 158) also notes this

theoretical part of metaphysics with objective reality. While the restriction Kant thus imposes on rational psychology, cosmology, and theology entails their incapacity to generate cognitions of objects, it entails neither their uselessness nor their impossibility.

5   The System Considered from the Standpoint of Ends

It has emerged from my discussion so far that Kant regarded his projected system of pure reason as a means rather than an end in itself. In order to put his thoughts on this system into perspective, this section briefly addresses Kant's account of the relationship between the system and the end it was supposed to serve.

In a letter written in 1773, quoted in Chapter 1, Kant tells Herz that the system he envisioned would be "much more favorable to religion and morality" than existing systems.[93] According to the 1787 Preface to the *Critique*, the pretensions of speculative reason must be tackled in order that "God, freedom, and immortality" can be assumed for the sake of morality (Bxxx). In a similar vein, Kant writes in the Architectonic that metaphysics protects religion and morality against the "devastations that a lawless speculative reason would otherwise inevitably perpetrate" (A849/B877). Accordingly, the propaedeutic critique of pure reason as well as the projected metaphysical system are said to further "the essential ends of humanity" by "relating everything to wisdom, but through the path of science" (A850/B878).

These remarks concur with Kant's distinction between the *Schulbegriff* and *Weltbegriff* of philosophy in the same chapter.[94] Kant here contrasts philosophy qua discipline that aspires to "logical perfection" with philosophy qua discipline that relates "all cognition to the essential ends of human reason" (A838–39/B866–67) and, hence, to the end of humanity at stake in practical philosophy as such (A840/B868).

---

tension. As was mentioned in Section 4, the Transcendental Dialectic uses the term 'transcendental' with regard to the various branches of former special metaphysics (A335/B392) and the concepts treated in them. These instances might also be considered to point to a much broader notion of first-order transcendental philosophy than the one Kant appears to defend in the Transcendental Analytic.

[93] Kant to Herz, 10:144. See Chapter 2, Section 4. Kant's view that metaphysics must be reformed for the sake of morality can already be found in *Dreams of a Spirit Seer* (2:349, 369) and is repeated on many occasions.

[94] I will leave the terms untranslated and disregard the problems these terms involve. On this, see Hinske (2013), who argues convincingly that the term *Weltbegriff* should not be associated with cosmopolitanism, but has a much broader meaning.

An example provided in the 1787 edition of the *Critique of Pure Reason* clarifies this point. Kant notes here that once all speculative so-called proofs of the immortality of the soul have been abolished, the useful proofs will emerge with all the more clarity. These proofs, he writes,

> move reason to its proper territory, namely the order of ends that, however, is at once an order of nature; but since reason is in itself at once a practical faculty and, in this capacity, *not limited to the conditions of the order of nature*, it is justified in extending the order of ends ... beyond the bounds of experience and life. (B425, emphasis mine)

Clearly, Kant considered an adequate conception of the moral order to be premised on the distinction between phenomena and noumena established in the *Critique*: it is only by dint of this distinction that philosophy can transfer the questions concerning God, immortality, and freedom from the theoretical to the practical domain.[95] On this basis, in turn, practical reason can provide guidance to the efforts of humankind to pursue the ends that ought to be pursued "if the will is free, if there is a God, and if there is a future world."[96]

Given these passages – as well as a number of later works that cannot be discussed here – one might be tempted to infer that Kant came to reject eighteenth-century school philosophy in favor of a mode of wisdom devoted to the practical ends of humanity.[97] I hope to have shown, by contrast, that he considered the shadowy, quasi-scholastic elaboration of the theoretical part of metaphysics announced in the *Critique* to be purposeful and worth pursuing for at least two reasons: first, it provides all other disciplines with the conceptual means to conceive of their domains as well-ordered totalities, and, second, it provides the practical part of metaphysics with the criterion, concepts, principles, and grid by means of which the discipline can be carried out in an adequate way and, hence, support the further enlightenment of mankind.

---

[95] A750/B778, cf. Bxxix. The question as to how this transition can be effectuated in an adequate manner plays an important role in Kant's late drafts titled *What Progress Has Metaphysics Made since the Time of Leibniz and Wolff?* (cf. 20:272–74, 293–94). On this, see Caimi (2017), who emphasizes that Kant considered this transition to involve a type of metaphysics – called practico-dogmatic – that relates the realms of nature and freedom by couching the idea of a final end in theoretical terms.

[96] A800/B828. The idea of a moral world is said to possess "objective reality" insofar as it is conceived by pure reason in its practical use (A808/809, cf. CPrR, 5:132).

[97] See Manchester (2003) and Ypi (2011). While Ypi's otherwise illuminating article considers the Architectonic to reject the scholastic understanding of philosophy (cf. 144), I contend, in line with Fugate (2014: 390–93), that Kant assigned the reformed version of this discipline a subordinate yet necessary task.

6   Kant's Later Remarks on His Projected System

As was mentioned in the introduction to this chapter, the idea of a system of pure reason that Kant presents in no uncertain terms in the *Critique of Pure Reason* did not fall on fertile ground. It is not possible here to deal with the intricacies of the early reception of Kant's critical philosophy and its impact on later commentators.[98] Yet in order to further support the reading elaborated so far, the present section contends that Kant never changed his mind as regards his intention to elaborate a reformed version of Wolff and Baumgarten's metaphysical treatises.

Since Kant did not publish the system he had announced in 1781, readers had a reason to conceive of the *Critique of Pure Reason* as Kant's 'system.' This tendency was reinforced by Kant himself in at least two ways. First, he in the *Critique* uses the term 'system' not only with regard to his projected system of pure reason, but also, more broadly, to denote any manifold of cognitions united by an idea.[99] Second, in line with the first generation of readers, he came to refer to the philosophy contained in the *Critique* as a system without specifying in which sense he used the term.[100]

The publication of the *Critique of the Power of Judgment* in 1790 made it even more difficult to discern Kant's original intentions. Yet I would like to claim that this work actually does not abandon the distinction between the preparatory task carried out in the three *Critiques* and the twofold metaphysical system announced in the *Critique of Pure Reason*. Thus, Kant writes in its Preface that in a "system of pure philosophy" the principles of the faculty of judgment ought not to constitute a separate, third, part of the system:

> A critique of pure reason, i.e., of our capacity to judge in accordance with *a priori* principles, would be incomplete if the critique of the power of judgment ... were not dealt with as a special part of this critique, *even though its principles may not constitute a special part of a system of pure philosophy, between the theoretical and the practical part....* For if such a

---

[98] For helpful accounts of the successive responses to Kant's notion of a system of pure reason, see Jaeschke and Arndt (2012) and Wellmann (2018).

[99] A832/B860. Thus, Kant uses the term 'system' in this broad sense to denote the sum total of the principles of the pure understanding (A148/B187; MFNS, 4:473), the sum total of the principles of pure reason (A333/B390), and the sum total of the categories (Prol, 4:322–26).

[100] In the *Metaphysical Foundations* Kant refers to his "system of the *Critique of Pure Reason*" (4:474n). In the 1787 Preface to the *Critique of Pure Reason*, Kant likewise refers to this work as a system (Bxxxviii). The *Critique of Practical Reason* distinguishes between a "system of science" and a "system of critique" (5: 8).

system, under the general name of metaphysics, is one day to come into being (something that can be done in an exhaustive manner and is highly important for the use of reason in all respects), then the critique must previously have probed the ground for this structure.[101]

In various letters, Kant affirms his intention to complement the propae-deutic *Critique of Pure Reason* with a metaphysical system – at some point. In 1783, he tells Mendelssohn he would like to write a short textbook on metaphysics, according to critical principles, but that it might take him rather long to finish it.[102] In 1786, he notes in another letter that he is further "putting off" the elaboration of a "system of metaphysics," because of his work on the practical philosophy and, moreover, because the forthcoming new edition of the *Critique* would allow "almost any insight-ful person" to carry out this task.[103] More than a year later, Kant tells Jakob in the letter cited above of his plan to move on to the "dogmatic part" of his work.[104] Echoing the letter he wrote in late 1773, Kant in a letter to Herz from 1789 – on Maimon – recalls his plan to elaborate "a system of metaphysics, of both nature and morals."[105] In his drafts for the prize essay *What Real Progress Has Metaphysics Made in Germany since the Time of Leibniz and Wolff?*, dated 1793–95, Kant reiterates that the predicables "could ... be completely enumerated and systematically pre-sented in a table" (20:272).

Kant's remarks on his projected metaphysical system are internally consistent as well as in accordance with the *Critique of Pure Reason* and the *Prolegomena*. Nevertheless, most commentators assume that Kant at some point reversed his view on the matter. They infer this primarily from Kant's famous open letter to Fichte, published in 1799. I contend, how-ever, that the meaning of the relevant passage has been misconstrued by most commentators from the time it was published until today. On my reading, Kant in said passage does not retract his earlier position, but reiterates that the *Critique of Pure Reason* paves the way for the system and that he from the outset intended to elaborate the latter:

> [T]he unwarranted claim according to which I merely should have wanted to deliver a propaedeutic to transcendental philosophy and not the actual

---

[101] CPJ, 5:168, emphasis mine, translation modified, cf. 5:417. See also the *First Introduction to the Critique of the Power of Judgment* (20:195, 201).
[102] Kant to Mendelssohn, August 16, 1783 (10:346–47).
[103] Kant to Bering, April 7, 1786 (10:441).
[104] Kant to Jakob, September 11 (?), 1787 (10:494), cf. Bxliii.
[105] Kant to Herz, May 26, 1789 (11:48–49), cf. Kant to Herz, late 1773 (10:145). See also Kant to Kästner, August 5 (?), 1790 (11:186), Kant to Beck, January 20, 1792 (11:313).

system itself is incomprehensible to me. Such an intention could never have occurred to me, since I myself, *in* the *Critique of Pure Reason, have lauded* (*gepriesen habe*) the completed whole of pure philosophy as the best indication of the truth of this philosophy.[106]

The preposition 'in' pertains not to what is actually *contained* in the *Critique of Pure Reason*, but to what is *recommended* in it. Read in this way, there can be no doubt that the passage concerns Kant's long-term *intention* to publish a metaphysical system, not the question as to what he took himself to have achieved.[107]

Apart from this fateful open letter, a letter to Schulz, written in 1783, might be taken to testify to Kant's doubts about the feasibility of his projected system. The table of categories, he notes, might give rise to "a possibly significant invention, one that I am however unable to pursue and that will require a mathematical mind like yours: the construction of an *ars characteristica combinatoria*." Kant admits that this idea is "obscured as by fog" in his mind.[108] However, he does not spell out what the difficulty is. What he does mention is the difference between the categories considered in themselves and the categories in their capacity as "predicates" of objects of sensibility. He tells his friend that he already in the final section of the *Dissertation* had touched on the issue, namely, I add, the insight that categories acquire a different meaning depending on whether or not the sensible condition of their actual use is taken into account.[109] Possibly, Kant struggled with the question as to whether his projected ontology should take into account the difference between, for instance, (1) the category of causality as such, (2) the meaning it acquires if used with regard to appearances, and (3) the meaning it acquires if used analogically

---

[106] 'Declaration Concerning Fichte's *Wissenschaftslehre*,' August 7, 1799 (12:370–71, translation modified). The term 'transcendental philosophy' here seems to refer to the projected system of pure reason as a whole. Zweig's translation of the letter canonizes the misguided interpretation mentioned above. Omitting 'gepriesen habe,' Zweig takes Kant to have considered "the completeness of pure philosophy within the *Critique of Pure Reason* to be the best indication of the truth of that work" (12:370–71). Repeating the standard account, he asserts in a note that "Kant's claim here is contradicted by many passages in the first *Critique*." Kemp Smith (1923: 72–73) claims that Kant, "having "forgotten his own previous and conflicting utterances on this point," ultimately "came to the conclusion that Critique, Transcendental Philosophy, and System all coincide." Commentators who misconstrue the passage along the same lines include De Vleeschauwer (1937: 547–48), Ameriks (2000: 50), and Ferrarin (2015: 247). See Theis (2012: 157–58) for an exception.

[107] While Kant in the *Critique* does not literally claim what he in 1799 purports to have claimed in this work, some passages, cited in the introduction to this chapter and Section 4 above, carry the same meaning (cf. Axix–xx, A82–83/B108–9).

[108] Kant to Schulz, August 26, 1783 (10:351); cf. Kant to Beck, September 27, 1791 (11:290).

[109] See Diss, 2:415, and Chapter 2, Section 4.

with regard to noumena such as God. If so, then predicables such as force should be treated in the same way. Obviously, in this case the text would become very complex.

More generally, the letter might be considered to testify to Kant's growing awareness of a tension between, on the one hand, his insight into the impact of pure sensibility on the meaning of categories and, on the other, the idea of a comprehensive account of the purely intellectual elements of any cognition of objects modeled on Baumgarten's *Metaphysics*. For this reason, or others unknown to us, Kant may have been less convinced of the exact way to carry out this plan than he appears to be in most of his remarks on the subject, and this may have played into his repeated postponement of the project.

Apart from that, Kant may have put off the publication of his system due to external circumstances. For one, in 1788 Eberhard argued in his *Philosophisches Magazin* that the insights of any value presented in the *Critique of Pure Reason* had already been achieved by Leibniz and Wolff.[110] Publishing a metaphysical treatise along the lines of Baumgarten's would evidently have given the Wolffian camp additional ammunition. Moreover, it is clear that Kant gradually shifted the focus of his attention to questions concerning the moral edification of mankind. Possibly, he came to think that addressing and answering these questions did not necessarily require the support of a full-blown metaphysical system after all or, at least, that providing one would be a waste of time given the indifference to metaphysics of his intended readers.

7 Conclusion

In this chapter, I have shifted the focus from the *Critique of Pure Reason* to the theoretical part of the reformed metaphysical system that Kant alluded to from the mid-1760s to the final years of his life. Notwithstanding the elusiveness of the issue, I hope to have shown that, for Kant, each of the branches of former metaphysics could be turned into an a priori science if it met a number of conditions. First, none of the metaphysical disciplines should contain synthetic a priori judgments about things. Second, each of them ought to develop its content, essentially consisting of concepts, definitions, and principles, by adopting the table of categories as a guiding thread. Third, this content should be completely devoid of empirical elements. Fourth, ontology and rational physics should treat the sum total

---

[110] Eberhard, *Philosophisches Magazin*, vol. 1, 289; quoted in Allison (1973: 16).

of pure concepts and a priori principles that allow the human mind to obtain knowledge of objects of experience and outer sense, respectively. Fifth, since rational psychology, cosmology, and theology, for their part, are not concerned with possible objects of experience in a direct way, their content should be limited to the purely intellectual predicates that allow the human mind to conceive of the ideas of reason – qua determinations of the unconditioned – in a determinate way.

It follows from these conditions, taken together, that only two of the branches of Kant's projected system of pure reason – ontology and rational physics – could have contained synthetic a priori judgments. The content of the other three branches – rational psychology, cosmology, and theology – would have been reduced to a limited number of quasi-empty concepts. As we have seen, however, Kant did not regard these concepts as useless: insofar as they allow scientists to represent the unconditioned of their discipline in a determinate manner, they indirectly contribute to the cognition of objects of experience. More importantly, he held that these very concepts can acquire objective reality, or content, insofar as they are put in the service of practical reason.

What has thus emerged from the fog, I hope, are the contours of a building that would have been quite different from the "intellectual system of the world" allegedly constructed by Leibniz (A270/B326) or the one that Wolff, according to *Dreams of a Spirit-Seer*, erected on the basis of "a few building-materials derived from experience and a larger amount of surreptitious concepts" (2:342). At least according to his own standards, the building Kant envisioned would have been more modest, more orderly, and more useful. Yet it would not have differed much from those of his predecessors in all regards: it would have been divided in a similar way, its materials would have been retrieved from the "ruins of collapsed old buildings" (A835/B863), and it would have been more Wolffian in spirit than most of Kant's readers were prepared to concede.

Conclusion

Kant's critical philosophy is reputed to impose strict limits on the cognitive activities carried out by the human mind. The mind is said to be able to generate empirical knowledge by means of two forms of intuition and twelve categories, and to delude itself whenever it illicitly ventures beyond these limits in search of a priori knowledge of the soul, the world as such, and God. Even if Kant may have been unable to demonstrate all of the claims he advances in the *Critique of Pure Reason*, we can be satisfied with the epistemological modesty his work proclaims: it allows us to pit Kant's work against the extravagancies of philosophers such as Fichte and Hegel as well as to follow his beacon in our own even more modest pursuits.

Yet this prevailing image of Kant does not fit well with many of his own utterances on the nature of his critical enterprise. In the 1781 Preface to the *Critique*, for instance, Kant writes:

> Every cognition that is supposed to be certain a priori proclaims that it wants to be regarded as absolutely necessary, and this holds true even more of a determination of all pure cognitions a priori that is to be the standard and thus even the example of all apodictic (philosophical) certainty. Whether I have performed what I have just pledged in that respect remains wholly to the judgment of the reader. (Axv)

Kant here considers the *Critique* to determine "all pure cognitions a priori." He carries out this task by identifying the a priori elements of any cognition of objects and investigating the conditions under which the human mind is warranted to employ these elements. What interests me at this point, however, is Kant's portrayal of transcendental critique as a mode of a priori cognition that can itself lay claim to apodictic certainty. His remark to this effect concurs with his assertion in the same text, cited in Chapter 8, that in metaphysics, considered as the "inventory" of everything that pure reason "brings forth entirely out of itself," nothing can remain hidden from the light cast by reason itself (Axx).

Is this modesty? Rather than ignoring the discrepancy between Kant's own account of the *Critique of Pure Reason* and those of most commentaries, I have approached the work from the vantage point of the end Kant had set himself, namely, the metaphysical system he referred to as the system of pure reason. Seen in this light, the *Critique* does not impose modesty on the human mind as such, but merely restricts the sphere within which metaphysics can obtain a priori knowledge of objects. The main idea behind the present book can be summarized by unpacking this claim.

Regardless of the distinction between appearances and things in themselves, which was discussed in Chapter 4, scientists can explore the universe in any direction they wish and to any extent they can. What Kant rather targets, on my reading, is the tendency of former metaphysics to objectify its various conceptions of the unconditioned. The Transcendental Dialectic identifies and counters this tendency by disentangling pure reason from the pure understanding: whereas the latter faculty aims to turn representations into objects of cognition, the former seeks to comprehend a sum total by positing an unconditioned condition. Accordingly, a critique of pure reason requires that the two faculties be assigned their own domain and, hence, that the branches of former special metaphysics be reduced to disciplines that specify the meaning of purely intellectual ideas by means of purely intellectual predicates. In this regard, Kant's projected system of pure reason is continuous with the outcome of the *Inaugural Dissertation*.

Yet, as we have seen in Chapter 2, the *Critique of Pure Reason* moves beyond the *Dissertation* by shedding the assumption that the act of specifying purely intellectual concepts by means of other purely intellectual concepts yields a priori knowledge of objects. Kant came to see, I assume, that the cognitive activity the pure understanding carries out in the applied part of metaphysics ought to be restricted to determining the ideas of reason in accordance with the table of categories. As long as this activity is purely intellectual, it does not entail the objectification of the unconditioned that deluded former special metaphysics. Seen in this way, Kant imposes modesty on the pure understanding insofar as it, in tandem with pure reason, carries out its determining activity within rational physics, psychology, cosmology, and theology.

Clearly, the diagnosis of former metaphysics carried out in the *Critique* is more complicated. Without doubt, Kant considered the problems afflicting former special metaphysics to be rooted in the objectifying tendency of former general metaphysics. The latter discipline, we know, treats the concepts and principles by dint of which the human mind can obtain knowledge of objects as such. As was argued in Chapter 5, Kant traces the production of a priori cognitions of objects to the effort on the part of the human mind to establish transcendental unity of apperception. Seen from this perspective, as was discussed in Chapter 6, any a priori knowledge of objects results from the unification of successive representations. Accordingly, it must rely on schematized pure concepts and, thus, on time qua form of intuition. If this is the case, I take Kant to infer, then the a priori objectification of representations is warranted on the condition that the activities involved are geared toward possible objects of experience. In this regard, Kant imposes modesty on the pure understanding by limiting its capacity to generate a priori cognitions of objects, in tandem with pure time and the pure imagination, to the realm of appearances.

However, this restriction is imposed not on the a priori cognitive activities carried out by the human mind as such but on the branch of metaphysics that used to be called general metaphysics and that Kant came to call transcendental philosophy. Whereas pre-critical elaborations of this foundational part of metaphysics laid claim to a priori knowledge of things as such, Kant's transcendental critique reduces the task of the pure understanding within this discipline to the systematic and purely analytic treatment of the concepts and principles that allow the human mind to obtain a priori knowledge of objects at all. Since the analytic activity carried out by the pure understanding does not rely on pure intuition, transcendental philosophy can be purely intellectual in this regard. As was suggested in Chapter 8, however, it cannot be purely intellectual in all respects, since the concepts it treats partly stem from pure intuition. As said, the same holds true of rational physics qua branch of special metaphysics.

Thus, I take Kant to hold that a thoroughgoing reform of metaphysics requires that the cognitive activities carried out by the human mind be analyzed so as to prevent them from encroaching on one another. As was mentioned above, I hold that transcendental critique primarily targets the objectifying activity of the pure understanding insofar as it is enacted in the element of former general and special metaphysics. To the extent that the Transcendental Aesthetic and Transcendental Analytic carry out this critique, they treat the sensible and intellectual conditions under which the a priori objectification of representations is possible and warranted. The critical strand of the Transcendental Dialectic, for its part, treats the purported a priori cognitions of objects that do not meet these conditions and that accordingly need to be abolished.

On this account, we can see how Kant's guiding question as to "what and how much the understanding and reason can know free of all experience" (Axvii) led him to explore vaults of the human mind where few had ventured before. Yet whereas these investigations were meant to prepare the ground for a comprehensive system of pure reason, they seem to have come to absorb Kant's attention to such an extent that the original aim lost much of its appeal. Even so, however, I hope to have shown that the idea of such a system constitutes the "inner end" of the *Critique of Pure Reason* (cf. A833/B861) to which all elements are subservient.

Considering the critical project in view of the idea of a system of pure reason, as I have done throughout this book, also sheds light on Kant's conception of the relationship between critique and system. As was argued in Chapter 3 in particular, Kant did not intend to carry out his second-order critique of metaphysics and his projected first-order metaphysics consecutively, but elaborated the core of the latter in the context of an analysis dominated by the former. In the end, it might be argued that Kant conceived of critique and system as nothing but two complementary ways in which pure reason, "concerned with nothing but itself" (A680/B708), seeks to illuminate everything that falls within its sphere. In the case of critique, pure reason, adopting the position of a judge, turns inward to determine the limits within which each of the a priori activities carried out by the human mind is warranted. In so doing, it can draw on the results of logic and empirical psychology, that is, on work previously carried out by the pure understanding. In the case of the system, conversely, pure reason, adopting the position of an architect, turns inward to identify and impose order on the products of the a priori activities carried out by the human mind, namely, forms of intuition, pure concepts, and a priori principles. In this regard, as we have seen, it can draw on the results of earlier elaborations of general and special metaphysics, which are likewise the work of the pure understanding.

In both cases, pure reason sets out to examine that which it – by means of the pure understanding – "brings forth entirely out of itself" and that accordingly cannot resist illumination. As was seen in Chapter 8, however, pure reason, in its capacity as architect, must impose order on material, handed down by the history of metaphysics, theology, and the sciences, that tends to resist its resolution into a limited number of pure intuitions and root concepts. Arguably, it is this intractable history that confronts Kant's own critical project with a boundary it cannot go beyond.

Insofar as the *Critique of Pure Reason* seeks to conceive of the concepts and principles that defined the scientific, philosophical, and cultural paradigm of the late eighteenth century as elements of a comprehensive system, it is itself part of a history that stretches – at least – from Wolff's *German Metaphysics* to Hegel's *Science of Logic*. Within this history, Kant's philosophy stands out not because it enclosed the human mind within the bounds of sense, but because of its relentless attempt to emancipate metaphysics from its self-incurred immaturity.

Bibliography

Works by Kant

All references to the *Critique of Pure Reason* are to the A and B pagination of the first and second editions (1781/87). All other references are to the volume and page of *Kant's Gesammelte Schriften*, 29 vols., ed. Königlich-Preußische Akademie der Wissenschaften, now Berlin-Brandenburgische Akademie der Wissenschaften (Berlin: De Gruyter, 1900–). English translations generally follow those of the *Cambridge Edition of the Works of Immanuel Kant*, edited by Paul Guyer and Allen W. Wood (Cambridge University Press, 1992–2012). With the exception of very minor modifications, I indicate in the notes where my translations deviate from the published versions or are my own.

Other Primary Sources

Baumgarten, Alexander G. 2013. *Metaphysics* [1739]. Translated and edited by Courtney D. Fugate and John Hymers. London: Bloomsbury.

Crusius, Christian A. 1964a. *Entwurf der notwendigen Vernunft-Wahrheiten, wiefern sie den Zufälligen entgegengesetzet werden* [1745], in *Die philosophischen Hauptwerke*, vol. 2, edited by Georgio Tonelli. Hildesheim: Olms.

  1964b. *Weg zur Gewissheit und Zuverlässigkeit der menschlichen Erkenntniss* [1747], in *Die philosophischen Hauptwerke*, vol. 3, edited by Georgio Tonelli. Hildesheim: Olms.

Fichte, Johann Gottlieb. 1967. "Zweite Einleitung in die Wissenschaftslehre," in idem, *Erste und zweite Einleitung in die Wissenschaftslehre und Versuch einer neuen Darstellung der Wissenschaftslehre* [1797], edited by Fritz Medicus. Hamburg: Meiner. Translated as "Second Introduction to the Science of Knowledge," in idem, *The Science of Knowledge*, edited and translated by Peter Heath and John Lachs. New York: Meredith Corporation 1970.

Locke, John. 1975. *An Essay Concerning Human Understanding* [1690], edited by Peter Harold Nidditch. Oxford: Clarendon Press.

Meier, Georg Friedrich. 1752. *Auszug aus der Vernunftlehre*. Halle: Gebauer. Reprinted in *Kant's Gesammelte Schriften*, Band XVI. Translated as *Excerpts from the Doctrine of Reason*, edited and translated by Lawrence Pasternack and Pablo Muchnik. London: Bloomsbury, 2016.

Mendelssohn, Moses. 1979. *Morgenstunden oder Vorlesungen über das Daseyn Gottes. Der Briefwechsel Mendelssohn – Kant*, edited by Dominique Bourel. Stuttgart: Reclam.

Tetens, Johannes N. 1913. *Über die allgemeine speculativische Philosophie. Philosophische Versuche über die menschliche Natur und ihre Entwicklung* [1775], Band I, edited by Wilhelm Uebele. Berlin: Reuther und Reichard.

Wolff, Christian. 1964. *Cosmologia generalis* [1731], in *Gesammelte Werke* II/4, edited by Jean École. Hildesheim: Olms.

    1973. *Ausführliche Nachricht von seinen eigenen Schriften, die er in Deutscher Sprache herausgegeben* [1733], in *Gesammelte Werke* I/9, edited by Hans Werner Arndt. Hildesheim: Olms.

    1978. *Vernünfftige Gedanken von den Kräften des menschlichen Verstandes und ihrem richtigen Gebrauche in Erkenntnis der Wahrheit* [1713], in *Gesammelte Werke* I/1, edited by Hans Werner Arndt. Hildesheim: Olms.

    1983a. *Der Vernünftigen Gedancken von Gott, der Welt und der Seele des Menschen, auch allen Dingen überhaupt, Anderer Theil, bestehend in ausführlichen Anmerckungen* [1740], in *Gesammelte Werke* I/3, edited by Charles A. Corr. Hildesheim: Olms.

    1983b. *Philosophia rationalis sive logica* [1740], *Gesammelte Werke* II/1.1–1.3, edited by Charles A. Corr. Hildesheim: Olms.

    1983c. *Vernünfftige Gedancken von Gott, der Welt und der Seele des Menschen, auch allen Dingen überhaupt* [1720], in *Gesammelte Werke* I/2, edited by Charles A. Corr. Hildesheim: Olms.

    1996. *Discursus praeliminaris de philosophia in genere. Einleitende Abhandlung über Philosophie im allgemeinen* [1728], edited and translated by Günther Gawlick and Lothar Kreimendahl. Stuttgart: Frommann-Holzboog.

    2005. *Philosophia prima sive ontologia / Erste Philosophie oder Ontologie* [1729] §§1–78, translated and edited by Dirk Effertz. Hamburg: Meiner.

Secondary Sources

Adams, Robert M. 1997. "Things in Themselves," *Philosophy and Phenomenological Research* 57/4, 801–25.

Adickes, Erich. 1889. *Immanuel Kants Kritik der reinen Vernunft, mit einer Einleitung und Anmerkungen herausgegeben von Erich Adickes.* Berlin: Mayer & Müller.

    1924. *Kant und das Ding an sich.* Berlin: Heise.

    1929. *Kants Lehre von der doppelten Affektion unseres Ichs als Schlüssel zu seiner Erkenntnistheorie.* Tübingen: Mohr Siebeck.

Allais, Lucy. 2015. *Manifest Reality: Kant's Idealism and His Realism.* Oxford University Press.

Allison, Henry E. 1973. *The Kant–Eberhard Controversy.* Baltimore: Johns Hopkins University Press.

    1981. "Transcendental Schematism and the Problem of the Synthetic *A Priori*," *Dialectica* 35/1–2, 59–83.

2004. *Kant's Transcendental Idealism: An Interpretation and Defense*, revised and enlarged edition. New Haven: Yale University Press. Originally published in 1983.

2015. *Kant's Transcendental Deduction: An Analytical-Historical Commentary.* Oxford University Press.

Ameriks, Karl. 1982/2000. *Kant's Theory of Mind: An Analysis of the Paralogisms of Pure Reason.* Oxford University Press.

1992. "The Critique of Metaphysics: Kant and Traditional Ontology," in Paul Guyer (ed.), *Cambridge Companion to Kant.* Cambridge University Press, 249–79.

2000. *Kant and the Fate of Autonomy: Problems in the Appropriation of the Critical Philosophy.* Cambridge University Press.

2001. "Kant's Notion of Systematic Philosophy: Changes in the Second Critique and After," in Hans Friedrich Fulda and Jürgen Stolzenberg (eds.), *Architektonik und System in der Philosophie Kants.* Hamburg: Meiner.

2003. "Kant's Transcendental Deduction as a Regressive Argument," in idem, *Interpreting Kant's Critiques.* Oxford University Press, 51–66.

Angelelli, Ignacio. 1972. "On the Origins of Kant's 'Transcendental,'" *Kant-Studien* 63/1, 117–22.

Arndt, Hans Werner. 1983. "Rationalismus und Empirismus in der Erkenntnislehre Christian Wolffs," in Werner Schneider (ed.), *Christian Wolff, 1679–1754: Interpretationen zu seiner Philosophie und deren Wirkung.* Hamburg: Meiner, 31–47.

Barker, Michael. 2001. "The Proof Structure of Kant's A-Deduction," *Kant-Studien* 92/3, 259–82.

Bärthlein, Karl. 1976. "Von der 'Transzendentalphilosophie' der Alten zu der Kants," *Archiv für Geschichte der Philosophie* 58, 353–92.

Bauer, Nathan. 2010. "Kant's Subjective Deduction," *British Journal for the History of Philosophy* 18/3, 433–60.

Baum, Manfred. 1986. *Deduktion und Beweis in Kants Transzendentalphilosophie.* Königstein/Ts: Hain bei Athenäum.

1993. "Metaphysik und Kritik in Kants theoretischer Philosophie," in Klaus Held and Jochem Henningfeld (eds.), *Kategorien der Existenz: Festschrift für Wolfgang Janke.* Würzburg: Königshausen & Neumann, 13–30.

2015. "Metaphysik," in Marcus Willaschek et al. (eds.), *Kant-Lexikon*, Band II. Berlin: De Gruyter, 1530–40.

Beck, Lewis White. 1969. *Early German Philosophy: Kant and His Predecessors.* Cambridge, MA: Harvard University Press.

1989. "Two Ways of Reading Kant's Letter to Herz: Comments on Carl," in Eckart Förster (ed.), *Kant's Transcendental Deductions: The Three "Critiques" and the "Opus Postumum."* Stanford University Press, 21–26.

Beiser, Frederick. 1992. "Kant's Intellectual Development: 1746–1781," in Paul Guyer (ed.), *Cambridge Companion to Kant.* Cambridge University Press, 26–61.

Benoist, Jocelyn. 1996. "Sur une prétendue ontologie kantienne: Kant et la néo-scolastique," in Charles Ramond (ed.), *Kant et la pensée moderne: alternatives critiques*. Presses Universitaires de Bordeaux, 137–63.

Blackwell, Richard. 1961. "Christian Wolff's Doctrine of the Soul," *Journal of the History of Ideas* 22, 339–54.

Blomme, Henny. 2011. "Kant et la matière de l'espace. Le problème d'une fondation transcendantale de l'expérience extérieure." PhD thesis, Paris-Sorbonne/Bergische Universität Wuppertal.

2015. "Kant's Conception of Chemistry in the Danziger Physik," in Robert R. Clewis (ed.), *Reading Kant's Lectures*. Berlin: De Gruyter, 484–502.

2018. "Sur la voie du problème de l'objectivité: concepts premiers et réforme de la métaphysique chez Tetens et Kant," *Astérion* 18, last accessed July 25, 2019; DOI:10.4000/asterion.3126.

Bouton, Christoph. 1996. "Ontologie et logique dans l'interprétation hégélienne de Christian Wolff," *Les études philosophiques* 1/2, 241–60.

Broecken, Renate. 1970. "Das Amphiboliekapitel der 'Kritik der reinen Vernunft.' Der Übergang der Reflexion von der Ontologie zur Transzendental-philosophie." PhD thesis, University of Cologne.

Caimi, Mario. 2001. "Zum Problem des Zieles einer transzendentalen Deduktion," in Ralph Schumacher, Rolf-Peter Horstmann, and Volker Gerhardt (eds.), *Kant und die Berliner Aufklärung: Akten des IX. Internationalen Kant-Kongresses*, vol. 10. Berlin: De Gruyter, 48–65.

2017. "Der Begriff der praktisch-dogmatischen Metaphysik," in Andree Hahmann and Bernd Ludwig (eds.), *Über die Fortschritte der kritischen Metaphysik. Beiträge zu System und Architektonik der kantischen Philosophie*. Hamburg: Meiner, 157–70.

Carboncini, Sonia. 1986. "Christian August Crusius und die Leibniz-Wolffische Philosophie," *Studia Leibnitiana Supplementa* 26, 110–25.

Carl, Wolfgang. 1989a. *Der schweigende Kant. Die Entwürfe zu einer Deduktion der Kategorien vor 1781*. Göttingen: Vandenhoeck & Ruprecht.

1989b. "Kant's First Drafts of the Deduction of the Categories," in Eckhard Förster (ed.), *Kant's Transcendental Deductions: The Three Critiques and the Opus Postumum*. Stanford University Press, 3–20.

1992. *Die Transzendentale Deduktion der Kategorien in der ersten Auflage der Kritik der reinen Vernunft. Ein Kommentar*. Frankfurt a.M: Klostermann.

Chance, Brian. 2012. "Scepticism and the Development of the Transcendental Dialectic," *British Journal for the History of Philosophy* 20/2, 311–31.

Chance, Brian, and Lawrence Pasternack. 2019. "Baumgarten and Kant on Rational Theology: Deism, Theism, and the Role of Analogy," in Courtney D. Fugate (ed.), *Kant's Lectures on Metaphysics*. Cambridge University Press, 214–32.

Chignell, Andrew. 2011. "Real *Repugnance* and Our Ignorance of Things-in-Themselves: A Lockean Problem in Kant and Hegel." in Jürgen Stolzenberg and Fred Rush (eds.), *Glaube und Vernunft/Faith and Reason. Internationales*

Jahrbuch des Deutschen Idealismus/International Yearbook of German Idealism 7, 135–59.

Cohen, Hermann. 1871/1987. *Kants Theorie der Erfahrung, Werke*, vol. 1 of 3. Hildesheim: Olms.

Courtine, Jean François. 1990. *Suarez et le système de la métaphysique*. Paris: Presses universitaires de France.

Cramer, Konrad. 1985. *Nicht-reine synthetische Urteile a priori. Ein Problem der Transzendentalphilosophie Immanuel Kants*. Heidelberg: Winter.

2001. "Peripetien der Ontologie – Wolff, Kant, Hegel," in Rüdiger Bubner and Walter Mesch (eds), *Die Weltgeschichte – das Weltgericht?*. Stuttgart: Klett-Cotta, 176–207.

Curtius, Ernst R. 1914. "Das Schematismuskapitel in der *Kritik der reinen Vernunft*," *Kant-Studien* 19/1–3, 338–66.

Daval, Roger. 1951. *La métaphysique de Kant: perspectives sur la métaphysique de Kant d'après la théorie du schématisme*. Paris: Presses universitaires de France.

De Boer, Karin. 2014. "Kant's Multi-Layered Conception of Things-in-Themselves, Transcendental Objects, and Monads," *Kant-Studien* 105/2, 221–60.

2015. "Heidegger's Ontological Reading of Kant," in Graham Banham, Dennis Schulting, and Nigel Hems (eds.), *The Bloomsbury Companion to Kant*. London: Bloomsbury, 324–29.

2018a. "Kant's Account of Sensible Concepts in the *Inaugural Dissertation* and the *Critique of Pure Reason*," in Violetta Waibel, Margit Ruffing, and David Wagner (eds.), *Natur und Freiheit. Akten des XII. Internationalen Kant-Kongresses*. Berlin: De Gruyter, 1015–22.

2018b. "Staking out the Terrain of Pure Reason: Kant's Critique of Wolffian Metaphysics in Dreams of a Spirit-Seer," in Dina Emundts and Sally Sedgwick (eds.), *Der deutsche Idealismus und die Rationalisten/German Idealism and the Rationalists. Internationales Jahrbuch des Deutschen Idealismus/International Yearbook of German Idealism*. Berlin: De Gruyter, 14, 3–24.

2019a. "Kant's Response to Hume's Critique of Pure Reason," *Archiv für Geschichte der Philosophie* 101/3, 376–406.

2019b. "The Prolegomena to Kant's Lectures on Metaphysics," in Courtney D. Fugate (ed.), *Kant's Lectures on Metaphysics: A Critical Guide*. Cambridge University Press, 31–52.

2020. "Pure Sensibility as Source of Corruption: Kant's Critique of Metaphysics in the *Inaugural Dissertation* and the *Critique of Pure Reason*," in Colin McQuillan and María del Rosario Acosta López (eds.), *Critique in German Philosophy: From Kant to Critical Theory*. Albany: SUNY Press.

De Boer, Karin, and Stephen Howard. 2019. "A Ground Completely Overgrown: Heidegger, Kant, and the Problem of Metaphysics," *British Journal for the History of Philosophy* 27/2, 358–77.

De Vleeschauwer, Herman J. 1937. *La déduction transcendantale dans l'oeuvre de Kant. Tome 3: La déduction transcendantale de 1787 jusqu'à l'opus postumum*. Antwerp: De Sikkel.

1939/1962. *The Development of Kantian Thought: The History of a Doctrine*, translated by A. R. C. Duncan. Edinburgh: Thomas Nelson.

Demange, Dominique. 2009. "Métaphysique et théorie de la représentation. La question des origines du transcendentalisme revisitée," *Revue philosophique de Louvain* 107/1, 1–21.

Detel, Wolfgang. 1978. "Zur Funktion des Schematismuskapitels in Kants *Kritik der reinen Vernunft*," *Kant-Studien* 69, 17–45.

Dörflinger, Bernd. 2000. *Das Leben theoretischer Vernunft: Teleologische und praktische Aspekte der Erfahrungstheorie Kants*. Berlin: De Gruyter.

Doyle, John P. 1997. "Between Transcendental and Transcendent: The Missing Link?," *Review of Metaphysics* 50, 783–815.

Dyck, Corey W. 2011. "Kant's Transcendental Deduction and the Ghosts of Descartes and Hume," *British Journal for the History of Philosophy* 19/3, 473–96.

2014. *Kant and Rational Psychology*. Oxford University Press.

École, Jean. 1979. "En quel sens peut-on dire que Wolff est rationalist?," *Studia Leibnitiana* 11, 45–61.

Edwards, Jeffrey. 2000. *Substance, Force, and the Possibility of Knowledge: On Kant's Philosophy of Material Nature*. Berkeley: University of California Press.

Engelhard, Kristina. 2009. "Kants physische Monadologie und dynamische Materietheorie. Die vorkritische Theorie und ihre Kritik," in Hans-Peter Neumann (ed.), *Der Monadenbegriff zwischen Spätrenaissance und Aufklärung*. Berlin: De Gruyter, 301–38.

Engfer, Hans-Jürgen. 1996. *Empirismus versus Rationalismus? Kritik eines philosophiegeschichtlichen Schemas*. Paderborn: F. Schöningh.

Ertl, Wolfgang. 2002. "Hume's Antinomy and Kant's Critical Turn," *British Journal for the History of Philosophy* 10/4, 617–40.

Favaretti Camposampiero, Matteo. 2015. "What Is Symbolic Cognition? The Debate after Leibniz and Wolff," in Cristina Marras and Anna Lisa Schino (eds.), *Linguaggio, filosofia, fisiologia nell'età moderna. Atti del convegno*. Rome: ILIESI – CNR, 163–75.

Ferrarin, Alfredo. 2015. *The Powers of Pure Reason: Kant and the Idea of Cosmic Philosophy*. Chicago: University of Chicago Press.

Ficara, Elena. 2006. *Die Ontologie in der Kritik der reinen Vernunft*. Würzburg: Königshausen & Neumann.

Fichant, Michel. 2014. "Leibniz a-t-il 'intellectualisé' les phénomènes'? Eléments pour l'histoire d'une méprise," in François Calori, Michael Foessel, and Dominique Pradelle (eds.), *De la sensibilité. Les esthétiques de Kant*. Presses universitaires de Rennes, 37–70.

Freuler, Leo. 1991. "Schematismus und Deduktion in Kants *Kritik der reinen Vernunft*," *Kant-Studien* 82/4, 397–413.

Friedman, Michael. 2013. *Kant's Construction of Nature: A Reading of the Metaphysical Foundations of Natural Science*. Cambridge University Press.

Fugate, Courtney D. 2014. *The Teleology of Reason: A Study of the Structure of Kant's Critical Philosophy*. Berlin: De Gruyter.

2015. "The Unity of Metaphysics in Kant's Lectures," in Robert R. Clewis (ed.), *Reading Kant's Lectures*. Berlin: De Gruyter, 64–87.

2019 (ed.). *Kant's Lectures on Metaphysics: A Critical Guide*. Cambridge University Press.

Fugate, Courtney D., and John Hymers (eds.). 2018. *Baumgarten and Kant on Metaphysics*. Oxford University Press.

Fulda, Hans Friedrich. 1988. "Ontologie nach Kant und Hegel," in Dieter Henrich and Rolf-Peter Horstmann (eds.), *Metaphysik nach Kant?* Stuttgart: Klett-Cotta, 45–80.

Gardner, Sebastian. 1999. *Kant and the Critique of Pure Reason*. London: Routledge.

Gava, Gabriele. 2018. "Kant, Wolff, and the Method of Philosophy," *Oxford Studies in Early Modern Philosophy* 8, 271–303.

Gawlick, Günther, and Lothar Kreimendahl. 1987. *Hume in der deutschen Aufklärung: Umrisse einer Rezeptionsgeschichte*. Stuttgart-Bad Cannstatt: Frommann-Holzboog.

Gerlach, Burkhard. 1998. "Wer war der 'Grosse Mann,' der die Raumtheorie des transzendentalen Idealismus vorbereitet hat?," *Kant-Studien* 89, 1–34.

Gram, Moltke. 1975. "The Myth of Double Affection," in William Henry Werkmeister (ed.), *Reflections on Kant's Philosophy*. Gainesville: University Presses of Florida, 29–63.

Grapotte, Sophie, and Tinca Prunea-Bretonnet (eds.). 2011. *Kant et Wolff: Héritages et ruptures*. Paris: Vrin.

Graubner, Hans. 1972. *Form und Wesen. Ein Beitrag zur Deutung des Formbegriffs in Kants "Kritik der reinen Vernunft."* Bonn: Bouvier.

Grier, Michelle. 2001. *Kant's Doctrine of Transcendental Illusion*. Cambridge University Press.

Grondin, Jean. 1989. *Kant et le problème de la philosophie: l'a priori*. Paris: Vrin.

Guyer, Paul. 1987. *Kant and the Claims of Knowledge*. Cambridge University Press.

Guyer, Paul, and Allen W. Wood. 1998. "Introduction," in Immanuel Kant, *Critique of Pure Reason*. Cambridge University Press, 1–80.

Hahmann, Andree. 2008. "Das Innere und das Äussere: Kant als kritischer Erbe der dogmatischen Schulphilosophie," *Perspektiven der Philosophie* 37, 179–215.

2009a. "Die Reaktion der spekulativen Weltweisheit: Kant und die Kritik an den einfachen Substanzen," *Kant-Studien* 100/4, 454–75.

2009b. *Kritische Metaphysik der Substanz*. Berlin: De Gruyter.

2020. "Crusius' Critique of the Leibniz-Wolffian Ontology and Cosmology," in Frank Grunert and Andree Hahmann (eds.), *Christian August Crusius. 1715–1775. Philosophy between Reason and Revelation*. Berlin: De Gruyter.

Hatfield, Gary. 2003. "What Were Kant's Aims in the Deduction?," *Philosophical Topics*, 31/1–2, 165–98.

Heidegger, Martin. 1929/1997. *Kant and the Problem of Metaphysics*, 5th, enlarged edition, translated by Richard Taft. Bloomington: Indiana University Press.

Heimsoeth, Heinz. 1924/1956. "Metaphysische Motive in der Ausbildung des kritischen Idealismus," in idem, *Studien zur Philosophie Immanuel Kants. Metaphysische Ursprünge und ontologische Grundlagen.* Köln: Kölner Universitäts-Verlag.

    1926/1956. "Metaphysik und Kritik bei Chr. A. Crusius. Ein Beitrag zur ontologischen Vorgeschichte der Kritik der reinen Vernunft im 18. Jahrhundert," in idem, *Studien zur Philosophie Immanuel Kants. Metaphysische Ursprünge und ontologische Grundlagen.* Köln: Kölner Universitäts-Verlag, 125–88.

Henrich, Dieter. 1969. "The Proof-Structure of Kant's Transcendental Deduction," *The Review of Metaphysics* 22/4, 640–59.

    1989. "Kant's Notion of a Deduction and the Methodological Background of the First *Critique*," in Eckart Förster (ed.), *Kant's Transcendental Deductions: The Three "Critiques" and the "Opus postumum."* Stanford University Press, 29–46.

Herring, Herbert. 1953. *Das Problem der Affektion bei Kant.* Köln: Kölner Universitäts-Verlag.

Hess, Heinz-Jürgen. 1981. "Zu Kants Leibniz-Kritik in der 'Amphibolie der Reflexionsbegriffe,'" in Ingeborg Heidemann and Wolfgang Ritzel (eds.), *Beiträge zur Kritik der reinen Vernunft 1781–1981.* Berlin: De Gruyter, 200–32.

Hessbrüggen-Walter, Stefan. 2004. "Topik, Reflexion und Vorurteilskritik: Kants 'Amphibolie der Reflexionsbegriffe' im Kontext," *Archiv für Geschichte der Philosophie* 86, 146–75.

    2014. "Putting Our Soul in Place," *Kant Yearbook* 6, 23–42.

Hinske, Norbert. 1968. "Die historischen Vorlagen der Kantischen Transzendentalphilosophie," *Archiv für Begriffsgeschichte* 12, 86–113.

    1970a. *Kants Weg zur Transzendentalphilosophie. Der dreißigjährige Kant.* Stuttgart: Kohlhammer.

    1970b. "Verschiedenheit und Einheit der transzendentalen Philosophien," *Archiv für Begriffsgeschichte* 14, 41–68.

    1973. "Kants Begriff des Transzendentalen und die Problematik seiner Begriffsgeschichte," *Kant-Studien* 64/1, 56–62.

    1998. "Transzendental – 18 Jh.," in Joachim Ritter, Karl Gründer, et al., (eds.), *Historisches Wörterbuch der Philosophie*, Band X. Basel: Schwabe, 1376–88.

    2013. "Kants Verankerung der Kritik im Weltbegriff," in Stefano Bacin, Alfredo Ferrarin, Claudio La Rocca, and Margit Ruffing (eds.), *Kant und die Philosophie in Weltbürgerlicher Absicht: Akten des XI. Kant-Kongresses 2010*, vol. 1. Berlin: De Gruyter, 263–75.

Höffe, Otfried. 2003. *Kants Kritik der reinen Vernunft. Die Grundlegung der modernen Philosophie.* München: Beck.

Honnefelder, Ludger. 1990. *Scientia transcendens. Die formale Bestimmung der Seiendheit und Realität in der Metaphysik des Mittelalters und der Neuzeit.* Hamburg: Meiner.

1995. "Die 'Transzendentalphilosophie der Alten.' Zur mittelalterlichen Vorgeschichte von Kants Begriff der Transzendentalphilosophie," in Hoke Robinson and Gordon G. Brittan (eds.), *Proceedings of the Eighth International Kant Congress*, Part I. Milwaukee: Marquette University Press, 394–407.

Howard, Stephen. 2017. "Kant and Force: Dynamics, Natural Science and Transcendental Philosophy." PhD thesis, Kingston University.

Jaeschke, Walter, and Andreas Arndt (eds.). 2012. *Die Klassische Deutsche Philosophie nach Kant: Systeme der reinen Vernunft und ihre Kritik 1785–1845.* München: Beck.

Jauernig, Anja. 2008. "Kant's Critique of the Leibnizian Philosophy: Contra the Leibnizians, but Pro Leibniz," in Daniel Garber and Béatrice Longuenesse (eds.), *Kant and the Early Moderns*. Princeton University Press, 41–63.

Kanzian, Christian. 1993. "Kant und Crusius 1763," *Kant-Studien* 84/4, 399–407.

Kemp Smith, Norman. 1923. *A Commentary to Kant's "Critique of Pure Reason,"* 2nd, revised and enlarged edition. London: Macmillan. Originally published in 1918.

Klemme, Heiner F. 1996. *Kants Philosophie des Subjekts. Systematische und entwicklungsgeschichtliche Untersuchungen zum Verhältnis von Selbstbewußtsein und Selbsterkenntnis.* Hamburg: Meiner.

Knittermeyer, Hinrich. 1953/54. "Von der klassischen zur kritischen Transzendentalphilosophie," *Kant-Studien* 45/1–4, 113–31.

Knoepffler, Nikolaus. 2001. *Der Begriff "transzendental" bei Immanuel Kant. Eine Untersuchung zur "Kritik der reinen Vernunft."* München: Herbert UTZ.

Kreimendahl, Lothar. 1990. *Kant: der Durchbruch von 1769.* Köln: Dinter.

2007. "Empiristische Elemente im Denken Christian Wolffs," in Jürgen Stolzenberg and Oliver-Pierre Rudolph (eds.), *Christian Wolff und die europäische Aufklärung*, vol. 1. Hildesheim: Olms, 95–112.

Krouglov, Alexei N. 2005. "Der Begriff *transzendental* bei J. N. Tetens. Historischer Kontext und Hintergründe," *Aufklärung. Interdisziplinäres Jahrbuch zur Erforschung des 18. Jahrhunderts und seiner Wirkungsgeschichte* 16, 35–75.

Kuehn, Manfred. 1983. "Kant's Conception of Hume's Problem," *Journal of the History of Philosophy* 21/2, 175–93.

Kuehn, Manfred. 1987. *Scottish Common Sense in Germany, 1768–1800. A Contribution to the History of Critical Philosophy.* Kingston: McGill-Queen's University Press.

1988. "Kant's Transcendental Deduction: A Limited Defense of Hume," in Bernard den Ouden (ed.), *New Essays on Kant*. Bern: Lang, 47–72.

1997. "The Wolffian Background of Kant's Transcendental Deduction," in Patricia A. Easton (ed.), *Logic and the Workings of the Mind*. Atascadero, CA: Ridgeview, 229–50.

2001. *Kant: A Biography.* Cambridge University Press.

La Rocca, Claudio. 1989. "Schematismus und Anwendung," *Kant-Studien* 80/1–4, 129–54.

Langton, Rae. 1998. *Kantian Humility: Our Ignorance of Things in Themselves.* Oxford: Clarendon Press.

Lanier Anderson, R. 2015. *The Poverty of Conceptual Truth: Kant's Analytic/ Synthetic Distinction and the Limits of Metaphysics.* Oxford University Press.

Laywine, Alison. 1993. *Kant's Early Metaphysics and the Origins of the Critical Philosophy.* Atascadero, CA: Ridgeview.

Leduc, Christian. 2020. "The Role of Experience in Wolff's General Cosmology," in Karin de Boer and Tinca Prunea-Bretonnet (eds.), *The Experiential Turn in Eighteenth-Century German Philosophy.* London: Routledge.

Longuenesse, Béatrice. 1998. *Kant and the Capacity to Judge: Sensibility and Discursivity in the Transcendental Analytic of the Critique of Pure Reason,* translated by C. T. Wolfe. Princeton University Press.

Lorini, Gualtiero. 2015. "The Contribution of Kant's Lectures on Metaphysics to a Better Comprehension of the Architectonic," in Bernd Dörflinger et al. (eds.), *Kant's Lectures/Kants Vorlesungen.* Berlin: De Gruyter, 233–46.

Lu-Adler, Huaping. 2018. *Kant and the Science of Logic: A Historical and Philosophical Reconstruction.* Oxford University Press.

2019. "Ontology as Transcendental Philosophy," in Courtney D. Fugate (ed.), *Kant's Lectures on Metaphysics.* Cambridge University Press, 53–73.

Malter, Rudolf. 1981. "Logische und transzendentale Reflexion. Zu Kants Bestimmung des philosophiegeschichtlichen Ortes der Kritik der reinen Vernunft," *Revue internationale de philosophie* 136–37, 284–301.

1982. "Reflexionsbegriffe. Gedanken zu einer schwierigen Begriffsgattung und zu einem unausgeführten Lehrstück der Kritik der reinen Vernunft," *Philosophia Naturalis* 19, 125–50.

Manchester, Paula. 2003. "Kant's Conception of Architectonic in Its Historical Context," *Journal of the History of Philosophy* 41/2, 187–207.

Martin, Wayne. 2006. *Theories of Judgment: Psychology, Logic, Phenomenology.* Cambridge University Press.

Marty, François. 2011. "L'ontologie dans le système wolffien: fortune et infortune d'un chemin de pensée," in Grapotte and Prunea-Bretonnet (eds.), *Kant et Wolff: Héritages et ruptures,* 163–70.

McQuillan, Colin. 2016. *Immanuel Kant: The Very Idea of a Critique of Pure Reason.* Chicago: Northwestern University Press.

Mensch, Jennifer. 2007. "The Key to All Metaphysics: Kant's Letter to Herz, 1772," *Kantian Review* 12, 109–27.

Merritt, Melissa. 2015. "Varieties of Reflection in Kant's Logic," *British Journal for the History of Philosophy* 23/3, 478–501.

Moledo, Fernando. 2016. "Die neue Auffassung der Metaphysik als reine Philosophie in der Inauguraldissertation und ihre propädeutische Bedeutung im Rahmen der Entwicklungsgeschichte der *Kritik der reinen Vernunft*," *Kant-Studien* 107/3, 485–95.

Mora, José Ferrater. 1963. "On the Early History of Ontology," *Philosophy and Phenomenological Research* 24, 36–47.

Paccioni, Jean-Paul. 2006. *Cet esprit de profondeur: Christian Wolff, l'ontologie et la métaphysique*. Paris: Vrin.

    2011. "Qu'est-ce qui est dogmatique? La pensée wolffienne et l'articulation du critique et du dogmatique selon la *Critique de la raison pure*," in Grapotte and Prunea-Bretonnet (eds.), *Kant et Wolff: Héritages et ruptures*, 101–18.

Parkinson, G. H. R. 1981. "Kant as a Critic of Leibniz: The Amphiboly of Concepts of Reflection," *Revue internationale de philosophie* 136–37, 302–14.

Paton, Herbert J. 1936a. *Kant's Metaphysic of Experience*, vol. 1. London: Allen & Unwin.

    1936b. *Kant's Metaphysic of Experience*, vol. 2. London: Allen & Unwin.

Pelletier, Arnaud. 2017. "On the Origin of Concepts: The Cognitive Continuum between the Senses and Understanding in Christian Wolff's German Logic," in Arnaud Pelletier (ed.), *Christian Wolff's German Logic: Sources, Significance and Reception*. Hildesheim: Olms, 29–51.

Pereboom, Derek. 1991. "Kant's Amphiboly," *Archiv für Begriffsgeschichte* 73/1, 50–70.

Perin, Adriano. 2015. "The Proof of the Principle of Sufficient Reason: Wolff, Crusius and the Early Kant on the Search for a Foundation of Metaphysics," *Revista Portuguesa de Filosofia*, 71/2–3, 515–30.

Pichler, Hans. 1910. *Über Christian Wolffs Ontologie*. Leipzig: Durr'sche Buchhandlung.

Pinder, Tillman. 1986. "Kants Begriff der transzendentalen Erkenntnis. Zur Interpretation der Definition des Begriffs 'transzendental' in der Einleitung zur Kritik der reinen Vernunft," *Kant-Studien* 77, 1–40.

Pippin, Robert B. 1976. "The Schematism and Empirical Concepts," *Kant-Studien* 67, 156–71.

Plaass, Peter. 1965. *Kants Theorie der Naturwissenschaft*. Göttingen: Vandenhoeck & Ruprecht.

Pollok, Konstantin. 2001. *Kants Metaphysische Anfangsgründe der Naturwissenschaft. Ein kritischer Kommentar*. Hamburg: Meiner.

Prauss, Gerold. 1974. *Kant und das Problem der Dinge an sich*. Bonn: Bouvier.

Proops, Ian. 2003. "Kant's Legal Metaphor and the Nature of a Deduction," *Journal of the History of Philosophy* 41/2, 209–29.

Prunea-Bretonnet, Tinca. 2011a. "De l'ontologie à la philosophie transcendantale: *dans quelle mesure* Kant est-il wolffien?," in Grapotte and Prunea-Bretonnet (eds.), *Kant et Wolff: Héritages et ruptures*, 147–61.

    2011b. "Crusius et la certitude métaphysique en 1762," *Astérion* 9, last accessed on August 27, 2018, http://journals.openedition.org/asterion/2137.

Rescher, Nicholas. 1972. "Noumenal Causality," in Lewis White Beck (ed.), *Kant's Theory of Knowledge. Proceedings of the Third International Kant Congress*. Dordrecht: Reidel, 462–70.

    1981. "On the Status of 'Things in Themselves' in Kant," *Revue internationale de philosophie* 35/2, 346–57.

Ritter, Joachim, and Karl Gründer (eds.). 1998. "Transzendental; Transzendentalphilosophie," in *Historisches Wörterbuch der Philosophie*, Band X. Basel: Schwabe Verlag, 1358–87.

Rivero, Gabriel. 2014. *Zur Bedeutung des Begriffs Ontologie bei Kant. Eine Entwicklungsgeschichtliche Untersuchung*. Berlin: De Gruyter.

Rosales, Alberto. 2000. *Sein und Subjektivität bei Kant. Zum subjektiven Ursprung der Kategorien*. Berlin: De Gruyter.

Rosefeldt, Tobias. 2013. "Dinge an sich und der Außenweltskeptizismus. Über ein Missverständnis der frühen Kant-Rezeption," in Dina Emundts (ed.), *Selbst, Welt, Kunst*. Berlin: De Gruyter, 221–60.

Rumore, Paola. 2018. "Kant and Crusius on the Role of Immortality in Morality," in Corey W. Dyck and Falk Wunderlich (eds.), *Kant and His German Contemporaries*, vol. 1. Cambridge University Press, 213–31.

Sala, Giovanni B. 1988. "Die transzendentale Logik Kants und die Ontologie der Deutschen Schulphilosophie," *Philosophisches Jahrbuch* 95, 18–53.

Schmucker, Josef. 1974. "Zur entwicklungsgeschichtlichen Bedeutung der Inauguraldissertation von 1770," *Kant-Studien* 65 Sonderheft, 263–82.

Schnepf, Robert. 2007a. "Metaphysik und Metaphysikkritik in Kants Transzendentalphilosophie," in Jürgen Stolzenberg (ed.), *Kant in der Gegenwart*. Berlin: De Gruyter, 71–112.

2007b. "Allgemeine Metaphysik als erste Philosophie. Zum Problem kategorialer Begriffsbildung in Christian Wolff's Ontology," in Jürgen Stolzenberg and Oliver-Pierre Rudolph (eds.), *Christian Wolff und die europäische Aufklärung*, vol. 1. Hildesheim: Olms, 181–203.

Schönfeld, Martin. 2000. *The Philosophy of the Young Kant: The Pre-Critical Project*. Oxford University Press.

Schwaiger, Clemens. 2019. "Christian Wolffs *Deutsche Metaphysik* und die Thomasianer Nicolaus Hieronymus Gundling und Johann Franz Budde," *Archivio di Filosofia* 87/1, 27–38.

Simmert, Sebastian. 2018. "Kosmologie," in Robert Theis and Alexander Aichele (eds.), *Handbuch Christian Wolff*. Wiesbaden: Springer, 197–218.

Smit, Houston. 1999. "The Role of Reflection in Kant's *Critique of Pure Reason*," *Pacific Philosophical Quarterly* 80, 203–23.

Strawson, Peter F. 1966. *The Bounds of Sense: An Essay on Immanuel Kant's Critique of Pure Reason*. London: Methuen.

Sweet, Kristi. 2013. *Kant on Practical Life: From Duty to History*. Cambridge University Press.

Symington, Paul. 2011. "Metaphysics Renewed: Kant's Schematized Categories and the Possibility of Metaphysics," *International Philosophical Quarterly* 51/3, 285–301.

Theis, Robert. 1982. "Le silence de Kant. Étude sur l'évolution de la pensée kantienne entre 1770 et 1781," *Revue de métaphysique et de morale* 87/2, 209–39.

2012. *La raison et son dieu. Étude sur la théologie kantienne*. Paris: Vrin.

Thiel, Udo. 2006. "The Critique of Rational Psychology," in Graham Bird (ed.), *A Companion to Kant*. Malden, MA: Blackwell, 207–21.

Thöle, Bernard. 1991. *Kant und das Problem der Gesetzmäßigkeit der Natur.* Berlin: De Gruyter.

Tolley, Clinton. 2012. "The Generality of Transcendental Logic," *Journal of the History of Philosophy* 50/3, 417–46.

Tonelli, Giorgio. 1969. "Vorwort," in C. A. Crusius, *Die philosophischen Hauptwerke*, vol. 1. Hildesheim: Olms, vii–lii.

1978. "Critique and Related Terms Prior to Kant: A Historical Survey," *Kant-Studien* 69, 119–48.

1994. *Kant's Critique of Pure Reason within the Tradition of Modern Logic: A Commentary on Its History*, edited by D. H. Chandler. Hildesheim: Olms.

Vollrath, Ernst. 1962. "Die Gliederung der Metaphysik in eine metaphysica generalis und eine metaphysica specialis," *Zeitschrift für philosophische Forschung* 16/2, 258–84.

Walsh, William H. 1957/1958. "Schematism," *Kant-Studien* 49/1–4, 95–106.

Watkins, Eric. 1998. "The Argumentative Structure of Kant's Metaphysical Foundations of Natural Science," *Journal of the History of Philosophy* 36/4, 567–93.

2001. "The Critical Turn: Kant and Herz from 1770 to 1772," in Volker Gerhardt, Rolf-Peter Horstmann, and Ralph Schumacher (eds.), *Kant und die Berliner Aufklärung*, vol. 2. Berlin: De Gruyter, 69–77.

2005. *Kant and the Metaphysics of Causality*. Cambridge University Press.

2006. "On the Necessity and Nature of Simples: Leibniz, Wolff, Baumgarten, and the Pre-Critical Kant," in Daniel Garber and Steven Nadler (eds.), *Oxford Studies in Early Modern Philosophy*, vol. 3. Oxford: Clarendon Press, 261–314.

2009. *Kant's Critique of Pure Reason: Background Source Materials*. Cambridge University Press.

Wellmann, Gesa. 2018. "The Idea of a Metaphysical System in Lambert, Kant, Reinhold, and Fichte." PhD thesis, University of Leuven.

Westphal, Merold. 1968. "In Defense of the Thing in Itself," *Kant-Studien* 59/1, 118–41.

Wilkerson, T. E. 1976. *Kant's Critique of Pure Reason: A Commentary for Students*. Oxford University Press.

Willaschek, Marcus. 1998. "Phaenomena/Noumena und die Amphibolie der Reflexionsbegriffe," in Georg Mohr and Marcus Willaschek (eds.), *Immanuel Kant. Kritik der reinen Vernunft*. Berlin: Akademie Verlag, 325–52.

2018. *Kant on the Sources of Metaphysics: The Dialectic of Pure Reason*. Cambridge University Press.

Wolff, Michael. 1995. *Die Vollständigkeit der kantischen Urteilstafel*. Frankfurt a. M.: Klostermann.

Wolff, Robert Paul. 1963. *Kant's Theory of Mental Activity*. Cambridge, MA: Harvard University Press.

Wood, Allen W. 1978. *Kant's Rational Theology.* Ithaca, NY: Cornell University Press.

Wundt, Max. 1924. *Kant als Metaphysiker: Ein Beitrag zur Geschichte der deutschen Philosophie im achtzehnten Jahrhundert.* Stuttgart: Enke.

1939. *Die deutsche Schulmetaphysik des 17. Jahrhunderts.* Tübingen: Mohr.

Wunsch, Matthias. 2007. *Einbildungskraft und Erfahrung bei Kant.* Berlin: De Gruyter.

2013. "Zum 'Schematismus' der reinen Verstandesbegriffe in Kants Inauguraldissertation von 1770," in Stefano Bacin, Alfredo Ferrarin, Claudio La Rocca, and Margit Ruffing (eds.), *Kant und die Philosophie in Weltbürgerlicher Absicht. Akten des XI. Kant-Kongresses 2010,* vol. 2. Berlin: De Gruyter, 505–16.

Ypi, Lea. 2011. "Teleology and System in Kant's Architectonic of Pure Reason," in Sorin Baiasu, Howard Williams, and Sami Pihlström (eds.), *Politics and Metaphysics in Kant.* Cardiff: University of Wales Press, 134–51.

Zöller, Günter. 1984. *Theoretische Gegenstandsbeziehung bei Kant: zur systematischen Bedeutung der Termini "objektive Realität" und "objektive Gültigkeit" in der "Kritik der reinen Vernunft."* Berlin: De Gruyter.

2001. "'Die Seele des Systems': Systembegriff und Begriffssystem in Kants Transzendentalphilosophie," in Hans Friedrich Fulda and Jürgen Stolzenberg (eds.), *Architektonik und System in der Philosophie Kants.* Hamburg: Meiner, 54–72.

2004. "Metaphysik nach der Metaphysik. Die limitative Konzeption der Ersten Philosophie bei Kant," in Karin Gloy (ed.), *Unser Zeitalter – ein postmetaphysisches?* Würzburg: Königshausen & Neumann, 231–43.

Index of Names

Index of Subjects

affection, 101, 103–5, 109
  transcendental, 107, 120
On the Amphiboly of the Concepts of
  Reflection, 14, 191, 193, 196, 211
Announcement, 51–52, 212
Antinomy of Pure Reason, 48, 56, 241
appearances, 90, 104–5, 110, 121, 130, 155,
  167, 170; *see also* thing in itself, noumenon
apperception
  empirical, 146–47
  pure / transcendental, 141, 147–49, 152, 155,
    181, 186, 239
  transcendental unity of, 68, 151–56, 181, 257
apprehension, 146–47, 154
Architectonic, 4–6, 86, 98, 122, 125, 215,
  217–18, 221–22, 231–34, 237, 239,
  242–43, 248–49

categories, 68, 89, 116, 127–28, 130–31, 137,
  149, 151–52, 154, 158, 176, 178, 186, 245;
  see also concepts, pure
  as conditions of possibility of experience, 136,
    141
  as deschematized pure concepts, 164, 180,
    182, 184–85, 187, 189
  as ontological predicates, 139, 186, 223
  objective reality of, 132, 158, 183
  objective validity of, 130, 132, 135, 137, 141,
    155, 157
  table of, 187, 214, 223–24, 227, 229, 231–32,
    235–36, 240, 242
  vs. pure concepts, 173, 176–77, 180–81, 187,
    189
  warranted use of, 127, 136–37, 145, 153, 156,
    161–62, 168, 209, 214
cognition
  empirical, 104, 118, 128
  a priori cognition of objects, 20, 82, 135,
    157–58, 189
  sources of, 136, 144, 148, 152, 203

symbolic, 62
vs. thought, 70, 102, 161, 209, 239–42, 248,
  256
concepts of reflection; *see* reflection, concepts of
concepts, pure, 57, 61, 68, 76, 78, 84–85, 89,
  92, 127, 139, 158–59, 178, 181, 187
  as rules, 68, 131, 139–41, 151, 155, 161, 163,
    174–77, 186
  deschematized, 164, 180; *see also* categories
  empirical / immanent use of, 90–91, 182, 184,
    188, 203
  thin vs. thick, 57, 68–69
  transcendent use of, 90–91
  transcendental use of, 88, 90–91, 99, 111,
    203
  two-aspect theory of, 165, 174, 183
continuism, 17, 19, 29, 39, 41–42, 58, 203, 205,
  239
cosmology
  rational, 60, 118, 219, 221, 241–42
  Wolff's / Wolffian, 27, 40, 53, 56, 59, 80,
    219, 242
critique
  in the 1770s, 61, 64–65, 67
  of Baumgarten, 52, 222, 247
  in the *Critique of Pure Reason*, 2, 18, 51,
    66–67, 71, 135; *see also* transcendental,
    critique
  of Crusius, 34–36, 39, 54–55
  in the early writings, 46, 50–52, 60
  of Leibniz, 195
  of Leibniz's / Leibnizian monadology, 191,
    203, 205, 208–9, 211
  as propaedeutic, 53, 61, 66, 74–75, 215–17
  of Wolff's / Wolffian metaphysics, 2, 17–21,
    34, 46, 48, 53–56, 65, 71, 96–97, 102, 112,
    115, 129, 143, 152–53, 157, 161–63, 165,
    169, 176–77, 184, 186, 190–91, 215, 247,
    256
Critique of the Power of Judgment, 250

277